Acclaim for *The New New Journalism*

"Fascinating and revealing insights into how writers really write."
—Tina Brown

"A must-read for any aspiring or experienced writer, *The New New Journalism* gives nothing less than a recipe for better storytelling, fact or fiction. . . . Boynton offers a journalism education bar none. . . . To journalists, this book is crucial. To writing students, undoubtedly next year's required reading. To avid readers of this genre, a light to illuminate the mystery of their best pleasure."
—Lydia Reynolds, *The Denver Post*

"Like a building contractor interviewing carpenters for a job, Boynton assesses his subjects based on what sort of tools he finds in their toolboxes."
—Jack Shafer, *The New York Times Book Review*

"If there has ever been a better book of author interviews, it has escaped my attention. [Boynton's] enormous labors show in the insightful introductions he writes about each of the nineteen authors, in the perceptiveness of his questions, in his determination to discover how the muckrakers of 100 years ago and the first wave of New Journalists forty years ago left their mark on these nineteen contemporaries, in the subtle ways he both instructs and entertains through the interviews he conducts."
—Steve Weinberg, *St. Petersburg Times*

"A compelling guide to the craft."
—Bob Cohn, *Wired*

"A gold mine of technique, approach and philosophy for journalists, writers and close readers alike."
—*Publishers Weekly*

"Boynton offers a valuable primer for how strong journalism and the attention to craft practiced by his featured writers have created a 'literature of the everyday.' *The New New Journalism* compels readers to seek alternatives to the current infotainment-soaked culture."
—Belinda Acosta, *The Austin Chronicle*

"A great compilation of astute interviews with a group of reporters who are both masterful story tellers and brilliant writers."

—Rita Radostitz, *Etude*

"A fascinating book that makes the reader want to go out and get every book the writers have written as well as those mentioned as sources of inspiration."

—*Booklist* (starred)

"Boynton's method offers a rare and quite nice example of asking simple questions about the complex task of good reporting and writing. . . . [F]or any journalist, 'new' or otherwise, this book serves as a necessary reminder that what we do is both an art and a craft."

—Christian Parenti, *The Brooklyn Rail*

"Reading the interviews was like eavesdropping on a literary dinner party held in honor of these accomplished non-fiction writers. Boynton, as host, certainly asked the right questions. And each 'guest' performed as expected—their answers were as fully-formed, interesting, and intriguing as their writing. They report. They decide. And we are grateful as readers."

—Bill Katovsky, coauthor of
Embedded: The Media at War in Iraq

"An important contribution on contemporary writers for which I can think of no other similar book. . . . When the literary history is written on the post-new journalism, I think *The New New Journalism* will be central to that effort. I have no doubt that it will become a standard in the field."

—John Harstock, author of *A History of Literary Journalism: The Emergence of a Modern Narrative Form*

The New New Journalism

Conversations with America's
Best Nonfiction Writers
on Their Craft

Robert S. Boynton

VINTAGE BOOKS

A Division of Random House, Inc.

New York

A Vintage Books Original, March 2005

Copyright © 2005 by Robert S. Boynton

All rights reserved under International and Pan-American
Copyright Conventions. Published in the United States by
Vintage Books, a division of Random House, Inc., New York,
and simultaneously in Canada by Random House
of Canada Limited, Toronto.

Vintage and colophon are registered trademarks
of Random House, Inc.

Cataloging-in-Publication Data for *The New New Journalism* is on file
at the Library of Congress

ISBN 978-1-4000-3356-0

Book design by Jo Anne Metsch

www.vintagebooks.com

Printed in the United States of America

To Helen

Acknowledgments

All books are collaborations, but this one has been more collaborative than most. I want to thank all the writers who talked to me for being so generous with their time and energy. The book benefited from the scrupulous research of Caroline Binham, Megan Costello, and Kris Wilton. Brooke Kroeger, Mitch Stephens, and Rick Woodward were kind enough to comment on the introduction, and Laura Marmor cast a critical eye on the entire manuscript. My friend and agent Chris Calhoun, and my editors at Vintage, Marty Asher and Lexy Bloom, have been supportive and enthusiastic throughout the project.

Contents

Introduction   xi

Preface   xxxiii

Ted Conover   3

Richard Ben Cramer   31

Leon Dash   53

William Finnegan   73

Jonathan Harr   103

Alex Kotlowitz   127

Jon Krakauer   154

Jane Kramer   183

William Langewiesche   206

Adrian Nicole LeBlanc   227

Michael Lewis   248

Susan Orlean   271

Richard Preston   293

Ron Rosenbaum   324

Eric Schlosser   342

Gay Talese   361

Calvin Trillin   379

Lawrence Weschler   404

Lawrence Wright   434

Introduction

In Tom Wolfe's now famous introduction to *The New Journalism* (1973), he argued that nonfiction—not the novel—had become "the most important literature being written in America today."[1] From Wolfe, who had toiled in the shadow of the novel for decades, this was a startling pronouncement. Even more startling was Wolfe's declaration that not just nonfiction in general, but journalism in particular, had become "literature's main event." But as Wolfe celebrated the triumph of New Journalism, evidence of an even more formidable next stage in American literary evolution was already taking shape.

In the thirty years since Wolfe's manifesto, a group of writers has been quietly securing a place at the very center of contemporary American literature for reportorially based, narrative-driven long-form nonfiction. These New New Journalists—Adrian LeBlanc, Michael Lewis, Lawrence Weschler, Eric Schlosser, Richard Preston, Alex Kotlowitz, Jon Krakauer, William Langewiesche, Lawrence Wright, William Finnegan, Ted Conover, Jonathan Harr, Susan Orlean, and others—represent the continued maturation of American literary journalism. They use the license to experiment with form earned by the New Journalists of the sixties to address the social and political concerns of nineteenth-century writers such as Lincoln Steffens, Jacob Riis, and Stephen Crane (an earlier generation of "New Journalists"), synthesizing the best of these two traditions. Rigorously reported, psychologically astute, sociologically sophisticated, and politically aware, the New New Journalism may well be the most popular and influential development in the history of American literary nonfiction. *The New New Journalism* explores the methods and techniques this new generation of journalists has developed, and looks backward to understand their dual heritage—their debts to their predecessors from both the 1890s and the 1960s.

The New New Journalists bring a distinct set of cultural and social concerns to their work. Neither frustrated novelists nor wayward

[1] Tom Wolfe, *The New Journalism* (New York: Harper and Row, 1973), preface.

newspaper reporters, they tend to be magazine and book writers who have benefited enormously from both the legitimacy Wolfe's legacy has brought to literary nonfiction, and from the concurrent displacement of the novel as the most prestigious form of literary expression. When experimenting with narrative and rhetorical techniques, they conceive of themselves as working wholly within the nonfiction genre, rather than parsing the philosophical line between fact and fiction, as Norman Mailer and Truman Capote did with their nonfiction novels, *The Armies of the Night* and *In Cold Blood*. And when this new group dabbles in fiction, it is without the anxiety about their place in the world of letters that afflicted the writers of Wolfe's generation. "Whereas journalists once felt humbled by the novel, we now live in an age in which the *novelist* lives in a state of anxiety about nonfiction," says Michael Lewis.

Society is a more complex phenomenon for the New New Journalists than it was for their immediate predecessors. They consider class and race, not status, the primary indices of social hierarchy. Ethnic and/or ideological subcultures ("terra incognita," as Wolfe called them)[2]—once perceived as bizarre tribes one studied anthropologically—are today considered different in degree, not in kind, from the rest of American culture.

This movement's achievements are more reportorial than literary, which is why this book consists of discussions of journalistic practice and method, as opposed to dialogues on the theory or state of the genre. The days in which nonfiction writers test the limits of language and form have largely passed. The New Journalism was a truly avant-garde movement that expanded journalism's rhetorical and literary scope by placing the author at the center of the story, channeling a character's thoughts, using nonstandard punctuation, and exploding traditional narrative forms. That freedom to experiment has had a tremendous influence on many of the New New Journalists. "Tom Wolfe and the other pioneers of New Journalism broke the ground that allowed me to write a book like *Into the Wild,* which isn't a flamboyant piece of writing by any measure, but it does have some

[2]Joe David Bellamy, "Tom Wolfe," from *The New Fiction: Interviews with Innovative American Writers* (Urbana: University of Illinois Press, 1974), reprinted in *Conversations with Tom Wolfe,* ed. Dorothy M. Scura (Jackson: University Press of Mississippi, 1990), 39.

quirks that don't seem quite so weird and quirky in the wake of the New Journalists," says Jon Krakauer. "In that sense I'm indebted to Wolfe's bold innovations."

Contrary to the New Journalists, this new generation experiments more with the *way* one gets the story. To that end, they've developed innovative immersion strategies (Ted Conover worked as a prison guard for *Newjack* and lived as a hobo for *Rolling Nowhere*) and extended the time they've spent reporting (Leon Dash followed the characters in *Rosa Lee* for five years; Adrian LeBlanc reported *Random Family* for nearly a decade; Jonathan Harr's *A Civil Action* took nearly as long). While some are literary stylists of note (Richard Ben Cramer and Michael Lewis, for instance), their most significant innovations have involved experiments with reporting, rather than the language or forms they used to tell their stories.

It is ironic, then, that this reportorial movement is exploring the very territory Wolfe once ceded to the novel. "There are certain areas of life that journalism still cannot move into easily, particularly for reasons of invasion of privacy, and it is in this margin that the novel will be able to grow in the future," he wrote.[3] What Wolfe didn't anticipate was that a new generation of journalists would build upon (and ultimately surpass) his reporting methods, lengthening and deepening their involvement with characters to the point at which the public/private divide essentially disappeared. Wolfe went inside his characters' heads; the New New Journalists become part of their lives.

Despite Wolfe's insistence that he is, first and foremost, a reporter, it is his baroque writing style and vivid imagination—the "fun house mirror," in Wilfred Sheed's words, he holds up to the world—that gives his work its power. We read Wolfe for the imaginative distortion he brings to reality, not the reality itself.[4]

Reporting, for Wolfe, means immersion reporting, the relentless accumulation of details that define an individual's status. "Perfect

---

[3]Wolfe, *The New Journalism*, 35.

[4]"Upon these truths he imposes his own consciousness, his own selection and rhetoric, and they become Wolfe-truths, and he is halfway over the border to the hated Novel," writes Wilfrid Sheed in "A Fun-House Mirror," *The New York Times Book Review*, December 3, 1972, reprinted in *The Reporter As Artist: A Look at The New Journalism Controversy*, ed. Ronald Weber (New York: Hastings House, 1974), 295.

journalism would deal constantly with one subject: Status," he once told an interviewer. "And every article written would be devoted to discovering and defining some new status."[5] How one dresses or where one lives takes on near-theological significance for him. His sensitivity to social status, combined with his fascination with the "new," secured his role as the New Journalism's chief trend-spotter. But Wolfe's status-fixated reporting so values fashion over substance that it robs much of his journalism (and, similarly, many of the characters in his novels[6]) of complexity and depth. Wolfe's writing is all about surface. Once described as possessing the "social conscience of an ant,"[7] Wolfe doesn't have an activist bone in his body.[8] For Wolfe "it is style that matters, not politics; pleasure, not power; status, not class," writes historian Alan Trachtenberg. "Wolfe's revolution changes nothing, inverts nothing, in fact is *after* nothing but status."[9]

Furthermore, Wolfe's notion of status did not include explorations of race and class—distinctions rarely explored in any meaningful way by the New Journalism, but which are often at the center of the New New Journalists' work. Subcultures in general, and impoverished subcultures in particular, provide material for writers like Ted Conover, William Finnegan, Leon Dash, Adrian LeBlanc, Alex Kotlowitz, and Eric Schlosser. These writers view the disenfranchised not as exotic

[5]Elaine Dundy, "Tom Wolfe . . . But Exactly, Yes!" *Vogue,* April 15, 1966, reprinted in *Conversations with Tom Wolfe,* ed. Dorothy M. Scura (Jackson: University of Mississippi, 1990), 9.

[6]Reviewing *A Man In Full,* James Wood writes that Wolfe "is like a man with a very loud voice who thinks he speaks like everyone else. . . . His characters are types: each is a special edition of generalities." James Wood, *The Irresponsible Self* (New York: Farrar, Straus and Giroux, 2004), 212–13. Wood shows that Wolfe frequently uses the exact same set of adjectives to describe different characters.

[7]Jack Newfield, "Is There a 'New Journalism'?," in *The Reporter As Artist: A Look at The New Journalism Controversy,* ed. Ronald Weber (New York: Hastings House, 1974), 302.

[8]"I think it's very comforting to be able to say that we've got the same old problems: we've got war, we've got poverty. That way we don't have to see that the main problem—if you want to call it that—is that people are free all of a sudden; they're rich and they're fat and they're free," says Wolfe in an August 19, 1968, *New York* magazine interview with Lawrence Dietz, reprinted in *Conversations with Tom Wolfe,* ed. Dorothy M. Scura (Jackson: University Press of Mississippi, 1990), 19.

[9]Alan Trachtenberg, "What's New." Review of *The New Journalism,* by Tom Wolfe. *Partisan Review* 41: 296–302.

tribes, but as people whose problems are symptomatic of the dilemmas that vex America. There is an activist dimension in much of the New New Journalism, an element of muckraking (Schlosser) and social concern (Dash, Kotlowitz, and LeBlanc). "Wolfe is concerned with where people stand in society," says Lawrence Wright. "I'm more engaged with the subterranean, sometimes deeply dangerous urges, and how these beliefs steer individuals and cultures into conflict."

Finally, the New New Journalism is the literature of the everyday. If Wolfe's outlandish scenarios and larger-than-life characters leap from the page, the New New Journalism goes in the opposite direction, drilling down into the bedrock of ordinary experience, exploring what Gay Talese calls "the fictional current that flows beneath the stream of reality." In this regard, writers such as John McPhee and Talese—prose poets of the quotidian—are its key figures in the prior generation. In Talese's quest to turn reporting on the ordinary into an art, we find an aspect of the New Journalism enterprise that Wolfe obscured in his manifesto. Both McPhee and Talese emphasize the importance of rigorous reporting on the events and characters of everyday life over turns of bravura in writing style. Reporting on the minutiae of the ordinary—often over a period of years—has become their signature method.

Talese draws the distinction between himself and Wolfe well. Unlike Wolfe, he prefers to write about failure. "It is a subject that intrigues me much more than success," he says. "Tom is interested in the new, the latest, the most current . . . I'm more interested in what has held up for a long time and how it has done."[10] And even when Talese does write about a subject as dramatic as the Mafia (as he did in *Honor Thy Father*), he shuns the story's most sensationalist dimension in favor of exploring the social and psychological reality of criminal life. Ronald Weber contrasts Wolfe and Talese differently. "If Wolfe could be placed on the literary end of the new nonfiction spectrum, Talese belonged on the journalistic end. If Talese was a

[10]Gay Talese, "The New Journalism: A Panel Discussion with Harold Hayes, Gay Talese, Tom Wolfe and Professor L. W. Robinson," *Writer's Digest*, January 1970, reprinted in *The Reporter As Artist: A Look at The New Journalism Controversy*, ed. Ronald Weber (New York: Hastings House, 1974), 69.

reporter reaching for the levels of art, Wolfe was an artist who also happened to be a reporter."[11]

McPhee's influence has been twofold. First, a generation of literary journalists has taken his "Literature of Fact" course at Princeton (including Eric Schlosser and Richard Preston). Second, McPhee's influence on the New New Journalism can be seen in the catholic approach he takes toward subjects: anything—from geology and nuclear weapons to fishing and basketball—is fair game for the literary journalist, as long as it is prodigiously researched and painstakingly reported. As William L. Howarth writes, he has "stretched the artistic dimensions of reportage."[12] The attraction of McPhee's work is the spirit with which he produces it, in his quietly defiant personal style, as much as the subjects he writes about. The informal, declaratory, almost deliberately inelegant tone one hears among many of the New New Journalists comes straight from McPhee. His authorial presence is the exact opposite of Wolfe's "hectoring narrator";[13] McPhee is rarely a character in his work, and if he does appear he is never in the foreground.

Wolfe's manifesto has long been considered the New Journalism's bible; and, as with the Bible, it contains a creation story and a set of guiding principles. The principles are fairly straightforward. The New Journalism uses complete dialogue, rather than the snippets quoted in daily journalism; proceeds scene by scene, much as in a movie; incorporates varying points of view, rather than telling a story solely from the perspective of the narrator; and pays close attention to status details about the appearance and behavior of its characters. Rigorously reported, the New Journalism reads "like a story."

Wolfe's epiphany came in 1962 while reading Gay Talese's "Joe Louis: The King as a Middle-aged Man," in *Esquire*. Here was a magazine article with the tone and mood of a short story, a piece that combined the intimacy of fiction with extraordinary journalistic reporting. The scales fell from Wolfe's eyes: the hierarchy had been

[11]Ronald Weber, *The Literature of Fact* (Athens, Ohio: Ohio University Press, 1980), 102.

[12]William L. Howarth, ed., *The McPhee Reader* (New York: Farrar, Straus and Giroux, 1977), vii.

[13]Wolfe, *The New Journalism*, 17.

overturned. Journalists might now "use any literary device, from the traditional dialogisms of the essay to stream-of-consciousness . . . to excite the reader both intellectually and emotionally."[14] Wolfe's baptism famously occurred while writing about a hot rod car show for *Esquire* in 1963. Suffering from writer's block, he summarized his reporting in a manic memo to his editor, who printed the text—"There Goes (Varoom! Varoom!) That Kandy-Kolored Tangerine-Flake Streamline Baby"—virtually unedited. "The sudden arrival of this new style of journalism, from out of nowhere, had caused a status panic in the literary community," wrote Wolfe.[15]

No longer was the novel the form to which great writing aspired, "a nationwide tournament" between giants like Saul Bellow, Norman Mailer, John Updike, and Philip Roth. No longer would journalism function as little more than the place young men went to gather experience of the world, "a motel you checked into overnight on the road to the final triumph" of the novel.[16] (As a *Herald Tribune* feature writer, traveling along this very road—which eventually led to *The Bonfire of the Vanities* and other novels—Wolfe knew what he was talking about.) From now on, Wolfe decreed, the novelist would fear the journalist.

The drama of Wolfe's account—Status panic in the literary world! The novel dead! The New Journalism triumphant!—rests on two hidden (and contradictory) premises. First, because he insists that the New Journalism sprang forth "from out of nowhere," Wolfe had to explain away the presence of writers whose work bore any similarity to it. Second, Wolfe, who is smart enough to know that nothing springs forth ex nihilo, needed to find the New Journalism a predecessor with a proper pedigree. Furthermore, it was essential that the New Journalism's literary predecessor *not* resemble anything as base as journalism; otherwise, Wolfe's "new style" would be little more than the next logical stage of the genre. And where is the fun in that?

Wolfe's solution was ingenious. What better literary precedent with which to upend the novel, he figured, than the novel itself?

[14]Ibid., 15.

[15]Ibid., 25.

[16]Ibid., 5.

Thus he argued that the New Journalism (and its practitioners, such as Michael Herr, Truman Capote, Norman Mailer, Joan Didion, John Sack, and Gay Talese) was not a new stage in American journalism, but instead a revival of the European tradition of literary realism—a tradition unjustly ignored by a generation of callow, navel-gazing MFAs. "He declaims about the end-of-the-novel while he hitchhikes on the novel," writes Michael J. Arlen.[17] In one fell swoop, Wolfe simultaneously "dethroned" the novel, broke from American journalism, and claimed the mantle of the eighteenth- and nineteenth-century European novel. Literary realism—particularly the work of Fielding, Sterne, Smollett, Dickens, Zola, and Balzac— became his *cri de guerre.*

With the New Journalism's pedigree established, Wolfe gave grudging acknowledgment to the fact that writers such as A. J. Liebling, Joseph Mitchell, Truman Capote, John Hersey, and Lillian Ross had been experimenting with various New Journalism techniques (scenes, dialogue, perspective, and status details) for years. But having trashed *The New Yorker,* the magazine where these writers' work appeared, in a two-part 1965 story in *New York,* the *Herald Tribune's* Sunday supplement,[18] Wolfe was in a difficult position. He couldn't very well turn around and praise the magazine, so what was he to do? Without batting an eye, Wolfe simply wrote *The New Yorker* out of the tradition, lumping Hersey, Capote, Ross, and Liebling along with other "Not Half-Bad Candidates" for historical forerunners of the New Journalism.[19]

Critics griped, but largely accepted Wolfe's account. Latching on to Wolfe's notion of the journalistic novel, literary theorists set off on a wild postmodern goose-chase to divine the line between fact and fiction, producing a rash of scholarly studies—"fables of fact," "the

[17]Michael J. Arlen, "Notes on the New Journalism," *The Atlantic Monthly,* May 1972, reprinted in *The Reporter As Artist: A Look at The New Journalism Controversy,* ed. Ronald Weber (New York: Hastings House, 1974), 253.

[18]"Tiny Mummies," in which Wolfe characterized *New Yorker* editor William Shawn as a "museum custodian, an undertaker, a mortuary scientist."

[19]Wolfe, *The New Journalism,* 46.

novel as history"—focusing on the same six writers (Wolfe, Mailer, Thompson, Herr, Capote, and Didion).

The skeptics, for the most part, focused on the question of whether the New Journalism was, in fact, new. Weren't there all sorts of precedents, especially in eighteenth- and nineteenth-century English literature? Wolfe anticipated most of his critics' candidates—the coffeehouse reports of Addison and Steele, Defoe's *A Journal of the Plague Year*, Dickens's *Sketches by Boz*, William C. Hazlitt's "The Fight," Twain's *The Innocents Abroad*, Lafcadio Hearn's portraits of prostitutes and criminals for *The Cincinnati Enquirer*—pointing out the significant ways in which they differed from the New Journalism. And Wolfe's rebuttal was convincing. Some of the techniques used by Dickens, Defoe, and others resembled New Journalism, but on closer inspection these writers had entirely different aims and methods. Addison and Steele were, essentially, essayists who occasionally used scenes and quotations to animate their work. Most of the other suggested candidates weren't writing journalism (as in the case of Defoe's *A Journal of the Plague Year*, which is technically a work of fiction). Others were merely autobiographers who peppered their work with scenes and snatches of dialogue. Important writers in their own right, they simply hadn't been playing Wolfe's game.

In the end, Wolfe's concern was less with the history of the genre than the future of his career. He was a salesman, and the New Journalism was his product. "If four-letter words, talk about drugs, appearances on television talk shows, continual references to a new genre, to nonfiction novels, to new journalism—and a suit with a vest—are necessary to sell the product, so be it," wrote George Hough.[20] Wolfe had declared war on the literary hierarchy that relegated him and his brethren to magazines and the feature sections of newspapers. Ultimately, Wolfe's argument was less a manifesto for a movement than an advertisement for himself.

As is common in an age of planned obsolescence, the New Journalism didn't remain new for long. "Whatever happened to the New Journalism?" wondered Thomas Powers in *Commonweal*, two

[20]George A. Hough, III. "How 'New'?" *Journal of Popular Culture* 9: 114–21, Summer 1975.

years after Wolfe's manifesto appeared.[21] By the 1980s, the consensus was that the New Journalism was dead.

Wolfe's self-serving history of the New Journalism makes it difficult to appreciate both the distinctively American quality of modern literary journalism and, looking forward, the continuity between nineteenth-century American literary journalism and the contemporary New New Journalists.[22]

Though Wolfe and his critics explored many aspects of literary journalism, no one asked why it had seemed to thrive almost exclusively in America during the second half of the twentieth century. Why, despite their highly developed novelistic and essayistic traditions, had neither Europe, Asia, nor South America embraced literary nonfiction? Even the birthplace of literary journalism, England—with the exception of *Granta*-affiliated writers like Bruce Chatwin, James Fenton, and Isabel Hilton—has produced few practitioners since Orwell.

The suggestion that there is something peculiarly American about the form is not new. "The tradition of reportorial journalism, which first attained literary quality more than a hundred years ago in Dana's *Two Years Before the Mast,* has become, since Mark Twain's time, one of the principal shaping forces in our literature," writes

---

[21] Wolfe's "attempt to divert the whole focus of American literary energy was met by indifference. It wasn't that no one believed he was serious; it was that no one believed he was right," Thomas Powers, "Cry Wolfe," *Commonweal,* October 24, 1975, 497.

[22] It has always struck me as odd that Tom Wolfe is considered the patron saint of the New Journalism. His work bears little formal resemblance to that of other New Journalists (Michael Herr, Truman Capote, Norman Mailer, Joan Sack, Gay Talese—all included in Wolfe's anthology). His subject matter (manners and morals, cultural trends) is distinct from those of his colleagues: politics (Mailer, Didion), war (Herr, Sack), and crime (Capote, Talese). His writing style—hyperbolic, frenzied, hectoring—is inimitable. "Wolfe was never in the same racket as Gay Talese or Dick Schaap—or they with each other," wrote Wilfrid Sheed in the December 3, 1972, *New York Times Book Review.* The obvious reasons he is identified with the movement—that he was among the first to call attention to it, and edited its first anthology—are, like most obvious answers, both correct and inadequate. They smack too much of "because I *said so*" logic, accepting at face value what Michael Arlen, writing in the May 1972 *Atlantic Monthly,* called Wolfe's "Me and My Pals Forge History Together" version of events.

John A. Kouwenhoven in his 1948 study *Made in America*. Reportorial journalism, he argued, is a distinctively American phenomenon, and he cites John Hersey's *Hiroshima* as an example of a work that gives "reportage a foundation of rigorously factual detail which is almost unknown elsewhere."

More recently, others have argued that there is something fundamentally American about the genre, suggesting that it "is inextricably connected with the effort to express the force and magnitude and sheer overpowering energy of the American experience."[23] *New Yorker* writer Jane Kramer, who has spent half her career writing in and about Europe, agrees. "People have tried to imitate the genre and somehow can't. It's really only in America—and in a different way England—that this narrative experiment has developed," she says.

One can trace this American exceptionalism to the second half of the nineteenth century, when a confluence of developments—demographic, economic, and cultural—provided conditions that encouraged nonfiction literature in general, and literary journalism in particular.

From the time of Benjamin Franklin, America has been an empirical, pragmatic culture—an impulse which came into its own in the mid-nineteenth century by way of the culture's embrace of science and social reform. "Ours is an age of facts. It wants facts, not theories," writes Jacob Riis in *The Children of the Poor* (1892). This hunger for factual information had its parallel in literature. "Scientists were gathering a torrent of facts, many of them strange and haunting to people's imaginations. While science struggled to fit all of these facts into a fabric of knowledge, writers struggled to embody facts . . . into a fabric of imaginative literature," writes journalist and literary historian Richard Preston.[24]

Among the most startling facts was the surge in America's wealth, size, and population. Between 1860 and 1890, the country's population and per capita wealth doubled, while its national wealth quadru-

[23]Chris Anderson, *Style as Argument* (Carbondale: Southern Illinois University Press, 1987), 2.

[24]Richard Preston, "The Fabric of Fact" (Princeton University dissertation), 1983, 6.

pled.[25] Between 1870 and 1900, a nation of seventy-five million people absorbed twelve million immigrants. Traditional journalism was simply not vivid enough to render the extraordinary changes in American life. Some have argued that the literary (or narrative) strand of American journalism was a reaction against the constraints of purely fact-based accounts. Instead a more narrative, subjective form conveyed such overwhelming data in a comprehensible manner.[26]

Thus the hybrid of the fact-rich, *narrative* history became a popular American literary genre. "Faced with a new continent full of strange forms of life and potentially useful or threatening mysteries, Americans have always placed a premium on the accurate survey, the reliable report," writes Preston. "There are many American classics in which facts become the girders of myth, from William Bradford's *History of the Plymouth Plantation* to *Leaves of Grass* to Tom Wolfe's *The Right Stuff*."[27]

There are a number of reasons that nonfiction dominated the nineteenth-century book market. First, novels were considered frivolous and potentially immoral.[28] Economics played a role, too. Publishers were more likely to offer an author an advance for a work of nonfiction than for a novel. Because no international copyright agreement existed between England and the U.S. until 1899, an American publisher was better off stealing British novels than paying for American ones. With the country's borders expanding and its population growing, readers were eager to learn more about America's new frontier. Sales for "true adventure" books were fairly predictable, and American nonfiction had a large, and reliable, international readership; America's was the story the world wanted to hear.[29]

One manifestation of America's thirst for nonfiction can be seen in the number of newspapers published, which quadrupled between 1870 and 1900. Much of this growth was the result of dramatic

[25]John C. Hartsock, *A History of American Literary Journalism* (Amherst: University of Massachusetts Press, 2000), 58.

[26]Hartsock, *A History of American Literary Journalism*, 59.

[27]Preston, "The Fabric of Fact," 34.

[28]Ibid., 16.

[29]Ibid., 19.

changes in the way the new newspapers conveyed information to their readers. Until the 1830s, the typical daily newspaper consisted of four pages, and was sold by subscription to a relatively small audience whose interests were business and politics.[30]

On September 3, 1833, *The New York Sun* began the transition from the partisan and mercantile press to the commercial Penny Press. Between the 1830s and the Civil War, the editors of the Penny Press discovered that news conveyed through "stories" drew a larger readership than the combination of editorial opinion and financial information that had theretofore dominated American newspapers. The *Sun*'s first issue sold out immediately, and contained numerous "human interest" stories (a form practically invented by the Penny Press) that drew an audience of readers "starved for information about other people like themselves, distressed souls from other lands or from upstate farms—people marooned in a rapidly growing city that was often inscrutable, uncaring, or unintelligible," writes historian George H. Douglas.[31] The Penny Press of the 1830s initiated the modern conception of news and reporting (the latter development coming to fruition during the Civil War). Newspapers turned their attention to stories with relevance to their readers' lives.[32]

The *Sun,* in its 1880s incarnation under Charles Dana, bridged the transition between the older press and the New Journalism that developed toward the end of the century. Dana's contribution was to combine a focus on the everyday with a concern for vivid, well-written stories: For Dana, a newspaper story was itself an art form.[33] That Dana's staff included reporters like Jacob Riis, who wrote about the New York slums he had inhabited for seven years, lent the *Sun*'s journalism a muckraking edge.

[30]Michael Robertson, *Stephen Crane, Journalism, and the Making of Modern American Literature* (New York: Columbia University Press, 1997), 3.

[31]George H. Douglas, *The Golden Age of the Newspaper* (Westport: Greenwood Press, 1999), 6.

[32]"The newspaper began to reflect, not the affairs of an elite in a small trading society, but the activities of an increasingly varied, urban, and middle-class society," writes Michael Schudson in *Discovering the News: A Social History of American Newspapers* (New York: Basic Books, 1978), 22.

[33]Douglas, *The Golden Age of the Newspaper,* 73–74.

It was no coincidence that when Joseph Pulitzer bought the *New York World* in 1883, he tried to hire some of Dana's best writers. The phrase "New Journalism" first appeared in an American context in the 1880s when it was used to describe the blend of sensationalism and crusading journalism—muckraking on behalf of immigrants and the poor—one found in the *New York World* and other papers. Pulitzer was not shy about his intentions, publishing his credo in his first issue of the new *World*: "There is room in this great and growing city for a journal that is not only cheap but bright, not only bright but large, not only large but truly democratic—dedicated to the cause of the people rather than that of the purse-potentates—devoted more to the news of the New than the Old World—that will expose all fraud and sham, fight all public evils and abuses—that will serve and battle for the people with earnest sincerity."[34] The New Journalism was a mass phenomenon, with Pulitzer's *New York World* reaching 250,000 readers a day by 1887—making it the largest paper in the country. Pulitzer argued that thorough reporting was a crucial component to his journalism. As he told the staff of the *St. Louis Post-Dispatch*: "Never drop a thing until you have gone to the bottom of it. Continuity! Continuity! Continuity until the subject is really finished."[35]

Although it was historically unrelated to Pulitzer's New Journalism, the genre of writing that Lincoln Steffens called "literary journalism" shared many of its goals. As the city editor of the *New York Commercial Advertiser* in the 1890s, Steffens made literary journalism—artfully told narrative stories about subjects of concern to the masses—into editorial policy, insisting that the basic goals of the artist and the journalist (subjectivity, honesty, empathy) were the same. "Our stated ideal for a murder story was that it should be so understood and told that the murderer would not be hanged, not by our readers," he writes in his *Autobiography*. "We never achieved our ideal, but there it was; and it is scientifically and artistically the true ideal for an artist and for a newspaper: to get the news so completely and to

[34]Quoted in Douglas, *The Golden Age of the Newspaper,* 103.

[35]Michael Emery, Edwin Emery, Nancy L. Roberts, *The Press and America: An Interpretive History of the Mass Media,* 9th ed. (Boston: Allyn and Bacon, 2000), 172.

report it so humanly that the reader will see himself in the other fellow's place."[36]

Steffens is best known for his work as a muckraker at *McClure's* magazine in the early years of the twentieth century. But throughout his career, his goal was to inspire his writers (and himself) to create "literature" about America's most important institutions (business and politics)—raising writing above mere journalism by infusing it with the passion, style, and technique of great fiction.

Steffens's *Commercial Advertiser* was not the only publication open to narrative literary journalism, as a look at Stephen Crane's wide-ranging publishing history shows.[37] Among his contemporaries, Crane was one of the best to put Steffens's vision into practice as he balanced the demands of literature and journalism in a manner that honored both. Crane thought nothing of chronicling an incident several times in several different genres, as he did when writing up his experiences in a shipwreck in a newspaper article, a short story, and a magazine piece.[38] "What didn't fit one genre was tailored to another," writes George Hough.[39]

Crane's career has often been used by Wolfe, and others, as evidence that journalism has always been merely the "warm-up" for the novel. But this simply isn't true in Crane's case. Crane's novels *preceded* his journalism on a subject. He wrote *Maggie: A Girl of the Streets* before he knew New York's slums, and didn't see a battlefield until two years after *The Red Badge of Courage*.[40] In this sense, it was fiction that was the warm-up for his extraordinary journalism, not the other way around.

---

[36]Lincoln Steffens, *The Autobiography of Lincoln Steffens* (New York: Harcourt, Brace and Company, 1931), 317.

[37]"At various times Crane published his true-life sketches of local color in every major New York paper," in addition to newspapers and magazines across the nation. Hartsock, *A History of American Literary Journalism*, 34.

[38]Robertson, *Stephen Crane, Journalism, and the Making of Modern American Literature*, 56.

[39]Hough, "How 'New'?" 117–119.

[40]Robertson, 57.

Crane's favorite journalistic form was the closely observed sketch of city life. These sketches—of the poor, of immigrants, of ordinary citizens—drew readers with the unsentimental, artful way he captured his characters and their pedestrian struggles. Experimenting with dialogue and perspective, Crane treated New York as a "mosaic of little worlds," a microcosm divided according to class and ethnicity, which he rendered with photograph-like clarity. Crane writes not as a social commentator or a polemical, muckraking journalist in the style of Jacob Riis or Lincoln Steffens, but rather as a detailed observer. "He is not concerned with converting the reader to social sympathy (perhaps distrustful or weary of the condescension of such a stance), but with converting the sheer data into *experience*. He writes as a phenomenologist of the scene, intent on characterizing the consciousness of the place (which includes its separate points of view) by a rendering of felt detail," writes Alan Trachtenberg.[41]

By the first decades of the twentieth century, the growing belief that newspapers should strive for objectivity left little room for literary journalism in their pages. Novelists were warned by Flaubert, Joyce, and others that writing journalism would harm their fiction, further diminishing journalism's status in the literary world. The novel gradually took on what Hartsock calls a "cryptotheological aura,"[42] a sense of importance and transcendence that journalism could never match. "The 'fall,' then, of journalism—and by extension narrative literary journalism—from literary grace was largely the result of the invention of a high literature in the nineteenth century," Hartsock argues.[43] And this, more or less, was the literary hierarchy when Wolfe started down the long road from journalism to the novel.

The writers who appear in this book do not constitute a coherent group in any social or institutional form. Some of them know each other, but most do not. They don't live in any one city or part of the country. They write for different magazines—primarily *The New Yorker*, *The Atlantic Monthly*, *The New York Times Magazine*, and

---

[41]Alan Trachtenberg, "Experiments in Another Country: Stephen Crane's City Sketches," *The Southern Review* 10: 278.

[42]Hartsock, *A History of American Literary Journalism*, 217.

[43]Ibid., 244.

Rolling Stone—but most of them make their livings writing books. It is a far cry from the clubby group of writers Wolfe describes in the *Herald Tribune* city room (Charles Portis, Dick Schaap, Jimmy Breslin), or at Harold Hayes's *Esquire,* or Clay Felker's *New York* magazine.[44]

What they do share is a dedication to the craft of reporting, a conviction that by immersing themselves deeply into their subjects' lives, often for prolonged periods of time, they can—much as Crane did before them—bridge the gap between their subjective perspective and the reality they are observing, that they can render reality in a way that is both accurate and aesthetically pleasing. In their devotion to close-to-the-skin reporting—a journalistic version of Keats's "negative capability"—they are the children of McPhee and Talese.

What this new breed represents is less a school of thought, or rule-defined movement, than a shorthand way of describing the reportorial sensibility behind an increasingly significant body of work. The list of writers I have focused on is neither exclusive nor complete—there are a dozen others I would have liked to include had I the time and space. Yet I chose these nineteen writers because each strikes me as representing a particular dimension of the New New Journalism.

Kramer, Talese, and Trillin are in some ways the "elders" of the movement, writers who have spent their careers alternatively reporting on the extraordinary lives of ordinary people, and the ordinary lives of extraordinary people—Talese's portraits of Frank Sinatra and Joe DiMaggio being the most famous example of the latter impulse.

In an era when the clash of convictions has led to terrorism and war, Lawrence Wright's writings on belief show why it is important for journalists to suspend their secular biases and examine religious ideas on their own merits. Wright's respect for the evangelical impulse, combined with his grounding in psychology and Arabic culture, makes him one of the most insightful of the New New Journalists.

A longtime reader of Stephen Crane, I was struck by the way that LeBlanc, Finnegan, Dash, Conover, and Kotlowitz resurrect Crane's capacity for drawing the accurate, sympathetic portrait of the vicissitudes of city life (a sensibility which Kotlowitz calls "the journalism of empathy"). To Crane's genius for subjectivity, they add an inde-

[44]Wolfe, *The New Journalism,* 5.

fatigable reporting stamina, returning to their subjects again and again, over months, and even years. There exists a sympathetic resonance between Crane's nonjudgmental renderings of his characters' experience and the New New Journalists' subtle pleas for justice on behalf of their vulnerable subjects.

Eric Schlosser's muckraking exposés about the fast-food industry and the underground economy of drugs, pornography, and migrant labor is exactly the kind of meticulously reported work I could imagine Lincoln Steffens or Jacob Riis producing were they still alive. Schlosser's background in drama and fiction only made the connection to Steffens's brand of literary journalism more obvious. And the steady placement of Schlosser's books on bestseller lists across the country is evidence both of his talent and of a public that is willing to be outraged by what he has discovered. Adrian LeBlanc, too, perceives herself as part of a tradition of journalists, like Riis, who have written about social justice. "It is a documentary tradition as well as a literary one," she notes.

One of the most successful genres in nineteenth-century American literary journalism was the travel adventure story: the young man who braves the elements and brings back news of his journey on the frontier was a perennial bestseller. Jon Krakauer's and William Langewiesche's work takes the genre in a different direction. Langewiesche's exotic journey deep into the bowels of the post-9/11 World Trade Center ("the heap") traces the extraordinary efforts to "unbuild" America's foremost symbol of global capitalism. Krakauer's trek into the wilds of Alaska traces the final days of a young adventurer, but whether writing about mountain climbing or Mormon fundamentalists, the terrain Krakauer explores is first and foremost psychological. The spectacular natural terrain is merely a bonus for the reader.

Although indebted to the experimentalism of Wolfe's New Journalism, the New New Journalism should also be understood as a movement that rehabilitates important aspects of its nineteenth-century predecessors. This latest generation of writers is not all directly or consciously influenced by nineteenth-century New Journalists—some have been, but most have not. Rather, participating in the tradition of American literary journalism, the New New Journalists are (often unwittingly) dwelling on questions that the genre has been posing since the nineteenth century: How does a fast-growing society of immigrants construct a national identity? How does a country built by capitalism consider questions of economic justice? The questions that pressed themselves upon nineteenth-century writers are posing themselves with new vigor today, which is one reason for the resurgence of American literary nonfiction.

Oddly enough, there are also many respects in which our cultural worldview bears more resemblance to that of Steffens and Crane than to Wolfe's. We are currently experiencing the fascination with "true stories"—news from the world—that is common during times of great unrest and turmoil. As in the nineteenth century, America is rethinking its place in the world, questioning whether it can absorb the huge number of immigrants who have flocked to its shores.[45] Once again, America's is the story the world wants to read about, although perhaps more out of spite than admiration. "Americans are lucky enough to be living in a place which, in relative historical terms, is *breathtakingly* important, not just militarily and politically, but also culturally," says Michael Lewis. "The stories we tell about life in America have a universal appeal that stories from no other place have." The subjects the New New Journalists write about—transnational immigration (Conover, Kramer), poverty (LeBlanc, Kotlowitz), race (Finnegan, Kotlowitz, Dash), the clash of faiths (Wright), big business (Lewis, Schlosser)—are the issues that the world cares about. The deep-rooted American desire for factual information has become exacerbated by our unease in the world, and it expresses itself in our thirst for drama "ripped from the head-lines," entertainment "based on a true story," or in the myriad "reality television" programs. Contemporary America is little more than Crane's "mosaic of little worlds, writ larger" a concatenation of sub-cultures bumping up against each other in previously unimaginable ways. The New New Journalists' recognition of this gives their work currency.

---

[45]Whereas the country underwent a similar process of self-reflection in the late 1960s, I would argue that the precariousness of the current situation is unprecedented in American history. The political and military uncertainty of the 1960s was cushioned by the tremendous surge of postwar wealth and power—the latter being precisely the sub-ject Wolfe chose to write about.

Much as it was in the nineteenth century, nonfiction today is as prestigious—if not more so—than the novel. Ours is an age of nonfiction, "the *de facto* literature of our time," the critic Seymour Krim once called it. This is as true commercially as it is culturally. There is nothing quaint or marginal about works of literary journalism like Jon Krakauer's *Into Thin Air*, Michael Lewis's *Moneyball*, Richard Preston's *The Hot Zone*, Susan Orlean's *The Orchid Thief*, Jonathan Harr's *A Civil Action*, and Eric Schlosser's *Fast Food Nation*—all of which have been enormous bestsellers. The New New Journalism is big business on a scale never before seen by serious literary journalism.

With their muckraking and intensive reporting on social and cultural issues, the New New Journalists have revived the tradition of American literary journalism, raising it to a more popular and commercial level than either its nineteenth- or late-twentieth-century predecessors ever imagined. The debates over "journalism" and "literature"—between "subjective" and "objective" reporting—weigh less heavily on this generation, freeing them to combine the best of both genres. Having done so without manifestos or public debates, the New New Journalism has assumed a premier place in American literature.

Anderson, Chris. *Style as Argument*. Carbondale: Southern Illinois University Press, 1987.

Applegate, Edward Cray. "A Historical Analysis of New Journalism." Diss., Oklahoma State University, 1984.

Beard, John. "Inside the Whale: A Critical Study of New Journalism and the Nonfiction Form." Diss., Florida State University, 1985.

Belgrade, Paul S. "The Literary Journalism as Illuminator of Subjectivity." Diss., University of Maryland College Park, 1990.

Benfey, Christopher. *The Double Life of Stephen Crane*. New York: Knopf, 1992.

Connery, Thomas Bernard. "Fusing Fiction Technique and Journalistic Fact: Literary Journalism in the 1890s Newspaper." Diss., Brown University, 1984.

Connery, Thomas B., ed. *A Sourcebook of American Literary Journalism*. Westport: Greenwood Press, 1992.

Crane, Stephen. *The New York City Sketches of Stephen Crane and Related Pieces*. Edited by R. W. Stallman and E. R. Hagemann. New York: New York University Press, 1966.

Dennis, Everette E., and William L. Rivers. *Other Voices: The New Journalism in America*. San Francisco: Canfield Press, 1974.

Douglas, George H. *The Golden Age of the Newspaper*. Westport: Greenwood Press, 1999.

Emery, Michael, Edwin Emery, and Nancy L. Roberts. *The Press and America: An Interpretive History of the Mass Media*. 9th ed. Boston: Allyn and Bacon, 2000.

Frankfort, Ellen. *The Voice: Life at The Village Voice*. New York: William Morrow, 1976.

Frus, Phyllis. *The Politics and Poetics of Journalistic Narrative: The Timely and the Timeless*. New York: Cambridge University Press, 1994.

Hartsock, John C. *A History of American Literary Journalism: The Emergence of Modern Narrative Form*. Amherst: University of Massachusetts Press, 2000.

Harvey, Chris. "Tom Wolfe's Revenge." *American Journalism Review* (October 1994).

Hellman, John. *Fables of Fact*. Urbana: University of Illinois Press, 1981.

Hollowell, John. *Fact and Fiction: The New Journalism and the Nonfiction Novel*. Chapel Hill: University of North Carolina Press, 1977.

Hough, George A., III. "How 'New'?" *The Journal of Popular Culture* 9: 121–23.

Huntzicker, William E. *The Popular Press, 1833–1865*. Westport: Greenwood Press, 1999.

Jensen, Jay. "The New Journalism in Historical Perspective." *Journalism History* 1.2 (1974): 37, 66.

Kaplan, Justin. *Lincoln Steffens: A Biography*. New York: Simon and Schuster, 1974.

Kerrane, Kevin, and Ben Yagoda, eds. *The Art of Fact*. New York: Scribner, 1977.

Kouwenhoven, John A. *Made in America*. Doubleday, 1948.

McPhee, John. *The John McPhee Reader*. Edited by William L. Howarth. New York: Farrar, Straus and Giroux, 1977.

Meyers, Paul Thomas. "The New Journalist as Culture Critic: Wolfe, Thompson, Talese." Diss., Washington State University, 1983.

Mott, Frank Luther. *American Journalism: A History, 1690–1960*. New York: The Macmillan Company, 1962.

Nocera, Joseph. "How Hunter Thompson Killed New Journalism." *The Washington Monthly* (April 1981).

Powers, Thomas. "Cry Wolfe." *Commonweal* 102 (October 24, 1975).

Preston, Richard. "The Fabric of Fact: The Beginnings of American Literary Journalism." Diss., Princeton University, 1983.

Robertson, Michael. *Stephen Crane, Journalism, and the Making of Modern American Literature*. New York: Columbia University Press, 1997.

Roundy, George. "Crafting Fact: The Prose of John McPhee." Diss., University of Iowa, 1984.

Schudson, Michael. *Discovering the News: A Social History of American Newspapers*. New York: Basic Books, 1978.

Scura, Dorothy M., ed. *Conversations with Tom Wolfe*. Jackson: University Press of Mississippi, 1990.

Sims, Norman, and Mark Kramer, eds. *Literary Journalism: A New Collection of the Best American Nonfiction*. New York: Ballantine, 1995.

Sims, Norman, ed. *Literary Journalism in the Twentieth Century*. New York: Oxford University Press, 1990.

Smith, Kathy Anne. "Writing the Borderline: Journalism's Literary Contract." Diss., University of Massachusetts, 1988.

Steffens, Lincoln. *The Autobiography of Lincoln Steffens*. New York: Harcourt, Brace, 1931.

Stephens, Mitchell. *A History of News*. New York: Harcourt, Brace, 1997.

Trachtenberg, Alan. "What's New?" *Partisan Review* no. 2 (1974).

Trachtenberg, Alan. "Experiments in Another Country: Stephen Crane's City Sketches." *Southern Review* 10.

Vare, Robert, ed. *The State of Narrative Nonfiction Writing*. Nieman Reports, 2000.

Webb, Joseph. "Historical Perspective on the New Journalism." *Journalism History* 1.2 (1974): 38–42, 60.

Weber, Ronald, ed. *The Reporter As Artist: A Look at The New Journalism Controversy*. New York: Hastings House, 1974.

Weber, Ronald. *The Literature of Fact: Literary Nonfiction in American Writing*. Athens, Ohio: Ohio University Press, 1980.

Winterowd, W. Ross. *The Rhetoric of the "Other" Literature*. Carbondale: Southern Illinois University Press, 1990.

Wolfe, Tom. *The New Journalism*. New York: Harper and Row, 1973.

Wolfe, Tom. *Hooking Up*. New York: Farrar, Straus and Giroux, 2000.

Wood, James. *The Irresponsible Self: On Laughter and the Novel*. New York: Farrar, Straus and Giroux, 2004.

I had neither studied nor taught journalism when I came to NYU. Instead, what I had to share with my students was a decade's worth of experience writing for *The New Yorker, The Atlantic Monthly, The New York Times Magazine,* and other publications. But I was always acutely aware that what I was teaching were simply my methods—not the best and (I hope) not the worst, but methods that were, for good or for ill, a reflection of me. Why should I assume they would work for anyone else? And if—as I believe—the only possessions a writer has are his talent and idiosyncrasies, was it even wise to recommend my hodgepodge of journalistic practices to my students?

I resolved my moral quandary by explaining, at the beginning of each semester, that it isn't so important for a writer to use one particular method rather than another (although some *are* inherently superior). What *is* crucial, I told them, is that *every writer have a method of some kind*: routines to cling to when everything goes wrong, rules to follow when you're blocked or frustrated. After all, there are an infinite number of ways to organize one's writing life. I had mine and knew other writers did, too. What were they? This book is my answer to that question.

The book grew out of my classes, during which I would invite in a journalist to discuss his work. What followed were conversations—extended interviews, really—on the *process* of writing: developing "beats," coming up with ideas, interviewing, research, writing, rewriting.

The results were often fascinating—both for my class and for myself (and for our visitors, who all confessed they, too, had no idea how their colleagues operated). Ren Weschler described playing with children's blocks to organize his thoughts. Ron Rosenbaum explained why he (manually) typed and retyped each draft. Jane Kramer told of the elaborate meals she cooks while writing, her ideas simmering along with the ingredients.

In the conversations that follow, I've tried to re-create the spontaneity and excitement of those classroom encounters. Each is the result of many hours of taped interviews, which I then transcribed and edited before giving the transcript to the writer to improve. The arc of each conversation is roughly the same, and follows a hypothetical work from conception to publication. The goal of this project was to find a way of talking about writing—as opposed to the *idea* of writing—that was at once demystifying and edifying; to make an often baffling process become more tangible and, perhaps, more manageable.

A bibliography of each journalist's work follows each conversation. For more information about their work and a complete bibliography of each journalist's articles, visit www.newnewjournalism.com.

The New New Journalism

TED CONOVER

The first time Ted Conover was asked if he was a tramp he wasn't sure how to respond. The son of a successful lawyer, Conover had been jumping on and off trains for months, riding the rails as research for his college anthropology thesis. He certainly *looked* the part; even his parents didn't recognize him when he showed up on their doorstep. In fact, he had entered the life so completely that when another tramp tried to jump into his boxcar (a violation of hobo etiquette), Conover barely hesitated before stepping on the man's hand, sending him flying off the moving train. "I guess I am," he answered uneasily, all too aware of the vast expanse—economic, social, intellectual—separating him from his veteran-tramp interlocutor.

It is this expanse that Conover has spent the last two decades exploring, first in *Rolling Nowhere* (1984), the cult classic he wrote about his hobo travels, and then in his three subsequent books—*Coyotes* (1987), *Whiteout* (1991), and *Newjack* (2000)—about Mexican illegal aliens, Aspen celebrities, and prison guards. Together, they have cemented Conover's reputation as one of the finest participatory journalists of his generation.

Those who have read only one or two of Conover's works might cubbyhole him as the bard of gritty, rough-and-tumble subcultures. While not untrue, the description is incomplete. It obscures Conover's real subject: the fine lines separating "us" from "them," and the elaborate rituals and markers—"parts of town, railroad tracks and boulevards, places in the heart and mind," he writes in *Coyotes*—that we have developed to bolster such distinctions.

In Conover's hands, migrant workers, rootless hoboes, and prison guards become vivid, morally ambiguous characters, deserving of praise *and* scorn, admiration *and* pity. Without sacrificing the commitment of the early-twentieth-century muckrakers, or the gusto of the nineteenth-century literary adventurers in whose footsteps he walks, Conover combines "a sociologist's eye for detail with a novelist's sense of drama and compassion," as *The New York Times*'s Michiko Kakutani wrote of *Coyotes*.

Born in 1958 in Okinawa, Japan, where his father was stationed as a navy pilot, Conover was raised in an affluent Denver neighborhood. In high school, he was bused to a newly desegregated school (50 percent black, 40 percent white, and 10 percent Hispanic), and he credits the experience with inspiring his love of anthropology (a discipline he calls "philosophy as lived by real people"). "I learned that one's own culture is not necessarily normative," he says, "that there are many ways of looking at the world."

In 1980, after three years of studying anthropology at Amherst, Conover wearied of the college's elitism. Conover proposed to ride the rails for his senior thesis. He wanted to learn whether hoboes were great American rebels ("renegades, conscientious objectors to the nine-to-five work world"), infantrymen in the army of homeless who were then inundating cities across America, or both. The college said they couldn't sanction an illegal activity, but Conover completed the fieldwork on his own time, hitting the road armed with little more than an emergency stash of traveler's checks.

Conover returned to Amherst to write his senior thesis gaining approval for the project after the fact, when his professor saw the notes he'd taken on the trip. He also spun off an autobiographical article for a student magazine, which caught the attention of several television producers. His enthusiasm for the subject bolstered by the attention, Conover turned down the reporting job he had been offered at *The Indianapolis Star* and decided to write a book about his adventures.

Rolling Nowhere was published in 1984. *Washington Post* staff writer Chip Brown noted the peculiarly American themes— expansion, restlessness, the myth of the West—that would mark much of Conover's future work. "Freight trains possess grandeur. They cast an epic spell. With their long whistles and their magical names, they summarize something in us, for they have carried not just the steel and wheat of America, but the nation's westwardness and some measure of its spacious dream," Brown wrote.

After graduating from Amherst summa cum laude, he won a spot as a Marshall Scholar at Cambridge University. It was not

long before Conover was back on the road, expanding on the
insight he had gained writing *Rolling Nowhere*: "Mexican farmworkers were the new American hoboes." For *Coyotes,* Conover
crossed the U.S.-Mexican border four times, traveling with migrant
workers through California, Arizona, Idaho, and Florida. He picked
lemons and oranges, and lived for a time in the village of Ahuacatlan,
Querétaro, the hometown of a number of the illegal immigrants
he met.

Again, some critics realized that Conover was writing about
something more fundamental than the immigration debate. "What
makes it really glow on every page is Mr. Conover's realization that
he is dealing neither with a crime nor a tragedy, but with another
of those human adventures that make America a country that is
constantly renewing itself," wrote T. D. Allman in *The New York
Times Book Review*.

Back in New York, Conover was rankled at a cocktail party
when a friend introduced him as "Ted Conover, a writer who
makes his living sleeping on the ground." The accuracy of the
remark disturbed him. "I was unsettled to feel so easily typecast at
age thirty, and began to wonder whether my participant-observer
method could be used to write about people who *weren't* remote
or poor."

The result was his 1991 book, *Whiteout: Lost in Aspen,* in
which Conover conducted what he described as "an ethnography
of hedonism," observing Aspen's celebrity culture from his perches
as a local cab driver and reporter at the *Aspen Times*. As with his
previous books, *Whiteout* was a meditation on the author's ambiguous relationship to the phenomenon he chronicled—the "great
celebrity laboratory" that Aspen had become. Some critics were
disappointed by Conover's turn away from the dispossessed.
Writing in the *Los Angeles Times*, Richard Eder felt that Conover's
considerable "talent overmatches his subject." Others perceived a
continuity. "His subject is Aspen, the glittering ski resort and
celebrity enclave in the Rocky Mountains of Colorado. The under-
lying theme, however, is similar to that explored in his earlier
books: the promise and betrayal of the American Dream," wrote
Kakutani.

In the early nineties, Conover asked the New York State Department of Correctional Services for permission to write an article for *The New Yorker* in which he would follow a guard through training. The U.S. prison population was at an all-time high, and he conceived of the story as being as much about economics as society. The Department is New York State's second-largest employer, and ailing communities throughout the region routinely bid for new prisons in the hopes they will revive the local economy.

When his formal request was rejected, Conover applied for a job as a guard, carefully navigating the ethical and legal minefield of undercover reporting. He offered no false information on his application, but did omit mention of his three books, and he vowed to himself not to write anything about the experience until after he had quit. "When I was a guard, I wanted to be 100 percent a guard," he says, living on a guard's salary and eschewing writing assignments. Fortunately, journalists and guards do share one thing—both carrying around notebooks in which to jot down their observations. Every night, from March 1997 to January 1998, when he returned from Sing Sing, Conover would type up pages of single-spaced notes (nearly five hundred in all), elaborating on the day's observations. It was part journalism and part therapy, as he tried to unburden himself of the awful things he'd witnessed—and taken part in—every day.

The project required complete secrecy, and Conover's double life took a toll. He was wracked with terrible headaches and found he was often sullen around his family. He feared he was allowing the anarchy of Sing Sing to seep into his placid home life. Published in 2000, *Newjack* won the National Book Critics Circle Award and was a finalist for the Pulitzer Prize. Conover was awarded a Guggenheim Fellowship in 2003 and is at work on a book about roads. In February 2004, Conover received the kind of compliment life pays to art. Using *Newjack* as their guide, a group of Sing Sing inmates hatched an ingenious (though unsuccessful) escape plan in which they would pose as guards.

———

Do you think of yourself as a "New Journalist"?

It isn't a phrase I use, although I wouldn't object if someone called me that. Wolfe's essay on the New Journalism was important to me because it articulated and validated many of the methods—saturation reporting, attention to detail, attention to status, etc.—I was already practicing. I feel lucky to have started my writing career at a time when writers like Wolfe were experimenting with the tools of the fiction writer.

So if not "New Journalism," what do you call your genre of journalism?

I write nonfiction narratives. I like that phrase because it doesn't have the pretensions of "literary journalism," and it stresses the fact that storytelling is the backbone of my work.

What subjects are you drawn to?

I guess mainly those that seem socially significant and underreported, particularly if they allow me to participate in the story in some meaningful way. I might discover a situation or group—sometimes a marginal or strange subculture—which I find fascinating. By participating in that world, I try to offer the reader a level of insight and detail he would not otherwise have. I prefer smaller, overlooked stories. I'd rather not be competing with the presidential press corps. I like to take my time and to be a bit contrarian.

Why subcultures?

In college I studied anthropology, which dovetails with journalism in fascinating and productive ways. If you're a journalist who has the luxury of time and a willingness to get your hands a little dirty, you will be able to get stories that nobody else gets.

An example is the story I told in *Newjack*. Here is an important subject, a worsening problem—incarceration, the boom in building new prisons—whose significance, I felt, was underappreciated by society at large. I found an unexplored angle from which to approach: guards are a stigmatized, insular subculture which have, for all their notoriety, rarely been written about. And guarding—working as a correctional officer—turned out to be something I could *do*.

So why not just interview prison guards?

Because I would only get part of the story. The interview will only take you so far, especially when you are talking to people who are uncomfortable with the press or who have things to hide. You can get further by conducting many interviews, over time, in different places. That was my original plan when I got the assignment from *The New Yorker*: I would follow a family of corrections officers at work and at home. But the New York State Department of Correctional Services turned down my requests for access to the prisons. And I thought, "Until you've seen somebody doing this kind of work, you probably won't know a thing about it."

I suppose what I'm getting at is like the distinction between *tourist* and a *traveler*. The tourist experience is superficial and glancing. The traveler develops a deeper connection with her surroundings. She is more invested in them—the traveler stays longer, makes her own plans, chooses her own destination, and usually travels alone: solo travel and solo participation, although the most difficult emotionally, seem the most likely to produce a good story.

Do many of your stories begin as an opportunity for role-playing, whether you are writing about hoboes, illegal immigrants, or prison guards?

I guess there's some role-playing involved. I'm fascinated by the idea of wearing different hats, of how one's outlook changes depending on one's position in the world, by the whole question of *identity*. For my first book, *Rolling Nowhere*—which started as a college thesis—I lived for four months as a hobo, with hoboes. The prospect was total wish fulfillment for me—several freight lines run through my hometown of Denver, and I grew up with a bit of an image of the hobo as a cultural hero, the kind of romantic figure you find in Kerouac. Riding the rails seemed, on the one hand, a great adventure.

But I knew it was something else, too. This was 1980, when the word "homeless" was just entering our vocabulary because of the large number of street people appearing in cities. I wondered to myself, Were the transients on freight trains homeless people? Or were they—as *they* insisted—something else entirely? Were they a social problem, or—the more romantic option—conscientious objectors to the nine-to-five world? I liked the dialectic. So the project was two things, as I guess all my books have been: an intellectual inquiry, and an adventure.

Why did you study anthropology in college?

I'd always been interested in philosophy, and anthropology seemed like philosophy as lived by real people. It was the study of how different groups of people view their experience of the world. Anthropology combines the abstractions of philosophy with the concreteness of lived experience.

What about the notion of multiple views and experiences of the world interested you?

I think it started a long time ago. One big piece comes from high school in Denver, where I was bused by court order from a predominately white school to a predominately black school. I was a racial minority for the first time in my life and it taught me a lot. The world looks different when your own group is not in charge. Also, there was a core of progressive teachers who were determined to defy the larger community's expectations that there would be a riot and that the experiment in integration would fail. The students embraced the possibility that it could be a new kind of school, one without the archetypes of jocks, freaks, and nerds. It was a place where you could be something new: a white person cheering the basketball team, or a black person cheering the soccer team. I found it profoundly liberating.

How do you connect those lessons to the kind of journalism you practice?

One result was that it made me want to avoid the kind of journalism that relies heavily on "credentialed" sources. I sometimes think of what I do as a kind of a guerrilla action. I try to find people and groups who have *not* been heard from. I depend on the *newness* of this information to keep my audience interested in my writing.

Is this why you've done so little celebrity journalism?

Well, it's one reason. Another is that there are lots of people who are more interesting than movie stars, and if I can contrive a way to spend my time with them, I'd rather do that.

That said, I do sometimes read celebrity profiles, and I'm thrilled by those rare journalists who manage to get past the mask that an actor wears. A couple of years ago I read a terrific profile of Leonardo DiCaprio in which the journalist convinced DiCaprio to allow him to go grocery shopping with him. We got to see Leo picking out his mesclun and tomatoes and Stim-U-Dents. The journalist was watching him make *real* choices, and it seemed fairly unmediated by the PR machine.

Whiteout is about the celebrity culture of Aspen. If you disdain celebrity journalism, why write a book about it?

"Disdain" is too strong a word. The genesis of *Whiteout* is basically this: In the late eighties, when I still lived in Colorado, I was at a New York cocktail party. David Remnick [now editor of *The New Yorker*] was there and introduced me to another guest as "Ted Conover, a guy who makes a living by sleeping on the ground." I was unsettled to feel so easily typecast at age thirty, and began to wonder whether my participant-observer method could be used to write about people who *weren't* remote or poor.

What was the answer?

Well, *Whiteout* is the answer—I wanted to watch the effects of wealth and celebrity on a small place like Aspen, a town I had known since I was a kid. And, yes, I think it worked. But the bigger question is whether it was as interesting as participant-observer journalism about less-familiar kinds of people. I'm not so sure about the answer to that question. I'm a little embarrassed by parts of *Whiteout* today. After all, what is more dated at the start of the twenty-first century than stories about Ivana Trump, Don Johnson, or Sheena Easton?

By contrast, *Rolling Nowhere* has maintained its interest because its subject has kind of disappeared. There are no more hoboes riding freight trains today. It is a lost part of the culture, a part of the country's history that people are intrigued by.

How do you develop specific stories from your interests and passions?

It's not always easy. I might look for people involved in a conflict, or a quest, some problem that does (or doesn't) get resolved. Some stories come with a built-in thread. For example, I reported a story for *The New York Times Magazine* about AIDS orphans by focusing on a single mom with AIDS. ["The Hand-Off," *The New York Times Magazine*, May 8, 1994.] She had a daughter but no other close relatives, and was looking for someone to adopt the daughter before she died. Can you imagine anything harder than that, seeking a replacement for yourself as a parent? Simply following her on this quest, and over all the bumps in the road, was the story's "thread."

What basic elements do you require for a good story?

The same as those required for good fiction: character, conflict, change through time. And, if you're *really* blessed, you get resolution. But life doesn't usually work out that way.

As you look for stories, do any parts of the world interest you more than others?

I'm partial to Latin culture. I speak Spanish and feel an affinity with Spanish-speaking people. But I'd go anywhere; the stranger the better.

What is the strangest place you've gone?

Well, I *almost* got to the moon. I was a semifinalist in the "journalist-in-space" project in the late 1980s, before the *Challenger* disaster led them to cancel the program. I think my approach would have worked well there. It was down to me and maybe twenty other people, including Tom Brokaw and Walter Cronkite.

How do you report a story somewhere you don't speak the language?

The closest I've come was when I did a story about truck drivers who travel along the so-called "AIDS highway" in Africa, for *The New Yorker*. When I got the assignment I asked whether the magazine would pay for some language instruction in KiSwahili, the African trade language. They said yes, and I took twice-weekly lessons from a Tanzanian diplomat, because no language school in New York taught it. It didn't make me fluent, but at least I would know the general subject area of a conversation the guys I was with were saying. And what I couldn't get from that language, someone could usually explain to me in English.

How do you decide which project to start when you've finished your last one?

When I finish a book, I sometimes seem unable to start anything big for months or years—much to the frustration of my agent and editor. I have to clear out the massive piles of books, folders, notes, and articles I've accumulated before I can make mental room for whatever is next.

Do you keep files of possible story ideas?

Yes, I have many files. I look through them when I'm starting to think about my next project. I recently came across a drawer I hadn't seen for years. It was filled with dead ends, with ideas that never went anywhere. I couldn't bring myself to throw them out because my ideas are my stock-in-trade. These files were dear to me, even if they had failed. They were like the kid who didn't do so well in school. Do his parents just chuck him out? Of course not!

What were some of your bad ideas?

Well, in the early 1990s, when everyone was getting online, I thought of doing a travel book about the Internet. My cyber-travel itself would structure the narrative. At the time it sounded good, but eventually I concluded it was more interesting as a sentence than a book.

How do you determine how much time to devote to a project?

For *Newjack*, I wanted to complete at least the seven weeks of training at the corrections academy. If nothing else, I knew I'd have a good *New Yorker* article. Once I got to Sing Sing, I thought four months would be enough. Working at that prison is a pretty intense experience, and I didn't think I could take much more. Four months later, I didn't really have the story yet. Two months after *that,* and then I was within four months of Christmas and New Year's. There's a natural, conclusory aspect to the holiday season, so I stuck it out. It is an emotional time that I knew would show me something new about the prison.

You didn't know precisely what you'd end up writing when you started the project?

There were *a lot* of things I didn't know at the start of this project. I didn't know until the last day of the academy that I'd be assigned to Sing Sing. That was crucial because Sing Sing was close enough to my home that I could conceive of working there for a while. And it was famous, had so much history: what if I'd been assigned to, say, Midstate Correctional Facility? How would you put that in a title? Would it have made a good book? I don't know. Could I have gotten a transfer to Sing Sing? I didn't know. I didn't even have a contract for *Newjack* until after I left my guard job.

Is that level of financial uncertainty—no contract—typical of your work?

No, but the project was so speculative that I didn't want to be on the hook to a publisher for thousands of dollars and *then* discover that I couldn't write a book based on the experience.

What were you afraid might keep you from writing the book?

I worried that I could be discovered and fired. Or, worse, that the other guards would suspect me of some kind of treachery and beat me up in the parking lot. I could have gotten injured by a prisoner and had to quit. Any number of things could have gone wrong. So I lived on my salary as a guard, and hoped that at the very least I'd get an article or two out of it.

The other reason I didn't want a book contract was so that it wouldn't look like I was serving two masters. After the book appeared, I didn't want New York State officials to be able to accuse me of *pretending* to be a guard, while actually working on a book for my publisher. When I was a guard, I wanted to be 100 percent a guard.

How do you pace your reporting when you are using the participant-observer method?

Well, patience is a huge part of it. Being able to live "without knowing" is crucial to the method.

Not knowing what?

All sorts of things: what the hobo will say to you, what the coyote will look like, what it will feel like to be threatened by an inmate. These are all experiences I anticipate—even hope for—when I begin. And yet, I *know* I'm going to have to wait and wait . . . And it may not happen at all. All that waiting can be pretty unnerving.

How do you deal with this uncertainty?

I try to let my instincts guide me. I conduct a bunch of interviews and then I digest them for a while and think, "What was most interesting about that? What did I learn that was new?"

How does this thought process influence your reporting?

As I've done more projects, I've gotten better at doing the two things at once, the participating and the observing. I can fully presence myself in the experience, while periodically stepping back and asking, "Now, how will *that* look on the page? Where would *this* fit into my story?"

My prison work was all about patience and forebearance. Every new guard at Sing Sing is a "floater" for the first few months, meaning that he is assigned to whatever section of the prison needs him. This gave me a good panoramic view of the prison, but not enough in-depth knowledge of particular inmates, officers, or jobs to tell the kind of stories I needed to tell. So I had to stick around, which, as I've mentioned, was not my number one choice.

How long did you end up staying at Sing Sing?

I was ten months in the system. There is something appealing about staying as close to a year as possible. *A Year in Provence,* for instance. That works, it sounds nice. It's a book, not an article.

How long did it take you to report Coyotes?

Between eight and nine months. Again, there were certain elements I needed in order to fill out the structure of the book. I wanted to be with them during different seasons, I wanted to be with them both in Mexico and in the U.S., I wanted to travel through different parts of the U.S., I wanted to cross the border more than once. I wanted to get to know a few *different* groups of illegals, in depth.

How many projects do you like to work on at once?

I'm best when I'm working on only one, but my finances often don't allow that. I find it hard actually to write on more than one subject in a single day, although I can report on a few. But shifting gears in order to write takes me a few hours.

Do you do most of your research before, during, or after your reporting?

I do a significant amount of research before, although I don't aim to be exhaustive. I don't want to get into too much detail, but it's important to understand the basic issues.

What's the danger of too much research?

I worry that if I do too much research I'll be following some other writer's cues or I'll develop a "take" that isn't my own. I want to come up with an original idea rather than absorb received wisdom.

Where did you learn how to do this kind of reporting?

I've never studied journalism. I worked for a chain of suburban weeklies around Denver in high school, and I worked on a bilingual Dallas community newspaper called *The People's Voice/La Voz del Pueblo*. In college I got an American Society of Magazine Editors internship and worked at *U.S. News & World Report*. It was so much fun to be in the heady world of Washington where I could talk to a senator or the secretary of defense. There's a rush in that.

Did you ever consider continuing in that career and writing about politics for one of the newsweeklies?

Well, not really. I was never comfortable with the fact that the more important you get as a journalist, the more important are the people you get to talk to. I didn't want to simply join the "club of eminences," where whom you know is everything. There's not a lot of meat in that for me. The goal of my career is not to achieve high status in Washington.

Do you have any reporting routines you follow when you arrive in a new town?

I pay a lot of attention to place in my writing, so when I arrive in a new town I try to do what Lawrence Durrell recommended in his essay "Spirit of Place," which is to get still as a needle, as he puts it.

["It is a pity indeed to travel and not get this essential sense of landscape values. You do not need a sixth sense for it. It is there if you just close your eyes and breathe softly through your nose; you will hear the whispered message, for all landscapes ask the same question in the same whisper. 'I am watching you—are you watching yourself in me?' Most travelers hurry too much . . . the great thing is to try and travel with the eyes of the spirit wide open, and not too much factual information. To tune in, without reverence, idly—but with real inward attention. It is to be had for the feeling . . . you can extract the essence of a place once you know how. If you just get as still as a needle you'll be there." —Ed.]

Think about what you hear, what you see, what you smell, what you feel. I try to remember that.

How would you describe your reportorial persona?
I'm the interested listener who is seldom disputatious. I am fairly self-revelatory so that people have a sense of who I am and why I'm there. I often try to position myself as a student to their teacher. Sometimes I am a person who doesn't know much: can you help me? Most people respond to that.

I try to blend in, whether I'm with hoboes or Mexican immigrants, or prison guards. I want to be spoken to in the same way they speak to each other.

How do you do this?
I tailor my vocabulary and body language. There is a degree of acting involved. And yet, on a deeper level, I'm always myself. If you pretend to be somebody you're not, people will see through it right away.

Do you tell your subjects *everything* about yourself and the project?
There are certain kinds of self-disclosures which will impede information gathering. For instance, if I'm talking to a rabid anti-

abortionist or racist, I'm not going to tell him why I disagree with him. It's more important for me to learn his point of view than to teach him about mine.

You told your subjects exactly what you were doing while reporting Rolling Nowhere *and* Coyotes, *but were completely undercover for* Newjack. *How does the degree to which you reveal yourself influence the kind of reporting you do?*

The differences are huge. *Newjack* was my first project that required secrecy. Perhaps six people knew what I was really doing, and I hope I never have to do that again. If you can't tell your friends what you're doing, and your experiences are as wrenching and upsetting as mine were, the result is that you lose some of those friends. If you can't tell your spouse about the horrific things you've seen all day because you don't want to upset her, you're not bringing her along with your life. I began to understand why the lives of undercover cops and narcotic agents so often fall to pieces. Living a double life isn't healthy.

Why couldn't you tell a few of your close friends what you were doing?

I did tell about three. But it's such a small world. Sing Sing is only twenty miles from Manhattan. I couldn't risk being discovered, and you never know whom you are going to run into. My well-being, as well as my work, was at stake.

What are the ethical dilemmas of undercover reporting?

Well, there's an ethical dilemma in almost all journalism, isn't there? In taking someone else's story and making it your own, in describing them on your terms, in ways they may not agree with.

Sure, but are the ethical dilemmas of journalism in general different in kind, *or in* degree, *from the dilemmas of undercover participatory journalism?*

Both. To go "undercover" strikes me as defensible only in extreme cases, such as the situation I was in with *Newjack*. The subject was of great social importance and I had already been thwarted in the more direct route. There was only one way left to get the story.

Okay, but what about once you've been forced into going undercover. What are the ethical dilemmas you face then?

I'm very concerned about the privacy of those who don't know that I'm writing about them. I change the names of anybody I portray in less than a positive way. In *Newjack,* I listed those names at the start of the book.

There were some kinds of information that I felt I could not ethically include in my book. For instance, an officer I was friendly with invited me home to watch a football game and have dinner with his wife. Ordinarily, this would be a journalist's *dream.* What better for the book than to see him at home? How does he act with his wife? Does he bring his work problems home with him? Is he short-tempered with his kids? It's a gold mine! But I made up an excuse and didn't go.

Why not?

Because I believe that there is an imperative not to betray a personal confidence. Reporting on him at work is different. But it's an intimate situation when someone invites you into his home. It seems sacred to me. I know that if I were in his shoes, I would have been *furious* to learn that I'd unwittingly invited a spy to my home.

Do you ever regret your decision to respect his privacy?

No. I do sometimes wonder, "Could the book have been better if I *had* gone?" The guy who reviewed the book in *The New York Times Book Review* seemed to think so. ["What are the stories of the men he is guarding and the officers he is guarding them with?" the reviewer wondered.] But I didn't think it was morally defensible for me to secretly learn about people's private lives for the sake of the book. I would have felt awful.

And on reflection, I *don't* think it would have made it a better book. That kind of reporting would have changed the character of the narrator, I think—he would have been not just a witness, but a spy.

Is there a limit to how far you can "go native" as a participant-observer?

Oh, sure. "Going native" means forgetting the observer part, los-

ing all perspective. If after eight months at Sing Sing I avidly partici-
pated in roughing up an inmate with other officers, you might presume I had lost my balance.

After all, if you truly "go native," you cease to be a writer. You *stay*
in Samoa with your local wife, you don't go home, and you stop
sending back letters. I'm always flirting with the line between
observer and participant, asking, "How much of the true me does
this role resonate with?" I like to joke that the prison job brought out
my "inner disciplinarian." What keeps me from going all the way and
losing the observer is the knowledge and expectation that I will
eventually go home.

**There is often danger inherent in the situations you've written
about. Do you *deliberately* expose yourself to danger in order to
get to the emotional heart of a piece?**

I don't mind a certain degree of risk. I may even be attracted to it.
It's instrumental, as well: the danger I experience often helps the
book's narrative, and therefore helps draw readers to my story.

For instance, it seems easy to entice readers into a story about
Paris or Provence or Tuscany. But I think it's hard to write a book
about illegal immigration that will attract a wide readership. It is
hard to write a book about prisons that many people will buy—they
just don't want to go there. Placing myself in harm's way is one way
of bringing readers along in the story.

**Okay, once you've come up with the idea and done some
research, how do you prefer to approach the people you want to
talk to? Directly? Or through intermediaries?**

If I'm working in another country, a personal introduction can be
very useful. Institutional affiliations, whether it is *The New Yorker* or
The New York Times Magazine, tend to mean less abroad. And the
whole activity of being a journalist is sometimes obscure overseas.
That role simply doesn't exist in some societies.

Do you have any routines for conducting interviews?

I like to interview in person, and will only do phone or e-mail
interviews if I have to. It is important for me to see someone with my

own eyes, to see how he reacts to his surroundings, and how he reacts to me.

For instance, I recently did an interview in Peru with the manager of a huge lumber mill. The mill is the town's leading industry, and this guy was the scion of a famous South American lumbering family. I interviewed him inside the mill's walled compound, across a table made of solid mahogany—a kind of wood he claimed was *never* milled there. I got to see him put his boots on the gorgeous table. I saw how his secretary acted toward him. I got a sense of what made him nervous. I'm not just after the facts, I'm after a character. So the more time I can spend with him in his element, the better.

Do you prepare questions in advance for your interviews?

I do write out questions beforehand. But it's more like a safety net: I often get completely sidetracked and never ask them.

I find that savvy interview subjects can be quite attentive to when you're writing and when you're not. I think it is counterproductive to try to hide your notes or questions. Fortunately, my handwriting is fairly illegible.

Will you send ahead questions if an interviewee requests it?

Almost never. I prize informality in my interviews.

Are there any places you especially like or dislike conducting interviews?

The only bad environment for an interview is a denatured one: a conference room, a bare office. I was writing a piece about Amadou Diallo's mother for *The New York Times Magazine* and had to do our first interview in the conference room of her PR agent in Washington, D.C. It was awful! And the PR agent wouldn't leave us alone.

So much of your reporting is done undercover or while you are on the run—how do you manage to record what is said and what happens?

With *Newjack,* I'd come home every night and write six to eight pages of exhaustive, single-spaced notes—and I wouldn't even get into much detail! I'd also take notes all day long.

What would you use?

My preferred equipment for participatory projects is a small, three-by-five-inch spiral notebook that fits in my shirt pocket or jeans pocket. It is unobtrusive and can be produced at a moment's notice. I probably filled up a dozen of those during my reporting for *Newjack*. Fortunately in prison, officers are told to carry these same notebooks, which they use to take down information about inmates. I would do that, and then add additional notes for my project. Then, when I got home, I'd expand on brief notes, transcribe quotes, etc.

Does your note-taking ever bother your subjects?

Sure, note-taking can be intimidating, particularly to those who are not used to writing. Hoboes and Mexican migrants associate note-taking with law enforcement, social workers, or employers, with powerful people who tell them what to do. My problem in those situations is that doing my job—reporting, taking notes—alienates the very people I need to get close to. So I work up to it slowly and try to make my note-taking less threatening.

With *Rolling Nowhere* I was very new to this. I treated my notebook as my diary. That made it easy to say, "That was a great joke! Tell it to me again so I can write it down."

The hardest thing to take notes on is dialogue, and those details are indispensable when I'm re-creating a scene later on. If it's inconvenient to have my notebook out, I'm pretty good at holding five or six lines of conversation in my head until I get a chance to go write them down.

It sounds as if you rely mostly on notes. Do you ever tape interviews?

I tape if I'm interviewing a sophisticated person who is good at stringing together complicated thoughts.

Do you transcribe your own tapes?

I do everything myself. I've never had a research assistant. I used a typist to redo drafts of *Rolling Nowhere,* but she introduced mistakes into the manuscript, so I stopped doing that. I'm a control freak about my writing. I like to think the work benefits from it.

How do you get people who have good reasons to be reticent—hoboes, illegal aliens—to talk so openly with you?

I spend a lot of time with them, tell them about myself, and listen carefully when they talk to me. In combination, those things will usually get people to open up. You have to bring your genuine concerns to people. You've got to tell them where you stand, not just on questions of policy, but also on personal issues. Self-disclosure is essential. I'll tell them, "I miss my kids. Do you miss your kids?" At Sing Sing I might say, truthfully, "I really *hate* that sergeant, don't you?"

In the beginning I might be the chatty one who initiates the conversation. But by the end they're usually doing most of the talking. The desire to speak about oneself seems a human universal.

How antagonistic will you become during an interview? How much will you challenge your subjects when they have incorrect beliefs?

It depends. For instance, I once contradicted a very explosive-tempered hobo named BB who'd done a lot of prison time. Like most white hoboes, he was at pains to distinguish himself from the Mexicans who rode the rails. He told me that when Mexicans die in the desert, the heat from the peppers they've eaten stays in their bodies so long that vultures won't touch their corpses. I laughed and told him that was *ridiculous*; and he threatened me, and challenged me to a fight.

I try to be sensitive to the situation. Some people you can push and challenge very productively. Some are used to the give-and-take of an argument. Others—like BB—feel challenged in a bad way.

Do you set ground rules for interviews? I somehow can't imagine a hobo telling you, "Okay, we can talk, but only on deep background."

When I'm reporting a story in Washington I play by the rules. But when I'm with people to whom journalistic conventions like these mean nothing, I am confronted with a set of moral questions, which

I have to resolve according to the situation. One thing that gets into is issues of protecting their privacy, which we talked about earlier.

In formal interviews, I try to avoid negotiations and minimize the amount of information given to me "on background," or "not for attribution."

You frequently mention certain aspects of your identity in your books, whether it is the fact that you are well-educated, upper-middle-class, or from Colorado. Why is it important to your writing that you disclose these facts?

I feel it's important, in first-person nonfiction, to establish the narrator's character as well as everyone else's. I try to let readers know, when appropriate, exactly who is doing the talking. I include personal information when it sheds light on a particular situation.

There are also times when, like a filmmaker's camera, the journalist's presence makes a difference; I want to make sure that the reader understands the *kind* of difference my presence might be making.

What kinds of situations require such self-disclosure?

For instance, in *Coyotes,* in order to accurately render the social dynamic in a rural Mexican bar, the reader needs to know that I am a blond-haired, college-educated guy standing there along with ten rural Mexicans who are destitute and about to risk *everything* to cross the border into the United States. My presence changes things: it changed what happened when we were caught by the Mexican judicial police on the border, it probably changed what the guys said to each other in front of me.

In *Newjack,* the reader needed to know that I'm not a large, muscular person, because physical presence makes such a difference in prisoner-guard interactions in prison.

In *Rolling Nowhere,* when I was trying to convey the feeling of dislocation, random fear, and rootlessness that dominates a hobo's life, I had to let the reader know enough about the relative *security* of my life for them to understand how I related to the hoboes. For instance, when I visited my hometown, Denver, as a hobo, it was important to let the reader know how I had previously experienced Denver as a member of a secure, upper-middle-class family.

How do you know when the interviewing and reporting phase of the project is done, and you can begin writing?

Either when the questions I set out with have been answered, or when I've reconciled myself to never finding an answer to them. Hopefully, by then, I can also see the shape of the book or article.

Let's talk about writing. Are you someone for whom reporting is easier than writing, or vice versa?

The two are very separate for me, both in time and in concept. I almost never do anything more than take notes while I'm doing my research and reporting. The real writing always comes after.

I love both parts, although for completely different reasons. I love the cloistered, cerebral, introspective phase of actually committing my knowledge to paper. And I love the travel, adventure, and excitement of gathering it. I think of them as two ends of a barbell.

Do you have a routine for writing?

My ideal day starts after a good night's sleep. The first thing I do when I wake up is make sure to spend enough time in bed to figure out what I'm going to write that day. A lot of my ideas take shape before I get out of bed. It is *murder* for me to arrive at the computer without having thought the day through. It is so frightening— true terror—to sit down in front of a blank screen with no forethought about what I'm going to write. I avoid that situation like the plague.

After sitting in bed and thinking about what I'm going to write, I have breakfast. I like to have breakfast by myself, and time to read the paper alone. Sometimes I'll take a short walk. I might check my e-mail in order to warm up my brain. Then I start writing.

How specific does your bed-inspired outline become?

It isn't so much an outline as a list of the topics I want to touch on during that day's writing. It is usually a list of scenes, ideas, and characters. I occasionally put an arrow or an asterisk next to items that are particularly important. But the weighting has already taken place in my head.

So your outline is more like a checklist?

Yes, a list of the specific parts that will be necessary in order to put together the whole.

You've told me about your notes, whether handwritten in little books, or the many sheets of single-spaced notes you typed up after, say, a shift at Sing Sing. How voluminous do these notes become, and how do you use them while writing?

In the case of *Newjack*, I had about five hundred single-spaced typed pages of notes. I spent a couple of weeks rereading and annotating them with a highlighter, marking those parts I wanted to include. My next step was to set the notes aside and try to imagine what the chapters of the book would look like. The notes are unmediated experience, and now it is time to mediate it, give it a structure. I have to decide what I'm going to *do* with my experience.

With *Newjack*, I knew I'd have a chapter about my training at the academy. And that it should come at the beginning of the book. I also knew I'd have a chapter about New Year's Eve and the fires that the inmates set in the cell blocks, which would come toward the end. I knew that somewhere past the middle of the book I'd write about the day I was slugged in the head and spit on. That was the point at which I began to hate *all* the inmates, and it was an important point in my personal story. Once I have a few of these fixed points, I use them to figure out where to put everything else.

Have you always been so organized?

No, when I was a beginning writer the structure often became apparent to me only after I'd begun writing—sometimes after I'd written a lot. I'd start without a plan and see where my interests took me. But that method wasn't very efficient. I wasted a lot of time on dead ends.

Once you've sketched a rough outline, or list, do you start writing the text in a linear fashion?

No. Next I try to fill in that list a little. I open up separate documents on my computer: "Chapter 1 notes," "Chapter 2 notes," etc. Then as I revise the notes I create subsequent files: "Chapter 2 notes 1.1," "Chapter 2 notes 1.2," etc. I go through revisions of the notes for each chapter in much the same way that I'll later revise the chapters themselves.

Do you do all your work on the screen of your computer?
No, not always. If something's really hard, I might write it out by hand first. Also, I'm not smart enough to keep track of all that information while it is still in the computer. I print things out frequently—it really helps me to have hard copies.

So what does your desk look like when you start to write?
On the day I begin work on, say, Chapter 2, I have the latest hard copy of "Chapter 2 notes" in front of me. To my left, I have my original five hundred pages of single-spaced notes, which I've annotated and marked up. To my right, I have the books I imagine I'll quote from or refer to. Then I do the actual composing on the computer.

How many drafts do you typically go through?
Anywhere between five and ten.

Do you write quickly?
I write more quickly about my personal experiences than I do when I am writing discursively about history or policy. Or than when I'm making an argument.

Do you write straight through a project, or do you stop and start, reading over and editing the work as you go?
I try to write a book in sequence. I *used* to start each morning by reading from the beginning of whatever I had written, but I don't do that anymore because I'm more confident of my voice, or more sure of my progress, or . . . you know, I really don't know why. But there are points when I just can't stand to look behind me; I've got to focus on what's ahead. Now I'm more likely to write through to the end of a section before I let myself read what I've done.

Once you've started writing, how do you organize the rest of your day?
I seldom spend more than a couple of hours at my desk without

taking a walk or a run, doing errands, etc. In a productive day I may have three two-hour periods when I'm actually writing.

How do you end the day?

At the end of each day I type myself a brief note at the end of the manuscript, using capital letters, describing what I want to do the next morning. I'm always nervous that I'll lose my train of thought, though I almost never do. I guess I'm superstitious.

Is there any physical place you need to be in order to write?

I don't need to be at my own desk. In fact, sometimes that is the worst place to be, because of all the distractions, like bills and phone calls.

One thing I've learned is that a room with a view is not necessarily a good thing for writing. The most productive I've ever been was when I was using the upstairs of a neighbor's garage to write *Coyotes*. My desk had a view of a blank wall, which is really what you want: no distractions.

Any time of day you especially like to write?

I tend to get going in the late morning and am usually tired by late afternoon. I seldom write at night. I don't write in the early morning unless I have a tight deadline and have to.

Almost everything you've written has been in the first person. Could you imagine writing as, say, a third-person, omniscient narrator?

I'm in the middle of writing a novel in the third person. I've written many articles that are third person, or just lightly first person, because those were cases where I didn't think my presence added much to the piece.

But the first person is how *I* best tell a story. Because my persona is so often that of the "witness," *not* using the first person would make me feel like a left-handed person who was forced to use his right hand. I'm glad the daily paper is written in the third person because I don't usually want to know about the writer in that context; I just want the information in the least obtrusive, most objective way possible. On the other hand, there are occasional news stories when the first person pronoun really is appropriate, and in those cases I'd much rather see an "I" than read a reference to "this reporter," or "a visitor," which feels stilted and false.

Do you think about the sound your words make?

A lot. When I've got a reasonably polished draft, I read chapters out loud to myself, or to my wife and friends. Bad writing usually reveals itself when it is verbalized. And particularly in first-person writing, I think—when you're being dishonest in your own, personal voice, there is nothing like reading it out loud to reveal it. It is sometimes quite painful to hear.

Do you believe that the kind of participant-observer journalism you practice leads to truth?

I'm a pretty straightforward, nuts-and-bolts guy when it comes to journalism. Either something happened, or it didn't. I have a contract with my readers according to which they can expect my material to be true, and I honor that. I believe in the literal truth of nonfiction, as opposed to the philosophical truth of fiction.

I think re-created dialogue is one of the biggest, most persistent problems of "creative nonfiction." Everything in my books is true, and yet dialogue is so difficult to record verbatim that it is a big gray area. And add to that gray area the fact that journalistic convention requires that dialogue be rendered intelligibly—edited, essentially— and the question of what "true" "creative nonfiction" *really* means gets even more difficult.

Is it a metaphysical or lasting truth? I hope there is a profundity in what I write. I hope that people feel they have received something "lasting" from it. But is it capital *T* "Truth"? I'm not sure about that.

Do you think long-form nonfiction is a peculiarly American form?

A number of British writers do it very well. But it *does* seem the form is most vital here. This is probably due to a few factors. The multiplicity of outlets that publish the form. The multiplicity of voices here, people from different backgrounds and experiences who find writing as a way to express themselves. Another reason is that we are closer to the engine of the entertainment industry, which options some of our books, and thereby provides us with the financial means to continue writing.

Who do you consider to be your colleagues and major influences?

As for colleagues, Jon Krakauer, Sebastian Junger, Scott Anderson, Adrian LeBlanc, Mark Salzman, and Nicholas Dawidoff are a few contemporaries. Tracy Kidder has been a model and a colleague. George Orwell is probably at the top of the list of influences. *Down and Out in Paris and London, Homage to Catalonia,* and his novels—I'm an aspiring novelist as well. John Steinbeck and Jack London, who did a lot of advocacy journalism. Joan Didion. Tom Wolfe. Peter Matthiessen, Bruce Chatwin, anything by J. M. Coetzee, the South African novelist. I guess I read more fiction than nonfiction.

Why?

Probably because fiction writers tend to be better storytellers. And they are usually more attentive to style and language than nonfiction writers are.

Are you hopeful about the future of long-form nonfiction?

The wave of New Journalism in the late sixties and early seventies, the old *Esquire* stuff, has had a great legacy, whether that legacy now takes the form of travel writing or memoirs. It manifests itself in new and unpredictable ways. For instance, I just read a memoir by Thomas DeBaggio, describing the progression of his Alzheimer's. What an amazing idea!

And long-form nonfiction seems to be thriving in the form of books and in magazines like *The New Yorker.* It is sad to see *Rolling Stone* thinning it out and running less ambitious, shorter pieces. It is sad to see that the men's magazines want only short pieces. But I don't think that those of us who write in this form are an endangered species. I don't think there is any kind of intellectual malaise. Quite the contrary, I think it is growing in all sorts of interesting ways.

BY TED CONOVER:

Newjack: Guarding Sing Sing, Random House, 2000
Whiteout: Lost in Aspen, Random House, 1991
Coyotes: A Journey Through the Secret World of America's Illegal Aliens, Vintage Books, 1987
Rolling Nowhere: Riding the Rails with America's Hoboes, Viking, 1984

RICHARD BEN CRAMER

Richard Ben Cramer is known for tackling "impossible" stories. Sometimes the impossibility lies in lack of access to the main character, as was the case with his legendary *Esquire* profile of Ted Williams, or his biography of Joe DiMaggio. Other times, a story may have been written about so often and at such great length that it seems impossible to cover freshly, as with presidential campaigns or international peace negotiations. In either case, these hurdles only serve to energize Cramer: "If I get really going on an idea, I just *can't* come home without it! It might take years, but I'll *eventually* get it."

Born in Rochester, New York, in 1950, Cramer attended Johns Hopkins. After being rejected by *The Baltimore Sun,* he got an MA in journalism from Columbia and was hired by the paper in 1973. Cramer covered city hall and local politics for three years before leaving for *The Philadelphia Inquirer,* where he was soon installed as the paper's New York bureau chief.

Although he had no foreign experience, Cramer was sent to Cairo in 1977 to cover the peace negotiations between Egyptian president Anwar Sadat and Israeli prime minister Menachim Begin. It was during his Middle East assignment that he successfully combined his dogged reporting with a vivid writing style that echoed Tom Wolfe's New Journalism literary experiments. Cramer's eye for telling detail and his appreciation for the impact of historic events on the lives of ordinary citizens enabled him to write about the peace negotiations with the familiarity and human scale that Janet Flanner had brought to her wartime "Letters" from occupied Paris in *The New Yorker.*

Cramer's dispatches earned him a 1979 Pulitzer for international reporting, as well as a seven-year job running the *Inquirer's* London and Rome bureaus (which, given the paper's financial difficulties, consisted of little more than Cramer and a suitcase). He covered the Iran hostage crisis in Tehran, and traveled with the anti-Soviet, mujahideen rebels in Afghanistan. In 1980, he won the Ernie Pyle Award for foreign reporting and an Overseas Press Club Award for his writing from Afghanistan. But despite his fame as a newspaper reporter and foreign correspondent, Cramer came into his own— professionally and aesthetically—as a magazine journalist.

Cramer met his wife, Carolyn White, an editor at the *Inquirer,* while visiting the paper's main office in 1983 (they later divorced). They soon quit their jobs and moved to New York, where she became an editor at *Rolling Stone* and he became a full-time free-lance magazine writer. He produced lengthy profiles for *Esquire* and *Rolling Stone* of Baltimore Mayor William Donald Schaefer, baseball legend Ted Williams, and baseball commissioner Peter Ueberroth. Still, Cramer wrote so slowly ("Richard has trouble writing his name in less than a year and a half," says David Rosenthal, his book publisher) that he found it difficult to make a living. "I lost money," Cramer told *The Washington Post*'s Martha Sherrill in 1992, "on every story I wrote."

Freed from the constraints of newspapers, Cramer reveled in the amount of space he could devote to his intensely reported articles. But even magazines have their limits. Cramer was not pleased when the thirteen-thousand-word Ted Williams profile he turned in to *Esquire* was cut to eleven thousand words. So the night the article was scheduled to close, he went to *Esquire*'s offices and (falsely) assured the art, production, and copy departments that he had received permission to reduce the typeface size in order to reinstate the two thousand missing words. Legend has it that this incident led to the magazine's policy of banishing writers from the noneditorial sections of the office. An expanded version of the article was later published as an illustrated book, *Ted Williams: The Seasons of the Kid* (1991).

Searching for a book topic, Cramer concentrated on the two subjects he felt he understood best: baseball and politics. "They're subjects much written about, that garner a lot of interest and a lot of ink, but in both cases I thought that there was a real space for someone to come in and do the hard work that never gets done," he says. He considered writing a book about Richard Nixon, but chose instead to tackle a larger subject in American politics: a presidential campaign.

The result was *What It Takes: The Way to the White House*, an epic chronicle of the 1988 election, a group portrait of presidential candidates (George Bush, Bob Dole, Michael Dukakis, Gary Hart, Joe Biden, and Richard Gephardt) as multidimensional *people*, rather than as "personalities" or stand-ins for various ideologies or policies. "I wanted to know not about the campaign, but about the campaigners," he writes in the "Author's Note." The book was propelled by a single question: what kind of life would lead a man to think that he *ought* to be president of the United States? As Cramer explained to Brian Lamb on *Booknotes*, "I had to go to a publisher, Random House, and tell them, 'Well, look, I don't have Chapter One yet and I don't have an outline for you. I can't tell you who the characters will be yet. I can't tell you what the story will be, but you just give me all this money and I'll see you in four or five years. Don't worry. It'll be great.' "

Cramer received a $500,000 advance for the book, which took six years to report and write (he conducted more than one thousand interviews). It was published in 1992, on the eve of the *next* presidential election. At 1,047 pages (a *Boston Globe* reviewer dubbed the book *What It Weighs*), the book is as much a work of journalism as a jeremiad against a political system in which a cynical media judges candidates by sound bites and ad hoc moral codes. Cramer quickly realized the limits of conventional political reporting. The book didn't carry quotes from "unnamed officials" and "important politicians." It didn't treat the campaign like a horse race or dwell on caucus votes and opinion polls. "When I finally did force my way into a few of the offices of these important Washington figures and I started asking about the candidates, I found that they really didn't know these guys. They knew them in a kind of Washington way," he says, "but they didn't know what was driving them onward or what was the real reason that they were climbing to the top of the pyramid." As a result, Cramer spent as much time reporting on the candidates' lives before the campaign, spending a year interviewing their cousins, grandparents, and friends before making an appearance on the campaign bus.

Longtime observers of American politics, like *New York Times* columnist Russell Baker, marveled that Cramer had managed to take a fresh look at presidential politics, calling *What It Takes* "a book that reopens a closed mind." He found the book compulsively readable. "It consumes weeks of my life, drives me up the wall every time it calls Dole 'the Bobster,' yet I can't stop turning the pages."

Others, like *New York Times* reporter (now columnist) Maureen Dowd, writing in *The Washington Monthly,* were put off by Cramer's New Journalism tone. "With a prose style more irritating than entertaining, the author takes Wolfe's faded New Journalism technique and sends it into fifth gear—VRO-O-O-OM! VRO-O-O-OM!—dousing each page with italics, ellipses, exclamation points, sound effects, dashes, hyphens, capital letters, and cute spellings."

Los Angeles Times political reporter Ronald Brownstein sensed that *What It Takes* was more about American ambition than electoral politics, and should therefore be judged alongside other overblown attempts to divine the national character. "Cramer has produced a work that should be put under glass: It's one of a kind, a hopped-up amalgam of Teddy White, Tom Wolfe and Norman Mailer—day-glo civics. Everything about this book is oversized: its ambition, its scope, its flaws, its energy. Presidential elections are the white whale of American journalism—and in Cramer they have found a manic Melville."

Cramer's next impossible assignment was a biography of Yankees legend Joe DiMaggio. A famously private, reticent man, DiMaggio had fended off all previous attempts to write about him. The project was suggested by Cramer's publisher, who had spent years trying to convince DiMaggio to write his autobiography.

DiMaggio's 1999 death provided Cramer with his biggest break. Already four years into the book, he hadn't been able to convince DiMaggio to help him ("We talked four or five times about *why* he wouldn't talk to me—which was quite interesting in itself"). Cramer found many of DiMaggio's friends were similarly reluctant to help, in deference to DiMaggio. Now information "came sluicing in—new recollections spurred by the event, new sources who felt free to talk and old sources who wanted to talk— to remember the man who had touched their lives," he says.

Published one year later, *Joe DiMaggio: The Hero's Life,* portrayed its subject in an unflattering light. DiMaggio's cheapness, greed, and coldness came to the fore, while Cramer subjected the "Hero Machine," the media and public's uncritical adoration that had produced DiMaggio's celebrity, to an unsparing critique.

Many reviewers seemed hurt at having their hero brought down. Russell Baker, writing in *The New York Review of Books*, questioned Cramer's sourcing ("With no attribution whatever, stories scandalous, shocking, and delightful are presented as gospel"). As with *What It Takes*, some critics, like *The Washington Post*'s Jonathan Yardley, objected to Cramer's writing style ("The prose careens wildly from he-mannish to maudlin to street-wise to coy to pseudo-hip to sarcastic to barstool confidential"). Others, like *The New York Times*'s Richard Bernstein, judged that the book was written "with utter command," and assigned a more respectable pedigree to Cramer's prose ("a cross between Ring Lardner and David Halberstam with dollops of Dreiser and Hemingway thrown in for good measure").

For his most recent book, *How Israel Lost* (2004), Cramer revisited many of the places he reported on in the late seventies and early eighties. He is currently working on a book about the American garment industry in the early twentieth century.

———

Do you see yourself as part of any particular journalistic tradition?

I think of what we do as going back to the kinds of profiles Joseph Addison did in the eighteenth century. Addressing the reader and telling him a story. Promising him that if he spends the time with your story then certain benefits will ensue, certain truths will be elucidated.

I write nonfiction with the same goal—though not necessarily the techniques—of a novel. I want my books or articles to have the same impact a novel has on a reader: something happens to the character in the story during which an emotional truth is revealed. That is a goal nonfiction and fiction can share. Both are capable of creating a life-changing experience for the reader.

Do you consider yourself a "literary journalist"?

No, I'm a *smith*. I occupy the position in our society that a good wheelwright would have occupied in his. Making wheels is a highly specialized *skill*. I don't consider myself to be an artist, I consider myself to be a skilled workman.

But I do feel part of a community of writers. I've been privileged to meet Halberstam and Talese, and I've told them how much their work meant to me, and how it showed me how big you could make this job. It's very nice to feel like there is a tradition that I am continuing. I don't know whether I'll leave it in as good shape as Halberstam and Talese did, but I certainly feel there is something they passed on to me. I *hope* there is somebody *I'm* passing it on to.

What kinds of subjects are you drawn to?

If there is a theme to my work, it is about people—usually men—working obsessively to create something larger than themselves. It may be larger than them, or they may just *think* it is larger than them. But the obsession is deep either way. I think I understand something about them.

Is that because you see yourself in them?

Perhaps. Or maybe I feel I *ought* to be more like them. But when I see one of those guys, I know that there is a world, of his creation, for me to write about. And if I can get the reader to see the world from behind that character's eyes, he will be taken on a wonderful journey.

How do you find stories?

I just get *on* something and can't let go. Sometimes an editor will call me up and say, "I think you should write about such and such." And I'll say, "Oh, no! I don't know a thing about that." And then a funny thing will happen. It won't go away.

How do you know when a story is right for you?

I'll mention the idea to my wife, and she'll say, "Ah, that's horseshit." And I'll get all defensive and argue with her, "*No it's not,* and the reason it's *not* horseshit is . . . !" *That's* when I know I'm hooked. It grows on me to the point where I start telling the story to people over and over again.

Do you prefer generating ideas or taking assignments from editors?

Some of my best stories have been other people's ideas. For example, Lee Eisenberg, then the editor of *Esquire,* sent me out to do a profile of Ted Williams, who was famous for not cooperating with writers.

Editors tend to call me with the stories that they can't get done otherwise. There's a certain kind of story that gets a reputation for being impossible. Great stories where the conventional wisdom is that they simply can't be done. Like, "Ted Williams won't talk to *anybody!*" or "Joe DiMaggio is *completely* unknowable!" or "*Nobody* can get inside national politics today because the process has been so sanitized."

But there are a *few* editors who have a feeling that perhaps these "impossible" stories *could* be done if they could just get a writer who was stubborn enough. They know that if they get me really going on the idea . . . well, I just can't come home without it! It might take years, but I'll *eventually* get it.

So you're the "go-to guy" when an editor needs a home run?

I guess, although sometimes I *wish* they'd send me a few singles or doubles. I could sure use more frequent paychecks.

Is it the same with book assignments?

Yes, that's what happened with my Joe DiMaggio biography. My editor, David Rosenthal at Simon & Schuster, had been trying to get DiMaggio to write a book for years. He'd written him letters, done research in the library about Joe's life so that he could really talk to him. And Joe was the way Joe *always* was. He was polite and said "no" because there wasn't enough money in it for him.

I had just finished *What It Takes* and was looking around for another book. I told David that the only two things I know anything about are politics and baseball. So he said, "I'll tell you the baseball story that *nobody* can do, and it's the only baseball story out there worth doing." That hooked me.

Is that what happened with What It Takes?

Sort of. I wanted to answer a fundamental question I had about American politics. I would watch the candidates on TV and they looked like *nobody* I knew—and not in a good way. They looked stiff and removed. Rehearsed, although not *well*-rehearsed. They looked like they were bound up in a million thoughts and doubts.

Now I've known a lot of politicians from when I worked for *The Baltimore Sun,* and that's not how those guys are. And all these presidential candidates had once been city councilmen and state reps and congressmen themselves, just like the folks I knew. So I knew that *something* had happened to them on the way to the presidential campaign. And I wanted to know what that *something* was. That was the question I wrote *What It Takes* to answer for myself.

How did you have the confidence to write such an ambitious first book?

I had read all the presidential election books: Germond and Witcover, the Teddy White books, *Dasher* by Jim Wooten, and *An American Melodrama* by three London *Sunday Times* reporters Harry Evans sent to America to write a minute-by-minute account of the 1968 election. That was a *really* wonderful book. And it seemed to me I could do something like that today.

So I called up my friend and ex-boss Jim Naughton, a veteran reporter who had covered the Carter campaign and administration for *The Baltimore Sun* and worked at *The New York Times* before that. I asked him, "Naughton, can this be done?" And he said, "Yes, but here is how you have to do it: you get in the plane, and when they come to you for your interview slot you say, 'You know what? I don't really need to interview the candidate. But, hey, would you mind if I just sat there while he does all the *other* interviews?'"

You don't ask any questions?

Not one. I'd sit there for the first day, and the second day, and the third day, and on and on. And sooner or later, the candidate is going to get so comfortable with my being there that he will lean over to me after one of the interviews and say, "*Damn,* I fucked up that agriculture question *again!*"

And at *that moment* I've moved from *my* side of the desk to *his* side of the desk. That's the judo move I try to pull off: using *his power* to throw him where *I* want him to go. I'm *always* trying to be on his side of the desk. If I come in with my notebook and my list of questions, then I'm just another schmuck with a notebook and questions to be brushed off with the "message of the day," or whatever form of manipulation is in vogue.

But if I don't *have* any questions—except for the basic one of *What the Hell is Going on Here?*—and I'm willing to hang around forever trying to see the world from his side of the desk, *then* I become something else entirely.

Is this "non-interview" interview technique effective?

Well, I can tell you what's *not* effective. I've been interviewed a lot during book tours, and I see how newspaper people, in particular, do it. They'll ask you a question. And as you start to talk they bend their heads to their notebooks and try to get down every word. They barely look at you again for forty-five minutes. Now that's *entirely* the wrong way to get any sense of anybody!

How do you conduct interviews?

When I go in to interview someone, I don't prepare any questions. And not only do I have no questions, I don't have a notebook—and if I *have* a notebook, I don't take it out of my pocket.

I just look at him and say, "Look, here's my situation . . ." And I explain my *problem.* When I was interviewing the presidential candidates I'd say, "You know what my problem is? I can't imagine the time when you say to yourself, 'It *ought* to be me.' Because *nobody* I've ever known would say something like that. So I want to know what you think *happened* that made you think 'It's *got* to be me'? What was the last thing you had to resolve before you traded your old life in for this one? And what about your wife? What did *she* think?"

And he *can't* brush me off with a prepared statement, because he's never rehearsed an answer to this kind of a question. All of a sudden I'm in a whole different territory of journalism. So he's either going to try to answer it, or he's going to make a joke about it, or he's going to say he needs time to think about it. *Whatever* happens, I'm going to see how he reacts when something unexpected comes at him—which is *really* what being president is all about!

Did this technique work immediately?
No, I completely fucked up for the first six months.

What was the first correct thing you did?
Well, whenever I do a profile, the first thing I do, out of respect, is let them know I'm doing it. You can't play straight up unless you *start* straight up. Sometimes I'll send a letter ahead, but what I really like to do is for them to lay eyes on me and shake my hand so I can tell them what I'm doing and answer any questions.

With *What It Takes,* I introduced myself to all the candidates and told them about the book. Then I disappeared for almost a year. I told them I'd be back, but I wasn't coming back until I really *knew* something about them.

You abandoned the campaign in the middle of reporting a campaign book?
Yep. I went to the candidates' hometowns. I talked to the people they played catch with when they were kids. I went to their high schools, their colleges, their next-door neighbors, and their first employers.

And by the time I got *back* to the campaign trail, I wasn't just the next journalist with a notebook who wanted a ten-minute interview. I was their mama's *friend,* or I was the guy their Aunt Sally had called them about. I knew all about their life. I had met the people they were genuinely close to. I had taken the time to steep myself in their world. And that made them look at me differently.

But how would the candidates know what you'd been doing?
Are you kidding? These guys are on top of their world like nobody else. Politics is all about gathering information. So the first thing they know is *where* you've been before, and *whether* you like them. They were receiving reports about me all during that year that I was getting to know their world. I want them to know how *hard* I'm work-

ing and that I'm not going away. I want the friends to tell him, "Well, he seemed okay to me."

Was the material you gathered during this year valuable?

Incredibly valuable. What amazes me is that most journalists won't bother talking to the people who *love* these guys. They only want to talk to the critics, or at the very least, people who have polit- ical reservations about him. Journalists think, "What the hell is his *sister* going to say? She's going to say that he's wonderful. Big god- damn deal!"

But they are missing the point. The important question is *how* is he wonderful! If you want to understand how someone got to the point where he is a credible candidate for president of a nation of 250 million people, you'd *better* goddamn-well know *how* he is won- derful. But most journalists don't care about that.

Do you ask peripheral characters the same questions you ask central ones?

Absolutely. I pose the *dumbest* questions in the world. I would talk for *six hours* with some guy who had given his life over to one of these candidates, or some woman who had been their girlfriend in college. And I'd ask only *one* question: "What's the good thing that he is getting out of all this?" I just wanted to know *that*. But, hey, that's a *pretty big thing* to know!

For instance, my researcher and I went out to dinner with Don Gephardt, Dick's brother, and his wife out on Long Island. We talked about *everything*: the mom thing, the dad, the house, the business—it was like striking gold! And then we go back to the house and look at the family picture album! I mean, *please*, it doesn't get any better than this!

And while we're driving back to their house I ask Don, "So have you been besieged by the press?" And he said, "Well, the Long Island bureau of *The New York Times* called once. But that's been about it." Now I *personally* knew 150 journalists who were doing Gephardt profiles—at a certain point, *everyone* had to do one. And they didn't call his *only* sibling? That astonished me.

The idea that a bozo like me could write a book after the *billions* of words that were written about that election shows that something was wrong with the billions of words. Look, this is *not* a smart guy's business I'm in. A *smart* guy's business is to prattle on every morning on CNBC. *Those* people are very smart. But they can't do what I do because they need to *show you* how smart they are. I couldn't care less whether the guy I'm interviewing thinks I'm smart. And it's no act. I am *so confused* when I am doing a story. I am *so tormented* by not knowing enough to write it. I don't have to *pose* at needing help.

Do you ever take notes?

Not at first. But after a while, when they say something really good I ask, "May I write that down?" *Then* I take out the notebook and in the process of writing it down, I tell them *why* it is such a good quote, and exactly *what* it means to me and the book. My goal is for them to understand my project as well as I do. Because we're going to build the boat together. They are part of it, they have a stake in it. Then I put the notebook away. And this drives them *crazy.* They'll spend the next six hours trying to make me *take my notebook out again!*

But how do you get their quotes without a notebook?

I'll call them up later and say, "I'm such an *idiot.* You know that great thing you said about Dick and such and such? Well, I haven't been able to get that out of my head. But I'm such a *moron* that I didn't write it down! Could we go over it again?" They're determined to help you get it right. I turn the traditional source-reporter relationship on its head.

How much research do you do to prepare for an interview?

I read a lot of stuff, but I'm no goddamn good at research. I trust God to send me something good. I'd rather read one good sentence than twenty books which leave me swimming. I don't have that kind of incisive, burrowing intellect. I'm not a head guy. I'm working from somewhere else.

You can read *Time* or *Newsweek* on the campaign until you're blue in the face, and you're no farther along than when you started. Because they are like those neatly-spun one-minute TV pieces: they have a little point, a sound clip, a scene to put on the screen, but they don't *know* the guy.

There is a scene in your Ted Williams piece where he yells at you because you hadn't read his autobiography. Did you avoid it deliberately?

Yes. After I got the assignment from *Esquire,* I just went down to the town he lived in in Florida. I didn't want to know anything, I didn't *want* to read all the received wisdom of the last fifty years, because then I'd be spouting the same crap as everyone else—which was *exactly* what pissed Ted off about journalists in the first place.

So you just showed up?

Yes. It's this little shitty town on the road to Key West. Ted wasn't there when I arrived, so I stayed in town for two weeks and I met *everybody* who knew him. They kept on asking me, "What are you hanging around for? Ted's not here." And I'd say, "Aw shucks, I don't know. I just kinda like the joint, I guess." And I did. It was cheap and warm and I had a nice hotel on the beach.

I met all his fishing guy buddies and I really got to know them. Once in a while I'd ask a *little* about Ted, but I didn't push it. So by the time Ted comes back everybody's saying, "Hey Ted, have you heard about this odd guy who's been hanging around for weeks?" And pretty soon, Ted had to check me out for himself.

Where did you learn to be a journalist?

I learned it in Baltimore when I was working for the *Sun.* It's the kind of town where everybody knows each other and you can't walk down the street without seeing somebody you know. So you have to deal fairly with the people you write about. It's not like you can play "gotcha" and then not show up again. So if you cheap-shotted them everyone is going to know. So I learned pretty quickly that I had to be straight up with sources. I'll do *anything* for my sources! I'll wash their damned windows if I have to.

This is just plain adaptive behavior. You do a lot better as a journalist if your sources help you than if they don't. And if you're going to *have* to fuck 'em, then you let them know man-to-man ahead of time *how* you're going to fuck 'em so they can be prepared. One politician who was my *friend* was sent to jail because of what I and others wrote in the paper. But I told him what I was doing every step of the way. I told him why it looked bad, what I was going to put in tomorrow's paper. I told him he might want to tell his wife before it hit. And he appreciated that. He sent me gifts from jail.

Who are your reporting models?

Gay Talese is *impeccable*. David Halberstam is great: a real hard-working sonofabitch. Tom Wolfe works his ass off, too.

I used to read Wolfe and think, "Well, *fuck you!* God touched you and made you a fucking genius, and that's the end of it!" Then in the mid-eighties I walked in to the offices of *Rolling Stone* one afternoon and saw him working at a desk. He was writing *The Bonfire of the Vanities* in biweekly installments at the time, and I looked in his eyes and saw the haunted, hunted animal look I *know* I have in my eyes when the shit is hitting the fan. And I thought to myself, "God bless you, Tom. You're a working stiff after all."

Do you alter your methods when writing an international piece?

Yes. There are whole areas of the world where a discussion of reporting ground rules would freak everybody out and cause a lot of problems. So I don't talk about that stuff much.

But what I really try to get across is the fact that I *really* want to hear what they have to say. My offer is, "Yes, show me your house. Yes, I'd like to meet your family. Sure, I'll sleep out in the desert with you tonight." And that willingness to engage transcends cultural boundaries.

How do you report a story when you are somewhere that you don't speak the language?

Half the battle is your interpreter. I get interpreters from universities because young people are better at it. Translating is a god-given gift. Because he has to be able to communicate *your* enthusiasm to them. And communicate *their* best to you. It is a job that requires a beautiful person of instant and subtle sympathies.

How do you get people to talk to you?

The thing is that people *want* to tell their stories. But only if you're really interested in them, which I am. When you're writing about a guy like Ted Williams or a presidential candidate, and you approach someone who *really* knows him, and you're not trying to prove some theory you dreamed up back in New York, it's the best thing that ever happened to him. Because this is the most amazing guy they've ever known. Their wives and girlfriends have long since tired of hearing stories about him, and here comes this kind of woolly guy who *really wants to know.* All the stuff they know about this amazing guy, but they've never been given the opportunity to really explain, is finally going to be heard. They're in heaven.

Aren't they suspicious about your motives?

Well, by the time I hang around for a while, they can see that I'm just not *capable* of duping them. I can't find my own ass with both hands! I don't have some big complicated scheme that I'm trying to fit everything into.

Do you ever talk to sources confidentially?

A lot of people want to be "in the conspiracy" with you. They'll agree to talk, but insist on all sorts of conditions. I always say no to that.

Do you establish ground rules for your interviews?

Yes, I tell them, "I probably won't end up quoting you at all. If I do, I'll tell you before. But if you say something *really* good, I'll probably just *steal* it and write it in my own voice." Because what I want them to know is that if *they* tell me the story and make me really understand, then *I'll* tell the story. I'll take the responsibility for it.

Do you allow them to change their quotes?

Only if they've got good reasons. But if changing the quote causes me insurmountable problems I tell them that I *have* to use their quote the way they said it.

You show subjects their quotes before a piece is published?

I find that reading them their quotes helps the piece. Hell, I'd *love* to read them the whole story if I had the time. With *What It Takes*, I sent every character every single page that I wrote about them before it was published. I didn't tell them I was going to do this when I started, but I realized by the end that I just *had* to.

Why did you do that?

First, I wanted *them* to know what is in it. Second, so much of the book takes place through dialogue that is running through their heads, they've *got* to sign off. You can't say what a guy is thinking unless you check with him. Third, although I won't let them be my editor, if something sounds wrong to them, I need to know.

How did they respond?

They were wonderful. They didn't try to dick around with their quotes or my descriptions. And it helped the book. I told them that if something is wrong I'll change it. But the *price* of my changing it is that they tell me what *really* happened.

How do you decide whom to interview?

Well, first off, don't waste your time interviewing a *guy* if a *woman* is available. Guys don't notice *anything*. I probably asked twenty of DiMaggio's teammates about the party after the 1947 World Series at the Waldorf-Astoria. And they'd say, "Aw it was great! There was a band and everything was first-class. Joe was real happy that night!" Then I'd ask one of their wives to describe the party. And she'd say, "Yes, it was a wonderful party. But the flowers were dreadful. And the food was late. And Phil Risutto's mother came in wearing the oddest hat . . ." They know *everything*. Guys are *hopeless*.

Does it matter in what order you interview your subjects?

It doesn't matter in what order I go in because I ask everyone the same question. There's no trickery involved, so it's easy. And I'm going to go back ten times anyway. And then one interview leads to the next, and to the next, and the next . . .

How do you get to famous people like George Bush and Joe DiMaggio?

In the case of then Vice President Bush, his son, George W., made all the difference. My researcher and I went to see Lee Atwater, who was the campaign manager. And because we tell him we want to know about Bush's personal/family side, Atwater shows us into George Jr.'s office. George is on the phone with his cowboy boots up on the desk, and a plug of tobacco tucked in his lip. Atwater introduces us, says, "Boys, just don't fuck me over," and leaves. George looks us over slowly. We looked pretty raggedy and I had a lot more hair. And he says, "Well, you certainly don't *look* like a bunch of young Republicans." And we all have a laugh.

He and I got off on the right foot. Junior just took me in. So every time I found myself in Washington and didn't have anything scheduled, I'd stroll over to Junior's office and sit around. It was the only place you could smoke cigars, so we'd smoke together.

I'd be sitting around and hear him talking on the phone about who was trying to screw him or his father. But I didn't care about that shit. And once he *saw* that I didn't care about that shit he let me see *everything*. Eventually, he brought me up to Kennebunkport to meet his dad. We played horseshoes together, and George Sr. totally kicked my ass. Junior knew how his dad would be comfortable with me. If I had gone in there with a straight interview it would have been a disaster.

How do you get busy, important people to give you the time you require for such in-depth reporting?

I never got as much time as I wanted with Bush. But I *was* able to do that thing where I sit with him while he was interviewed by other journalists. And I would ride in his motorcade, and when he was about to do something, his aides would hustle me into a spot where I'd be standing behind him and could see what he was seeing.

Do some people balk when they realize how much time you're asking of them?

Sure, some people just can't do it. Jack Nicklaus, for instance. *Esquire* assigned me a piece on him, but it was too much for him. He told me, "I was out on the green today and I wasn't thinking about the *putt,* I was thinking about *you.* I can't do that." I didn't hold it against him, but if I can't get enough time with my subject then it isn't my kind of story. I don't have the chops to pull off a story after spending only a few hours with someone.

Why didn't DiMaggio talk to you for your biography of him?

Well, he *talked* to me, but he just wouldn't help me. We talked four or five times about *why* he wouldn't talk to me—which was quite interesting in itself. I learned a lot about him from those non-conversations. I guess I thought that maybe he'd see my smiling face and decide to unload his tale on me. But once I knew something about him I knew he wouldn't, because his life's method was always to withdraw.

How do you report *around* someone who won't give you access?

I don't skulk around. If I'm at a car show or someplace where Joe's appearing, I'd wave to let him know I was there. But I didn't approach him. Actually, I think he was kind of satisfied that this well-financed, serious inquiry into his life was under way. If I had quit I think he would have been miffed.

Where do you most like interviewing?

I like to eat and I often take people out to dinner. I'll take a guy out to dinner six times and never ask a question. Then on the *seventh* time I'll say, "Let's go out to this place for brunch on Saturday, and don't make any other dates that day." And we'll sit there and talk, and I'll fill four notebooks with notes. We'll stay there so long that I'll buy him dinner—in the same place. Because at a *certain* point you've got to get it down. But only at the point where he and I are building the boat together. I say, "The stuff you've told me during these six dinners is *fabulous.* But I don't know it well enough to tell the story. So now you're going to help me understand it well enough to tell it."

Where do you least like interviewing?

Living rooms. People don't talk well in living rooms. The living room is the place where you sit with your hands folded in your lap.

Most of the people I interview never use their living rooms unless the parson is coming over.

If I find myself talking to someone in a living room I'll say, "Could you do me a favor? Could we do this at the kitchen table? Because it's so much easier for me to take notes there." I don't actually write anything down, but the conversation is *so* much better in the kitchen.

What does your researcher do, and why do you bring him along while you report?

God, he's doing *everything*. I bring him along with me because he's got *fabulous* eyes. The other reason is that he has information about the guys I'm interviewing that I don't. He's the one who goes to their high school, xeroxes the yearbook, and calls up the classmates. So he's got a depth of research knowledge that I don't have at that point in my reporting.

How do you then combine your reporting and his research?

We created a system when I was writing *What It Takes*—a book that *could easily* have been a logistical nightmare. When I had finished my reporting, I'd *read* the contents of my hundreds of notebooks onto a tape recorder. The notebooks have all the scenes I've witnessed, speeches, meetings, quotes, everything. So I read them— not necessarily word for word—onto the tape. And at this point I'm beginning to *tell the story.* Then my researcher has those tapes transcribed into computer files, which are digitally moved into giant time lines. Then we print out the whole thing and bind it in giant notebooks, each of which is probably about a foot thick.

What exactly is in this notebook?

Everything. One volume might have every *moment* of, say, Bob Dole's career. I might have five different eyewitness accounts of the day Dole became state's attorney in Russell, Kansas. It will have some notes I wrote when I visited his old office. There will be newspaper clips from the *Russell Daily News* from that day, as well as the certified vote totals. It's all there.

How do you start writing?

The first thing is to get my butt in the chair. Then I write the lead. Don't try to cutesy-up the lead. Just tell the reader what the book is about. The longer and more ornate the project is the faster you tell the reader what it is about.

For instance, the lead of my Ted Williams piece is, "Few men try for best ever, and Ted Williams is one of those." That's the story. No fucking around.

Do you have a daily routine for writing?

I make myself do a thousand words a day—and they have to be keepers. *If* I get my thousand words done, I can get out of the chair. If I don't, I have to sit there for eight hours. I tend to do my thousand words because I *really* want to get out of the fucking chair!

Where do you like to write?

For the DiMaggio book I had a backhouse, an old tenant farmer's house. No phone. I used a shitty laptop with a big monitor and a spare keyboard. No cool programs, like solitaire, I could waste time with.

How do you start your writing day?

I go to the beginning of the text I've been working on and read through the entire thing, fixing as I go. I've got to add a thousand words.

Are the experiences of writing a newspaper story, a magazine piece, and a book radically different?

The difference is pace. You've got to move a newspaper story at a breakneck pace since the reader is only going to be with you for five minutes. A magazine story has to make the reader *want* to commit more time. If you get a magazine reader to commit to only five minutes you've failed.

A book is something else entirely. Not to be too grand about it, but a book ought to alter the reader's life, add to the reader's life, in some fundamental way. You have a compact with the reader that if he gives you the time then something will be better for him. His understanding will increase, an emotional satisfaction will ensue, a cathartic

RICHARD BEN CRAMER 51

experience will take place. A book *has* to make something happen. A newspaper story informs, a magazine article entertains, and a book has to move you.

Do you use outlines?

I'm not much of an outliner. The whole of *What It Takes* was outlined on the back of a placemat in a Greek diner on Sixth Street. I was trying to explain to my researcher how I'd structure it, with all the stories running parallel to each other. So for the next three years we worked off that placemat.

Why do you like the profile form?

I think writing about a human is the hardest thing to do. But it is the most satisfying for the reader because most people learn most easily through personal acquaintance. So if I can, in effect, introduce them to a person who shows the reader their world, it is a much more organic process than, say, a story by John McPhee, which is carefully constructed and impersonal. McPhee is fabulous, but his is a lot headier than my work. My work soaks in like one of those magic creams where you rub it on and it's gone. It goes down so easy that the reader doesn't know they're getting it.

Why are you seldom a character in your pieces?

I'm never in a piece unless the subject does something *with* me that is revelatory about *them*. There's no other reason for me to be there. I *get* my innings. I get my licks in. I don't need any more exposure. For instance, when Ted Williams took me in after he was so happy about his girlfriend, Lou, that was an occasion where I *had* to be in the piece. I put a few "I"s in the lead so that the reader wouldn't be startled when I popped up in the middle of the piece, when Ted finally opens up. Ted was famously guarded, so this *moment* when he opens up shows the reader the boy who is so dear underneath all the gruffness.

What kind of a presence do you like to have in your work?

I'm the guy on the barstool who is telling them the story. And they're in the armchair listening. As long as I can keep them from remembering that they've got to go home tonight, we're good.

My wife, who's my best editor, says you can't give them a chance to put it down. Because if you give them a chance, they will. And they may never come back. Not because they didn't like it, but because there are so many other distractions. But if the last sentence they read *got* them something they'll read the *next* sentence.

How would you describe your theory of reporting?

I've always said I practice the "feet" theory of journalism. That is, if you want to talk to an elevator guy about something that happened in the building last Tuesday, don't walk in and ask him what happened in the building last Tuesday. Ask him about his *feet*. Because if there is *one* thing an elevator guy thinks about, it's his *feet*. And if you want to get to know this elevator guy, all you've got to do is ask him about his feet. I'm betraying my age because there aren't any more elevator guys.

Can journalism lead to truth? Or is it simply another version of reality?

I'm not out there busting my ass to give people just another "take" on reality. I'm out there to clean the plate. Once they've read what I've written on a subject, I want them to think, *"That's it!"* I think the highest aspiration people in our trade can have is that once they've written a story, nobody will ever try it again.

BY RICHARD BEN CRAMER:

How Israel Lost: The Four Questions, Simon & Schuster, 2004
Joe DiMaggio: The Hero's Life, Simon & Schuster, 2000
Bob Dole, Vintage Books, 1995
What It Takes: The Way to the White House, Random House, 1992
Ted Williams: The Seasons of the Kid, Prentice Hall, 1991

LEON DASH

April 18, 1995, was a bittersweet day for *Washington Post* reporter Leon Dash. At four a.m., Rosa Lee Cunningham, the principle subject of his eight-part series "Rosa Lee: Poverty and Survival in Washington" (September 18–25, 1994), entered the hospital where she would die from AIDS three months later. That morning, Dash attended the funeral of her fifteen-year-old grandson, Rico, who had been murdered in drug-related violence. When he returned to the *Post* offices, he learned that the series had been awarded the Pulitzer Prize.

Dash entered journalism in 1966 while an undergraduate at Howard University, a self-described crusader determined to "right all the wrongs in the world." After a while, he became disappointed when he realized his readers weren't going to "rise up and change the system" whose corruption he had revealed. But Dash's early frustration didn't deter him from employing his rigorous journalistic methods to explore controversial subcultures—prisons, teenage pregnancy, drugs, adolescent violence—that few other reporters have the skill, patience, or emotional fortitude to write about in depth. "My precise intention is to make the reader as uncomfortable and alarmed as I am," he writes in *Rosa Lee* (1996), the book he adapted from the series.

It is fitting that Dash dedicated *Rosa Lee* to "unfettered inquiry." Dash's extraordinary brand of immersion journalism sets his work apart from most writing about people mired in poverty, drugs, or crime. The key to his success is time.

Dash will only write about people whom he is living among, and spends months, sometimes years, interviewing them. For his six-part 1986 series on teenage pregnancy, he lived for a year in a roach-infested basement apartment in the section of Washington, D.C. with the highest rate of adolescent pregnancy. *Rosa Lee* was the result of a four-year-long effort.

Dash's reporting routine is methodical. The initial cycle of interviews lasts between eight and sixteen hours (Rosa Lee's took *nine days*), and requires multiple sessions. The sessions are divided between the four spheres Dash believes dominate one's life: home, school, church, and social life. The interviews, which Dash tapes and transcribes himself, yield a skeleton of a subject's life, a rough map with which he then explores specific episodes in detail during subsequent interviews.

The point of such lengthy interviews is not merely to accumulate facts. Dash's goal is to remove the public mask every subject dons when talking to a journalist. "I've learned that you don't really begin to get the truth of a circumstance or a person's life until you've known that person for at least four to six months," he says. Unlike reporters who write on tight deadlines, Dash tries to understand his subjects in their full historical context, analyzing the poverty, crime, or drugs that vex them as *inter*generational phenomena. In *Rosa Lee*, Dash escorts Rosa Lee to North Carolina to explore the legacy of her family's sharecropper past. Dash's determination to pose what he calls the "Why" question earned him the moniker of "staff anthropologist" at *The Washington Post*.

Dash gained his most important journalistic insight while teaching history and geography at a Kenyan high school while in the Peace Corps from 1969 to 1970. Living among the pastoral Nandi people, he saw firsthand that middle-class norms were far from universal. Back in the U.S., this insight helped him learn information from subjects who routinely lied to reporters who condescended to them. "At delicate points in the interviews, every one of them would watch my eyes and listen intently to my questions. They were watching me to see if I would judge them. Only months after they had not seen condemnation in my eyes or heard a judgmental nuance in my voice did they begin to open up," he writes in *When Children Want Children* (1989).

Born in New Bedford, Massachusetts, on March 16, 1944, Dash was raised in New York City, living in Harlem and the Bronx. His parents were middle-class civil servants: his father a postal clerk (and eventually a supervisor) and his mother an administrator for New York City's Health Department. Dash's interest in journalism began while he was the editor of the school newspaper at Lincoln University in Pennsylvania, where he studied for two and a half years before transferring to Howard University, which offered the courses in African studies he wanted to take.

While at Howard, Dash worked the "lobster shift" as a copy aide at *The Washington Post*, leaving the paper at 2:30 a.m. He was promoted to reporter in 1966 and received his BA in history from Howard in 1968. After two years in the Peace Corps, he returned to the *Post* in 1971, where he coauthored *The Shame of the Prisons* (1972) with Ben Bagdikian, contributing a section on intergenerational family crime. In 1975, Dash was one of forty-four journalists who founded the National Association of Black Journalists.

From the mid-seventies to the mid-eighties, Dash was primarily a foreign correspondent. In 1973, he trekked four hundred miles over four months with the UNITA guerrillas in Angola as they tried to oust the Portuguese. In 1974, the Portuguese military authorities, who had read his series on UNITA, invited him back to Angola to report on the colonial side of the conflict. The series won Dash a George Polk Award from the Overseas Press Club, and from 1979 to 1983, Dash was the *Post*'s West African bureau chief, based in Abidjan in the Ivory Coast.

Dash's six-part series on teenage pregnancy, which he undertook upon returning to Washington, D.C., to join the *Post*'s special projects unit in 1984, was a finalist for the Pulitzer Prize. He began his research with the common assumptions that the high incidence of teenage pregnancy among poor, black urban youths was the result of ignorance about birth control and adolescent reproductive capabilities. After months of exhaustive interviews, he learned that neither was the case. "He spent two years as a kind of spy, cultural anthropologist, visitor from Mars," writes the novelist John Edgar Wideman in a *Washington Post* review of the book version of the series, *When Children Want Children*. "The slow, painstaking cultivation of mutual intimacy between himself and his subjects carries Dash's research far beyond the level of social science eavesdropping and statistics; he doesn't allow the reader to forget the complexity of people's lives and problems in Washington Highlands."

In 1990, Dash published "Drugs in the Ranks: Getting High in

D.C. Jail" (June 10–14, 1990), about rampant drug use by the *guards* in D.C.'s jail system. He stumbled on the story while interviewing Rosa Lee Cunningham, a heroin addict, mother of eight, who was doing time for selling heroin to feed two of her grandchildren. Dash wanted to write about the explosion in the population of Washington's "underclass," as defined by the Urban Institute (female-headed, chronically unemployed, marginally educated, criminally recidivist families), and initially planned to follow four families. When that became logistically impractical, he settled on Rosa Lee's family, interviewing Rosa and her children from 1990 to 1994. Published in eight parts, the series elicited heated responses from thousands of readers, 4,600 of whom left messages on a special response line set up by the newspaper. "When are you going to do a story about a white person who moved from Appalachia and is still in a trailer park three generations later?" one complained. Dash made a point of calling every reader who left a critical comment, explaining that he had no particular ideological agenda in writing the series. "There is something in her life story to confirm any political viewpoint—liberal, moderate or conservative," Dash writes in *Rosa Lee.* "The reality however is much more complicated and difficult to grapple with." The series won the 1995 Pulitzer Prize for explanatory journalism (with photographer Lucian Perkins). It was made into a PBS documentary and published in book form as *Rosa Lee: A Mother and Her Family in Urban America.* The book was well reviewed. "Dash's candor and his painstaking accumulation of details overcome any dehumanizing effect that the story he gives us might have," writes Nicholas Lemann in *The New York Review of Books.*

Dash's final investigative series for the *Post,* "21st and Vietnam: The Making of Teen Killers" (November 29–30, 1998), was coauthored with *New Yorker* writer Susan Sheehan. He used his trademark immersion technique to try to understand why children like Rosa Lee's grandson had been murdered, and how young male killers were formed—a process which had led to a 700 percent increase in the local homicide rate for young victims between 1985 and 1996.

The two-part series was criticized by readers, and some colleagues, who believed Dash was perpetuating stereotypes of young black men. "Leon Dash has done it to me again. My friend and *Post* colleague has coauthored a pair of excruciatingly detailed stories on the underside of black life in Washington," wrote *Post* columnist William Raspberry. "Where does news value end and exploitation begin?" wondered E. R. Shipp, the *Post*'s ombudsman.

As in the past, Dash responded that he was only doing his job. "I always do this with no more interest than informing the public how these circumstances are creating the things you read about on a daily basis. You know we seldom tell people what the circumstances are that lead to the phenomena that claim so much of our journalistic attention. Your suggestions suggest that I ought to be prescribing instead of describing. But that's somebody else's job. I'm a reporter, not a policy wonk," he told Raspberry.

In 1998, Dash left the *Post* to take a professorship in Journalism and Afro-American Studies at the University of Illinois at Urbana-Champaign, where he was later awarded the first Swanlund chair in 2000.

What kinds of subjects are you drawn to?
I want to understand the lives of people trapped in poverty. The myths which the middle class uses to describe the poor, and formulate policy, are just that: myths. Not only are they inaccurate, they also don't do anything to help the poor get out of the situation they're in.

How do you manage to portray poor people more accurately?
The form of immersion journalism I practice requires that I spend a lot of time with the people I write about. People who write about poverty don't usually spend the amount of time with poor people it takes to *really* understand their lives.

I operate on the theory that everyone has a public mask. This public mask applies to every ethnic group, at every class level, throughout the world. The stories most reporters get—because of time constraints and deadline pressures—rarely penetrate beneath that mask. Unless you're able to get someone to remove his public mask, your story won't reflect his genuine motivation or behavior.

Even when I was writing a short piece for *The Washington Post,* I was always trying to figure out *why* the people I was writing about were behaving the way they were—what circumstances led them to behave this way. One colleague at the *Post* used to call me the paper's "staff anthropologist." I liked that.

Do you prefer coming up with your own story ideas, or do you like to work on stories that editors and others suggest?

I generally come up with my own ideas. And when I was at *The Washington Post*, I *always* planned my next project in great detail, and then presented it to my editors as a done deal. I had to operate that way or else I'd be assigned some foolish piece. I made sure to stay ahead of the process. I also get ideas from friends.

For example, in 1984, when I returned from Africa, where I was a foreign correspondent for *The Washington Post*, a friend mentioned to me that 53 percent of all black children were born to single mothers, and that one-third of those single mothers were adolescent girls growing up in poverty. I didn't believe her at first. But I did some research and discovered that she was right. That, to me, was a *major* phenomenon. I started reading books and articles about it, and found that everyone was all over the map. They had lots of information, but no real explanations. Nobody knew what motivated these girls. Some said they were ignorant. Others said they wanted the welfare checks. I had written enough about poverty to know that being on welfare is not a sufficient economic incentive. So I wrote *When Children Want Children* in order to answer that question.

Does one story sometimes lead directly to the next?

Yes. After I'd spent some time hanging out in jail to report on Rosa Lee, the officers became comfortable with me. One day an officer asked me, "Have you noticed the large number of drug-addicted officers here?" In fact, I had noticed that a lot of them wore long-sleeved shirts on even the hottest days (to cover up the needle marks on their arms), and I knew that one officer had overdosed. I eventually wrote that story, quoting all the officers on the record. They talked about their drug use, about female officers selling sex in the jail to buy drugs—all of it. Then I went back to reporting the Rosa Lee story.

Do you discuss your work as it progresses, or do you keep it to yourself until a project is complete?

When I was living in Washington I had a coterie of friends (white and black), and a few colleagues, with whom I discussed my work. I got ideas from them and shared my research with them. They weren't experts, but they were critical thinkers. And they were not afraid of the controversial topics I was exploring. A lot of my black middle-class acquaintances were uncomfortable with my work and tried to discourage me. I lost friendships. It was a small circle of friends, and after I wrote about adolescent childbearing, the circle got even smaller.

This got worse after I started writing about adolescent male killers. And they'd say, "Oh Leon, leave it alone!" And I'd ask them, "You have read enough to know that there has been an astronomical increase in adolescents killing adolescents since 1985. Most of it is black-on-black violence connected to the crack trade. Why do you think we should *ignore* that?" And their response was, "Yes, but you always want to go into these subjects in so much detail!" And I'd explain that it was all interconnected, it was all intergenerational. And their posture was, "But white people are going to ascribe that behavior to all of us."

But I can't help what racists think. If they want to read my books and twist them around for racist purposes, so what? They aren't going to be converted by anything I write. I'm not responsible for American racism. And it's not going to stop me from doing the work that I want to do.

Are there parts of the world or country that are more or less interesting to you?

I'm interested in any group of people that I'm living among. It doesn't matter whether it is a small town or a big city. The key factor for me is that I must be living among them. I don't do commuter journalism.

How did your experience in the Peace Corps, from 1969 to 1970 in Kenya, influence your ideas about journalism?

Being in the Peace Corps was very important because it taught me about cultural relativity. I lived among the Nandi people in a very rural, relatively isolated part of northwest Kenya, and I learned very quickly that I had to adjust to the local culture, rather than trying to get the local culture to adjust to me. It made me realize in a profound way that people who have different upbringings from me end up having very different values—whether they live in Kenya or right here in the United States. There is an unspoken assumption in American journalism that white, middle-class values are the norm. The fact is that they aren't in most places.

I teach my students that you can't be a journalist if you are going to be judgmental. If you have a judgmental reaction in your eyes during an interview, or a judgmental nuance as you pose a question, people will close down.

You haven't done any celebrity journalism. Would you ever?

Sure. A celebrity wouldn't turn me off. Because if a celebrity came into the interviewing project, I would put them through an interview process they had never been through before. The first few months of the project would be dominated by the celebrity's rehearsed responses, his public mask. But that would fall away eventually. I'd keep going until I got them to drop their mask. But I'd need a lot more time than they would probably be willing to give me, which is the whole problem with celebrity journalism.

The subjects you write about—race, poverty, crime, drugs— are so widespread. How do you focus your curiosity about them enough to develop a specific story?

In the case of *Rosa Lee,* it all came from a small article in *The Washington Post* I read while I was on leave from the paper. The Urban Institute had issued a very good study of the American underclass, which contained a succinct definition of the term "underclass." I got a copy of the report and read it carefully. I knew it would provide my intellectual framework for a series on poverty. Their definition of the underclass had five parts. An underclass family was female-headed, welfare-dependent, and only marginally educated. The adults in the family were chronically un- or underemployed. And they supplemented their welfare stipend with petty crime. They cycled in and out of prison. They'd get a year's sentence and be out on good behavior in eight to ten months.

How did the report help you focus the story?

First, it gave me an intellectual framework, which most journalism doesn't have. Second, it gave me an idea of where to look for the subjects of my project.

Where did you look?

For *Rosa Lee*, I started hanging around the D.C. jail in 1987. Jail officials initially had me on a very tight leash, and wouldn't let me roam around the building, as I wanted to. One officer there really helped me. I gave him the Urban Institute's definition, and he identified the inmates who fit it. It turned out that there were entire families traveling through the prison system simultaneously. There was a father on one cell block, who had a son on another cell block, and a grandson on another. Three generations—men and women—in the same jail, on separate charges, at the same time. That information wasn't in any central computer, but the officer knew the inmates so well that he directed me to all the family units in the jail. I couldn't have found my characters if I hadn't had his help.

How do you prefer to approach someone once you've decided you want to interview him?

It is best to go directly to someone, and to tell him how you got his name. If you are doing a project on people in poverty, you don't want to be introduced by a social worker. You need to find some other mechanism. For example, when I was reporting the adolescent childbearing book, the first mechanism I used was going through the minister at the neighborhood church, who introduced me to the head of the church's youth council. I met one sixteen-year-old girl, Tauscha Vaughn. She started telling me about pregnant girls she knew, and she provided me entrée to them. Tauscha was a better mechanism than the minister or the director of the youth council. I wanted to get to the teenagers *through* a teenager.

How did you choose your characters for Rosa Lee?

I used the five categories from the Urban Institute's definition of the "underclass." If someone didn't meet all five requirements, I'd eliminate him. I did extensive interviews with twenty men and twenty women. I selected four families to follow: two male-headed families, and two female-headed families. One was Rosa Lee's. I eventually had to drop the other three families because the reporting was overwhelming.

What is the most important literary factor when you are choosing the people who will be in your story? Narrative? Character? Plot?

I'm not sure I look for any one of those elements. Perhaps "character" comes closest to what I'm seeking. In order to write the kind of "anthropological" immersion journalism I do, I have to find characters who allow me to pose—and answer—the "Why" question. "*Why* is she in this terrible situation?" "*Why* is it that six of her eight children are drug addicts and criminal recidivists?" "*Why* did two of Rosa Lee's eight children turn out so differently?" "*Why* were they able to resist being swept up into this lifestyle? And how did Rosa Lee get into this lifestyle?" "*Why* does a strong family, coming out of the rural South, end up with a daughter like Rosa Lee and a family of drug-addicted criminal recidivists?"

I'm looking for the kind of character who will explain to me why she does what she does, give me lots of access, and have a commitment to the project. Most people aren't willing to undergo my kind of process of intensive, long-term interviewing.

What attracted you to Rosa Lee as a character?

She was fifty-one, and addicted to heroin, when she was arrested in October 1987 for selling drugs to feed two of her grandchildren. She went through the most debilitating withdrawal she had ever experienced. She thought she was going to die. After she began to feel better, she told her counselor, "I almost *died* last fall. I need to tell my life story to somebody."

When the counselor told me about her—a drug-addicted grandmother who sold drugs to feed her grandchildren *and* who wanted to tell her life story to someone—I was immediately interested. She fit into my definition of the "underclass" (her youngest sister was in the adjoining cell block, her youngest daughter had just left the jail, four of her six sons cycled in and out of prison, her oldest son was in a medium-security facility, and her youngest son was at a minimum-security facility), and she seemed like someone through whom I could pose the "Why" question I wanted to explore.

We started meeting for daily interviews in jail. It became immediately clear that her memory was excellent and that she was a good storyteller who loved detail. She was the perfect subject.

How do you determine how much time you need for a particular project?

I never know. I *do* know that I don't really begin to get the truth from someone until you've known her for at least four to six months. But it depends on the person. For example, with Rosa Lee, there were so many layers to her life story that we talked hundreds of times. When we started I didn't know that it would take me four years to learn the truth about Rosa Lee.

Do you ever do interviews by phone, e-mail, or letter?

No, I need to have face-to-face contact with the people I interview. I must establish a relationship with someone before he will take off his public mask, and I can do that only if I can make eye contact and see his body language. Most people give themselves away through their body language, and you can't pick that up over the phone.

Do you do most of your research before, during, or after your reporting?

I *start* by interviewing the people I want to write about. After I'm well along in the interviewing process, I start to read the literature.

When I came up with the idea for *When Children Want Children,* I told Bob Woodward that I'd start by interviewing some experts. He told me not to talk to them because if I did the reporting properly, I would know more than the experts. And he was right. Experts always end up interviewing *me!* I now see that conventional technique as totally pedestrian.

So what *is* your research routine?

It differs from project to project, but the first thing I usually do is find the relevant statistics. For example, when I was doing research for *When Children Want Children,* I went to the National Institutes of Health, the child development section, and looked at the statistics.

Then I looked at the Washington, D.C., census data, which lists the rates of birth to adolescent girls, as well as the rates of poverty, for each neighborhood. And I found that every neighborhood that had the highest rate of people living in poverty *also* had the highest number of girls having babies out of wedlock. That was how I chose the area of Washington Highlands to concentrate my reporting: of nineteen thousand residents there, 26 percent lived at *sub*standard federal levels of poverty, meaning they were subsistence survivors. And it had the highest level of adolescent childbearing of any census track in Washington, D.C. That's where I rented an apartment and started conducting my interviews.

What kinds of ground rules do you set during your reporting?

It changes with every project, but the basic rule is to keep a professional distance. I'm very strict about not crossing ethical lines while the project is ongoing. For instance, some of the adolescents I interviewed for *When Children Want Children* gave me gifts for Christmas. It was very painful and difficult, but I had to explain that I couldn't accept the gifts because I was there *working.* I gave the presents back, and if they wouldn't take the gift back, I gave it, unopened, to Goodwill. I don't want them to see me as their friend. I'm a reporter.

With *Rosa Lee,* I was dealing with a family of drug addicts. I explained at the beginning of the project that under no circumstances would I give anyone in her family money. I know how drug addicts collect little bits of change from different people until they have enough to buy drugs. I knew that they would simply use my money to buy drugs.

Every member of Rosa Lee's family tried to scam money off of me. Rosa Lee's daughter, Patty, even offered me *sex* in exchange for money. But they eventually learned that this was a rule I was never going to break.

So there was no exchange whatsoever for the entire four years you were reporting her story?

No, I just didn't give anyone *money*. I told Rosa Lee that if she was hungry we would go to a restaurant, and I would pay for the food. And if she wanted a pack of cigarettes, I'd buy them. But I will not give you money to buy food or to buy cigarettes—because I knew where that money would go.

But Rosa Lee inevitably broke some of your rules. You told her you wouldn't be witness to any criminal behavior, but she went shoplifting when she was with you. She also tried to use your connection to The Washington Post to help her navigate government bureaucracy. You write, "I'm angry at Rosa Lee for violating my trust, and I'm angry at myself . . . Why did I think she would behave differently around me?"

In retrospect, it was very egotistical of me to insist that when she was with me she behave so differently from the way she normally behaved. After all, this is a woman who has been shoplifting since she was thirteen years old! She *never* paid attention to the rules! So why did *I* think I was going to be able to impose rules on her? It was a mistake, although a well-intentioned one.

Rosa Lee obviously looked up to you. At one point, she asked you whether she should stop teaching her granddaughter to shoplift. She asks, "So you think I should stop?" And you reply, "No, no. I'm not getting into whether you should stop. I'm asking you how do you justify it?" Do you ever worry about becoming too involved with your characters?

It is a very fine line between maintaining my role as a reporter and developing the kind of humane relationship that inevitably occurs between two people who spend a lot of time with each other.

In the case of Rosa Lee's teaching her granddaughter to shoplift, she crossed the line. I didn't want my opinion influencing her behavior. I wasn't taking a moral position on what she was doing. All I wanted was to understand her justification for it.

How do you convince your subjects to talk to you so openly?

I'm a pretty gregarious guy, and I'm very flexible and open about myself. I am very accessible. Most of my subjects get addicted to the interview process and don't want to stop talking.

Time is the most important factor in doing this sort of project. For example, when I was reporting *When Children Want Children*, I rented an apartment in the community. So I was very accessible. I was walking on eggshells in the beginning because the adults thought that I had a sexual interest in these girls. And when I hung out with teenage boys they thought I was homosexual. It was only with time that they realized that I was actually doing what I said I was going to do: interviewing kids about adolescent childbearing.

How much do you reveal about yourself during interviews?

I tell them everything. If you can't speak honestly about yourself then you shouldn't be in this business. Nothing about my life is out of bounds.

For example, I interviewed Joye Jackson, a girl who was the mother of two children by the age of fifteen, for *When Children Want Children*. I asked her, "When you were thirteen, your mother told you that you were to notify her if you became sexually active so that she could get you birth control pills. Why didn't you go to her?" She kept blowing me off with silly answers. But I kept asking her again and again. Finally, she said, "Mr. Dash, let me ask *you* this question. When *you* were a teenager, and *you* were about to start having sex, did you ask *your* father for condoms?" And I said, "No, I *never* would have done that!" And she said, "Well, what makes you think that I'm any different? Sure, my mother made the offer. But I wasn't going to announce to her that I'd decided to start having sex." She wouldn't have told me the truth if I hadn't been willing to open myself up to her.

Do you share information you've discovered from other sources with the people you are interviewing?

Yes, I find it helps get people to talk more freely. For example, a woman I interviewed for *When Children Want Children* told me this horrendous story about being raped. I was very upset about it and had a headache—as I often do after I'm told something upsetting. I had promised to have dinner with another woman I was interviewing. When she came by I said, "Look, I'm not in good shape tonight. One of the young women in the project told me about being raped." And she said, "Well, I was raped, too. I just didn't tell you about it . . ."

Will you negotiate what is on, and off, the record?

Sure, but I continue to tape when someone asks me to keep something in confidence. When I transcribe it, I indicate that it is off the record or confidential, etc.

Do you ever use pseudonyms?

Never. When I was reporting *Rosa Lee,* one of her daughters didn't want me to use her name, so I had to drop her from the book. It was too bad, because I had already interviewed her for a couple of years.

Do you ever confront, or argue with, your interview subjects?

No. I'm never adversarial or antagonistic. I'll confront them with false *information* they've told me, but I try to stay very relaxed when I do it. For instance, when I told Rosa Lee's son, Ducky, that I knew he was a crack addict—and not a born-again Christian, as he claimed— my voice didn't rise above a monotone, I didn't point my finger at him, I didn't scold him. I just told him not to play me for a fool.

What is your interviewing method?

I divide the initial interviews into four sections: home life, school, church life, and social life (by which I mean life outside the family). Each complete interview (which consists of all four sections) takes at least eight hours—and usually a lot more. I start each section by asking them to think of their earliest childhood memory: "What is your earliest childhood memory growing up in your family?" "What is your earliest childhood memory going to school?" By the time I get to the section on growing up outside the family, they are addicted. People get annoyed if I cut it off after only two hours. I've had those interviews go for three or four hours at a stretch.

I start with no more than two hours for each session, even if we haven't completed, say, the school history. I don't want them to become overwhelmed or worn out. The people in my projects have never been interviewed before. So it can be unsettling for them.

The interviews take longer and longer as we move from the early to the later sections. This is the first time in their lives that they understand that they are *themselves* the end product of *multiple* influences by *many* people and experiences over a *long* period of time. They know that they could never put their story together in this organized fashion on their own, so they want me to pull it out of them. They are hooked.

How did you settle on these four sections?

School is very important to all of us. Sixty percent of one's young life is spent in school. And school is also a fairly neutral, safe area to start from (rather than, say, asking them about their sex lives). I've found that once I get someone to recall his school memories, I can take them forward, year by year, and correlate the events of their lives with the grades they were in when those events happened. If I can remind him what grade he was in, or the teacher he had—and we can date the experience. After we complete the school section, we move on to the family life, and then church life.

What if he didn't attend church?

It doesn't matter. Even if he didn't grow up in the church, he has *some* relation to the universe. Everyone has *some* concept of God and religion, even if it comes from family and friends. Even if he rejects God, the "church" section tells me about his moral core.

Where do you most and least like conducting interviews?

I don't like interviewing people in their homes, unless they are alone. If other people are there, they won't be candid with me.

I like doing interviews over meals at restaurants. It helps to break bread with someone. The only problem is that restaurants are noisy, so I have to be aware of the sounds that will drown out someone's words and ask them to repeat themselves.

Do you ever "stage" encounters in which you can observe the people you are writing about?

No. Rosa Lee was always trying to get me to take her out to a nightclub. I told her, "Look, this is *not* that kind of party!" She was always trying to make people think I was her lover, and I didn't like that. Now if *she* chose to go to a nightclub with her girlfriends, I might join them. But I wouldn't "take her out" to a club just for the sake of doing it.

Do you tape, or take notes?

Both. I write longhand, and use a small notepad that I keep either in my suit jacket or in my back pocket.

Taping allows me to maintain eye contact. I use microcassettes, and label each tape with the name of the interviewee, and the date of the interview. I star the most important interviews with a red ink pen.

Do you transcribe your own tapes?

Yes, because if I gave the tapes to a transcriber, I would have too many transcripts to deal with once I started writing. I summarize most of each interview, and transcribe only those exact quotes I think I'll want to use when I sit down to write.

Also, I had a bad experience with a transcriber. I taped 205 hours of interviews for *When Children Want Children. The Washington Post* transcriber became so offended by the sexual content of the tapes that she complained to Bob Woodward. The funny thing was that the interviews about sexuality didn't come until the last tapes, at the *end* of the project. The transcriber complained right away, so she had obviously skipped over the interviews on school, church, and family *in order to get to* the sexual material that so offended her! I ended up transcribing all 205 hours myself. And I've transcribed my own tapes ever since.

Is writing more difficult than reporting for you?

Writing is always painful and slow. I always need the help of a good editor.

Once you've done all your reporting and research, how do you begin to write?

Once I've transcribed my major interviews, I organize them into hanging folders, according to the names of the families. Each family has a folder, and that folder is broken down into smaller folders on each member of the family. For example, I had an enormous file on Rosa Lee's family: sections on her six brothers and sisters, each of her eight children, and then all her grandchildren.

What do you do once you've organized the transcripts?

I decide which themes I'm going to use. For *Rosa Lee* the themes were "how drugs ran through the family," "adolescent childbearing," "Rosa Lee's criminal life," "Rosa Lee's mother's legacy," etc. Once I've established the themes, I read through every transcript, selecting the passages that are relevant to the section. I type those passages into the outline. Once I'm done with the outline, I no longer refer to the transcripts.

What kind of authorial presence do you strive for?

I want to be the observer, the fly on the wall. But I also want to depict the interaction I have with my subjects. For example, the exchange I had with Rosa Lee when I pushed her to explain to me how she could justify teaching her granddaughter how to shoplift. That was a powerful scene, and I was clearly more than a fly on the wall. I was involved in every way. It showed my dilemma as well: I want to understand her, but don't want to influence or judge her. But I was upset by what she did.

My editor argued that my very presence had an impact on the adolescents in *When Children Want Children* and on Rosa Lee. He said, "Even if you didn't give them a word of advice, your presence influenced those kids. Your presence had an impact on Rosa Lee. You can't get around that, as much as you want to be a pure reporter." So I just had to acknowledge that I am a participant-observer in the story by introducing myself as a character.

Rosa Lee was the first time I put myself into a piece in a major way (although I had done it before when I wrote about the guerrillas in Africa in 1973 and 1977). With *Rosa Lee,* I *wanted* to step back as the anthropologist and write it in the third person. But it just didn't work. My editor told me that I had to put myself into the story, and he was right. It was very difficult the first time. I didn't want my ego to take over and obscure the real story.

How important is your identity in your journalism?

Very. I was once at a conservative gathering in D.C. after *Rosa Lee* was published, and someone asked me, "How can you be so sympathetic to these people?" I was a little stung by it because I thought I was simply being honest and nonjudgmental. I told him, "But I *do* feel empathy for Rosa Lee and for people trapped in their circumstances. Because I recognize that, given the history of this country—and the role race has played—that 'there, but for the grace of God, go I.'"

My father worked in the post office and my mother was a registered nurse in the New York City Health Department. That made me middle-class, growing up in Harlem in the fifties. But if my parents had had the same limitations as Rosa Lee's parents, I might not be able even to read today.

What kind of tone do you strive for in your writing?

I try to strike the tone of the honest observer. I'm not there to preach; I'm there to guide the reader through an experience, a world. I want to open your eyes, and perhaps even shake you up a bit. But I want to be as understated as possible.

Do you believe journalism can lead to truth?

There is no such thing as absolute truth. There are people who have been married to each other for seventy years and they still don't completely know each other. We all have some secrets we don't share with anyone.

What I am seeking to do in my writing is to get as close as I can to the whole truth about someone's motivations as I can. I'm pursuing something that, while not "absolute truth," is a lot closer to the truth than most people have, including the policy formulators and so-called experts.

What name do you give to your journalistic method?

I call what I do "immersion journalism" because I immerse myself so deeply in someone's life.

What do you think about the prospects for the kind of long-form nonfiction you write?

I'm somewhat optimistic. There are so many media outlets available competing for someone's time, but long-form nonfiction does something that none of the other media do. We take people on an extraordinary kind of a voyage, a voyage that can change them and the way they look at the world. Television can't compete with the experience of reading a really powerful piece of long-form nonfiction.

BY LEON DASH:

Rosa Lee: A Mother and Her Family in Urban America, Basic Books, 1996

When Children Want Children: The Urban Crisis of Teenage Childbearing, William Morrow & Co., 1989

The Shame of the Prisons [with Ben Bagdikian], Simon & Schuster, 1972

WILLIAM FINNEGAN

In William Finnegan's writing there is often a turning point, an aporia, when the author realizes his assumptions have been skewed and all is not as it seems. The war in Somalia hasn't simply devastated the country, it's also brought forth a strange but bustling form of wild-frontier capitalism; Mozambique's rebel army *isn't* merely a proxy force supplied by neighbors, but a dark, complicated brew concocted from indigenous African ingredients.

A self-described "specialist in the unexpected," Finnegan writes stereotype-defying descriptions of the kinds of people—young, black, poor, foreign—mainstream journalism tends to dismiss with a pastiche of clichés and statistics. Finnegan reports in real time, returning to the scene again and again, watching characters develop and scenarios play themselves out over months and even years. His goal is to transcend the snapshot frame of standard journalism by creating something more documentary in scope and feel. While any good journalist will hazard a guess as to his story's *next* development, Finnegan is aware that genuine change takes place slowly, perceptible "only" over the long term, and usually only in retrospect.

Finnegan is master of the genre that Joyce Carol Oates calls "memoirist-reportage." Reviewing *Cold New World* (1998) in *The New York Review of Books,* she defined it as "a hybrid of investigative research and interviewing, sociopolitical analysis and first-person narration that is often couched in the present tense." Memoirist-reportage is personal, but not only that; the writer neither idealizes nor dismisses his characters. It is an ambitious form that, in order to be done well, requires a writer to be many things: crack reporter, social critic, storyteller. Writing in *The Village Voice,* Robert Christgau praises the compassion of Finnegan's writing: "Not the fact of it, which we have a right to expect from any personal reporting about the oppressed, but its coolness, its clarity, its ductile strength." Finnegan writes about people in such a way that their "talents, their aspirations, and their struggles toward self-hood also seem ordinary, in the best way—organic attributes of a shared American humanity."

Born in New York City in 1952, Finnegan moved between Los Angeles and Hawaii while growing up. His father worked in the movie business, and it was during these years that Finnegan developed his love of surfing—a preoccupation that would later inspire him to travel the world in search of the perfect wave. While he was working toward his BA in English literature at the University of California in Santa Cruz he would occasionally hop a freight train for family visits to L.A. After graduating in 1974, Finnegan took a job as a railroad brakeman for the Southern Pacific in California, a job Neal Cassady once had on the same line. It was seasonal work, and when winter came, Finnegan would move to Missoula, Montana, to work toward an MFA in creative writing, which he received from the University of Montana in 1978.

Finnegan spent the next four years traveling through South Asia, Australia, and, finally, Africa. Supporting himself through odd jobs and freelance travel writing, he spent his spare time surfing and working on the unpublished novel he had started in Montana. Finnegan was strapped for money when he reached Cape Town, where he got a job as an English teacher at the Grassy Park High School, a non-European school whose students gave him his first close look at the world of apartheid. He quickly realized that the school's curriculum was designed to reinforce his black students' subservience.

It was in South Africa that Finnegan, who until then thought of himself as a novelist, became interested, suddenly and almost exclusively, in political nonfiction. His first piece of political journalism was a long *Mother Jones* essay about his experience living in a village in Sri Lanka in 1979. Finnegan's year at Grassy Park coincided with a nationwide school boycott, which became the subject of his first book, *Crossing the Line: A Year in the Land of Apartheid* (1986). "This may be the best book to give to an American trying for the first time to understand the agony of South Africa. Even those familiar with the structure and history of apartheid will encounter much that is new and important to think about," wrote Norman Rush in *The New York Times Book Review.*

In 1986 *The New Yorker,* for which Finnegan had started writing in 1984 (he became a staff writer in 1987), sent him back to South Africa, where he took up residence in the newsroom of the white, liberal *Johannesburg Star.* Unbeknownst to its owners, he attached himself to a group of black South African reporters whose responsibility it was to gather news from areas white reporters couldn't visit. Led by the enterprising and gutsy Jon Qwelane, these men and women ventured into black townships and "bush ghettos" in search of stories they had no assurance would be printed. Much like the students of his first book, these reporters became the lens through which Finnegan observed the country. His two-part series was subsequently published in longer form as *Dateline Soweto: Travels with Black South African Reporters* (1988). Critics marveled at the depth of Finnegan's reporting. Calling it "one of the few books written by a white non–South African that capture the spirit of the South African people," *The Washington Post*'s Jill Nelson identified Finnegan's strategy: "Finnegan became a minority within a black majority to get the story. At his best, Finnegan sees, as clearly as possible, through black eyes."

Finnegan's next book, *A Complicated War: The Harrowing of Mozambique* (1992), also grew out of a *New Yorker* assignment, this time a series of dispatches from a country at war. The book is more loosely constructed and meditative than his earlier work. The conflict is a shadowy, "complicated" war. There is no front, no beginning, or end. Although Finnegan finds ample evidence of the fighting (devastated villages, terrorized villagers), the conflict takes on a ghostlike character and the combatants are rarely seen. Likening it to a "novel on war-torn Mozambique," *The Black Scholar*'s Mario Azevedo said that it "deserves to be placed among the best works, if not the best, in the literature on contemporary Mozambique."

During the nineties, Finnegan alternated between foreign and domestic pieces, covering wars in Somalia, Sudan, and former Yugoslavia, and writing portraits of places—New Haven, East Texas, suburban L. A.—that proved his compassion and reporting skills were as applicable to America as they were to foreign countries. Finnegan refashioned these pieces into *Cold New World,* in which he offered a bleak assessment of the lives of young Americans—black, Mexican, neo-Nazi—all living in poverty of varying kinds. Despite America's affluence, he argues, the very people who should most be benefiting from the surging stock market are experiencing a general decline into a state of anomie. The pieces gave him an opportunity to try out his theory about the way teenagers influence a culture: "The story of youth culture is always the story *beneath* the official story. Following it is a way of getting ahead of the received wisdom, of getting a jump, as it were, on the story of the future."

For all its drama, *Cold New World* is a quiet, subtle book that chronicles the dark underside of the American dream. "His stories do not concern a trial of the century, a perfect storm or the ascent of a tall mountain. Instead, they are about powerless people left battered and grounded by an economy that may be richly rewarding the educated, but is cruelly punishing many others," writes Jack Hitt in *The New York Times Book Review.* Some reviewers questioned Finnegan's choice of such unrepresentative characters and, by extension, disputed his diagnosis of America's malaise. "Finnegan ends up with a remarkably muddled view of America. In fact, he often seems as lost as the youth about whom he writes," writes Abigail Thernstrom in *The Times Literary Supplement.* "Finnegan is gloomy and, in fact, wrong. He has woven disparate scraps of economic reality into a dismal, and fanciful, tapestry."

Finnegan is currently working on a surfing-themed memoir about male friendship.

———

In the introduction to *Cold New World* (1998) you call yourself "a specialist in the unexpected." What does that mean?

I used that phrase because I rarely have a well-formed idea of the story when I begin a project, although I don't tell my editors that. The truth is that the story I end up writing is almost always very different from the story I set out on.

For example, I went to Somalia in 1995 to cover the end of the failed U.N. mission for *The New Yorker* ["A World of Dust: Letter from Mogadishu," March 20, 1995]. The intervention had helped end the famine, but had then become a fiasco. The pullout was very tense and complicated, and that was naturally the story that the few foreign reporters there were focused on. But because I'm not a conventional news reporter, I had other options, and I soon realized that I basically had the whole country to myself.

And when I looked at *Somalia,* rather than at the U.N. pullout, my preconceptions about starving, suffering, "anarchic" Somalia were quickly undercut by the reality of a bustling, functioning, obviously very interesting place. There was no government, and a lot of violence, but new structures had clearly emerged to replace the state, and lots of business was being transacted. Newspapers were being published; people were eating; they were living their lives. The question was how. There was no office to tell you *anything.* No banks, no post offices—no ordinary modern services.

So how did you handle the reporting?
I ended up hanging out with the editor of one of the more popular Mogadishu papers—the only one that wasn't aligned, in fact, with one of the warlords. The paper was a primitive operation, run out of the editor's house, but it had a big circulation, and the editor was a fascinating guy. Following him around let me start to see how a post-nation-state Somalia worked—a place where Islamic or traditional clan-based Somali nomadic social institutions or, in some cases, whole new administrative concoctions had risen to fill the vacuum, as it were. There's actually something to be said for statelessness in some of the worst-governed parts of Africa, which would definitely include Somalia—beginning with the press freedom that can come with having no dictator around.

Somalia at that point was also kind of a country-sized experiment—the ultimate in deregulation, a true wild-frontier capitalism. And it had all these bizarre, postindustrial contrasts: people starting up new satellite communications businesses in neighborhoods that were simultaneously imposing sharia law, which can be quite medieval. So I ended up writing about this new country that was no longer a recognized country—a place that was both ancient and postmodern, and that was just then molting into a series of city-states around the port towns and their hinterlands—a place that I had never heard or read anything about before I went there and saw it.

Intellectually speaking, it was actually a relatively painless piece, which isn't always true, because a lot of my stories have a turning point, an aporia, a moment of disabling perplexity when I realize that the situation is not at all what I thought it was. That can be a miserable, disorienting experience, although sometimes my confusion itself—my change of heart—becomes a part of the narrative. It can even become the main intellectual suspense of a piece. Sometimes the narrative utility of my own confusion feels like a kind of consolation prize for all the anxiety of having things come unglued, of having not understood what I was getting into.

How do you get story ideas?

Some stories are generated by earlier stories. The logic of one piece propels me toward another. For instance, I wrote a piece about a family in inner-city New Haven ["A Reporter At Large: New Haven," *The New Yorker,* September 10–17, 1990], then later went looking for a story that would let me deal with some of the same topics—race, drugs, crime, the lives of working-class African Americans—in the rural South, to which almost everybody I'd written about in New Haven traced their roots. That's how I ended up writing about a little rural community in East Texas ["A Reporter At Large: Deep East Texas," *The New Yorker,* August 24–31, 1994], which had just undergone the forceful colonic of a federal drug raid. The two stories went together in my mind—and, indeed, in my book, *Cold New World.*

What elements make a good story for you?

I look for compelling characters who are in the midst of a morally complex conflict. I look for the unexpected twists and turns in the story.

Why is it that you've so seldom written about celebrities?

I have an aversion to writing about people who have press agents. Journalistically, it's already a very crowded field, obviously. Some writers can play with the formula, and be amusing, writing about celebrities. But getting access to subjects, the suck-up factor, seems like it can get pretty demeaning. The truth is, though, I don't know anything about it. I've written a lot about politics, and I've interviewed a few famous people in the course of reporting stories, but I don't think I've ever written anything you could call a celebrity profile. Being part of somebody's publicity machine would probably make my skin crawl.

Why do you write so frequently about teenagers?

Nearly everywhere, nearly always, there's a generation coming along that is developing a perspective that is likely to be quite different from their parents'. For me, nosing around a place that I'm trying to figure out, the most interesting story is often the disconnect between what the kids are saying and what the adults are saying. I've found this to be just as true in the Republika Srpska of Bosnia as in the suburbs of Los Angeles. The story of youth culture is always the story *beneath* the official story. Following it is a way of getting ahead of the received wisdom, of getting a jump, as it were, on the story of the future.

What is your thought process while you are trying to figure out what kind of story you're going to write?

It depends on the piece. If I'm trying to portray a place, a community, I look for sympathetic protagonists. Sympathetic main characters make the reporting richer, more fun, and simply more doable, since we usually have to spend a *lot* of time together. If I don't enjoy the company of the people I'm writing about, the project can get kind of arid.

But how, then, do you write well about someone you aren't sympathetic to?

I make a fairly sharp distinction, for journalistic purposes, between public figures and private citizens. If I'm trying to report on the lives of people who were basically minding their own business before I came along, and I realize at some point that the portrait I'm going to produce is likely to be unflattering, I have to have some very good reason to proceed. Lacking that reason, I generally think I should stop and go looking for other characters. With public figures, which in my work usually means politicians but can also mean powerful businesspeople or soldiers, I have a completely different standard.

Which is what?

For a start, I'm probably not going to be spending months hanging out with them, so the question of whether we get along well isn't usually so pressing. More than that, though, if somebody's position, their line of work, gives them power over many other people's lives, then I'm likely to be interested in them, in what they do and think, quite apart from my feelings about them, and my readers are, too—this assumes I can make them interesting on the page. And the feelings of my subjects about how I portray them are, in such cases, relatively unimportant to me. In fact, there's some inverse relationship there, I guess—the more powerful the person I'm writing about, the less I care what they themselves may think about what I write. The public interest in their personalities, their attitudes, their activities, takes precedence, so to speak. I don't mean I never find a public figure to be a sympathetic character. It's just that, if I find them unsympathetic, I'm not deterred from writing about them. A good critical portrait—one that captures a subject fully and fairly—can be a real challenge to write (and to read, I expect, if you happen to be the subject).

What kinds of people do you most like writing about?

People whose experiences are radically different from mine, and who are therefore initially difficult to understand, but whom I think I will eventually be able to render a decent likeness of.

For example, I wrote a piece about a guy named Moctar Teyeb, who is about my age and lives in the Bronx, but who was born a slave in rural Mauritania ["Profile: A Slave in New York," *The New Yorker,* January 22, 2000]. Moctar's childhood and adolescence, herding camels in the Sahara, his escape from slavery—and the incredible odyssey that had brought him to New York, via Senegal, Morocco, and Libya—all made a story that was so dramatic, so good, that it pretty much wrote itself. But his character was, for various reasons, much trickier to describe with any nuance. His deep religiousness, his sadness, his self-discipline, his fierce desire to expose the slavery still being practiced in his country . . . We're all prisoners of our pasts, but Moctar was, in my experience, uniquely so. Getting to know him actually opened up strange, difficult questions about the nature of freedom.

He was in a lot of pain. He was also extremely erudite in Arabic literature and Islamic history—he had really made up for lost time after he finally managed to get some formal schooling, as an adult— he had an advanced degree in Islamic law by the time I met him— and so his understanding of life was heavily embedded in a cultural, religious context that was, at the same time, part and parcel of his oppression. He had a lot of enemies, too, some of them in his own family, people who didn't like what he was saying about social institutions they accepted. Getting Moctar right was difficult, and I'm not sure I succeeded, but in some vital way he felt like my kind of character.

I also like writing about people who suffer from extensive stereotyping, like gang kids. The challenge there, of course, is to dig up material that contradicts, or humanizes, or at least avoids, the clichés and formulas of most magazine journalism.

Do your stories gestate for a long time?

I keep a lot of files on places, people, issues, and situations that I think I might eventually want to write about. I've been aware, for instance, of Robert Kiley's career for some years, and always thought he'd make an interesting story. He was in the CIA in the sixties, then he was a deputy mayor of Boston, and in the eighties he ran the Metropolitan Transportation Authority in New York. Now he's the transport commissioner of London, where they're hoping he can "save the Tube." But he's having to fight the Blair government, which is bound and determined to privatize the Tube—a truly terrible idea. I'm interested in railroads and in privatization—I've written about both subjects in other contexts—so it now seems like the right time to write about Kiley. ["Underground Man: Can the Former C.I.A. Agent Who Saved New York's Subway Get the Tube Back on Track?" *The New Yorker,* February 9, 2004.]

Following *places* also lets stories develop over time, of course. I've written a lot about southern Africa and try to keep an eye on events there, and I'll sometimes decide the time is ripe to write about something in the region that I've been following for years. But working anywhere far from home tends to lead to a lot of new story ideas. I recently wrote a piece, for instance, about a failed water privatization in Bolivia ["Letter From Bolivia: Leasing the Rain," *The New Yorker,* April 8, 2002], which gave me a chance to look at the U.S. from a Bolivian angle. And I was struck by the fact that Otto Reich, a Cuban American Republican activist who was, until very recently, our assistant secretary of state for Latin America, was such a prominent figure in Bolivia, while nobody in the U.S. knew who he was. I don't often write about diplomats or public officials, but I thought Reich was someone Americans should know about. ["The Political Scene: Castro's Shadow," *The New Yorker,* October 14–21, 2002.]

How much research do you undertake before you start a project?

It depends on the project. If I'm going to a country I've never visited before, I know I have to do a lot of reading, a lot of research, before I leave home. Otherwise, I won't know where to start reporting, won't know what questions to ask, and will probably waste a lot of time, mine and other people's. If I'm going to write a profile, then I'll try to read everything I can about the person—assuming there's been anything published—and about their area of expertise, certainly before I interview the profile subject. On a lot of stories, though, my initial notions are so vague, and subject to change, that it's not necessarily clear what sort of prior research I should be doing. When I decided I wanted to write about downwardly mobile white kids in a California aerospace suburb, I didn't know that I would end up having to research the history of white supremacist movements in the West. That only came out during the reporting.

I'm always collecting books and clips and articles as I go, usually to read after I get home. I'm thorough to a fault—"this story over-reported by Bill Finnegan"—which makes me a slower writer than I'd like to be.

What kinds of resources do you use in your research?

Libraries, bookstores, Nexis, the Internet. If I'm going to a new place, I like to start reading the local papers online before I go. If they're not available online, I'll try to spend some time in the papers' morgues when I get there. You can learn a lot in a short time from newspapers.

Do you consult experts?

Sure. And if I've read something particularly helpful, I'll often go and talk to the author—assuming our interests aren't so similar that we're crowding each other. Very often, I only really figure out the policy issues of a story *after* I've done a lot of the street reporting. So I usually save the analytical discussions with experts until after I'm done with my other reporting.

You frequently draw on academic texts, whether about poverty or drugs. What role do statistics, public policy, etc., play in your work?

Again, that kind of knowledge usually comes relatively late in the course of a project. For instance, I knew I wanted to write about downwardly mobile families and kids for *Cold New World*. But I had done five or six years of reporting for that book before I started developing an *explanation* for what I was seeing. I knew little or nothing about twenty-five-year wage trends, or any of the other statistics and trends that helped explain downward mobility in America, when I started. Once I'd done my reporting, I used the academic literature to confirm—or amplify, or moderate, or, in some cases, contradict— various explanations I'd heard or come up with myself for what I'd seen.

One not-very-happy example: I was reporting on Mexican immigrants in the Yakima Valley in Washington ["A Reporter At Large: The New Americans," *The New Yorker*, March 25, 1996], and I stumbled on a very disturbing, counterintuitive pattern. It seemed that the children of recent Mexican immigrants were doing better in school than the children of Mexican immigrants who had been in the U.S. for a few years, and that all the immigrant kids were doing better than the Mexican American kids who were born in this country. Simply put, the longer they stayed here—learning English, becoming acculturated—the worse these kids performed in school. I thought this couldn't be broadly true, that I must have landed among an unrepresentative group of kids. But later, when I read the academic literature on immigration and education, I found a number of studies that documented exactly the pattern I had found. So it was generalizable, and the question became why—what was it about these immigrants' experience that allowed a healthy percentage of newcomers to succeed, while so many of their predecessors, who had obvious advantages, failed?

Once you settled on that question, where did you look for answers?

In the schools themselves, in families, in the streets, in the gangs, but mainly the answers I found were in mainstream U.S. youth culture, and inside the kids' heads, and in the changing structures of economic opportunity. Suffice it to say that the American Dream is not alive and well except as a fantasy among a lot of poor kids, and that alienation and disillusionment are major problems among poor and working-class Latino kids.

How do you decide where to go and report your stories?

Occasionally—very occasionally—editors decide for me. Tina Brown suggested I go to Somalia—she was *The New Yorker*'s editor at the time. But that actually happened more often when I was freelancing—editors calling and asking if I'd go to, say, Nicaragua. I've sometimes had a subject in mind, but haven't settled on a place in which to go looking for a story, and have solicited the advice of editors. I knew, for instance, that I wanted to write about a deindustrialized city, and I was looking at a number of towns in the Rust Belt—Detroit, some places in upstate New York. But when I mentioned New Haven as a possibility to Bob Gottlieb, who was *then* the editor at *The New Yorker,* his eyes lit up. He liked, in the faintly evil way that editors like such things, the high contrast between Yale University and this terribly poor, crime-ridden city that it sits in the middle of. And the more I told him about New Haven's troubles— that it had more murders per capita than New York or Chicago, that it was the seventh-poorest city in America—the more Gottlieb liked it. And he was right: the heavy contrast did help the story I eventually found there stand out, I think, from the background of some of the other stories that were being done about deindustrialization, the illegal drug trade, and so on. I'd only known New Haven myself through the dim and highly distorting lens of Yale before I started reporting on the city.

Most of the time, though, I've just followed my own nose. My first story meeting with David Remnick, who's now *The New Yorker*'s editor, lasted about thirty seconds. He asked me what I wanted to do. I said, "Punk band from Montana." He said, "Go." After I did that story ["Onward and Upward with the Arts: Rocket Science," November 16, 1998], our next meeting was about the same length. I said, "Civil war in Sudan." Remnick didn't look *quite* as happy as he did about the Montana punk band. But he said, "Go." ["A Reporter At Large: The Invisible War," January 25, 1999.]

How do you find your main characters?

Digging around, talking to people, waiting for somebody to strike me just right. Soon after I got to New Haven, for instance, I knew I wanted to write about kids in the drug trade. But I wanted to keep the piece connected to politics. I wasn't interested in writing a crime story. So I didn't talk to the cops first. Instead, I hooked up with the local NAACP Youth Council, which was a hotbed of activism at the time. They had just conducted a big voter registration drive and managed to elect the city's first black mayor. I met some interesting kids there—high school students who were politically sophisticated, and were working hard on getting into college, even though some of them came from very poor and troubled families. Most of them had friends who were in the drug business. But their friends wouldn't talk to me. "He doesn't talk to white people"—that kind of thing.

What happens when you hit those kinds of stumbling blocks?

In this case I backed off for a while, and was just doing general reporting on local black political history when I met a guy named Warren Kimbro, who had been a Black Panther in New Haven, had gone to jail, then gone to Harvard, and who was by then running a halfway house for juvenile ex-offenders. Warren introduced me to some of the kids he was looking after, including Terry, who was sixteen and had been dealing cocaine for some time. And Terry was the boy I ended up writing about. We just hit it off right away. He had a great, unguarded, self-questioning way of talking about his life. And everything he said checked out—which was really a rare combination of qualities in the very dangerous world he was scuffling in. He'd only been to the NAACP Youth Council once, and that was only because a judge had ordered him to go. And Terry had found the scene there "corny." But his—and his family's—deep alienation from conventional politics, and from conventional ways of getting ahead, interested me in itself. I knew right away that he was the kid I wanted to write about.

How would you describe your reportorial stance?
On certain kinds of stories, my reporting goal is just to get people to ignore me. I'll put my notebook or tape recorder away, and not bring them out for days at a time. Insofar as possible, I want people to forget I'm there.

How do you get people to ignore you?
I hang out and hang out and hang out. I ask a lot of questions, tell a few stories, do whatever they're doing—whether it's watching TV, going to clubs, snowboarding, logging pulpwood, going to political rallies. I spend so much time hanging around that people sometimes really seem to forget what I'm actually there to do. When I was reporting *Dateline Soweto* [1988], my book about black South African journalists, I faked out a lot of people at this big Johannesburg newspaper called *The Star* by simply setting myself up at a desk in the newsroom. Most of the reporters and editors assumed I *worked* there. I'd answer the phone, take messages, go out on stories. The handful of black reporters whom I was there to write *about* knew what I was doing, of course, but that was about it. A few people told me I should get permission from the newspaper's bosses, but I never did. I just continued to breeze in and out every day. The security guards all figured I worked there, too.

I remember a moment when I was reporting the last section of *Cold New World.* This was in the Antelope Valley, in California. I was trying to ingratiate myself with a gang of "antiracist skinheads." They weren't very friendly at first, but I got to like them, and I spent a lot of time with them. Their "headquarters" at the time was this horrible, graffiti-covered bedroom in a rundown tract house. And one day I was in there, lying on a bed watching a Mike Tyson video for the hundredth time, and I overheard this conversation at the front door. Two girls had come by, looking for something to do, and they were asking one of the skinheads, "Hey, who's here? What's happening?" And the kid at the door said, "Nothing. Nobody's here. Just Bill." So the girls said they'd come back later. And I thought, "*Great!*" I was exactly where I wanted to be—barely worth mentioning.

So your "reportorial stance" is not to have one?
In that case, yes. But, as it happened, when I started reporting, a few weeks later, on that gang's big enemies—a *racist* local skinhead gang called the Nazi Low Riders—I had to take a completely different, more aggressive tack. The racist kids were much harder to approach than the antiracists. They were more paranoid (and rightly so, when it came to the press), more violent, often drunk, and usually tweaking—high on crystal methamphetamine.

The only way I finally got my foot in the door—literally—with them was by learning everything I could about them from a young woman who had just left their gang to join the antiracists. She told me all these stories about life with the boneheads, as everybody called them, and lots of stuff about each of the main neo-Nazi kids. So when I went to talk to them, and I had all these barriers of mistrust to get over, I could casually drop little details about their lives into our conversations on the doorstep—the name of an old girlfriend, somebody's father's hometown, whatever. It stopped them cold. They were incredulous. "How do you know *that*? You know *him*?" They were so unnerved that they eventually let me in.

How did you get them to talk to you?
Well, I knew I'd never get anything from them with the passive, hanging-out method that worked with the antiracists. The mood at their "headquarters" was totally different. A lot more aggression, a lot more anxiety about authority. So I became a really aggressive interviewer. I'd wear a coat and tie, always. Carry a briefcase. Kind of act like I owned the place. I wanted them to see me as an authority figure. I developed a routine. I'd walk in and order everybody out of the kitchen so that I could interview one kid, alone, at the kitchen table.

And they'd usually get quite meek and mild. Everybody wanted to be interviewed. They'd tell the others to keep quiet. "Turn off that amp!" This was while somebody was probably down in the basement putting together pipe bombs. I'd bark my questions, beginning at the beginning. "Sit down! Okay, when were you born? Where did you grow up? . . ."

And I'd take down their stories on legal pads. It was kind of absurd, but usually it worked. And if this routine wasn't working, for some reason, on a given day, if things were just too rowdy, I'd invite one kid out for pizza, try to cut him from the herd, as it were, and then interview him while he ate. They were usually hungry—in more ways than one. They were really starved for adult attention. And they did a lot of awful things to get attention.

Is reporting abroad different from reporting in the U.S.?
Yes.

How?
You need a passport.

Are you now being A Difficult Interviewee?
Precisely. Buy me some pizza.

Okay. How is reporting an international story different from reporting a national story?
In international reporting, you can be much more conventional and presumptuous—assuming, of course, that your readers are the folks back home. I can try to explain what I mean by comparing the reporting I did on the civil war in Mozambique [*A Complicated War,* 1992] with the reporting I did in New Haven for *Cold New World.*

In Mozambique, I traveled around the country, interviewing a lot of people, often with a translator. And I found that pretty much everybody, even the most oppressed, illiterate peasants, understood perfectly well what I was doing: I was a foreigner, interviewing them so as to understand something about their country. The journalistic conventions held steady. Nobody seriously questioned the purpose of what I was doing, or my right to be doing it.

Of course, I could never make the same kinds of generalizations about my own country, if only because my readers—Americans—know too much about it already—it's their country—and would therefore know endless exceptions to any big, gauche generalization I might throw out there. Since virtually none of my readers know anything about Mozambique, though, I'm free to plunder the country's history, say, for the flashiest, most unforgettable stories, to simplify wildly for economy and effect, and to generalize flamboyantly and shamelessly. It's as if you were asked to describe the American landscape to someone who had never heard of the Great Plains, or the Rocky Mountains, or the Grand Canyon. Or, to stick to the history example, as if you were asked to tell the story of the American nineteenth century to someone who had never heard of the Civil War. It's not hard—the best material is lying right there on the surface, still fresh.

Whereas in a place like New Haven . . . ?
The job is different in almost every respect. The journalistic conventions *don't* hold steady. I'm less sure about what I'm looking for, and the poor black New Haveners I'm interested in are far more suspicious about my motives—and far more likely to ask the obvious question: "What's in this for me?" And then, after a while—after a few months of my hanging around—some of the harder questions, too. Like: "What are you *really* after?" Or: "Aren't you just here to find a lurid story with which to titillate other white people, and make a buck yourself?" And, of course, when it comes to writing the story, I have to be mindful of a vastly more knowledgeable audience—the same readers who know little, if anything, about Mozambique, have read plenty about inner-city poverty, the illegal drug trade, race in America, etc. So I have to be much subtler, more selective, in my descriptions, in my stories—I've got to come up with something *new*, details that other commentators haven't already noted.

It's also loaded with more and different nerve endings. In America, the white writer's right to speak for black people has steadily diminished over the past several decades—or, you might say, conversely, black people's right to speak for themselves has expanded. So when I come to write about the lives of poor black Americans in New Haven, my options for choosing a narrative voice are not the same as they would have been forty years ago, nor are they the same ones I have when it comes to writing about Mozambique. Omniscience is really not a possibility. My fallibility, my presumptuousness, have to be acknowledged. My own implication in the lives of the people I'm describing is just so much greater. The right of the characters in the piece to tell their *own* stories seems much greater. I feel compelled to show how I am constructing the story, how my opinions are just my opinions, how the people I'm writing about may have different opinions, and how this is all about not simply *their lives,* but my interaction with them—and their efforts to understand me. It all requires a much greater degree of self-reflexivity than writing about Mozambique does.

It also requires more originality. For that New Haven piece, with a subject that was, in a sense, already overreported, I tried to do something different from most of the journalism that was then available on inner-city teenagers and the drug trade, a lot of which I found unsatisfying—sensationalistic, decontextualized. I tried to take what social scientists call a longitudinal look at the subject. That is, I tried to look at a longer time line, at a community and a family not only in a present-day snapshot, but also over several generations. Blessedly, my editors gave me the space, the leeway, to do that. But other journalists have since carried that approach to similar subjects much farther, taken it much deeper, than I did, Adrian Nicole LeBlanc's *Random Family* being the supreme example.

What do you do when you're reporting from a country where you don't speak the language?
Use interpreters.

What qualities do you look for in an interpreter?
A good interpreter tells you what people *actually* say. This sounds obvious, but it's sometimes difficult to find an interpreter who will do this. I often interview my interpreter first, just to make sure he isn't going to bring his own political or ethnic baggage and introduce complications into my interviews. I've often had to switch translators when I noticed an odd pattern emerging and realized that something was being distorted.

Do you have a reporting routine?

It's different with every piece. But the local college is often a good place to find someone who knows something about a story you're chasing. I've mentioned local newspapers—other hacks can be terrific guides in a new place. On some stories, political organizers—they survive by knowing what's going on, though you have to stay aware of their agendas, of course. I've also worked in a lot of places where it's imperative to check in with the local boss man as soon as you arrive, and let them know who you are and what you're doing. It might be a military commander, the police chief, a party official, a traditional chief, even just some kingpin local businessman—but it has to be the right person.

How do you pace yourself when reporting a long piece?

When I'm reporting in the U.S., I try to take breaks and go home. I probably made five separate trips to report on the skinheads in the Antelope Valley, and when I was writing about New Haven, I'd sometimes go up for the day. (I live in New York, two hours away.) These breaks help me recharge, but they also give the *story itself* some time to unfold. I usually write about people's lives, not about breaking news, so events tend to play out more slowly, sometimes over months or even years.

Given that you spend so much time with your characters, do you worry about maintaining sufficient distance from them?

I try to maintain some distance, but I don't always succeed, especially when I'm writing about kids. When I was reporting *Cold New World,* I came up with some ground rules. They were pretty arbitrary. The big one was that I would not intervene in the lives of my characters until after the magazine piece I was writing about them had appeared. My reporting after that was purely for the book, and I decided I could be more lenient then—that it would be my call whether to cross, in some emergency, the traditional line separating journalists from their subjects. Books are, after all, different from magazines. They're a less fixed form, and responsibility for their contents is far more concentrated with the author.

In the middle of reporting Cold New World you paid for one of your characters (Juan) to take a trip to San Francisco in order to avoid a rival gang.

First, it was after the magazine article ran. Second, it was a real emergency because that gang had tried to kill him, and a drive-by shooting on his family's house, where a number of little kids were living, was almost certainly going to be next. So I panicked and gave Juan money to go to San Francisco. It's pretty hard to stand by passively when some terrible thing is about to happen to a kid you've gotten to know well—or to his parents or his little brothers or his nieces. I couldn't do it, anyway.

There were other aspects to that situation, though, I must admit. Because I wasn't just trying to save Juan, or somebody in his family, from getting hurt. I was also interested in challenging Juan—as part of a dialogue that he and I had been having over a couple of years by that point. I was saying, "Okay, Juan, you *claim* you're this footloose, individualist American, not bound by the ties of community, ethnicity, and class that your parents are, and that they believe in. So go out, hit the American road, prove it!" My first thought was to get him to safety, but I also saw it as a kind of narrative experiment. And it ended up costing me quite a bit of money. From San Francisco, he went to New Mexico, and then to Texas, all on my dime. Maybe that'll teach me not to go around breaking cardinal journalistic rules.

How do you convince people to spend so much time with you?
Most of the people that I write long documentary pieces about don't have jam-packed schedules. So time isn't usually a problem.

Do you ever tell them how much time you'll need?
No. Partly because I don't really know beforehand. Also, if I have to have a discussion with someone about time, then he or she probably won't end up being one of my main characters. I don't mean that their time's not valuable. It's just that they have to be open to the idea that spending a lot of time with me will be worth their while. If someone I'm interested in is skeptical because they think I won't spend *enough* time with them to really understand their story, I'll assure them that I'll be around "for a long time." But I don't get more specific than that.

How much do you tell people about yourself and your project?

Not much, usually. If somebody asks me about myself, I'll tell them, of course. I'll show them a *New Yorker* if I have a copy. If they ask about my project, I'm usually pretty vague—partly because it's usually still taking shape, and I'm not yet sure what it is. I just say I'm collecting information to put together into a story. I tell people that I want to know as much as I can about their lives, their neighborhoods, their thoughts, their experiences. Basically, I just hang around as long as they'll have me. In some situations, I've become a kind of local curiosity: The White Man on the Couch. I can practically hear people saying, "Hey, come over and see our white man! He's still here!" Of course, some people get suspicious, even paranoid. They may believe at first that I'm a news reporter, but when you talk to a news reporter something comes out in the paper that weekend, or the following week. Meanwhile, here I am, hanging around for months on end, and nothing ever appears in print. People have accused me of being FBI, CIA. Why else would I be collecting so damn much information?

How do you begin an interview?

I don't have a set opening—although, if I hit on a good litmus-test question on a given story, I'll ask that question of everyone I interview. It might be simply their opinion of some public figure, or their version of a story that everybody knows, but that different sides tell differently. It's usually just to help me judge what I'm seeing and hearing. But it's something that can be particularly helpful when you're trying to understand a complicated conflict, where the truth is really up for grabs. For example, when I was doing a piece about the psychology of militant Serb nationalism ["Letter from the Balkans: The Next War," *The New Yorker*, September 20, 1999], I developed a set of questions that I found most Serbs rose to. I'd ask about the various myths of Serb nationalism, including recent events. After having heard responses from fifty different people, I felt slightly more comfortable generalizing about Serb nationalism. I could actually write in good conscience a sentence about Serbs' "xenophobia, their psychologically mangled ethnocentrism, their war culture of paranoia and denial, and their isolation, disappointment, and guilt."

Will you agree to send questions ahead?

Not usually. Under some circumstances, if I'm really desperate for an interview, I might, but I hate doing it. Sending questions ahead usually kills the life out of an interview. There was a British official I wanted to see for my piece about Robert Kiley and the London Underground. His assistant said he needed to see all my questions before we met. And I realized that that request alone really told me everything I needed to know about the guy. He probably never intended to talk to me, anyway. He just wanted to see the questions to learn what I was up to.

But if the supreme leader of Sudan wants to see my questions, that's another story. He's so important to the piece that I'll probably send him some questions. Then I'll try to slip in some new questions when we meet.

Do you only do interviews in person? Or will you interview someone by phone or e-mail?

I do some interviews over the phone. Experts—people who probably aren't going to be characters in a story, but who may contribute a quote or two, or may just help me understand some question—I'm usually happy to interview over the phone. I don't need to know what they look like, or what their office looks like. But if you want to evoke a "world," a real place and setting, e-mail or the phone obviously won't cut it. You have to meet people face-to-face. In fact, for me, formal interviews often aren't that important. They're just the foreground activity, while I'm hanging around, waiting for things to happen.

Do you tape or take notes?

I tape if I'm interviewing a high official or somebody who talks exceptionally fast or someone who, for whatever reason, is hard to understand. Or if the person I'm interviewing is taping our conversation, which occasionally happens. But usually I take sloppy longhand notes, which I have to reread immediately after the interview so that I can decipher them.

Has taking notes openly ever been a problem in the more restrictive countries—Sudan, the Serb Republic, apartheid South Africa—that you've reported from?

When I was reporting *Dateline Soweto,* I deposited my notes at the end of each day with a sympathetic guy who worked in a library across the street from the headquarters of the newspaper I was writing about. He'd stash them in the library overnight, make a copy of them the next morning, and mail a set to me in the U.S. That way, I could be fairly sure that, whatever happened, I'd have most, if not all, of my notes when I got home. Foreign reporters were being thrown out of the country every day at that point, so I never knew how long I'd last, especially since I was there on a tourist visa.

When I was working in Sudan, and traveled from the south, which was rebel held, to the north, which was government held, via Kenya, I had to destroy *all* evidence that I'd been in the south. The cops and the army in the north were scary—really fierce. I had to use different passports and totally purge my luggage—every scrap of paper, even my address book.

How did you preserve your notes from the south?
Mailed the originals home from Kenya, and stashed copies in Nairobi as a backup.

Do you ever arrange for an interview to take place somewhere that will provide a scene for the piece?
I have, although it's hokey and I don't like doing it. When I was writing about Moctar, the former slave, we drove to Washington to see some friends of his. On the way down, we stopped at Gettysburg, which he actually wanted to see, but which I also wanted to see *him* in. It was a hokey move, but we had fun, and it helped the piece.

How confrontational will you become in an interview?
I almost never argue with the people I'm interviewing. I usually just laugh along with the things I disagree with and write it all down. The more dubious or debatable stuff is often the best material. The more outrageous, the better—that's one of the not-very-secret tawdry little secrets of journalism.

What kinds of negotiations will you do before an interview?
I'll agree, reluctantly, not to name government officials, or anybody, really, who's taking a risk by talking to me and doesn't want to

be named. I often reassure people that a fact-checker will verify that I've got all the facts right, and will give them a chance to correct any mistakes I make. But I won't read quotes back to people.

Do you reconstruct scenes you haven't witnessed firsthand?
Rarely. When I do, I'm careful to be clear that I'm being told about the scene by someone, rather than imagining it for myself ("He said such and such . . ."). I never write a scene *as if* I were there, if in fact I wasn't.

How do you know when you're done reporting?
When the story seems to have a beginning, middle, and end. When I think that the action, the narrative arc, is complete. But I'm often wrong about that, and more action often takes place while I'm writing. New endings appear. New beginnings, even.

Is writing or reporting more difficult for you?
Reporting can be lonely, boring, depressing. But writing is definitely harder.

Do you make outlines?
Yes. I make detailed outlines of entire pieces, but at least half the time they fall apart after I start writing. I've always wished I were better at visualizing a piece. And I'm always surprised when, for instance, a major section that I've carefully placed three-quarters of the way through my outline turns out to be just three lines. Where's the big rant I had in mind? Can it all really be said in just three lines? It seems so. Then I'll come to a tiny, marginal note I've scribbled on the outline, and *it* explodes into an *enormous* scene. Why couldn't I see that beforehand? I've been writing for a long time now and I'm appalled that I still can't outline better.

What do your outlines look like?
They can get pretty big. When I was writing *Crossing the Line* [1986], the outline, which was on brown butcher paper, took up the whole wall of my study. It was about eight feet by ten feet. I had to

stand on a chair to write on the top lines of it. And the plan for the book kept changing. Originally, it was going to be nine chapters. It ended up being ninety-one.

Do you write straight through a piece, or do you revise as you go along?

I try to advance the piece each day. I tend to back up and then run forward, editing in the morning and then moving it along. But once it catches fire I just write straight through. I used to be afraid to leave anything in the computer. I'd print out my new stuff every night. But nowadays I often don't print out anything until I complete the first draft of the entire piece. I'll probably live to regret this trust in technology, which is really just laziness. Before I quit for the day, I like to sketch the scene I'm going to write the next morning. When that works, it gives me a nice running start. But usually I doubt myself too much to just plunge on, and instead start rereading, and fall into that pattern of backing up and editing.

Do you show your work-in-progress to people?

I used to show drafts of pieces to friends. I was never sure if I was on the right track, or if anything I was trying to do was getting across, and I thought a piece had to be perfect before I turned it in. People were incredibly generous, I now realize, with their time and insights. But I don't do that anymore. I trust my editors more than I used to— trust myself more, I suppose.

How many drafts do you typically go through?

I'll do fifteen to twenty drafts of the first few sections. Backing up, running forward. I do fewer as I get closer to the end.

Is there any particular place you like to be when writing?

I prefer to face a wall. I daydream less than when I'm looking out a window. I used to go to writers' colonies. Or off to cheap, quiet spots where the surf was good. Indonesia, Sri Lanka. My wife and I have a young daughter now, so I stay closer to home.

What kind of authorial presence do you strive for?

It varies with each piece. Leaving aside a few straightforwardly autobiographical things I've done, I find that establishing a connection between the narrator, the "I" character, and the subject of a story can often be useful. It can help the reader get into the story, even if it's just a matter of placing them in a car with you as you travel through some landscape. But you have to judge closely if and when the "I" character is actually going to help a story.

It was actually kind of a turning point for me, as a younger writer, to realize that the first person *could* be a very useful character. It's a character who can change—within limits, of course—from piece to piece. It can have different uses, play different roles. Yes, everything that the "I" character says in one of my stories is something I actually said, but that's less confining than it sounds, simply because, by selecting *what* to quote, I can, in virtually every case, make myself out to be a jerk or a genius or anything in between.

In other types of pieces—particularly pieces where my narrative authority seems questionable, for whatever reason—I try to reveal my biases, my own fallibility. In those cases, I imagine myself standing in for my readers, who are broadly likely, for reasons of shared culture and class, to see things more or less the way I do. Writing about the illegal drug trade in New Haven, for instance, I had my little theories about why kids went into it, and what it all meant, and I laid those out—the terrible collision of grinding poverty with the ideology of consumer individualism, and so on. But then, having offered my analysis, I felt obliged immediately to hand over the microphone, as it were, to someone who was actually living in the thick of it all. So I quoted an antidrug activist, a grandmother who lived in the projects, who *completely* disagreed with my liberal moral relativism. "*Wrong!*" she said. "I'm sorry, but these kids know right from wrong . . ." And she went on to give a straight-ahead Christian moralist's analysis of the drug trade. I actually gave her ideas more space than my own because her authority on the subject—based on personal experience, based on neighborhood history—was in so many ways greater than mine.

What kind of a tone do you strive for?

Some stories seem to impose a certain austerity of tone. On those, the less the writer gets in the picture with writerly flourishes, the better. The power resides in the facts. War reporting can have that quality, obviously, but so can other genres, and tragedy and violence aren't necessarily part of it—just a story that's sufficiently taut or somber, or characters who can somehow carry it themselves, with their eloquence or strangeness or unusually powerful presence. With other subjects, other pieces, the main interest may lie somewhere *between* the writer and the subject, allowing for more commentary, more flash, more intrusiveness. What I strive for, tonally, is just to figure out what voice will work best on a given story. But even on the pieces that let me fool around—going on the road with an obscure but witty punk band, say—I still want my prose to feel sturdy, and reasonably well built. I want readers to trust me, and I'm always afraid that loose writing might squander that trust.

Do you think a lot about the sound your words make?

Too much, I'm told. But not nearly as much as I used to. There was a time when I was almost *more* interested in the sound of my sentences than in whatever sense they made. Working as a journalist for a couple of decades has pretty much knocked that out of me, and I've long stopped letting myself write the kinds of rhetorical glissandos and crescendos that I still hear in my head. On balance, that's a good thing, I'm sure.

Do you believe the kind of journalism you practice can lead to truth?

There are "facts," which you need to get right. And then there is the "truth," which is a larger issue. If there's a question about whether individual incidents or facts are true, I think one should try to provide the reader with all the credible versions and let him or her decide what's true.

If I'm telling a family story, the truth as I understand it is my best, fullest, most accurate sense of how people talk, feel, interact, and what happened. And yet my view, my understanding, of someone else's family is inherently terribly limited—especially when compared to the understandings of the people *in* the family. So I never stop worrying that I'm not getting it right.

With political stories, including war pieces, I tend to worry less about getting the meaning of things wrong. It's public life and, even if my understanding is flawed, giving it my best shot at an interpretation, at a truthful depiction, feels essentially legit. A lot of people may disagree with my version, but that's the nature of political life, which includes political journalism. It's a world in which the "truth" *is* the most persuasive argument—assuming, always, that nobody's cooking the facts.

Do you think there is something peculiarly American about the kind of literary nonfiction you write?

There's literary nonfiction in many countries—essays, memoirs, biographies, high-style long-form journalism—but the kind of rigorous interest in facts, giving little or no license to embroider or preen, is particular to this country. And of relatively recent vintage. The journalistic standards in Britain are markedly lower. A lot of British nonfiction writers have great style, but on the whole they care less about factual accuracy than we do.

Do you see yourself as part of an historical tradition?

Well, the line between nonfiction and fiction wavers, often, in great pieces of reportage from the past. *Life on the Mississippi* and *Roughing It* are my favorite Mark Twain books, but they both take big, amusing liberties with the facts. Andy Adams's *The Log of a Cowboy*, which was published in 1903, is another extremely close study of work, which actually has comparable power and depth, and a different kind of eloquence. But it's a novel—except I've always read it as impeccable reporting. To contradict what I just said about the standards of British nonfiction, there are Henry Mayhew and George Orwell. Mayhew was an amazing, utterly scrupulous journalist in the mid-nineteenth century. His masterpiece was *London Labour and the London Poor*. Orwell's reporting on poverty, war, colonialism, and revolution—*Homage to Catalonia, The Road to Wigan Pier, Down and Out in Paris and London*—is simply nonpareil.

The New Yorker has published some great writers of nonfiction, who might be said to constitute a sort of in-house tradition, different as their styles have been. A. J. Liebling and Joe Mitchell deeply influenced the next generation or two at the magazine, including me. John McPhee, Jane Kramer, Ian Frazier. The magazine has also managed to run major pieces so timely that they end up defining an issue, even an era: John Hersey's *Hiroshima*, James Baldwin's *The Fire Next Time*, Rachel Carson's *Silent Spring*, Hannah Arendt's *Eichmann in Jerusalem*, Jonathan Schell's *The Fate of the Earth*. That's a lineage any journalist would be happy to be associated with, and I certainly am.

But the collision of major talents with major events, which can't usually be organized by an editor, has a way of creating great journalism. The Vietnam War gave us Michael Herr's *Dispatches* and Neil Sheehan's *A Bright Shining Lie*. The antiwar movement begat Norman Mailer's *The Armies of the Night*. Desegregation occasioned Tony Lukas's *Common Ground*. More recently, the Balkan wars produced tremendous books by American reporters—Roger Cohen's *Hearts Grown Brutal*, Chuck Sudetic's *Blood and Vengeance*, Brian Hall's *The Impossible Country*. I'm not an investigative journalist, but I admire the great ones—Seymour Hersh, above all, who's been doing it since the sixties, and Eric Schlosser, who's just getting the attention he deserves, with the success of *Fast Food Nation*. Internationally, the working nonfiction writers I most enjoy, and have tried to learn something from—although, again, with each of them, the lines around fact and fiction can get blurry—are Eduardo Galeano, Ryszard Kapuściński, Jonathan Raban, and John Berger.

What do you think about the prospects for the form?
The prospects for literary nonfiction in book form are as good as ever. Until the late eighties there was a cottage industry publishing long *New Yorker* pieces as books. The books rarely sold, and that industry dried up. Meanwhile, *New Yorker* pieces have gotten shorter and shorter, so one doesn't write book-length pieces for the magazine anymore. But the good news is that good literary nonfiction books are fully viable now.

BY WILLIAM FINNEGAN:

Cold New World: Growing Up in a Harder Country, Random House, 1998
A Complicated War: The Harrowing of Mozambique, University of California Press, 1992
Dateline Soweto: Travels with Black South African Reporters, Harper & Row, 1988
Crossing the Line: A Year in the Land of Apartheid, Harper & Row, 1986

JONATHAN HARR

I n February 1986, Jonathan Harr was considering writing about a lawsuit that had been brought by eight families in Woburn, Massachusetts. They alleged that their children (several of whom died) had gotten leukemia by drinking water polluted by a nearby tannery and a factory owned, respectively, by Beatrice and W. R. Grace, two enormous corporations. The case had been running for four years and had yet to go before a jury. Ominously, it had already generated 196 volumes of sworn depositions. A number of Harr's friends, such as Pulitzer Prize–winning author Tracy Kidder, thought the Woburn case was a good opportunity for Harr. Others, like Dan Okrent, the editor of *New England Monthly*, where Harr was a staff writer, had severe doubts. "Don't do this book," Okrent warned. The case was so complex and the trial was likely to be so protracted that Okrent feared Harr would be left poor and miserable long before the project was completed. "You'll be digging out quarters from behind the car seat," Okrent warned.

In the end, *both* Kidder and Okrent were right. *A Civil Action* was a hit, although writing it nearly destroyed Harr's life. Eight years and five extensions later, long since having spent his $80,000 advance, Harr submitted the eight-hundred-page manuscript to his editor at Random House. After a slow start, the book sold one hundred thousand copies in hardcover and sat on the paperback bestseller list for two years. It won the National Book Critics Circle Award for nonfiction and the film rights were purchased by Robert Redford for $1.25 million.

In many respects, *A Civil Action* set the pattern for Harr's journalistic life: years of detailed reporting on a complicated technical story, followed by more years of painstakingly slow writing. If this weren't frustrating enough, the stories Harr chooses seldom have happy endings (the main lawyer in *A Civil Action* is driven bankrupt and loses a significant part of the case—"an uncomfortably untidy ending," in the words of one reviewer) and in some cases they're left completely unresolved. The miracle of Harr's work is that, despite such obstacles, it reads not just like novels, but like *great* novels. "Be forewarned," writes T. H. Watkins in *The Washington Post,* "once you start *A Civil Action* you probably will not be able to pull it from you until it is finished, and it will stay with you for a long time even then. As it should."

Writing *A Civil Action,* Harr's choice to focus on the lawyers—rather than, say, the victims—was risky (given our society's dislike of lawyers), and criticized by a number of the Woburn families. But his focus is precisely what raised the book above the realm of advocacy journalism and into the realm of art. There are no heroes or villains, only thoroughly ambiguous characters whose lives Harr enters completely. The book "isn't written the way most journalists, myself included, would have written it," environmental journalist Mark Dowie writes in the *Los Angeles Times Book Review.* "As a result it is both readable and riveting."

A number of reviewers raised the question of how Harr could have gathered such intimate details—the dialogue from a day-long negotiation session between lawyers, the intimacies of a couple in bed—without using a tape recorder or being present for every event. Harr was wounded by these criticisms, but felt vindicated in 2002 when an eight-hundred-page *Documentary Companion* containing the raw transcripts and the court documents was published. "The quality and thoroughness of Mr. Harr's presentation make *A Civil Action* a book that is likely to have broad appeal to readers interested in the law or courtroom tactics," writes Gregg Easterbrook in *The New York Times Book Review.*

Harr was born in Beloit, Wisconsin, in 1948, the son of a Foreign Service officer whose assignments took the family to France, Germany, Israel, Chicago, San Francisco, and Washington, D.C. Harr attended the College of William and Mary, but left in 1968 to serve as a VISTA volunteer in Appalachia. He later attended Marshall University.

Driving a New York City cab to support himself, he wrote short stories and dreamed of becoming a novelist. He held a succession of brief jobs— at ABC News, at a literary agency—before moving to New Haven where his wife-to-be was living. Harr worked briefly for the *New Haven Register* before getting a job at the local alternative paper, the *New Haven Advocate,* which allowed him to write lengthy stories with literary style.

In 1984, Harr was hired as a staff writer by the *New England Monthly,* a newly founded journal that published long-form non-fiction by writers—Joseph Nocera, Adrian Nicole LeBlanc, Susan Orlean, Barry Werth—who went on to write important books of their own.

The idea for *A Civil Action* came to Harr indirectly. Harvard Law School professor Charles Nessen had contacted Tracy Kidder to see whether he was interested in writing about the Woburn case. Kidder wasn't looking for a project. But he had a friend who was. Although he had no legal background, Harr was attracted to the story by the extraordinary access he had negotiated with the plaintiff's lawyers, and with Jan Schlichtmann, the lead lawyer, in particular. Harr took a three-month paid leave of absence from the *New England Monthly,* after which he agreed either to write an article for the magazine, or pursue a book, which the magazine would excerpt on publication.

Harr contracted with Random House to deliver the manuscript in two years, but it quickly became apparent that the task before him was enormous. He accumulated twenty-seven feet of deposi-tions and transcripts with which to re-create the four years of events that occurred before he began following the case. The court proceedings (which lasted for nine months) generated seventy-eight days of trial testimony, and fifty-seven volumes of pre- and posttrial hearings. "The documents in this case, not including trial transcripts, were, if you stacked them up, as tall as a three-story building," he says. Three years into the project, Harr had spent a large part of his advance, but was far from finishing the book.

Harr's economic circumstances mirrored those of his main character, who eventually filed for bankruptcy. He worked part-time teaching writing at Smith College to make ends meet, and had it not been for his wife's job as an art teacher he probably would have had to declare personal bankruptcy, too. At one low point he applied for a job as a night proofreader at a local New Age publisher, only to have his application rejected. Two serious bicycle accidents delayed him by another six months.

The main problem was that Harr was at a loss for a way to structure his enormous trove of material. He originally conceived of structuring the book like a Russian novel, with many "main" characters who all converge in the courtroom. He finally decided to focus on Schlichtmann, using him as the story's hub, with all the other elements emerging from him.

Tracy Kidder played a crucial role in the construction of the book. Often, after finishing his own writing, he'd come over to Harr's house in the afternoon and read what Harr had written, scrawling editorial notes all over the manuscript. "I got you into this, and I'll make sure you get out," Kidder assured his friend.

"It was the hardest thing that I've ever done, and there were many times when I regretted getting involved in it. What interested me was the process of storytelling. I knew that I had stuff, that I could make characters come to life on the page. I'm a story-teller. That's what I do," Harr told a group of Harvard's Nieman Fellows in 1997.

With *A Civil Action* behind him, Harr turned to three very different stories. On August 5, 1996, the week after a TWA airliner exploded on its way from New York to Paris, *The New Yorker* published "The Crash Detectives," Harr's investigation into the still-unsolved crash of USAir flight 427 in 1994. In "The Burial," Harr was back in the courtroom, with the story of Willie Gary, a flamboyant Mississippi lawyer who won one of the largest civil settlements in American history.

Harr also wrote about a lost Caravaggio painting that was found hanging in a small monastery in Dublin ("A Hunch, An Obsession, A Caravaggio," *The New York Times Magazine,* December 25, 1994). Given the success of his first book, Harr received a substantial advance to expand the article into a "quick, short book." For his next project, he says he is interested in writing a novel. "I'm tired of following people around."

What kinds of ideas get you excited?

I can get excited about virtually anything, as long as it contains the elements of a good story. At its most basic, a good story is about people engaged in an endeavor where there is some degree of tension, mystery, or suspense. Something must be at stake for the people involved. If I can succeed in getting the reader interested in the people I'm writing about it doesn't matter what the field is, or how technical or simple it is. As long as it has a narrative arc and something to discover.

Does it matter what's at stake or how the story ends?

The outcome of the narrative isn't vital to me. The outcome in *A Civil Action* [1995] was, in several respects, disappointing. The lawyer doesn't win the way he thinks he will, and in the process learns a lot about himself and the underbelly of the law. The book I'm writing now is about a young woman looking for a lost Caravaggio painting. She doesn't actually find it—somebody else does. If I were writing fiction, it's not the narrative outcome I'd choose, but in some respects it's more interesting because of that. Anyhow, I did okay with a legal story in which the protagonist more or less loses the case, so perhaps this will work out, too.

I'm drawn to mysteries, which are natural engines for narrative. In the case of an article I wrote about a plane crash ["The Crash Detectives," *The New Yorker,* August 5, 1996], the mystery is obvious at the outset: why did a plane fall from the sky on a perfectly clear day? But even more than the mystery, the story gets its energy from the people involved in trying to solve the mystery and the pressures on them.

That's awfully generic, isn't it?

What makes a story idea good or bad, or banal or interesting, has nothing to do with the subject matter, but everything to do with how well or poorly the story is told. I wrote a story about a funeral home ["The Burial," *The New Yorker,* November 1, 1999] that was basically a legal story. Okay, there have been thousands of legal stories written, but I found both the characters and the circumstances fascinating. For example, I hadn't known anything about the history of the funeral industry and how it has changed in America, and that is something that sooner or later *everybody* has to deal with. I wouldn't have set out to write an article based on some vague idea that the business of death and dying might be an interesting place to look for a story. But I got taken there because I was interested in one of the people involved in the case—a lawyer named Willie Gary.

A Civil Action was about toxic waste, dead children, and a lawsuit that drags on almost for a decade. Sounds like a dreadful idea for a book, and when people asked what I was working on, I'd watch their eyes glaze over while I explained it. But if I can succeed in making the characters come to life on the page, and in illuminating the process they're caught up in, I'll have succeeded in telling a good story. Interesting people caught in difficult circumstances—those are the basic requirements I look for.

Lots of stories meet those requirements. What makes the difference between an "interesting" story and one you dedicate years of your life to?
There's no science to this, just what interests you. Often the business of choosing a story isn't rational or fully thought out. You can't possibly know all the contours, all the dimensions, to a story when you embark. I've also given up on a few stories that I'd devoted time to—not years, but maybe weeks, or even months.

How do you come up with stories?
I tend to find them by accident. I might read a short article and sense there's a larger story embedded. That's what happened with my current book. The idea to write about this lost Caravaggio painting came from reading a short article in *The New York Times* about the painting being unveiled in Dublin. Something of great value that had been lost for hundreds of years and had just been discovered. Where had it been? Who found it? How did they find it? Why does it matter? Those are the sorts of questions behind every story ever written.

Do you prefer coming up with your own ideas, or will you take suggestions from editors?
Mostly I prefer to choose my own ideas. Usually if an editor suggests a story to me, that means he or she has a preconceived idea of how the piece should turn out. I keep a file of clippings, some of them pretty old and yellowed by now, and I also keep lists of story ideas.

What do your lists look like?

The list has gotten pretty long, given all the ideas that don't go anywhere, or that I never act on. Each item in the list is anywhere between a short paragraph and a half a page. Most of them, as I say, never go anywhere.

Are there any particularly good ones that haven't worked out?

Sure. I was set to do a piece for *The New Yorker,* and then maybe a book, about an archaeological dig at the Turkish-Syrian border, where the remains of an ancient city had been discovered. The dig involved a large group of people—professors, graduate students, archaeologists—not many of whom knew each other. My idea was that the piece would have two levels: the story of the archaeological discoveries and their significance, and the story of these people thrown together, working and living in the middle of a desert for months at a time.

What happened?

I was ready to head to Syria when the lead archaeologist told me that he wanted a percentage of whatever I earned from writing about the dig. Basically, he wanted me to pay for the access, for the privilege of writing a book. That effectively ended it.

Why is paying for access a problem?

If I pay someone for access, he becomes my de facto "partner." It was easy to say no, although I did feel a little bad about it, because it wasn't a case of his being venal. After all, I was going to be using them to write a book, and I hoped to make money doing it. It wasn't, from their point of view, unreasonable to expect something in return. All the more because the money would have been used to finance the dig, which was a perfectly honorable motive.

I briefly considered a creative arrangement, like agreeing to give them money if the book got optioned in Hollywood. I've been lucky in the past with movie options and I consider money from Hollywood at a far enough remove from the book. But it seemed like too big a hurdle. Besides, they make their living being professors and doing archaeological digs. I make mine as a writer. Why should I give part of my living away?

You described the Woburn story as being "about toxic waste, dead children, and a lawsuit that drags on almost for a decade." What about it attracted you?

A lot of people presume that I wrote *A Civil Action* because I had an environmentalist agenda, but that was the furthest thing from my mind. I think I would have written a bad and boring book if I had such an agenda. The truth is that I wasn't very excited about it initially. A friend of mine who then worked for *The Boston Globe* wrote a lengthy piece about the case for the *Globe* Sunday magazine, just before the trial began. It was so dense I don't think I even finished reading it. It just sounded utterly boring and didn't arouse my interest at all. But when my friend Tracy Kidder suggested that I write about it, I thought I'd take another look.

What changed your mind?

Access, in a word. The lawyers decided, after some negotiation, to allow me in, behind the scenes, with very few restrictions.

How did you get the access you wanted?

That was difficult. I met with the lawyers in their conference room in Boston and I told them I wanted to follow the trial from the inside. I wanted to witness their discussions and decisions, how they prepared witnesses, everything. They were a bit taken aback because no journalist had ever been granted that kind of access. But they were also interested—they thought they were doing a great and wonderful thing, and they thought they would win big. So the idea of somebody chronicling it appealed to them.

The next day, one of them invited me to lunch. He explained that there were all sorts of legal problems with having me behind the scenes (my presence would violate the attorney/client privilege, which meant I could be called as a witness by the defense). He offered a compromise. Every evening after the trial, they would brief me on what was happening in the case, who they were preparing, etc. I told him that I wasn't interested in writing the book that way. For me, it was either complete access or nothing.

A few days later, I met back in the conference room with all the lawyers again. They made essentially the same offer their colleague had made over lunch. I told them I still wasn't interested. Then Jan Schlichtmann, the senior partner at this firm and the guy who became the main character in *A Civil Action,* said, "Okay, we'll try it your way." That was it. I never had another discussion about access. After that, I was in Schlichtmann's office every day for nine months. I'd be there in the morning, before they went to the courthouse, I'd go to the courthouse and watch them, and then I came back to their office and stayed until midnight or later.

Do you ever tell someone how much of their time you'll need?
No. If I were to announce it up front, I might scare them and derail the project. I just kept showing up. I tried to keep out of the way, the proverbial fly on the wall. After a while, they accepted me as one of them.

How did you get so much access to the defendant's lawyers?
I got to know Jerry Facher, the chief defense counsel, and the other defense lawyers during the seven months I watched the trial. Facher took a liking to me and invited me to sit in on his Harvard Law School class, which I did for two successive years. The thing Facher likes best is mentoring young lawyers, so he was a natural teacher. We would have dinner at the Harvard Law School cafeteria after his class, talking about the case and the law. He got to the point where he let me watch him prepare and take to trial another case in New Hampshire, after the Woburn case ended.

Did the contrasting degree of access you received from the defense and the prosecution distort your reporting?
I would have no doubt written a different book had I been behind the scenes with the defendants. But I knew from the beginning that I'd never get the same kind of access from Facher that Schlichtmann had given me. Facher's client was a big corporation (Beatrice Foods), and it is unheard of in the world of corporate law to allow a journalist behind the scenes. And even if Facher had been inclined to permit it, his client wouldn't have allowed it. Moreover, I was worried that if I had simultaneous access to both sides, I might become an unwitting conduit of information between the two camps. Or Schlichtmann

might start mistrusting me because I was spending time with Facher. It wouldn't have worked.

The book got good reviews, except for *The New York Times* reviewer who complained that I didn't depict the defendants in the same detail as I depicted the plaintiffs. Well, I did what was possible. The only other possibility would have been for me to have access to neither camp, and to sit in the gallery with all the other journalists, and then write an impossibly dull book. In the end, I wrote the book I wanted to write, not the book the *Times* reviewer thought I should write. So fuck him.

The sweet thing was, I got some degree of vindication with the publication of a law school textbook called *A Documentary Companion to A Civil Action* [Foundation Press, 1999]. It was put together by two law professors at George Washington University and consists of a compilation of all the most important documents, motions, and rulings, along with commentary and page references to my book. It's about eight hundred pages long and is used with my book in civil procedure classes in at least fifty law schools. To me that's validation of the fact that I didn't distort either the facts or the process.

A lot of your stories obviously gestate for years. Are you continuously aware you're working on a particular piece?

They may seem to gestate for years because they take me so long to write. I'm always working on a story, because I'm always past a deadline. I work on only one thing at a time. When I'm stuck in the middle of something, I get lots of ideas for other things that I think might be more interesting than what I'm actually supposed to be doing.

How do you determine how much time to give a project?

I'm too optimistic about time. That's partly because I don't account for the long periods when I'm completely buffaloed by the story. I had a two-year contract for *A Civil Action,* but it took me seven years, and five contract extensions, to finish.

What took so long?

I originally had this notion that everything important would simply unfold in front of me, either at the lawyers' office or in the courtroom. It didn't work out that way. The case was divided into two phases.

The question in the first part of the trial was who had dumped the chemicals that had poisoned the wells from which the families got their drinking water. The wells were clearly contaminated—nobody disputed that—and I assumed the families would win that phase. I thought the second phase, in which the jury would decide whether the contamination in the wells actually caused leukemia among the children of East Woburn, was going to be the most interesting part. But seven months into the trial, the judge ruled that the second phase wouldn't even be tried.

So what does a writer do when the part of the trial he thinks will be the meat of his book doesn't take place?

Well, in a sense, it *did* take place—just not in a courtroom. All the doctors and scientists—ninety-nine of them—who would have testified in the trial had been deposed before the case came to trial. These depositions were the bedrock of the entire case, so I ended up reading thousands of pages of deposition testimony and documents in order to re-create for the reader the information that never came to light in the trial. I realized—rationalized, maybe—that during the nine months I had immersed myself in the case, I had observed a lot of high drama, people who were stretched to the breaking point, psychologically, financially, morally, so I knew I had enough good material for the book to work.

Where did you learn how to be a reporter?

I was never formally taught, and I never took any journalism classes. I think it comes more or less naturally. You want to find out about something, you ask questions. My first writing job was at a weekly newspaper in New Haven called the *New Haven Advocate*. The editor, an experienced journalist and a good friend named Andy Houlding, taught me a lot about journalism. I liked the *Advocate* because they cared as much about how a piece was written as about what it said. And they published relatively long articles.

Then I worked for *New England Monthly,* where I got more time to report and I got to write longer pieces. I did some traditional investigative stories about corporate CEOs who had a lot to hide. It was fun—late-night phone calls with sources, documents passed through third parties, that sort of thing. I also did the sort of pieces where you just hang out with regular people—a story about loggers who drove these immense trucks weighted down with tons of timber in Maine.

Do you think of yourself as practicing immersion journalism?
For some types of stories. Perhaps *inundated* or *drowning* journalism would be more accurate.

How do you conceive of your role as a reporter?
I guess I don't think of myself as a reporter. I think of myself as a writer who needs to gather information in order to write. Having said that, I'm a pretty diligent reporter. I feel like I was put on this world to be an observer, not an actor. I like to watch what other people do. My form of "action" is writing: creating something on the page. The paradox of my life, of course, is that although I think of myself as a writer rather than a reporter, I enjoy the reporting much more than the writing.

It sounds as if your problems come during the writing more than during the reporting.
True. Writing is always torture. If I can avoid it by doing more reporting, I will. For example, I'm writing a scene in the Caravaggio book in which the two main characters find an archive in a dilapidated old villa on the Adriatic coast. I went to the villa with one of them and thought I had asked every question possible. I had *forty-five* interviews with one of these women, and twenty with the other, but now I realize I need to know more.

What more could you *possibly* need to know?
Let's see. I know which of them drove the car, what kind of car it was, how old the car was, how long the trip took . . . But I want to know what the weather was that day, and what they talked about during the four-hour trip. That sort of stuff is evanescent—their conversation in the car, about what they might find in the archive, about their boyfriends, about their professor at La Sapienza. Sometimes I feel silly coming back and asking these kinds of questions. They seem so trivial. But they give a narrative its texture.

How do you begin the interview process?

I like to do interviews in the character's own environment, whether that's an office, home, laboratory, courtroom—anywhere he spends time. I notice what books are on the shelves, what paintings are on the walls, how they keep their house, what kind of car they drive. The setting of an interview functions as a way to let me look around their lives. I'm always thinking about how I can construct a scene that will reveal something about a character.

Do you have a standard way you open an interview?

I explain a bit about what I'm working on. Then I begin by asking some general questions, the answers to which I usually know.

Why?

Just to get the motor turning over. Plus, they serve to triangulate the answers against the answers I've been hearing from other people. It gives me a sense of who I'm dealing with.

Do you prepare for an interview?

I always prepare at least a dozen questions, which I type up in advance. I never want to be at a loss for where to go next. But that doesn't mean it's a script I stick to. Interviews can become—should become—quite circuitous, discursive. But I always want to get answers to the questions I've prepared. I usually list them in order of priority, and I always try to keep it to a single page.

Why only one page?

Because I don't want to walk in to an interview with a thick stack of papers. That might look too daunting to the person I'm interviewing. I want to show someone that I respect his time. I never think of myself as so interesting or diverting that someone will want to spend time with me just for the hell of it. So I've got to be organized.

Do you ever send questions ahead?

I've rarely been asked to do that. I do it only when I have to. In an investigative piece about a corporate CEO, I had to. In the Woburn case, with the lawyers for one of the defendants, W. R. Grace, their client made me submit questions at the beginning. Then they grew more relaxed about it. My preference is to tell people what I think is necessary for them to know about my project, but not much more. I don't think it is wise to lay everything out.

Do you talk about yourself during an interview?

Well, I don't see any reason to tell people much about myself. If I am asked, I'll answer, but my response will be pretty bland. Sometimes we'll become friendly and I'll share more about myself. But, in the end, this is a business. I'll do what I have to do to get what I need. Well, within reason. I won't lie, I wouldn't pose as somebody I'm not, and I wouldn't misrepresent what I'm doing.

Is there anywhere you especially like or dislike interviewing people?

I've had good experiences interviewing people in restaurants. They sometimes reveal amazing things when they are eating and drinking. Especially drinking. During *A Civil Action,* I was having dinner at a fancy restaurant with Schlichtmann and a very pretty woman, a talented lawyer he admired and had once dated. Their romance didn't go very far, but they were still friends. I was asking them about a particular moment, when Schlichtmann had gone to New York to appear on *Good Morning America,* near the end of the trial. I hadn't gone with him, but she had, so I was trying to get some additional details. She started telling me how she and Schlichtmann had slept together for the first time that night in New York. We'd all had a lot of wine.

What did you do?

I put down my pen, because I could see the look on Schlichtmann's face. She said to me, "No, no, I *want* you to write this down!" So I did. Schlichtmann's face was in the soup by then. I debated about whether to use it. I told Schlichtmann I wouldn't if it bothered him. He said, "Do whatever you want." So I did use it.

Do you take notes or tape?

I take notes with a pen and a narrow reporter's notebook. I use my own illegible shorthand, which even I can't read sometimes. I'm religious about typing up the notes, usually every night. The memory of the interview is fresh, and I sometimes add things I didn't get into the notes. I always print a copy of the typed notes and put them into a physical file. Once I have a hard copy, I don't usually look at the notebook again. The hard copy is important to me: I annotate it, cover it with marginalia. I get to know the hard copies intimately. I can visualize them and remember where certain pieces of information are. During *A Civil Action,* I accumulated two file cabinets' worth of typed notes. More paper than I ever want to see again.

Do you ever tape?

I have done it a few times. But when I tape I get so much peripheral, unimportant material, and of course you have to transcribe the tape. It costs a lot of money, and there's so much dross in it.

How do you capture page after page of dialogue if you don't tape?

The writer Anthony Lukas, who read the manuscript of *A Civil Action,* asked me the same question. He said, "The only part I had a problem believing as nonfiction was when the lawyers were talking about the settlement negotiation at the Helmsley Palace. You had three straight pages of dialogue. How did you get that if you didn't tape?"

It really isn't so astonishing, if you think about it. Those three pages take the reader perhaps ten or twelve minutes to read, but the actual event lasted for four hours, and it was, as long discussions often are, endlessly repetitive. I filled an entire notebook, probably thirty single-spaced typed pages of dialogue. The hard part was deciding what to leave out. I wanted to capture the atmosphere, the feeling, the psychological state of these guys, and at the same time have the narrative move ahead and not bore the reader to tears with repetition and circumlocution.

Did you indicate gaps in the discussion by using ellipses?

Of course not. I'm not writing a formal legal document, I'm writing a narrative. There are a whole variety of ways of signaling to the reader that he is reading a condensed version of what took place. For example, after an exchange between two lawyers, I'll write, "An hour passed, and then they continued talking about the problem." Or I'll break the scene with a phrase like, "And Conway looked out the window and thought . . ."

But how do you know what he thought at that moment?

I don't read minds, and I don't invent, so obviously I had to ask him. Or he may have turned around and said, "I think you guys are nuts . . ." In which case he announced what he had been thinking. Or he may have told me a day later, two days later, a week later, that during that afternoon he had been thinking, "These guys are nuts . . ." And I use a bit of license to put it in his head at a given moment, while he's looking out the window. The point is, it doesn't have to be *precisely* what he was thinking at that *precise* moment—at 1:47 p.m., say, on Wednesday afternoon—although it might have been. It might also have been more generally what was going on in his brain during the time he was listening to others talk. If the laws of nonfiction dictate that you can only write the absolute, literal truth, then I would be compelled to write: "Writer sees Conway looking out window, asks Conway what he is thinking (because writer cannot read minds), and Conway tells writer, 'Before you interrupted my thoughts, I was thinking . . .'"

Does that mean I'm taking some unforgivable license with the perfect, absolute truth? If I'd had a camera and was filming the scene, rather than taking notes, would that constitute the perfect absolute truth? Even a camera wouldn't capture the absolute "truth," presuming there is such a thing, and I'd argue there isn't. There'd still be questions like: What *angle* should I use? Which *person* should I focus on? What do I leave in, what do I take out, to make it coherent to a viewer? Unless of course you're presenting the whole thing unedited. And a camera will never reveal what someone is thinking, unless they announce it or you ask them.

I try to capture the *essence* of what took place. The thing about the past is that it is *past*: it will never happen again. We can reconstruct it, interpret it, cast it in one light or another. One person's version of an event will always differ in detail and often in significance from another's.

I don't invent dialogue. I sometimes compress dialogue—even trial testimony—but that's totally different from inventing. And if

I'm not present, I have to rely on someone else's recollection of what was said. If someone has a different version of an event, and the two versions are completely irreconcilable, then I'll present it by saying to the reader, "X remembered it differently . . ."

Aren't you concerned that if you compress trial dialogue then your rendering of the dialogue will be different from that in the court transcript?

By compression, I don't mean paraphrasing. If I paraphrase, I wouldn't use quotation marks. My goal is to be as faithful as possible, while also making the passage readable. For example, it sometimes took a dozen questions for a lawyer to get a single answer. In the book I would eliminate the endless repetition without using ellipses, and get to the answer. Or I might write, "It was a question to which he couldn't seem to get an answer, even after trying a dozen times." If I'm not allowed that license, then I'm put into the position of simply reprinting the entire trial transcript. And that's not writing.

Let's talk some more about ethics. Do you think it is important to keep a distance from your characters? If so, how do you do it?

While reporting, I'm always thinking about how something—a scene, a quote, a character—fits into my "story." I have to be able to determine if somebody is giving me a lot of bullshit. And the only way I can do that is by constantly evaluating how well the information fits. Of course, the fact that a character is full of bullshit, or twists events to reflect his own virtues, might well be part of a story.

Joe McGinnis had a simple but apt line about this. He had to defend himself against the accusation that his book, *Blind Faith,* had betrayed the main character, Jeffrey MacDonald. McGinnis had entered into an arrangement with MacDonald to write about his murder trial, and McGinnis professed at first to believe that MacDonald was innocent. (This goes back to why arrangements are a bad idea, by the way.) Anyhow, by the end of the trial, McGinnis was convinced *not* of MacDonald's innocence, but of his guilt. McGinnis defended himself by saying, "When you sit down at the typewriter, it is between you and the typewriter. You have to be true to what you believe."

There's something very ethically sticky about this, because he'd made this arrangement. Janet Malcolm dissected this—and McGinnis got cut up badly by her scalpel—in a long *New Yorker* essay called "The Journalist and the Murderer." The first line of her essay is unforgettable: "Every journalist who is not too stupid or too full of himself to notice what is going on knows that what he does is morally indefensible." So, if you write nonfiction, you've bought yourself a ticket to Dante's ninth circle.

The distance I keep from a character—the point is, I have a story to tell and it has to make sense. If I am too enamored of someone, or someone's point of view, and in the end it doesn't cohere, if I can't pull away and see the larger picture, then I'm screwed.

Will you negotiate about what material you can and can't use?
My feeling is that just about everything can be used. If an interviewee tells me that something is "off the record," and he knows I'm sitting there, taking notes, trying to gather information for a book or a story, then why is he telling me it? On the one hand he wants me to *know* it, on the other he's telling me I *can't* use it. What's the purpose in that, the motive? My interpretation is that he wants me to be discreet about where I learned this information, or wants to influence me to his point of view. That gives me the license to find other ways of confirming the truth or falsity of the information, and using it, if it is significant and worth using. I guess that constitutes proof of the Janet Malcolm paradigm.

How do you prepare to write? Do you make an outline?
For a magazine story, even for *The New Yorker,* which has been about twenty thousand words for me, I can usually hold the details of the narrative arc in my head. I do write down a list of things I want to cover, but I wouldn't dignify it by calling it an outline.

Do you outline a book?
Actually just the same sort of thing, a list of scenes I want to get into the story, usually a list done as I'm working on a particular section. But a scene that takes twenty pages in the book might be only a single line of my outline. I did more or less outline each section of *A*

Civil Action, but I never outlined the entire book. I didn't really understand the shape of the book until I'd been working on it for a few years. In retrospect, the shape seems obvious, but it wasn't obvious to me for a long time.

What do you write on?

I use a laptop, but I keep a manual 1948 Royal typewriter around for when I get blocked.

How does a manual typewriter help unblock you?

For one thing, it's physical. The problem with a computer is that I spend forever going back over the text. A manual typewriter is great because it's difficult to go backward. Sure, you can x-out a line, but it is very laborious. So you just have to go ahead—even though I know what I've written is imperfect.

Another thing I do to trick myself into writing is use canary yellow paper. White paper feels permanent, almost like a book. But yellow paper? I tell myself, "I'm just putting some words down on the page." Facing the blank page is the hard part. Once I have a page with words on it, I can start having fun.

Anything else you do to get past your block?

Yes, when I'm stuck on a section, I juggle three little yellow beanbags. I count how many times I can juggle them. It's very important to me whether I do it one hundred times, or a thousand times, if I decide that's the magic number, without dropping one. If I drop one, I know it's going to be a difficult day at the office. I used to juggle oranges, and then my wife bought me these beanbags.

Describe your writing process.

I have a very well-developed self-censoring mechanism, which has proven to be a great impediment, sort of like being a fat marathoner. I choose a word and immediately think, "No, that's wrong." I rework a sentence endlessly to make it clear, to make it flow. I spend hours on a sentence, or days on a paragraph. I go back every day and make changes, which makes me feel like I've done something that day.

I make myself write only when I'm forced to by the panic of immi-

nent failure. I write when I know that I'll fail if I don't get it done by
a certain point, and that all of the work I've done up until that point
will be lost. Panic is the great motivator.

Have you ever thought of trying a different method?
It would be so much more efficient—both in terms of time and
psychic energy—to get an entire draft done before revising it. My
writer friends are always telling me to write the first draft quickly
and then revise it. Rewriting is, in fact, when real writing happens.
The first draft is just a template, an outline. But I have a fear that if I
write a draft and then revised it I would lose sight of what works and
what doesn't work, that I'd delude myself into believing a section is
working okay when in fact there are still lots of things wrong with it.
I would rather always be in doubt and constantly revising. But the
price, of course, is that I go ahead at a snail's pace. And despite all
the labor and doubt, I generally don't see what's working or not working. That's why I need an editor.

Do you like to show your work-in-progress to people?
Not to editors. My rule about editors is that I don't want to give
them something that I know isn't ready. Because if a manuscript isn't
right, then the editor will force solutions—some of which I might
not like—upon me. I'd rather find the solutions myself.
There is only one person who reads my stuff before I hand it in,
and that is Tracy Kidder. He's like my boss, and he's a very close
friend. He'll come over and rip pages away from me, or sit at my
computer and read stuff. He's the only person I allow to do that.
He'll cover the front and back of each page with notes. He tells me
his opinion, and he can be very opinionated. He's usually right about
what's not working. Sometimes his solutions are not the ones I like,
though. Or he may be right, but I just don't see it. And if I don't see
it, he's got to beat me up for a while before I make the change.   ·

Do you have any other editors you trust?
Yes, a great editor at Random House named Bob Loomis. I trust
his judgment without question or hesitation. His editing style is very
different from Tracy's. Whereas Tracy will tell me exactly what he
thinks I need to do to fix something, Bob is more elliptical. He'll put

these little dots under a passage and a question mark next to it. He doesn't usually tell me precisely what is wrong, and that forces me to go back over it again and figure out what's gone wrong.

Do you mind talking about your work-in-progress?

I'm not big on it, but it's not because I'm secretive, or that I feel talking about it will suck the energy out of it. It's just tiresome. Also I've had some disheartening experiences when talking about my work in the past. When I was writing *A Civil Action,* I developed an abbreviated explanation to give when people asked what I was doing. I could see them losing interest within the first fifteen seconds. That depressed me. I've got a two-minute pitch about the book I'm writing now, which I give at dinner parties, just so I'm not perceived as rude. This book tells very well, which also worries me. If I can tell the story with such fluidity, I don't understand why the hell it's taking me so long to write it.

Do you need to be anyplace in particular to write?

I like to have all my stuff with me: notes, books, computer. Even if I'm not going to use them, I need to be surrounded by everything that is relevant to the project. For the last few years, I've been splitting my time between Northampton, Massachusetts, and Rome, Italy. So I bought double copies of every book, and made second hard copies of all my notes. But I don't like making copies of my notes because the sets don't have the same marginalia and comments on them.

More important than the ambience of my workplace is how much time I have before and after I write. I can't just come back from vacation, turn on the computer, and begin writing where I left off. I need a sort of buffer on either side of my writing. It is a psychological transition, a decompression period to get used to things before I write. And then, once I start writing, I need a seemingly limitless amount of uninterrupted time in front of me.

I get upset if I have to go out to a dinner or to a party during a week I'm supposed to be working, because then my time won't be completely free. I need to be able to think about my project at any moment that week. Weeks with social engagements or dentist appointments are fucked-up weeks for me. They feel too broken up for me to use properly. I don't mean to make it sound too monastic, but it is a rather plain life.

What does a typical writing day look like?

I try not to go out the night before, so I won't have a hangover. And I always wake up at 6:30 a.m., no matter when I've gone to bed. The first thing I do is have a cup of coffee and read *The New York Times*. Then I work until around one or two in the afternoon. When I really get going, I work at night. I need to do some kind of physical activity every day—running, riding a bike, or going to the gym. It's gotten pared down to just the gym since I nearly killed myself twice on a bike, and my knees aren't what they were.

What kind of authorial presence do you strive for in your work?

I strive to be invisible. I don't like to write in the first person, or to be a character in my work. I'm an observer, not an actor. I try to construct a narrative that flows naturally, so the reader doesn't notice me pulling the strings behind the scenes.

What kind of tone do you aim for?

I tend to be a little formal, a little distant. I want the writing to be evocative, but not to call attention to itself. I believe in Orwell's dictum that good writing is like a windowpane, that it shouldn't interfere with what the reader is trying to see. I tend to write short, simple sentences. Tony Lukas told me my writing was "muscular." I think he was complimenting me. I took it that way, anyhow.

What writers have influenced you?

Wow. How about every writer I've read that I liked? My father had Arthur Conan Doyle's *Complete Sherlock Holmes,* and I started reading it when I was about twelve years old. Maybe that's where I get my affinity for mystery.

In nonfiction, John McPhee has been a big influence, especially for what I guess you would call his tone—detached, slightly ironic—but also for how he builds characters. Edmund Wilson, in a collection of articles published as *The American Earthquake,* all written in the 1930s. There's one piece called "A Bad Day in Brooklyn," only about four pages long, and he constructs a complete world. He was literary and journalistic at the same time. I think he was perhaps the first to do the sort of thing that has become "the New Journalism." Orwell, in his nonfiction—*Down and Out in Paris and London, Homage to Catalonia*—but also of course his fiction. A writer named C. D. B. Bryan, whom I met when I was in my early twenties, wrote a book called *Friendly Fire* that I loved and studied diligently. My friend Tracy Kidder, with *The Soul of a New Machine* and *House*—both of those were seminal for me. Norman Mailer with *The Executioner's Song*. Early Joan Didion. Early Gay Talese. And then of course Truman Capote. The opening of *In Cold Blood,* this beautiful scene describing the town of Holcomb, Kansas, so vivid and clean, with no characters other than the town itself. When I was trying to describe the town of Woburn in *A Civil Action*, I reread that dozens of times. I didn't come close to him, though.

Do you believe your brand of journalism can lead to truth?

Ahh, the truth. Jerry Facher, one of the lawyers in *A Civil Action*, once said to me: "The truth is at the bottom of a bottomless pit." A line I used in the book, of course.

I was sued by one of the characters in *A Civil Action*—it was ultimately thrown out of court as meritless, but not before I was deposed under oath. The lawyer for the aggrieved character asked me whether I had written "a true novel." I replied, "First of all, it's *nonfiction,* not a novel. And what do you mean by true?" I went on to say that, after all, the entire trial was an exercise in trying to discover the truth, about which there was vast disagreement. The Woburn families believed the chemicals in the water killed their kids, and the companies who dumped the chemicals believed it didn't. So what is gospel truth for one person is not always true for another.

I'm not a complete relativist, I don't believe that everybody's version of the truth—Holocaust deniers, for example—has to be accorded legitimacy. But I also don't believe we can know the absolute truth. That's such a loaded word. Some *facts* are indisputable. But beyond those, the truth lies in the interpretation of the facts, and different people will assemble them and interpret them in different ways. A writer who tells a compelling story about these different interpretations comes as close to the truth as one can get.

Do you think of yourself as a New Journalist as defined by Tom Wolfe?

"New Journalism" has sort of an antique ring to it by now, but I guess I'm working in that tradition.

What do you think about the prospects for literary nonfiction?

I think they're great. I believe that literary nonfiction will be to the twenty-first century what "the great American novel" was to the twentieth. The "great American novel" was the big prize for writers like Mailer, Bellow, and Roth. I think the new competition will be to write the great American work of *nonfiction*.

That said, the next thing I want to try my hand at is fiction. It's exhausting to follow people around, and the facts of a real event sometimes don't occur in a way that lends itself to narrative elegance. The great thing about nonfiction is that it gives you a sturdy framework. I don't have to ask myself whether something I'm writing is plausible, since I know it actually happened. My job is to make it plausible to the reader.

BY JONATHAN HARR:

A Civil Action, Random House, 1995

ALEX KOTLOWITZ

One Christmas Day, Alex Kotlowitz was strolling through Chicago's Henry Horner projects with Lafeyette and Pharoah, the protagonists of his first book, after sharing a holiday meal with the young black boys and their family. Suddenly, they were approached by a white, female police officer. "Are you okay?" she asked, looking directly at Kotlowitz. A few weeks later, Kotlowitz and Pharoah were shopping for sneakers in downtown Chicago when a black man approached them. "Is everything okay?" he asked. This time the question was directed at Pharoah. In a white neighborhood, Kotlowitz was perceived as imperiled; in a black neighborhood, the two boys were potential victims. "Such is the state of race relations today," Kotlowitz says. "We view the world through such distinct prisms, having everything to do with our personal and collective experiences."

America's vexed relationship with race, the drama of ordinary lives on either side of a divide—these are Kotlowitz's subjects. In *There Are No Children Here* (1991), he chronicles two years in the lives of Lafeyette and Pharoah, who, even as adolescents, had confronted more terror and violence than most people experience in a lifetime. His second book, *The Other Side of the River* (1998), explores the death of a black teenager in Michigan as a screen onto which two adjacent towns—one black and one white—project their resentments and fears.

Kotlowitz calls his work "the journalism of empathy," by which he means writing that seduces the reader into standing in his subjects' shoes. He often writes about children, drawing stories from reticent, underaged subjects who leave less patient interviewers with empty notebooks. Children, he says, "are our own most vulnerable, and I think that how we come to view them defines us as a culture."

That conviction became the framework for *There Are No Children Here*—an intimate exploration of the lives the boys managed to carve out, the family they create, in circumstances defined by grinding poverty and brutality. Writing in the *Los Angeles Times Book Review*, Samuel Freedman praised the book as "a triumph of empathy as well as a significant feat of reporting." While not removing responsibility from Lafeyette and Pharoah's mother, Freedman notes, Kotlowitz poses "the rhetorical question to whites inclined to judgment: Just what would you do in her place?"

The son of writer Robert Kotlowitz, Alex Kotlowitz grew up in a book-filled house in New York City. He graduated from Wesleyan University and originally planned to pursue a career in zoology. After college, he worked on a cattle ranch in Oregon before landing his first reporting job at an alternative weekly paper in Lansing, Michigan. He spent much of the next five years freelancing for National Public Radio and various publications before seeking a job at a newspaper. With no daily journalism experience, Kotlowitz was rejected by the first dozen papers to which he applied before being hired in 1984 by the Chicago bureau of *The Wall Street Journal*. At the time, *The Wall Street Journal* was known as a "writer's paper," a publication that allowed its reporters to compose long, narrative articles on topics that had little, or nothing, to do with business. Talented *Wall Street Journal* writers like Tony Horwitz, Susan Faludi, Brian Burrough, and Erik Larson were nurtured by editors like John Koten and James Stewart. Kotlowitz credits Jim Stewart's urgings to "think cinematically" with his desire to pursue long-form nonfiction.

Kotlowitz had been asked to write the text for a *Chicago* magazine photo essay on children of poverty when he first met Lafeyette, then ten, and Pharoah, seven, in 1985.

In 1987, Kotlowitz again met with the brothers, and wrote an article in *The Wall Street Journal* about the effect growing up amidst violence was having on their lives. When he suggested to the boys' mother that he might one day write a book about "The Story of Two Boys Growing Up in the Other America," she responded, "But you know, there are no children here. They've seen too much to be children." Kotlowitz took an eighteen-month leave of absence from the newspaper to write the book. The reporting was so grueling—and so emotional—that he became distant from many of his friends. "I just couldn't imagine they would believe or understand what was going on there," he told the *Chicago Tribune*.

Published in 1991, the book was a surprise bestseller and became a made-for-television film by Oprah Winfrey. Kotlowitz set up a trust fund for the two boys with money from the book's royalties. He paid their tuition at a private school and helped the family move out of the projects. In 1995, the New York Public Library listed it as one of the 150 most important books of the century.

In 1992, when riots broke out in Los Angeles in response to the verdict of the Rodney King trial, Kotlowitz suggested to his editors that he write about the reaction to the trial in two small communities in southwestern Michigan, Benton Harbor and St. Joseph. The assignment was Kotlowitz's way of avoiding the "center of the storm." It was also an opportunity for him to explore racial politics in America through two towns, divided by a river, one black, one white, one poor, and one well-to-do.

While there, Kotlowitz heard the story of Eric McGinnis's death. A sixteen-year-old black boy, McGinnis had been found floating in the St. Joseph River. Each town had reached starkly different conclusions about the circumstances of his death—and that divide became Kotlowitz's subject. "As would any journalist, I wanted to uncover the truth, but it wasn't to be that simple. When race is involved truth becomes myth, myth becomes truth, and your perspective—myth or truth, truth or myth—all depends on which side of the river you live on. In the end all that matters is what *you* believe. Or so it seems," writes Kotlowitz. He left *The Wall Street Journal* in 1993 and spent four years on *The Other Side of the River*.

The reviews of this second book were mixed. Some faulted Kotlowitz for failing to solve the mystery of McGinnis's death; others found the narrative too digressive. Kotlowitz's discussion of race raised the most criticism, with critics like *The Nation*'s Allison Xantha Miller accusing him of settling for the liberal status quo. "For all his thorough reporting, solid writing and admirable compassion, he comes up with the same old conclusions: White and black Americans are physically, and spiritually, isolated from one another. We live on opposite sides of the bridge. We believe in different histories. We speak different languages," she writes.

Still, Tamar Jacoby praised Kotlowitz's skill in "flushing out the inherited fears, personal slights and pent-up resentments that shape the color-coded lens through which many people see the world. It is a harrowing ride, and by the end, the black view of McGinnis's death emerges so sharply that it makes a kind of sense even for skeptical white readers," she writes in the *Los Angeles Times*.

Aside from its poetic language and narrative daring, the most remarkable thing about *The Other Side of the River* is its utter break—structurally, thematically—from *There Are No Children Here*. Beyond Anthony Lukas's *Common Ground* and William Finnegan's *Cold New World*, few books have so successfully examined the ways in which race manifests itself in *both* black and white America. In *The Other Side of the River* Kotlowitz appeared for the first time as a character in his own work—serving as an impartial guide to the two towns. In contrast to the third person narrative of *There Are No Children Here*, which reads like a novel, Kotlowitz's second book has the feel of a murder mystery, in which the reader is led by the story's chief investigator. Both are profoundly intimate books, but in completely different genres.

In addition to his writing, Kotlowitz returned to radio in 2003, winning a Peabody Award for coproducing "Stories of Home," a collection of audio essays that aired on Chicago Public Radio. His most recent writing project is *Never a City So Real* (2004), a book about Chicago.

You've described your work as "the journalism of empathy." What is that?

I've come to realize that in my writing, I'm looking for empathy. And it works on two planes. First, I try to put myself in the shoes of my subjects, to be able to look at and understand the world through their eyes. To do so, I have to set aside my preconceptions. I have to open myself up. But secondly, I look to achieve empathy with my readers. To get them to a place where they, too, are in the shoes of my characters, and in some cases, as with my second book, in my shoes, empathizing with me, the narrator.

What kinds of subjects are you generally drawn to?

I'm drawn to stories along the margins, to communities that are tucked away in the crevices of the country, to the sorts of people who reporters don't typically spend much time with. For me, the joy of what I do is finding and telling stories that haven't been told publicly before. Nothing's as exhilarating—and ultimately as intimidating— as discovering that untold tale. There are plenty of reporters out there writing about the powerful and the wealthy and doing a hell of a good job at it. But for me, I find myself running from the center of the storm.

What do you do when forced to write about a big story?

I guess I think of most of my stories as "big" in the sense that they all, I hope, give us reason to reflect on the human condition. But you're right that I don't often find myself reporting and writing on a story which is front-page news. But it happens on occasion, as when for *The New Yorker* I wrote on a case in Chicago in which two boys were falsely accused of killing an eleven-year-old girl ["The Unprotected," February 8, 1999]. And in that instance, I found a way to report and write the story in a more intimate and thoughtful manner than the daily press could afford.

But as I said, more often than not, I'm inclined to run *away* from the center of the storm. In 1993, when the first of the verdicts in the Rodney King case came down, the minority community in Los Angeles exploded. At the time, I was a Chicago-based correspondent for *The Wall Street Journal,* and before my editors could ask me to go to L.A., I told them that I didn't think I could add anything more to the story there. Part of it, to be honest, is that I don't fare particularly well on tight deadlines and in highly competitive arenas, which is why I don't work at a newspaper anymore. So I suggested that instead of going to L.A., I head for St. Joseph and Benton Harbor, these two small towns in Michigan. St. Joseph is virtually all white and Benton Harbor all black. The two are separated by a river. I was hoping to find—which I did—a story that would help us reflect on why it is that blacks and whites often come to the same event—like

the Rodney King beating—from such extraordinarily different perspectives. And I found this Rashomon-like story, one so peculiar to
this country, one that centered on the personal and collective experiences of the residents in these two towns, which had everything to
do with race. The story—about the mysterious death of a sixteen-
year-old African American—ended up being the subject of my second book.

How do you come up with story ideas?

How I wish there was some clear, established path to follow.
There isn't. Which can make life enormously frustrating—as well as
exhilarating. Consider the St. Joseph/Benton Harbor story. I sometimes feel like I live on hunches. I had lived in Michigan for a while,
and had for many years been haunted by these two towns, their geographic proximity to each other, and yet their spiritual distance.

When I got there, the first thing I did was go to the public library
and read through the recent newspapers. The head librarian asked
me what I was doing, and I told her. And she began to tell me a story
about a sixteen-year-old African American, Eric McGinnis, who had
drowned in the river that separates the two towns. It turned out each
town had its own theory as to what had happened to him. I was
hooked.

Do you often stumble on a story in this way?

"Stumble" is the key word. So much of it is luck, not dumb luck,
but a kind of informed good fortune. It's like panning for gold; you
know what you're looking for, and you have a notion where to look
and how to look for it, but whether you find it or not has everything
in the end to do with chance.

What elements do you generally look for in a story?

First and foremost, I'm drawn by the power of narrative. So, I'm
always looking for a *story*, a tale with a beginning, middle, and end.
And all those elements were present in this situation. The longer I'm
at this, I find myself more and more attracted to stories riddled with
ambiguity. It's more reflective, I think, of how most of us view our
own lives. Grace Paley once wrote that characters, both fictional and

real, are entitled to their own destinies, that is, nothing needs to be neat and tidy in storytelling. It's not how life works.

I also look for stories that surprise me. Unpredictability is especially important given the kinds of topics—like race and poverty—that I write on. People aren't inclined to read articles, let alone books, about such well-traveled subjects, and so my challenge is to figure out how to engage readers.

What is your thought process as you decide whether to pursue a story?

I ask myself a series of questions: Are these people I want to spend time with? Is it a place I want to spend time in? Is there a larger point I can draw from it? Is it a book, or an article? Are these issues engaging enough to wrestle with for two months, or for two years?

What kinds of people do you *most* like writing about?

People who have never been interviewed before and who've never dealt with the press. It's a privilege to be let into people's lives, and I'm continually astonished at how generous people can be, with their time, with their emotions, with their stories. I especially like writing about children and teenagers, in large part because they look at the world with such a fresh perspective. But they're also very tough to write about. The temptation is to be facile and to fall into all those hoary clichés about how kids "say the darnedest things." Most reporters don't take children seriously. They're too often used as means to telling a story rather than the story itself. They're our most vulnerable, and I think how we come to view them defines us as a culture. We're conflicted about how we think of children and of childhood. Young enough to execute or to try in adult court, but not old enough to drink, or to drive, or to marry. I guess I also cherish their existential nature. They live in the moment. They lack the self-consciousness of adults. And, man, they're fun to be around. Which counts for a lot.

Children are not terribly reflective, so getting to know them well, getting information from them can be difficult. I remember when I was first reporting *There Are No Children Here,* I'd ask Lafeyette and Pharoah (the two main characters), "What did you guys do yesterday?" And they'd just shrug their shoulders. I thought, "Oh, no! How the *hell* am I going to pull this off?" They didn't have a good sense of time. They didn't know precisely *when* something had happened to them, or even what had happened. And my questions were so general that they didn't even know how to *begin* to answer them.

How did you solve this problem?

I learned *how* to ask them questions, how to jog their memories, how to avoid the open-ended questions. What I discovered was that if I interviewed the adults in their lives (who *did* have a sense of when events took place) before I talked with Lafeyette and Pharoah, I'd get the information I needed in order to ask the children more precise questions. After that, whenever I interviewed Lafeyette and Pharoah, I found I could ask them about events that took place three days—or even three months—ago, and they'd remember every detail as if it happened earlier that day.

What kinds of people do you *least* like writing about?

Public figures. Often when I write about public figures, one of two things happens. If I admire them, I admire them too much, and I fall in love with them. Or the opposite happens: when I write about someone in a position of influence or power, and they're not fulfilling their responsibilities, I get angry. Anger's not a bad thing, mind you, but in a controlled form. You can't let it get the best of you. In either case, I have trouble maintaining my perspective, and that's not a good thing to let go of.

The New Yorker once assigned me a profile of Cathy Ryan, who had just been appointed Chicago's new chief prosecutor in the juvenile courts. I'd been trying to figure out a way to write about the juvenile courts for years, and I thought she was it. She intrigued me. She was a nun, and a longtime child advocate. The irony, of course, was that as chief prosecutor for juveniles, she was a nun whose job was putting kids in jail. She was a dedicated reformer and was trying to make significant changes in the prosecutor's office. I came to admire her too much, and it showed in my writing. So I put the profile aside, and figured out another way to write about the juvenile courts. Readers are pretty savvy, and they'll sense when a writer has become too enamored of his subject.

Do you conceive of your work as variations on a few themes? Variations on one theme?

We're a country with a deep, profound sense of fairness, and so I often find myself drawn to stories that somehow wrestle with the notions of fairness and justice, notions of what is right. But in the end, I'm drawn to the dramas in everyday lives.

Are you aware from the beginning that you're working on a story, or do you sometimes stumble on a story and realize it has been in front of you all along?

It happens both ways. Occasionally, I'll tell my wife about someone I've met and she'll realize that they would make a great story. She's usually right.

On the other hand, I'll find someone or someplace that particularly intrigues me, and I'll take my time—sometimes a year or two— to find the story. I'm so intrigued, for instance, by the new-immigrant experience, and there's a particular story that I still haven't figured out how to write. There are five INS detention centers around the country that hold immigrant kids who have either been smuggled into the country or have come in on their own. The one in Chicago has children, mostly teenagers, from China, the Ukraine, India, and Central America. I periodically visit the center, looking for a narrative. I've come close, but haven't quite figured out how best to tell this story. It'll come.

Why do you keep going back to this detention center?

The children's stories. They're riveting. They're the story of these times. Stories of migration, of our search for home. It's human nature to want to belong, to a tribe, to a community, to a country. And each of these children have come here, sometimes by extraordinary means, looking for home, and for reasons as varied as safety, money, and love. It's also, in some ways, a reminder of how much smaller the world is becoming, that is, how much easier it has become to find our way from one corner to the other, and sometimes back again.

Do you prefer long-term stories, or do you also like stories that get you in and out relatively quickly?

I'm not the most efficient reporter or writer. My inclination is to find stories that don't have an immediate deadline, stories that will be as powerful if they're published next month or next year. I get invested in my subjects, and intimacy takes a while. There aren't any shortcuts in that regard. But having said that, I do like taking on short, quick projects from time to time. It keeps me energized, keeps me writing. And often the shorter material becomes the basis for a longer project.

Do you have a research routine?
I have no routine whatsoever, at least when it comes to work.

Is that a problem?
No, I like that I don't have one. Each time out feels like an adventure, like traversing unnavigated terrain—which I guess in the end is what I find so invigorating about this work, and at the same time so damn intimidating.

Some writers prepare a lot before they begin their reporting. Others don't want to know anything that will prejudice them. Where do you place yourself along this continuum?
I'm closer to the latter. I'm nearly a blank slate when I start a project. I do most of my research while I'm reporting the story because I don't know what to look for until I start asking questions and listening to the people I'm writing about.

Where did you learn to be a writer?
Well, my father's a novelist. And he can write such taut, precise prose. So undoubtedly he influenced me, in ways that I'm still probably not aware of. Virtually every wall in our apartment was lined with books. Those books became my refuge in adolescence—that and the basketball court.

After college, I got a job at an alternative weekly in Lansing, Michigan, then freelanced for five years, mostly for NPR. They taught me how to do radio by phone. Finally, I worked at *The Wall Street Journal*, which was then a real reporter's paper.

What did you learn there?
I learned a lot about narrative. Jim Stewart, who was page-one

editor and later went on to write *Den of Thieves,* had a mantra: "Write cinematically." Jim also had this fierce commitment to story. I remember once I had a hunch, which proved to be true, that the rates of police brutality were going up, and I thought much of it could be attributed to the war on drugs. The "war" rhetoric, after all, set the police against the very communities they were supposed to protect. I wanted to do a general story that probed this notion, but Jim urged me to find a police officer who had committed an act of brutality, and profile him. I said, "You've got to be kidding. How am I ever going to get a cop in that position to talk to me." He persisted. And sure enough, I found a police officer in Dayton, Ohio, who had been fired from the force after taking a hot iron to a drug suspect's chest. He was black, on a predominately white police force, and was used on undercover assignments in the very neighborhood he'd grown up in. You can imagine what an intense emotional experience this was for him. And the kind of danger he faced. One day, he cracked. It was a tragic story about the rise and fall of this one police officer, and of how the war on drugs had created a sense of "us" versus "them." And how, in the end, this one officer felt betrayed, by his fellow police officers, by his own community, and ultimately by himself.

Do you ever worry that you become too involved with the people you write about?

Always. When you spend a lot of time with somebody, you inevitably develop a relationship, and presumably intimacy since that, after all, is what you're after. And usually—though not always—I'm writing about someone because I admire something about them or about their life. Truthfully, one of the joys of my work is the friendships I make, and with the unlikeliest of people.

Do you abide by any specific ethical guidelines?

There are some barriers I won't cross. I won't, for instance, offer money for someone's story—or allow my subjects to read what I've written before it's published. I'm also careful not to make promises I can't keep. And, indeed, I tell people—no matter how close we've grown—that I need to check out everything they tell me, and that I need to write about them in an honest, full way. Again, readers are savvy. They'll know if you're pulling your punches—or if, on the other hand, you're crucifying someone who doesn't deserve it. My one general rule is that I let people know what I'm going to write about them, if for no other reason so that they have a chance to respond, and, equally important, to correct any errors.

In your "Note on Reporting Methods" at the end of There Are No Children Here *you mention that you set up trusts for Lafeyette and Pharoah, and helped them get into private schools. Did those actions color your story?*

I was very careful to balance the demands of the relationship I developed with Lafeyette and Pharoah with the ethical demands of journalism. But it probably seems tidier in hindsight. I didn't get them into private school or set up the trusts until *after* I had finished the book. And on other occasions in which I intervened in the lives of my subjects, I've always told the reader about it in the text. I'll always remember, in those first few months with Lafeyette and Pharoah, all they wanted to know was "was I going to leave after I finished the book." They asked me that repeatedly. And eventually I did promise them that I would not move, and I didn't. Our relationships, in fact, only deepened in the months and years following the publication of the book.

Do you ever worry that you aren't involved enough in the lives of your subjects? I'm thinking of an episode from There Are No Children Here *in which a* Wall Street Journal *article you wrote inadvertently causes LaJoe to lose her public aid.*

I felt awful about that. I originally had written an article for *The Wall Street Journal* about a summer in Lafeyette's life, and in passing mentioned that his father occasionally slept on the living room couch. What I later learned—remember, this is during the Reagan years, during the myth of "the welfare queen"—is that local welfare officials were reading newspapers daily to find so-called "welfare cheats." It was a perversion of what public assistance is supposed to be about, which is watching out for those in need. The result of all this was that they cut the family off of public aid, arguing that there was a man in the house. There wasn't. And, what's more, the father at the time was unemployed.

silences, whereas I'm fine with silences in person. I'm confident that face-to-face with someone, I can convince just about anyone to talk with me. And moreover, it's sometimes just as important to see people's reactions to questions. Do they flinch? Do they smile? Do they turn away? Do they get fidgety?

I remember this *New Yorker* story I did about a small-town newspaper reporter, Dave Silverberg ["I Got the Sheriff," September 25, 2000]. Dave, who for twenty years had been covering county board meetings, stumbled onto the story of a lifetime, exposing a corrupt sheriff. When I first called him he said he didn't want anything to do with me. He didn't want to be the focus of any story. It wasn't about him, he told me. So I went to see him in person. I told him I was going to be in town anyway (which was a bit of a fib). We spent two hours talking. I was almost on my knees begging him. As we talked, I kept searching for things we had in common. We were both reporters. He was half Jewish. I told him about my books, and it turned out that, of all things, he was passionate about the subject of race. That's ultimately what connected us. I could never have gotten him to cooperate if we had just spoken on the phone.

Once you've struck on a story, how do you decide whom to interview? How do you find characters?

A lot of it is serendipitous. To be honest, when I met Lafeyette and Pharoah, I didn't think to myself, "Boy, these kids are representative of thousands of others." I was doing a *Wall Street Journal* piece about violence in the inner city, and I wanted to write about it through the eyes of a child.

What I do in a community like that is find an institution that is respected in the neighborhood. So I spent three weeks hanging out at the local Boys and Girls Club. I went three or four afternoons each week to hang out, play basketball, and shoot pool with the kids. I didn't take any notes, although I did tell them I was a reporter and wanted to write a story about their community. The toughest thing was convincing them I wasn't a cop.

What were you looking for in these kids?

It was simple. I wanted to find a kid I connected to, a kid with whom I identified with on some level.

What about Lafeyette and Pharoah did you identify with?

With Lafeyette, I identified with his sense of responsibility. Dutiful. Too much so. That describes me as a kid. And that was Lafeyette's problem, as well. Pharoah, on the other hand, struck me as terribly vulnerable, a boy who so much wanted to belong, to be connected, to be liked. That's how I think of myself, as someone who wants to belong, the only difference being that I can never quite figure out what it is I want to belong to.

How have your ideas about empathy influenced your choice of characters?

I wrestled with how to open *There Are No Children Here*. The obvious place to begin would have been with a moment of violence. It's what astonished me. It would have startled readers, as well. But I ultimately chose to open it with a fairly benign scene of the boys hunting for garter snakes on nearby railroad tracks. Looking back on it, I was looking for ways to create empathy with my characters. As kids, we all looked for places of refuge, and so readers, I hoped, could immediately see some of themselves in Lafeyette and Pharoah.

In a *New York Times Magazine* piece about a jury in a death penalty trial ["In the Face of Death," July 6, 2003], I wrote the story from the viewpoint of the jurors, and so I had to remind myself throughout the piece that I couldn't introduce anything—like what the defendant was feeling—that the jurors weren't privy too. I wanted to put the reader in the shoes of those jurors, for them to hear what they heard, to see what they saw.

When I was reporting *The Other Side of the River*, I interviewed a former police officer who was an out-and-out racist. He was filled with venom for African Americans, and would have made an easy target. He was incidental to the plot, so whether I used him or not was clearly a judgment call. I chose not to. I feared that if I did it would have made it easy on my white readers; it would have been easy for them to condemn him, and then say, "But that's not *me*." I didn't want to make it that easy for my readers. I wanted readers to grow fond of the characters, yet also see how their disconnection from the other side of the river poisoned their relations with their neighbors. I wanted to challenge people's perceptions of themselves, and I couldn't do that if I chose a completely unsympathetic character. It's not that I don't look for heroes and villains. They after all make for compelling stories. But I think the world's a more complicated place than that.

Do you prefer to approach your subject cold, or via an introduction?

I prefer to find people myself. Having an introduction can open up doors, for sure, but it can also create problems of its own. I don't, for example, know how my subject perceives the intermediary. Being introduced by the "wrong" person might color the entire relationship.

How do you convince your subjects to give you so much time?

I don't go away. I push myself into someone's life with a kind of quiet, determined persistence. I also work at being patient. If it's clear that my presence is becoming an intrusion, I back off for a while. And then try to reenter. I become a slave to people's schedules.

Do you tell them immediately how long you're going to hang around?

Problem is, I don't know. I don't know whether I'll need two meetings or twelve to get someone to open up. And there's always the chance that it turns into a much larger, or different, story than the one I anticipated. I'm frequently shifting gears. *There Are No Children Here* began as a two-month commitment, to write a *Wall Street Journal* piece that followed Lafeyette for a summer. Those two months turned into a year, and that turned into two years.

Do you prepare for interviews?

I prepare very little for interviews because my assumption is that I'll go back and talk to someone again, and again. But if it is a situation in which I'll get only one shot at someone—like when I interview a busy public official, or a prisoner—I do prepare written questions in advance. But they just serve as a guide. I don't want to kick myself later for not asking some question.

Where do you least like to conduct interviews?

There's a formality to offices, and usually too many interruptions. Having said that, someone's office can give a lot away about the individual. Photographs on the wall. Plaques. Even choice of furniture and design can often tell you something about someone's personality. I also can't bear conducting interviews in restaurants; there's too much going on and, besides, I like to eat too much. It's virtually impossible to eat and take notes at the same time.

Where do you most like to conduct interviews?

At someone's home, or anywhere else that's informal and quiet. It's important for me to get to know people in all aspects of their lives. With Lafeyette and Pharoah I hung out a lot at their home. With Jim Reeves, the police lieutenant in *The Other Side of the River,* I first interviewed him in his office, then while we drove around the two towns, and finally at his home, where I got to know his family.

How do you typically begin an interview?

I ask my subject to tell me a story. Maybe it's just an anecdote. Maybe it's a full-fledged narrative. Stories are so much a part of who we are, and it's after people tell me their tales that I begin to poke and prod. The more specific they get, the more reflective and truthful they become.

For example, the first time I sat down with Jim Reeves for *The Other Side of the River,* I asked him, "Tell me about the moment you got the phone call about Eric's death." When he answered that question he started to relive the experience. He told me that he was about to go golfing when the police chief called and told him that they'd found a body down by the river, and that he ought to get down there. I walked him through every minute: what he did, what he said, what he thought, what he was wearing. I want him to go into so much detail that I can close my eyes and see the events, as if I had been there with him. Now if I had simply said, "Tell me about Eric's death," he would have said something vague like, "Well, it was a terrible thing . . ."

Do you think people's inclination is to lie?

No. But I do think that—and this is only natural—that people want to present themselves in the best light possible, so it takes time to sort through people's stories to find the truth. Sometimes I learn the truth by doing more interviews, or by just hanging out. But more often than not I learn it by talking to other people in their lives. Not long ago, I'd met a young couple on Chicago's West Side for a documentary I was doing for *Frontline*. They had just had a child together, and the father told me that he worked for the phone company. But when I met his uncle a few weeks later, he mentioned in passing that he was helping his nephew find work. "Find work?" I asked. It turns out that he'd been laid off about two months before we'd met him. That kind of lying is understandable. Here I am, this complete stranger walking into this young man's life, and telling him I'd like him to be a part of a television documentary, and so he wants the world to see him in the best light possible. It's when people lie and then lie again that I get nervous—and have to work doubly hard to verify everything. And sometimes the fact that people color or hide the truth is very much a part of the story.

How much do you tell the subjects you're interviewing about what you've discovered so far in your investigation?

I try not to be a messenger between my subjects, or become identified too clearly with one camp or the other. But it is a delicate balance because talking about your story, trading information, is the way you get people to open up to you. Sometimes you need and want people's reactions to what others have had to say.

What is your policy about information someone tells you either "not for attribution," "off the record," or "on background"?

"Off the record" is such an ambiguous term. People often mean very different things by it. That you can't use the material. Or that you can use it but you can't attribute it to them. So when someone tells me they're willing to tell me something "off the record" I make sure that I'm clear about what they mean. It's fine with me if people want to tell me something without my attributing it to them. But I have a *very strict* policy about "off-the-record" information (by my reckoning, "off the record" is when I'm told something, but am *not* allowed to use it—unless I verify it elsewhere). Too often it's a way for sources to try to convert a journalist to his or her version of the story. Besides, I feel confident as a reporter that I can find out what I need to know, and find out in ways that I can use it.

When I wrote *The Wall Street Journal* story that grew into *The Other Side of the River*, the prosecutor in the case told me, "Listen, I want to tell you something—off the record—that will help you understand this case a lot better." I remember thinking, "Boy, I can't wait to hear this!" But then I realized that it was probably best left unsaid. So I told him I didn't want to know anything that was off the record. I figured I was a good enough reporter that I'd eventually learn it on my own.

Did you?

I did. He wanted to tell me that Eric McGinnis had been caught breaking into a car the night he disappeared. And that he fled. Which might have suggested that in order to avoid the police he tried to swim the river to get home, and drowned. And in fact I was able to learn that on my own, through my own reporting. It turns out that the reason the prosecutor held back this piece of information from the public was that he feared that the black community would riot if he released it. Which to me was just evidence of the myths the whites held about their neighbors across the river. And that of course became part of the story.

What's your policy for when you choose to change the names of your characters?

Most of the people I write about aren't public figures. If changing their names affords them some protection or measure of privacy I'm happy to do it.

In the case of *There Are No Children Here*, I was the one who insisted on changing Lafeyette and Pharoah's last names. Their mother wanted me to use their real names because she felt such a sense of pride in their story. But I insisted. There was no way, of course, to know what kind of impact the book might have on their lives. I mention at the beginning of the book that I had changed their last names.

I should underscore something, though. I always tell people, if they tell me they want their names changed, that in the end it won't afford them the privacy from the people they most care about, their family, their friends, their neighbors, their coworkers. They'll know it's them, pseudonym or not. It only affords them a measure of privacy from the larger public.

Do you take notes or tape your interviews?

I rarely use a tape recorder, although there are a few occasions when I will. If I'm talking to a public figure and suspect it will be a contentious interview; or if I'm interviewing a prisoner who is difficult to get access to, and I know there's no way to ask follow-up questions, to confirm my notes.

Another reason I sometimes tape is in order to get somebody's speech patterns down. For example, for *There Are No Children Here,* I made sure to tape two or three interviews with each of the main characters so I could get down the rhythms and syntax of their speech.

What do you have against taping interviews?

It makes me a lazy interviewer. When you're taking notes, it forces you to concentrate on what you're hearing, to think of the next question. On a more practical level, transcribing tapes takes forever.

What do you use to take your notes?

I used to use reporter's notebooks, then I used legal pads, and now I use small spiral notebooks. But I'm an inveterate note-taker. Flaps of books. Scraps of paper stuffed into my wallet. On the back of my kids' homework. I have my own shorthand, and I make a point of transcribing all my written interview notes into my computer soon after I conduct an interview.

How do you know when you've finished interviewing?

I'm so obsessive and thorough that I never think I've interviewed enough people, or asked enough questions, or acquired enough details. Often the only thing that makes me stop is when my editor, or my wife, suggests, rather diplomatically mind you, that perhaps I ought to consider taking pen to paper.

After you've come up with an idea, found the story, done your research, reporting, and interviewing, how do you prepare to write?

I'm hopelessly disorganized. But I do my best. The computer has helped. I sort files by character and by moment in time. And I can use the computer to cross-reference everything. When I was working on *The Other Side of the River*, I printed all my notes out and created fifteen to twenty loose-leaf notebooks, with each notebook covering a different subject. Also, each major character had a separate notebook, as did each major incident. I could lay them out on the floor, and on my hands and knees piece together material I needed for each chapter.

I'm pretty good, though, at mentally organizing my material. I'm a storyteller, so I'm instinctively looking for a chronology or narrative of some kind. Then I print out all my notes (the ones I've transcribed into my computer from my reporting notebooks), and read them over. As I read them, I mark quotes or incidents and moments I want to remember. Before writing, I read through all my notes once, then put them aside. I begin writing from memory. I write for as long as I can without looking at my notes. Then, after I've written for a while, I start to look back over them to fill in details and quotes. And as I begin to work from draft to draft, I'm using my notes more and more.

Do you write from the start to finish, or do you write sections out of sequence?

I begin at the beginning. The opening of a piece is incredibly important to me, so I spend an enormous amount of time on it. If you can't get your reader in at that point, you're lost. When I teach, I begin every class by reading the opening page from a piece of nonfiction. Those opening lines set the tone for the book. But my initial goal is to get through a complete rough draft. Psychologically, it helps me to have something down, to confirm that I really do have a story. As you can tell, I'm filled with insecurities when I'm writing.

You don't write from an outline?

I guess my first very rough first draft is sort of a rudimentary, impressionistic outline. I work from it the way that some writers might work from a more formal outline. It won't have the quotes, and details are missing, but it's all down there.

What do you do once you've written your first draft?

I go back and rewrite, scene by scene, detail by detail. It's the part I love the most. It's all I think about. I'll awake in the middle of the night with a perfect sentence. Or during a game of basketball will find a word I'd been looking for. I'm sure, to some, I must seem like an unholy, scatterbrained mess.

Do you discuss a story while you're working on it?

No, I'm incredibly private. I don't talk about my work-in-process. I worry that if I talk about it too much, it'll get stale, and I want the writing to be as fresh as it can. I'm sure people think I'm rude, but I just can't get myself to talk about what I'm writing on.

When do you show your writing to other people?

Once I've finished four or five polished chapters, I give them to a couple of friends. And I give everything to my wife, who is such a careful reader, and so blunt and critical. She has saved me from myself on numerous occasions.

Do you show it to your book editor, Nan Talese?

I've tried. But she won't look at an unfinished manuscript. She doesn't even want to hear about it. She wants to come to it fresh. I remember the first time she turned me down, when I was writing *There Are No Children Here,* I just about panicked. But I admire it now. It's how it should be. It's so important to have her fresh eyes on it once I've got it to a place where I feel good about it.

How much do you work with your editor after you've finished writing?

When I was at *The Wall Street Journal* I realized that the worst writers were the obstinate ones, those who resisted their editors' suggestions. Having a great editor is a blessing, and more often than not they'll improve your writing, not dampen it.

Is writing more difficult than reporting or vice versa?

For me, the reporting is the most difficult. I'm fairly quiet, somewhat reserved, so sometimes it's hard to put myself out there and meet people. And reporting can be tedious, even boring at times. Writing's also hard, but in a different way. After all, I'm at home. I can go for a bike ride—or take a break to read a magazine. My time is my own.

What's your writing routine?

Mornings are best for me. If I have any routine in my life, it's breakfast. I'm an obsessive reader of newspapers, and we get three of them delivered (*The New York Times, The Wall Street Journal,* and the *Chicago Tribune*). So I read them, sports and culture sections first, then the news, and have my coffee. Then I help get the kids off to school and am back at my desk at eight. I'm usually good for four hours of writing. The mistake I sometimes make is to spend all day at my desk, which doesn't mean I'll produce all that much more material than I would in the first four hours. If I'm smart about it, I take a midday bike ride, or walk, when I feel I've gotten enough done. Then I come back and spend the afternoon making phone calls and doing more reporting. I try to finish up at five thirty so I can hang out with my kids. I'm not much of a night person, though when I'm deep into a story, I'll go back to work after I get the kids down.

The authorial presence you have in There Are No Children Here *(which is written in the third person) is drastically different from the one you adopt in* The Other Side of the River *(in which you are a main character). Which do you prefer?*

I'm not comfortable writing in the first person. A nonfiction writer has to be careful about using the first person because the truth of the matter is that readers don't really care much about us. There are exceptions, of course, like Tony Horwitz and Ted Conover, who are incredibly skillful at using the first person, at doing what I think of as experiential journalism. But for me, the power in writing comes from using the third person. Get out of the way, and tell the story.

If I had written *There Are No Children Here* in the first person it would have been an entirely different story. It would have become a tale about my relationship with Lafeyette and Pharoah, and I wanted to avoid that. In *The Other Side of the River,* my inclination was to write in the third person. But it wasn't working. Nan urged me to try the first-person voice. The reason it seemed appropriate was that I was writing about these two towns, and didn't have a clear protagonist. And even if I did have a clear protagonist to focus on, I feared that doing so would weigh the book toward one town or the other. I needed to write it with a neutral voice, and the most obvious voice was mine.

What kind of tone do you strive for?

I have a fairly direct, understated style. I don't think of myself as a loud or particularly lyrical writer.

What writers have influenced your choice of tone?

For me, Anthony Lukas's *Common Ground* is the gold standard of understated storytelling. Another book that had a great influence on me is Truman Capote's *In Cold Blood.* You read that book and have to remind yourself constantly that this is all true. What better, more gripping way to write nonfiction? I'm also a fan of E. B. White's essays. Sentence by sentence, he's among the best. I actually read more fiction than nonfiction, and so much of my writing is influenced by novelists as much as by nonfiction writers.

Do you think about the *sound* of your words when you write?

Yes, and I owe that to my working for NPR's *All Things Considered* and *Morning Edition* before I started writing. It made me a much better listener.

You're a well-educated, literary, Jewish liberal. How does your identity influence your journalism?

I'm always an outsider wherever I go—if not by class or race, then by geography, age, or religion. I'm always conscious of who I am and where I've come from. I need to constantly remind myself that the people I write about have had different experiences in their lives. That's what "the journalism of empathy" is all about: trying to understand how people experience their lives, and why they might see things differently from others.

Do you believe that journalistic inquiry can lead to truth?

I think what I'm writing is genuine, but *truth,* that's elusive. The *search* for truth is what makes a good story. I'm not so presumptuous to think that I'll necessarily find it at the end of the day, but I do hope that my writing prods readers to join that search, to think about themselves and the world just a little bit differently.

McPhee calls this the literature of fact, and that's what it is. People always ask me, "How much can you bend the truth?" The answer is: not one bit; it is what it is. The nonfiction writer is both constrained and freed by his or her allegiance to the facts. It's the one absolute dictum for nonfiction writers, that what you write must be genuine, must be authentic, must be real. It must be verifiable. We can't stray from that. It's freeing because often the dramas of real life are more powerful than anything that one could possibly make up.

Truth, though, well that—as I said—can be elusive, and sometimes it's that very slipperiness of truth which is the story itself. That was very much the case in *The Other Side of the River,* where these two towns couldn't agree on what had happened to Eric McGinnis, and in fact we may never know for certain.

What do you call the kind of journalism you do? "New Journalism"? "Literary nonfiction"?

I think of myself as a writer of nonfiction. "Literary journalism" feels awfully presumptuous. I guess I'd rather let others decide whether what I do is literary. I don't like the phrase "creative nonfiction," because it suggests that we take liberties with the facts. I think of myself as a storyteller, a teller of authentic, genuine stories.

Do you think of yourself as part of a historical tradition? And, if so, who are your "colleagues"?

A fairly young historical tradition, but yes, I do. I'd be honored to be associated with writers like Tony Lukas, Tracy Kidder, Philip Gourevitch, Melissa Fay Greene, David Halberstam, Gay Talese.

What do you think are the prospects for this kind of writing?

I got a call recently from somebody who's doing a book about the end of New Journalism. I didn't quite know what to say. The end? I think of narrative nonfiction as so vital at the moment. Look at the popularity of nonfiction books, or the success of public radio's *This American Life,* a show completely committed to the notion of nonfiction storytelling, or the continuing powerful presence of publications like *The New Yorker, The New York Times Magazine,* and *The Atlantic.* That's not to say there couldn't be more outlets. I wish there were. But overall, I feel pretty optimistic about narrative nonfiction's prospects. I've got to. I don't know what else I'd do with myself. Telling stories. I can't think of anything else I'd rather be doing.

BY ALEX KOTLOWITZ:

Never a City So Real: A Walk in Chicago, Crown, 2004

The Other Side of the River: A Story of Two Towns, a Death, and America's Dilemma, Nan A. Talese/Doubleday, 1998

There Are No Children Here: The Story of Two Boys Growing Up in the Other America, Nan A. Talese/Doubleday, 1991

JON KRAKAUER

Jon Krakauer's pride was wounded by his editor's lukewarm reaction to an early draft of his most recent book, *Under the Banner of Heaven* (2003). After having published *Into the Wild* (1996) and *Into Thin Air* (1997), Krakauer's two bestselling works of adventure writing, the editor was puzzled by this next work—a grizzly tale of Mormonism and a 1984 ritual murder, punctuated with long chapters on the history of the religion. "Where are the mountains?" she asked.

What she didn't appreciate was that *Under the Banner of Heaven* was a continuation, not a departure, from Krakauer's central themes: the delicate balance between faith and reason as seen through individuals who are drawn to extremes, whether they be youthful idealists, mountain climbers, or religious fanatics. Rather than rework the book, Krakauer switched publishers and *Under the Banner of Heaven* became his third bestseller.

Krakauer has given a personal twist to the tradition of American adventure writing. His identification with his subjects, his intense personal investment, distinguishes Krakauer's writing from the work of others in the nature/adventure genre.

Jon Krakauer was born in Brookline, Massachusetts, in 1954. His family moved to Corvallis, Oregon, when he was two. When he was eight years old, his father took him to (unsuccessfully) climb Oregon's ten-thousand-foot South Sister, sparking Krakauer's lifelong obsession with mountaineering.

Krakauer's ambition stood at odds with his father's desires for him. His father was a doctor whose establishment credentials (Williams College, Harvard Medical School) he wanted his son to pursue. When Krakauer was a high school junior, his father sent him to Boston for two weeks for interviews at elite New England colleges. While waiting for his Amherst interview, Krakauer got some advice from a fellow applicant: "Dude, you should check out this hippie school just down the road."

An experimental school, Hampshire College was only in its second year of operation. The very first student Krakauer saw there was a girl wearing a see-through blouse. The school had no grades, an outdoors program, and a pond for nude swimming. Without consulting his father, he applied early decision and was accepted. "Hampshire was harder to get into than Harvard at the time and I thought my father would be proud," he says. Father and son didn't speak to each other for two years.

Krakauer received a degree in environmental studies and devoted his senior thesis to pioneering an arduous new route up an Alaskan mountain called the Moose's Tooth. After college, Krakauer worked intermittently as a carpenter and a commercial fisherman to support his climbing. His first writing assignment was in 1974 when he was asked to write about his climb of three previously unexplored peaks in Alaska for the journal of the American Alpine Club. The piece eventually led to more assignments, particularly for *Outside* magazine, and in 1983 Krakauer quit his job as foreman of a house-building crew to concentrate on writing.

In 1992, a party of moose hunters found the decomposing body of a young man in the Alaskan wilderness. *Outside* asked Krakauer to write about this young man, Chris McCandless, a bright idealist from Washington, D.C. The resulting article drew more mail than the magazine had ever received. Many readers thought McCandless was a reckless fool; others sympathized with his spiritual quest.

Krakauer saw a lot of himself in McCandless. "I was haunted by the particulars of the boy's starvation and by vague, unsettling parallels between events in his life and those in my own," he said. As a young man Krakauer had made a particularly dangerous solo ascent of the Devil's Thumb, a remote Alaskan peak and a feat a number of critics thought to be suicidal—perhaps pushed by the same inexplicable force that pushed McCandless to the edge. As Krakauer wrote, "In coming to Alaska, McCandless yearned to wander uncharted country, to find a blank spot on the map. In 1992, however, there were no more blank spots on the map—not in Alaska, not anywhere. But Chris, with his idiosyncratic logic, came up with an elegant solution to this dilemma: He simply got rid of the map. In his own mind, if nowhere else, the *terra* would thereby remain *incognita*."

A year after the *Outside* article was published, Krakauer couldn't get McCandless out of his mind. He received a small advance for a book and spent two years retracing McCandless's route. *Into the Wild* was Krakauer's first bestseller. Writing in *The New York Times Book Review,* Thomas McNamee wrote, "Mr. Krakauer's elegantly constructed narrative takes us from the ghoulish moment of the hunters' discovery back through McCandless's childhood, the gregarious effusions and icy withdrawals that characterized his coming of age, and, in meticulous detail, the two years of restless roaming that led him to Alaska. The more we learn about him, the more mysterious McCandless becomes, and the more intriguing."

On May 10, 1996, Krakauer climbed to the top of the 29,028-foot-high Mount Everest with an expedition of twenty-three people. An afternoon blizzard hit the peak, exacerbating errors made by guides on several teams. Eight lost their lives, including Scott Fischer and Rob Hall, two of the best-known guides in the Himalayas.

Barely surviving the climb, Krakauer initially said he didn't want to write a book about the experience. But after the magazine article was published (it won the 1996 National Magazine Award for reporting), he discovered that he had made several significant errors he wanted to correct. "The Everest climb had rocked my life to its core, and it became desperately important for me to record the events in complete detail, unconstrained by a limited number of column inches," he wrote in the introduction. After the tragedy, he conducted countless interviews, weighed multiple contradictory accounts of the climb, and combed through base-camp radio logs in a quest for the truth. *Into Thin Air* was on the bestseller list for two years and was a finalist for both the Pulitzer Prize and the National Book Critics Circle Award.

Few of those who climbed Everest that day—including Krakauer himself—were spared from criticism. "The plain truth is that I knew better but went to Everest anyway. And in doing so I was party to the death of good people, which is something that is apt to remain on my conscience for a very long time," he wrote. "The controversy over Everest changed him," said John Rasmus, the editor of *National Geographic Adventure Magazine.* "Jon felt the Everest book was somewhat the result of being in the right place at the right time and that he had profited from what turned out to be a tragedy." It was his criticism of the guides that caused the most controversy. Krakauer faulted Anatoli Boukreev for leaving the summit before all of his clients were down the mountain and for not using supplemental oxygen. In a postscript in a later edition of the book, Krakauer wished that he had been "a little less strident" in his post-Everest debate with Boukreev, who died shortly after his own book on the Everest disaster appeared. In 1998 Krakauer established the Everest '96 Memorial Fund, endowing it with royalties from his book.

The success of *Into the Wild* and *Into Thin Air* had made Krakauer wealthy, giving him the freedom to stop writing for magazines and choose his next book carefully. For his third book, he wanted to further explore the themes that run throughout his work. Many of Krakauer's childhood friends had been Mormons, and he had always marveled at the intensity of their faith: "The faith of my Mormon friends was so sure and clear. I, on the other hand, came from a family of agnostics."

When he stumbled on the existence of Colorado City, a large Mormon fundamentalist community astride the Utah-Arizona border, he had an inkling that it might provide a context for his musings. When Krakauer was granted an interview with Dan Lafferty—a fundamentalist Mormon who had slain his sister-in-law and niece in a ritual murder—he knew he had found the narrative through which to tell his story.

Stylistically, *Under the Banner of Heaven* is a complete break from Krakauer's earlier work. Although it was motivated by deeply personal questions, he doesn't appear until the author's note, and there only to provide his theological credo: "I don't know if God even exists, although I confess that I sometimes find myself praying in times of great fear, or despair, or astonishment at a display of unexpected beauty."

The book received mixed reviews, with a number of critics faulting him for ignoring Mormonism's positive characteristics. "Something must explain the vibrancy of mainstream Mormonism, and I doubt it's just the dark energy of residual authoritarianism," wrote Robert Wright in *The New York Times Book Review. In These*

Times's Mark Engler judged Krakauer theologically unsophisticated. "In reviving religion and science as mutually exclusive options, he dredges up a long-stale debate that has lately produced few insights into questions of ethics and meaning. Krakauer's own religious search would be more compelling had he not ignored the vast swaths of modern theology that have proposed more subtle accommodations between reason and faith." Writing in *The Washington Post*, Ann Rule called it "a tour de force that must be read carefully and savored."

The Mormon Church was more upset and issued a five-page, single-spaced rebuttal of the book two weeks before publication, calling it "a full frontal assault on the veracity of the modern church." The church accused Krakauer of using the violent actions of a fundamentalist sect to smear the whole religion: "His basic thesis appears to be that people who are religious are irrational, and that irrational people do strange things."

Krakauer defended his reporting and accused the church of whitewashing its history. "I am especially disappointed that they feel such an urgent need to attack writers, like me, who present balanced, carefully researched accounts of Mormon history that happen to diverge from the official, highly expurgated church version." He insists that his intentions in writing the book were honorable. "I wanted to write about how they dealt with their history. I didn't realize how rankled they would become about it."

———

What kinds of ideas are you drawn to?
I've been pegged as a writer whose beat is extreme ideas, extreme landscapes, individuals who take actions to their logical extreme. And there is some truth to that. I'm intrigued by fanatics—people who are seduced by the promise, or the illusion, of the absolute. People who believe that achieving some absolute goal, say, or embracing some absolute truth, will lead to happiness, or peace, or order, or whatever it is that they most desire. Fanatics tend to be blind to moral ambiguity and complexity, and I've always had a fascination with individuals who deny the inherent contingency of existence— often at their peril, and at the peril of society.

How do you come up with ideas?

The majority of the magazine pieces I've written over the past twenty-plus years were proposed by editors. As a freelancer having to churn out a crippling number of articles each year to pay the rent (one year I had to write something like sixty pieces), I found it was easier and more efficient to write what editors asked me to write, rather than try to sell an editor a story that I, personally, was itching to do. In my early years as a freelancer I took almost any assignment offered to me. More than a few of these assignments were less than scintillating, but I reaped certain benefits by accepting whatever was tossed my way. I'm a self-taught writer. I've never taken a writing course or a journalism course. I learned the craft on the job, through trial and no small amount of error.

Although my best magazine work has explored subjects that I already knew a lot about, many of the ideas for those pieces came from editors. Two of my books—*Into the Wild* and *Into Thin Air*—originated as magazine pieces suggested by editors.

How do you come up with ideas of your own?

I keep my antennae up all the time. Whenever I read a local newspaper, or talk to the guy selling me a doughnut at a small-town coffee shop, I'm reflexively on alert for a compelling story. Living in the West is an advantage, I think, because there are fewer writers per square mile on the far side of the hundredth meridian, and there's much to write about. The West is a big place that's home to a whole lot of people whose stories remain untold. It seems like I'm constantly stumbling across things that have the potential to become the germ of an interesting article or book.

For example, I originally intended *Under the Banner of Heaven* to be a meditation on the nature of faith and doubt. It turned into an examination of fundamentalism pretty much by accident. One July day I was driving to Colorado and I stopped for gas at a mini-mart in the middle of nowhere. A sign identified a decent-size town just off the highway as a place called Colorado City. When I went inside to pay, the girl who took my money was wearing a nineteenth-century costume that could have been lifted from the set of a John Ford western. Even though the temperature that day was 104 degrees in the shade, she was wearing a long dress, with a high collar and long sleeves. There were several other women and girls inside the mini-mart and I noticed that they were all dressed in the same distinctive style.

I decided to drive into Colorado City proper for a quick look around. Immediately I was struck by how immense most of the homes were: many of them looked like large apartment complexes. About thirty seconds after I entered the residential district, a police cruiser pulled behind me and stayed on my tail until I left the city limits. A little ways down the road, I saw a National Park Service vehicle and I pulled over to ask a ranger what the hell was going on back in Colorado City. He said, "You don't know? Colorado City is the country's largest community of Mormon fundamentalists. They believe that if you want to go to heaven you have to practice polygamy." I'd lived in the West a long time, yet until that moment I knew nothing about Colorado City or the several thousand polygamists who lived there under the absolute control of an elderly tax-accountant-turned-prophet named Uncle Rulon who had married seventy-five women, many of them when they were in their early teens.

Okay, so you have a general interest (faith, religion) and stumble onto a specific context (Colorado City). How, then, do you develop a "story"?

I was raised among Mormons in small-town Oregon, and was fascinated by the power of their belief. I grew up surrounded by kids who were utterly convinced that they were going to the celestial kingdom in the afterlife, where each would become a god, ruling his very own planet. Coming from an agnostic family, I was blown away by the intensity of their faith. I've wanted to understand the roots of such faith ever since. Blundering upon Colorado City gave me my first inkling that the story might be found somewhere within the shadowy culture of Mormon fundamentalism.

I'm a storyteller. I need a narrative chassis on which to assemble my ideas. If I determine that a potential story is sufficiently fertile, and decide to go for it, I commence a feverish hunt for material that will drive the narrative forward while simultaneously illustrating the points I wish to make.

What kinds of characters do you look for?

I look for interview subjects who not only play a central role in the story I want to tell, but also happen to be articulate and complicated and outspoken. If they are angry, or unexpectedly brilliant, or have an eccentric sense of humor—well, that's huge. A single fascinating personality can make a book—one can't state this strongly enough. It's an invaluable lesson for a writer of nonfiction—a lesson I learned by reading Tracy Kidder, Janet Malcolm, and John McPhee.

How did you find the characters for *Under the Banner of Heaven*?

Relatively early in my research, I wrote to Mark Hofmann, a one-time Mormon missionary who had lost his faith. Hofmann had gained infamy by forging some historical documents that were damaging to the Mormon Church, selling them to church leaders (who wanted to keep them out of the hands of nosy scholars and journalists) for a lot of money, and then killing two people with bombs in a vain attempt to hide the fact that the documents he'd sold were bogus. Hofmann was caught, convicted, and sent to prison. He'd been locked up since 1985, and had never given an interview to a journalist. I wrote to him anyway, and politely requested an interview. Within a couple of weeks I got a letter back—not from Hofmann, but from his cellmate, a fellow named Dan Lafferty, who was serving a life term for the ritual executions of his niece and sister-in-law. In Lafferty's letter to me, he wrote something like, "Mark doesn't give interviews. But I'd be happy to talk to you instead. And I'm the most fanatical believer you'll ever meet."

Believe it or not, I almost declined Lafferty's invitation. I'd wanted to talk to Hofmann, and my disappointment that he'd blown me off blinded me to the opportunity staring me in the face. But I decided to go through the motions and interview Lafferty and spent an afternoon talking to him in maximum security. When I walked out of those prison doors into the bright Utah sunlight, my head was spinning. I was staggered by the things Lafferty had described to me, and appalled, but I knew right then and there that I had just tripped over the central narrative of my book, and its most important character.

Did others agree it was a good story?

Not at first. I knew it would be a tough sell, because religion is a subject that induces terminal boredom in a great many folks, and because publishers are made nervous when authors abandon their home turf to write about something new. I didn't see the subject of the new book as much of a departure for me at all, since these were themes I had been exploring in my writing all along, if sometimes below the surface. Random House had an exceedingly lukewarm reaction, which wounded my pride. They said, "Where are the mountains?" Fortunately, an astute editor at Doubleday immediately understood what the book was about. So I ended up with a contract from them.

What is your thought process when deciding whether to pursue a story?

Writing a book is so hard and painful—it demands such a huge commitment of time and energy—that I won't embark on a book-length project unless the subject matter has me by the throat and won't let go.

For example, after I wrote about Chris McCandless for *Outside* magazine in 1992, I found that I just couldn't get this kid out of my mind. I was obsessed with his story and wanted to know more about his last days. Everyone told me that there was no book in the saga of a misguided kid who died in the Alaskan wilderness, and that I was wasting my time. I didn't get a big advance—in the low five figures. Then, a year after I delivered a sixty-five-thousand-word manuscript, my editor was fired. An eminent editor at another Random House imprint—an editor widely regarded as a demigod, whom I admire immensely—sent my agent a letter explaining that the manuscript was deeply flawed, and perhaps even unpublishable. That was a huge blow. Fortunately, another editor at Villard convinced her boss to take a flyer on it. This is a cold and capricious business. To make a living at long-form journalism you have to possess at least a modicum of talent, but it's perhaps even more important to be stubborn and determined and, above all, lucky.

Are you always so determined and stubborn?

No. One story I abandoned—after a lot of reporting and research—was about three antigovernment renegades in the Four Corners region who gunned down a cop with automatic weapons, in broad daylight on a busy street, in Cortez, Colorado, a few years back. The police chased the bad guys into the desert, where two of them eventually turned up dead. The third fugitive was never caught and might still be out there. I love spending time in the desert, and I had a wonderful time researching the story. I got to explore some beautiful slot canyons in remote parts of the Colorado Plateau, but the main subject of the story—the fugitive who may still be alive—wasn't someone I found sympathetic. He was a creep. The guy wasn't likeable enough for me to invest years of my life writing about him.

Is likeability a criterion in deciding whether to write about someone?

Not likeability exactly. Dan Lafferty certainly isn't very likeable and he's the central figure in *Under the Banner of Heaven*. But I found him complicated and intriguing. The main character in the fugitive story I abandoned lacked sufficient moral complexity and depth to sustain my interest. He was merely a pathetic, hate-filled young man. Although Lafferty is abhorrent in all kinds of ways, there are sides to him that I find fascinating, even sympathetic. He tells us some very disturbing things about ourselves.

What kind of research do you do?

Essentially, I grab a shovel and start digging hard, for a long time—in the case of *Under the Banner of Heaven*, I spent more than three years doing the research before I began to write. On a couple of occasions in the past I've hired private investigators to help me find elusive fugitives (in each case they failed), but I've never hired a researcher to help me with background for a book or magazine project. I enjoy doing the research—I enjoy it a hell of a lot more than writing. I always begin by combing library card catalogues, bookstores, rare-book dealers, the Internet, and newspaper archives. A sense of place—a familiarity with the particulars of the landscape in question—is always important to me, so I buy lots of maps.

For *Under the Banner of Heaven*, I spent a lot of time at Brigham Young University, the Salt Lake City Public Library, and the Utah State Historical Society combing through card files. The Mormons are such compulsive chroniclers of their past that any archive associated with Mormon history is crammed with a staggering amount of material.

I pay special attention to names or events that may help me connect disparate narrative threads. For instance, early in my research for *Under the Banner,* I learned that Dan Lafferty and his brother Ron had joined a group called the School of the Prophets, where they learned how to receive revelations from God—including the revelation in which God commanded them to slash the throats of their sister-in-law and her baby girl. So I read the school's sacred texts, unearthed the names of all of its members, and then looked for connections to some of the other narrative threads in the book. Thanks to my research into the School of the Prophets, I was able to draw solid connections between the Lafferty brothers, Colorado City, Elizabeth Smart, Joseph Smith, Brigham Young, and polygamous communities in Canada and Mexico.

Are there any particular resources you return to?

Trial transcripts are a gold mine of information. Usually you must purchase such transcripts directly from the court reporters, which is astoundingly expensive (I spent several thousand dollars on trial transcripts for *Under the Banner*), but they can be worth every penny. You learn things you won't find anywhere else. Individuals who you would otherwise have no hope of ever finding are subpoenaed to testify. And the transcripts often reveal where such individuals live, as well as other details about their lives. Transcripts are also a great source of narrative. Such narratives seldom resemble the one I construct, but the lawyers are each trying to tell a coherent story to advance their aims, and these competing narratives are frequently edifying.

Where, or from whom, did you learn to report?

I became a journalist in the early 1980s when I found myself broke and out of work—I was a carpenter at the time, and the construction industry had plunged into a bad recession. I had just gotten married, and my wife didn't have a paying job, either. I was so fucking desperate that I contemplated applying to law school—I went so far as to study for the LSAT. I was rescued from that fate by my friend and climbing partner, David Roberts, who had recently left academia to become first an editor at *Horizon* magazine, and then a freelance writer. He argued that journalism was "a lot more fun than pounding nails." He told me, "Magazines pay you to travel to interesting places and talk to interesting people. Just start doing it. You'll figure it out as you go."

I bought a book that taught me how to type with all my fingers, and then I bought another book on how to become a magazine writer. It was largely full of shit, but it did teach me how to write an effective single-page query letter, which is an invaluable art. You've got to write stylishly, use fresh language, and convey with extreme economy what's interesting about your idea. This how-to book suggested setting a quota and sending out something like ten queries a week, which I did. I didn't know anybody in the magazine industry, but I figured editors lower on the totem pole were more likely to read their own mail than the big cheese at the top, so I directed my query letters to them. My first query to *Outside* magazine resulted in an assignment on spec, as did my first query to *Rolling Stone*. It took a few tries to get into *Smithsonian,* but eventually I started getting assignments there, too.

How did you go from writing about climbing to writing about other topics?

I realized that I couldn't afford to write only for the adventure niche because there are too few outdoor magazines to give me enough work to live on. I had held many different jobs over the course of my short life, so I tried parlaying what I had learned in other spheres into writing assignments. I pitched a story to *Smithsonian* about a commercial herring fishery in Sitka, Alaska, where the entire season lasts *six hours* and yet can make a skipper and his crew filthy rich; I only knew about it because I'd worked on a fifty-eight-foot Alaska seine boat. I used what I'd learned building houses to write about architecture for *Architectural Digest*. For two or three years I wrote a monthly column for *Playboy* about health and fitness.

How would you describe your reportorial stance?

I try hard to be fair and objective, but if I care enough about a subject to write about it, I tend to have an agenda. There is almost always a case I'm trying to make, although I usually prefer to present it indirectly rather than beat readers over the head with it. I want to provoke people, to expose readers to unsettling truths. But I don't write polemics. No matter what the subject, I try to write with compassion and empathy.

For example, when writing *Under the Banner of Heaven,* I struggled with how to convey my respect for people with deeply held religious beliefs, while simultaneously advancing my ideas about the perils of unyielding faith. Although I'm an agnostic, I'm profoundly moved by demonstrations of religious devotion. When I hear people earnestly explain how prayer has transformed their lives, or I listen to, say, Emmylou Harris singing in her angelic voice about Jesus, I'm sometimes moved to the point of tears. I understand the ache to know God. I feel that same longing myself—I feel it down to my bones. But that doesn't deter me from reporting the venality that's so often committed under the cloak of piety. I admire many things about Mormons, and in *Under the Banner* I tried to express that admiration while at the same time sharply questioning some of the actions of the men who run the Mormon Church.

How do you pace yourself while reporting?

I tend to work until I crash and burn. The people I'm writing about will often invite me to stay in their homes, which can be incredibly valuable from a reporting perspective, but it can also be dangerous, because if I don't have a refuge to escape to, I'm likely to burn out prematurely. I generally prefer to spend six to eight hours a day with them, but then retreat to my tent or motel room.

You become so deeply involved with your subjects. How do you manage to maintain enough distance to write about them?

The writer-subject relationship is always fraught with thorny complications. Janet Malcolm's book, *The Journalist and the Murderer,* should be a required text in all schools of journalism. Her first line— "Every journalist who is not too stupid or too full of himself to notice what is going on knows that what he does is morally indefensible"—

is intentionally harsh and provocative, but contains more truth than most journalists admit. The writer *is* a confidence man. The journalist never has *any intention* of telling the story your subject wants told. Your job is to tell the story as you see it. Once a subject has talked to you, he has surrendered all control. For my own conscience's sake, I try to begin almost every interview by quoting Malcolm's infamous first line. I tell the person I'm interviewing that he'll have no control over the process, that I won't show the article to him before publication, that he will tell me things he'll regret . . . and none of that ever deters anyone!

What are the ethics of a situation like the one you found yourself in while climbing Mount Everest for *Into Thin Air*, when you were a participant in the activity you chronicled?

Those were odd circumstances. Two competing commercial expeditions courted me because they thought the resulting article would be good publicity. I made it clear to the owners of both guide services that if I came along, I would describe the ascent exactly as I saw it, and that they would have no control over what I wrote. The problem was that the leaders of the expeditions never told the other team members—their paying clients—that a journalist would be climbing with them. At first, most, maybe even all, of the clients were delighted I'd be documenting their climb of Everest. After things went horribly wrong, I did exactly what I always had said I'd do: I reported what happened. And that made some of the people I wrote about profoundly unhappy.

Although I still feel terrible about my complicity in the deaths of those who perished on Everest—and I think all of us who were up there that day share some blame for what happened—I don't feel guilty that I wrote about the disaster. I deeply regret that I ever went to Everest in the first place, but having gone, I'm glad I wrote the book. The fact that I was part of a commercial expedition made it easier to report with complete candor. It allowed me to describe the actions of other climbers without remorse. I was climbing with a group of individuals who for the most part felt no great bond for one another, each of whom had paid a huge amount of money to be led up the mountain. We were all there for our own selfish reasons. If I had been a member of a traditional climbing team, reporting what happened would have been ethically murkier. Two contradictory ethical responsibilities were at play: you can't be loyal to the basic standards of journalism—to tell the cruel truth as you see it—and at the same time be loyal to your fellow climbers. There's no way to rec-oncile these responsibilities. You have to be willing to be the worm in the apple if you want to do your job. I've had strangers walk up to me in the street and scream into my face that I'm an asshole. It's not fun. Routinely betraying the trust of subjects is but one of the conun-drums that shapes the difficult moral topography of journalism.

Do you have any particular ethical guidelines you work by?

I don't pay subjects for information. A subject will sometimes ask, "What's in it for me?" And I explain that if they decide to talk to me it will have to be for their own reasons, and they had better be good reasons, because what I write could turn their lives inside out. But as I said before, that little speech rarely deters anyone. I mean, hell, when I've been on the other end of the relationship—when journal-ists have interviewed me during my book tours—I've said things that came back to bite me in the ass. When someone sticks a micro-phone in our face, we are afflicted with this inexplicable compulsion to tell all.

Why is it so important not to pay for information?

The notion that writers should never pay their subjects is taught in every journalism school in the country and accepted unquestion-ingly as one of the Ten Commandments of our peculiar profession, but lately I've begun to wonder about it. It seems like such a self-serving axiom. I understand why paying subjects can corrupt the process, but on certain occasions it seems like subjects deserve to be compensated for their contributions to a book or article. I once addressed a seminar for mid-career journalism fellows who attacked me when I made this very point. I said, "I've made a boatload of money off of the books I've written. Don't you think I owe anything to some of my subjects, who got nothing for the crucial assistance they provided except, in some instances, unwanted publicity?" The journalism fellows were incensed and argued that paying a subject would compromise my integrity as a journalist. I was determined to shake their complacency. Writers for magazines like *The New Yorker,*

The Atlantic, Vanity Fair, GQ, and *Esquire* are quite well paid. Do they never owe anything to their subjects?

How have you worked through this moral quandary?

One thing I've done is buy one-time literary rights to a subject's letters or journals, or any other material to which he or she may own the copyright. I bought the rights to one Mormon fundamentalist's memoir. It was an unpublishable mess, and I didn't really need it since she had already told me everything in it. But she was dirt poor, and struggling to overcome some serious problems, and I wanted to compensate her for helping me.

. By the standards of our profession, it was entirely *ethical* for me to pay her $20,000 for the rights to her book, yet it would have been *unethical* for me simply to pay her $20,000 for talking to me. This strikes me as a self-serving stricture, a legalistic distinction that too often allows journalists to stiff their subjects. According to the accepted standards it's okay to buy a subject a nice dinner, but it's not okay to pay them cold hard cash? That's so patronizing. We have the right to enrich ourselves off of these people whose lives we may ruin, but we never, under any circumstances, owe them anything? Give me a fucking break. I grow impatient with smug, self-righteous reporters who refuse to consider the subjects' side of the argument simply because these reporters were taught in J-school that subjects should never, ever be paid.

What is your policy for using pseudonyms?

If I think that an innocent bystander's life is going to be upended by appearing in my book or article, I may elect to give them a pseudonym. If the subject is a minor, I will be even more inclined to do so.

Do you ever use the promise of a pseudonym to get someone to talk to you?

If it is the *only* way for me to get an interview, I'll sometimes offer to use a pseudonym. In *Under the Banner,* one of the key members of the School of the Prophets didn't want to talk to me. He'd served time in prison for a financial scam, was trying to put his life back together, and had no desire to be associated with an unsavory double murder. But this guy's inside knowledge was so important for my book that I told him that if he would consent to be interviewed, I'd give him a pseudonym. His friends and acquaintances in Utah County would no doubt figure out who he was, but his identity wouldn't be revealed to most of the world.

When you start a story, how do you decide whom to interview?

I contact every single person I've read about or heard about who has any connection to the story. I've learned that it almost always pays to check out every potential interview subject. Often, after conducting a whole bunch of long, exhausting interviews (most of which, inevitably, will not have been very useful) I've thought, "What is this next gal on my list really going to know? Why should I waste my time calling her?" But I make myself call her anyway, and the interview will turn out to be amazing. Remember, I almost didn't respond to Dan Lafferty's letter. What a mistake *that* would have been!

Do you prefer to approach interview subjects directly or via an introduction?

I've found that phoning from out of the blue can freak people out, so I like to approach a potential subject by letter, and maybe even send them copies of my books as a way of introducing myself. On several occasions the books have persuaded otherwise reluctant subjects to talk. They'll think, "Oh, this guy's no threat. He's just a mountain climber." A few people who have actually taken the time to read, say, *Into the Wild,* have been convinced by that book, in particular, to talk to me. The family of Dan Lafferty's victims decided to talk to me after reading it. They told me, "We thought you were very fair to that young man, Chris McCandless, so we decided we could trust you."

Where do you most and least like conducting interviews?

I hate interviewing people in restaurants. The background clatter makes it hard to transcribe the tapes, and the public setting can inhibit the subject. Too often he or she is worried about who might be eavesdropping at the next table. I prefer to interview subjects in their homes, or at a place with a strong connection to the story, or while driving. Driving is especially good if the trip is long and the road is relatively empty. On a long drive the subject is captive and maybe bored, and unexpected stuff is likely to pop out of his mouth. If the car is old and noisy, background noise can render a tape unusable, so you have to clip a lapel microphone to your subject's shirt, or let the subject hold the recorder in his or her lap while you drive. The latter can be good because it gives the subject a sense of power—he can turn the damn recorder off whenever he wants—which may embolden him to speak more candidly.

How do you get people to confide in you?

One of my gifts as a journalist is that, for some reason, people see me as innocuous and harmless. So people tell me all kinds of stuff that isn't in their best interest. A lot of people I write about have been marginalized in one way or another, like the Mormon fundamentalists, who live outside the norms of middle-class society. I was a carpenter and a fisherman in places like rural Colorado and the Alaska bush. I've pumped gas, worked in a psychiatric hospital, a tarpaper factory, a cannery. When I'm on a construction site I can talk about glue lams and sidewinder saws. I've spent a lot of my working life hanging out with people like that. I'm generally comfortable with them, and they in turn are comfortable with me.

Do you use any particular persona to encourage them to talk to you?

I'm a listener by nature. I grew up in a big family—three sisters, one brother—that was very contentious, with everybody jabbering all the time. I was the quiet one. My mom says that I was the kid with the Norwegian temperament (she's descended from Scandinavians). I can listen to women talk among themselves for hours. I don't go into an interview with a long list of questions. I just get my subject talking, make sure there are fresh batteries in the tape recorder, and sit back and listen. The interview takes the form of a pleasant, largely one-sided conversation.

How confrontational will you become during an interview?

I sometimes engage in good-natured debate. I'll say, "Really? Do you *really* believe that?" I won't outright argue with someone. In my experience, people don't generally need to be provoked. If they agree to talk to you, they really *want* to tell you what they believe. And I won't deceive someone about my agenda. With Dan Lafferty, I made it clear that I didn't agree with him and that I found what he did to be reprehensible, and it never slowed him down for an instant.

Do you only do interviews face-to-face, or will you do them via phone, letters, or e-mail?

Face-to-face interviews are invaluable, but they are so draining. The first time I interview an important subject, I like to do it face-to-face. Then I like to follow up with phone interviews. The initial meeting breaks the ice and makes the subject comfortable with me, but I've found that many people will talk to you more easily on the phone than they will in person. It may have something to do with being a disembodied voice. The interviewer isn't "there." It's the same reason that a psychoanalyst sits behind the couch, out of sight. Phone interviewing is incredibly efficient: you don't have to fly thousands of miles, rent a car, get a hotel room—all for a two-hour interview I might not use.

Letters are also a great way to conduct interviews. After I interviewed him in prison, Dan Lafferty and I had an extensive correspondence, which has been of incalculable value. For one thing, it helped me get the details right because everything was in writing. He has absolutely no remorse for the brutal things he did; he believes he was doing God's work. He wanted me to report what really happened, to get the facts right. Lafferty also happens to have a very personable side. In his letters he'd frequently ask about my wife and family, he'd inquire about my problems . . . and I'd have to keep telling myself, "Wait a second. This is a guy who calmly slit the throats of a blameless young woman and her baby girl."

Did you ever confront him with this discrepancy?

Yes, and he told me, "It's what God commanded me to do. And when God commands you to do something you'd better do it. You'll understand this someday, Jon, when the Judgment comes."

Do you take notes or use a tape recorder?

I do both, and I use my notebook and tape recorder like a professional photojournalist uses a camera. He doesn't wait for the "perfect" shot. He turns on his motor drive and shoots *everything*. He burns through rolls and rolls of film. So I try to tape every conversation I have with a subject. My notebook is always out. I'm like a human sponge. Anything that happens anywhere near me gets recorded, whether on paper or on tape.

I think a tape recorder is an important tool that is used too little in journalism, and I don't understand journalists who don't record their interviews. Sure, there are situations where you can't record—like when you're in the backcountry for weeks and have to use your batteries sparingly—but it is *always* better to tape if you can. I understand that newspaper writers facing daily deadlines don't often have time to tape and transcribe—it's an incredibly slow and tedious process—but magazine writers should tape more than they do.

I've conducted an experiment that I would encourage any journalist to try. Do an interview in which you simultaneously use a tape recorder *and* take notes by hand. Then transcribe your tapes and compare this to the handwritten record. I bet you'll find that you got many of the quotes wrong in your handwritten notes. Often you may get the intent or the meaning right, but you miss the idiosyncratic phrasing, the precise inflections, the unique qualities that make a quote ring true. Quotes not based on a taped interview often sound more like the writer than the interview subject.

Why take notes in addition to taping?

Because I don't want to miss anything. When I tape *and* take notes, the person I'm interviewing usually thinks I'm using the tape as backup. In fact, most of what I'm writing down are my observations: what the guy is wearing, the way his eyes dart, the nervous way he pulls at his earlobes. If I'm not using a tape recorder, I have to focus all my attention on writing down what the subject says, making it impossible for me to make these other crucial observations. I don't think anyone can do both things at once, no matter how fast they are at shorthand.

Not all of the notes I take during an interview are about the subject. I grew up admiring writers who could render landscape well, so I fill my notebooks with observations of the weather, the scent of the wind, what plants are growing in the vicinity. When I'm in the desert, I don't want merely to write that the subject "brushed against a cactus," I want my notes to show whether he bumped into a jumping cholla or an ocotillo cactus. If we are walking beneath towering cliffs, I want my notes to indicate whether the cliffs are Wingate sandstone or Navajo sandstone or Kaibab limestone. Details are important. When I'm at my computer writing the damn book, I want to have lots of stuff, telling particulars I can insert into the narrative.

What kind of a notebook do you use?

I rely on two kinds of notebooks. I have my "overnight" notebooks, which are thick, six-by-nine-inch spiral notebooks I use to write stuff down at the end of the day. And I always carry several small reporter's notepads that I keep in the back pocket of my jeans, or the breast pocket of a jacket. I always have a pen and a notebook at my fingertips. Stuff bubbles up in my mind when I'm walking or driving or climbing, and I want to be able to record it.

What do you write with?

I use a blue fine-point Pilot Precise Rolling Ball pen for taking notes and a red one for underlining important passages. When I was on Mount Everest I wrote in pencil, or with one of those "space pens" that will function underwater and in zero gravity. It was too cold for a tape recorder to work, and the subzero temperatures would have frozen the ink in an ordinary pen.

Do you transcribe your own tapes?

Yes, and it takes me forever. I transcribe them word for word, passage for passage. Lots of typos, but every word is there. It's an agonizingly tedious process, but I do it because I hear all sorts of things while transcribing that I didn't hear during the interview. At the time, I tend to be so focused on getting someone to answer my questions that I often don't hear the other, more important stuff he's trying to tell me, if I would only shut up and listen. The best material in interviews so often comes when the subject is *not* answering my questions!

*How do you organize your research and reporting material in
preparation to write?*

I keep a file folder for each interview subject, which holds a
printed copy of the interview transcript, my written notes, and any
press clips I've dug up. By the time I begin writing I will have stacks
of interviews, stacks of notebooks, and stacks of photocopies that
I've made of relevant articles and book passages.

Before I begin writing, I reread all my transcripts and notes,
underlining any useful passages. Once I'm done, I go back to the
passages I've underlined and tag them with sticky, colored plastic
flags in order of significance: red means most important, blue means
second most important, etc.

How much do you think about structure before you write?

A lot. But I don't think of structure in terms of chronology.
Chronological order often means nothing to me. It can be a really
stupid way to organize a book. I'm looking for whatever elements of a
story (character, dramatic events, the development of an idea) best
propel my narrative forward—no matter what those elements are, or
in what chronological order they occur.

For example, in *Into the Wild* (which I like better than anything
else I've ever written), people have told me I was crazy to start the
book with Chris McCandless's death. Doing so gave away the "ending," and utterly scrambled the chronology. But in my view it was a
powerful and effective way to bring readers into the story.

Do you make an outline?

Yes. There is no fucking way I could ever keep all the information
I've gathered for a book in my head. I have the opposite of a photo-
graphic memory: information flees my brain as quickly as it enters.
So I need a map to tell me what I've got and where it fits. The first
thing I do is make a very general outline. If I am writing a book, I
winnow my material down to the forty or fifty most interesting
scenes or incidents. And then I write a two- or three-line précis of
each scene. This fills three to five pages of a yellow legal pad. Each
page might have ten or twelve scenes, in no particular order.

I stare at this list long and hard, asking myself, "How can I shape this material into a story? How should I arrange these scenes to give the most weight to my ideas and at the same time keep the narrative flowing?" Then I take a single page of paper and outline the whole book, using only ten or twenty of the strongest scenes. Each of those scenes will become the basis for a chapter. Once I have that crude, overarching outline, I go back through all my material and figure out how and where to incorporate each of the remaining scenes into the designated chapters. The result is a preliminary flowchart for the book, a skeleton of a narrative, handwritten on perhaps six or seven pages. I pin this outline—the map that's going to lead me through the wilderness to my salvation—onto a bulletin board over my desk.

At this point I'm more or less ready to begin writing. I'll start with the first chapter, study my outline, then go back to my notes and transcripts and review all the relevant material, underlining and flagging more passages as I go. Then I make a much more detailed revised outline—a more accurate map—for a chapter, and write directly from that. I repeat this same process for each subsequent chapter.

My methodology requires me to go through my notes over and over again. I think there is great value in rereading your notes as many times as you can stand it. Late in the process, I often stumble on crucial quotes or information that appeared unimportant to me at the beginning.

Where did you learn to outline a piece like this?

Rock climbing. When you embark on a really big climb like, say, the Salathé wall of El Capitan, which rises three thousand vertical feet from the floor of Yosemite Valley, the enormity of the undertaking can be paralyzing. So a climber breaks down the ascent into rope-lengths, or pitches. If you can think of the climb as a series of twenty or thirty pitches, and focus on each of these pitches to the exclusion of all the scary pitches that still lie above, climbing El Cap suddenly isn't such an intimidating prospect. By following an outline I can focus on the chapter that's in front of me, without having to worry about all the inevitable problems to come. It makes writing a book much less terrifying.

Do you write and revise, or write through to the end?

I am not a good writer; I'm a good editor—at least when it comes to my own writing. So I have to get a bunch of junk down on the page and then rework it endlessly. I'm one of those perennially blocked writers you hear about. The first sentence is agony, and I rewrite that goddamn first sentence from the beginning every single day for weeks. It's not an efficient way to work, although it gets a little faster as I go along. I'll often spend a week writing the first few sentences, and then write the rest of the chapter in a few days.

Once you get going do you write quickly or slowly?

I'm a slow writer, except when circumstances demand that I write fast. I took three years to research and write *Into the Wild,* but I wrote *Into Thin Air,* a longer book, in just three months. When I got back from Everest in May 1996, I told everyone that there was no fucking way I was going to write a book about it—I was simply going to fulfill my obligation to write an article for *Outside* magazine, and then walk away from Everest for good. But when *Outside* published the article in September of that year, I realized that I was still obsessing over what had happened on Everest. Although the magazine had run my piece at eighteen thousand words, I felt like it wasn't enough space to tell the story right. Plus I'd gotten some facts wrong and felt it was important to correct them. So in September 1996 I signed a contract to write a book about the Everest disaster. I had already committed to join an expedition that was scheduled to leave for Antarctica on December 1, which left me less than three months to write the book. I estimated that it would be somewhere between ninety to a hundred thousand words. I wrote more than a thousand words a day, every day, for those three months, and delivered the manuscript the same day I left for Antarctica. The writing in *Into Thin Air* isn't particularly stylish or elegant, but the book has an immediacy and emotional honesty derived in large part, I believe, from the fact that I wrote it so quickly.

How do you pace yourself when writing?

I try to write at least six hundred to seven hundred words per day. I often fail to meet that goal, however.

Do you show your work to people as you write?

I don't show it to anyone until I have a draft completed and I feel that I'm going in the right direction. At that point, I show whatever I've got to my wife, Linda, who is a good, brutally honest critic. I may also show it to my main climbing partner, a writer and mathematics professor named Bill Briggs; my literary agent, John Ware; and my mentor, David Roberts. Roberts doesn't tend to like my writing—he's not a fan—so he's a particularly valuable reader.

What is your routine for a perfect writing day?

I used to have this fantasy of completing all my research and then moving to an isolated cabin in the mountains, where I'd wake up, write until noon, and spend the rest of the day climbing. Nothing remotely like this has ever happened.

The reality is that even though I'm not a morning person, I wake up at six and have breakfast with my wife, because she likes to wake up early. I get back to my computer by seven thirty and waste an hour or two fucking around with e-mail and reading the newspaper. When I finally get to work, I waste the next two hours writing the first sentence. Then I break for lunch and get really jacked up on coffee. At three in the afternoon I realize, "Shit, I haven't gotten anything done and the day's almost over!" Desperation kicks in and the words start to flow. I don't stop for dinner and I find it is two a.m.—but I've written my seven hundred words! My brain chemistry seems to kick in between late afternoon and three a.m.

Do you have to be anyplace in particular in order to write?

No, I can write anywhere. I learned to be flexible when I was having to write dozens of magazine pieces every year. I'd be out reporting one story and realize that another story was due the next day. So I'd find a library in, say, Phoenix, and write the piece there. I have a wonderful ability to focus. When I'm focused, I shut everything else out. My wife sometimes comes into my office and will have to shout to get my attention.

Still, I try to minimize distractions. I work in a nine-foot-by-nine-foot basement cubicle with a low, six-foot-five-inch ceiling. There is nothing to look at but my work. The one luxurious feature of my cubicle is an abundance of shelf and counter space. Instead of tall vertical stacks of books and papers, I now have many shorter piles spread over a much greater area. It's easier to find stuff, and the stacks don't topple over as often.

What kind of a desk do you use?
It's a U-shaped countertop built along three walls of my cubicle. When I sit down at my computer in the crook of the U, I feel like I'm at the helm of a submarine. But instead of being surrounded by dials and sonar screens, I'm surrounded by stacks of notes, transcripts, file folders, and books, all at my fingertips.

What kind of a relationship do you have with editors?
I rely on magazine and book editors, the good ones, to save me from myself. It doesn't take much to sink a book or article, and sometimes the deadliest material is the stuff the writer is most enamored of. Writers often fail to appreciate that removing 5 percent of a book can make that book *twice* as good.

What kind of an authorial presence do you strive for?
My instinct is to write in the third person, and keep myself off the page, but magazine editors almost always push a writer to work in the first person. They'll say, "We want the reader to see what you see, to smell what you smell, to feel exactly what you feel as you're out there getting the story." I sometimes enjoy writing in the first person because it gives me a wealth of material to work with (i.e., my entire personal history), although I have this fear that if I go to the well of personal experience too often, it may eventually run dry.

It feels safer to write in the third person—less exposed, less vulnerable—but sometimes including personal material enhances a book or article tremendously. For example, in *Into the Wild*, I included two first-person chapters about my experience as a headstrong young man who took a reckless solo trip into a mountainous corner of Alaska. I felt like I *knew* McCandless, and knew what he was trying to accomplish, so I used my own experience to argue, in a roundabout way, that he wasn't a nutcase. I was telling the reader, "You know, I was just as reckless and stupid as he was in my youth, and I wasn't suicidal. So perhaps *he* wasn't suicidal either."

Do you think that journalistic inquiry can yield truth?

I think it can shed light on the truth, but our understanding of the truth is always in flux and often contradictory. Although I may have my own sense of where the truth lies, and I always go to great lengths to report the facts as accurately as I can, I accept that nothing I write is ever going to be the last word. I nevertheless aspire to persuade readers to regard old truths in a skeptical light, and to at least consider other, newer perspectives that I believe have more merit.

Do you think of yourself as a New Journalist as Tom Wolfe defined it?

No. My work isn't much like Wolfe's. I don't have the skill, or the chutzpah, to attempt the literary fireworks that are his stock in trade. I think Wolfe's finest book, *The Right Stuff,* is absolutely brilliant— it's one of the seminal works of nonfiction written this century, certainly—but time hasn't been terribly kind to most of Wolfe's writing. Upon rereading his work today it can seem overly mannered and self-conscious, and sometimes completely over-the-top. When I was starting out I was more impressed by flashy writing—I thought what a writer said was less important than how he said it. Nowadays I'm inclined to applaud clarity, economy, and subtlety (to say nothing of substance) more than literary flash.

But Tom Wolfe and the other pioneers of New Journalism broke the ground that allowed me to write a book like *Into the Wild,* which isn't a flamboyant piece of writing by any measure, but does have some quirks that don't seem quite so weird and quirky in the wake of the New Journalists. In that sense I'm indebted to Wolfe's bold innovations.

What writers have influenced you?

I learned almost everything I know not only about reporting, but about the craft of writing in general, by reading luminaries like Joan Didion, Tracy Kidder, David Quammen, Richard Ben Cramer, Philip Caputo, Tom Wolfe, Edward Hoagland, Barry Lopez, Janet Malcolm, Neil Sheehan, Michael Herr, David Roberts, Tobias Wolff, Richard Ford, William Styron, Annie Dillard, John McPhee, Charles Bowden, William Kittredge, Paul Theroux, Joy Williams, Tim Cahill, Terry Tempest Williams, E. Jean Carroll, and Peter Matthiessen.

Whenever I would come across a passage by one of these writers that blew my socks off, I would read the sentences over and over until I understood what gave the writing such power. That's how I learned technique. I paid close attention to what these authors quoted and whom, where they went, what they observed. I studied how they began their books and/or articles, and how they ended them. Reading these writers is what I did instead of attending journalism school.

If there is an historic tradition of long-form nonfiction that you'd put yourself in, who else is in it?

There is of course no way to answer a question like that without sounding like a presumptuous ass. I will say, however, that I've been inspired by such notable writers as Bernal Diaz del Castillo, who in 1568 wrote *The Discovery and Conquest of Mexico*; Alexis de Tocqueville, author of the incomparable *Democracy in America*; Francis Parkman, the nineteenth-century prose stylist who wrote *The Oregon Trail* and *LaSalle and the Discovery of the Great West*; the underappreciated Russian explorer Valerian Albanov, author of *In the Land of White Death*; Wallace Stegner, who in my opinion was better at nonfiction than fiction (I think his finest books are *Beyond the Hundredth Meridian* and *Mormon Country*); the outspoken British historian Roland Huntford, author of *The Last Place on Earth* and *Shackleton*; and Michael Herr, author of the haunting Vietnam memoir *Dispatches*.

Your question brings to mind a quote from *The Adventurer,* by Paul Zweig, which I used as an epigraph in my first book, *Eiger Dreams*: "The oldest, most widespread stories in the world are adventure stories, about human heroes who venture into the myth-countries at the risk of their lives, and bring back tales of the world beyond men . . . It could be argued . . . that the narrative art itself arose from the need to tell an adventure; that man risking his life in perilous encounters constitutes the original definition of what is worth talking about."

Are you optimistic about the prospects for long-form nonfiction?

I'm as optimistic as one can be in this postliterate era, where culture the world over has been shanghaied by television. As a writer who found his voice by doing long, deeply reported pieces for magazines, I'm discouraged by the trend toward shorter and fluffier magazine features. On the positive side, the public's appetite for well-crafted nonfiction books remains strong. As a form of entertainment—as a source of pure, unalloyed pleasure—the best examples of literary nonfiction remain equal to the best novels, and far surpass all but a tiny handful of films. Moreover, a really good work of nonfiction can edify—and in rare cases even enlighten—in ways that fiction and film seldom can.

BY JON KRAKAUER:

Under the Banner of Heaven: A Story of Violent Faith, Doubleday, 2003
Into Thin Air: A Personal Account of the Mount Everest Disaster, Villard, 1997
Into the Wild, Villard, 1996
Eiger Dreams: Ventures Among Men and Mountains, Lyons & Burford, 1990

JANE KRAMER

J ane Kramer writes about two kinds of people: anonymous, marginal characters; and powerful politicians and business-men who are at the center of their world. But in both cases, Kramer's goal is the same: to explore the space between what's in their heads and what they *say* is in their heads. "It's in that space—that negotiated space—that you can find the person," she says. It is this talent for limning a character's inner reality, for ren-dering someone's subjective perceptions as well as their objective actions, that led *Newsweek*'s James N. Baker to describe Kramer as "a writer who combines the skills of a social historian with those of a novelist."

Kramer has split her forty years at *The New Yorker* between writing about America and Europe, alternatively leaving one and reintroducing herself to the other—a dialectic that keeps her per-spective toward each fresh and open. She has had an astonish-ingly productive career (nine books and hundreds of articles, essays, and reviews), all the more impressive because of the vari-ety of subjects and countries she writes about.

Her greatest talent is for writing concretely about enormous, abstract questions (the meaning of the Holocaust, the future of the American West, the function of art). "Ms. Kramer's methodol-ogy is to start at the grass roots and work upward, musing on an intriguing personality or a quirky situation; her generalizations fall not as sweeping declarations from the pulpit, but as astringent aphorisms, mordant throwaway lines," writes James M. Markham in his *New York Times Book Review* of *Europeans* (1988).

Kramer's favorite literary form is the profile. "I like looking at a larger story through a particular personal lens so that I'm not sim-ply analyzing or asking 'Whither the world?' I try to find the people within the larger story. I look for marginal figures who by defini-tion look at the world with the skepticism of a journalist. There is something almost collegial about looking at life through the eyes of another outsider," she says.

Jane Kramer was born on August 7, 1938, in Providence, Rhode Island. She received a BA in English from Vassar College in 1959, and an MA in English from Columbia University, where she studied seventeenth-century and contemporary English and American literature. Her first journalism experience was at *The Morningsider,* a free weekly run by two Columbia graduate students. This led to a job at the recently founded *Village Voice,* where she wrote feature stories about such people as Jane Jacobs and Marcel Marceau, and the life of downtown New York. These stories were collected in her first book, *Off Washington Square: A Reporter Looks at Greenwich Village, N.Y.* (1963).

Her *Village Voice* writing caught *New Yorker* editor William Shawn's eye, and she became a staff writer in 1964. Her second book, *Allen Ginsberg in America* (1968), grew out of her two-part *New Yorker* profile of the Beat poet. In 1969, Kramer accompanied her husband, anthropologist Vincent Crapanzano, to do fieldwork in Morocco. Kramer helped Crapanzano—interviewing Moroccan women was difficult for a Western male—and in doing so developed some of the reporting methods that would become her journalism's trademark: intensive interviewing, attention to detail, and nuance. "I became sensitive to the way people tell their stories, by the seemingly unrelated details that connect them. I learned how picking up on those details—noting precisely *where* and *when* people chose to start their own narratives—was what gave any richness to any account of their life then," she says. In addition to the article they coauthored for *The New York Times Magazine,* Kramer gathered material for a three-part series, and her next book, *Honor to the Bride* (1970), about the spiritual and legal machinations a Moroccan family undertakes to "reclaim" its thirteen-year-old daughter's lost virginity.

In the 1970s, Kramer began splitting her time between America and Europe, becoming *The New Yorker's* European correspondent in 1981. While Kramer wrote her share of articles about certifiably important events and powerful European leaders, she grew more fascinated with those who did not fit into the "new Europe," those who scratched out their lives—whether for economic or political reasons—in the nooks and crannies, the fault lines, of the continent. "She is, after years of experience, disgusted with the official 'Europe' which pretends that the west of the continent is just one happy extended family sharing a broad political view," writes Neal Acherson of Kramer's *Unsettling Europe* (1980) in *The New York Review of Books.* "She asks: 'What does "Europe" mean, then, if these nineteen or twenty million people are not included in the word?'"

Kramer first reintroduced herself to America in 1977, with *The Last Cowboy,* a portrait of Henry Blanton, a twentieth-century man clinging desperately to the nineteenth-century American myth of the cowboy—a myth largely sustained in movies. In it, she posed questions she would revisit in *Lone Patriot* (2002). "What is downward mobility in America? How do you get from the immigrant who succeeds to the immigrant who fails?" The book won the 1981 American Book Award for best paperback nonfiction.

Her second collection of European reports, *Europeans,* displayed Kramer's breadth with a pastiche of portraits of the infamous (Kurt Waldheim, Klaus Barbie) and the anonymous (Madame Goncalves, Kramer's concierge). "She fills her boat with individuals whose heritage, habits, and concerns are as different from each other's as they are from the Americans' who are her audience. Only Kramer's fine eye for detail, her wicked turn of phrase and a steady tone of surgical detachment unite her subjects," writes *The Washington Post*'s Jim Hoagland. Some critics felt Kramer's collections didn't hold up as books. "When we first read these pieces in *The New Yorker,* we mistook their stylishness, allusiveness, indirectness and learning for true depth. Now, old and cold, the articles stand revealed for what they are," complained Stuart Miller in the *Los Angeles Times Book Review.*

Kramer wrote *Whose Art Is It?* (1994), which won a National Magazine Award, when she returned from living in Paris and wanted to understand the culture wars that had been raging. It is the story of sculptor John Ahearn, a white Soho artist who has decided to live in the South Bronx. After receiving a commission to create public art for the neighborhood, he creates sculptures depicting some characters from the community, and thereby falls into a controversy more political than aesthetic. Kramer's questions—Who has the right to represent a community? What happens when one citizen's notion of celebration is another's notion of denigration?—are at the core of the debates over political correctness and multiculturalism. Kramer avoids the easy answers, scrutinizing Ahearn's motives as closely as his ideological opponents'. It is in the space between what each says and means that she finds her richest material. "[Ahearn] talks about making people in the South Bronx 'happy.' He does not easily admit that he needs to make them happy, or why he needs to make them happy, but anyone who really looks at the work he does in the South Bronx knows that his community—the people he loves and casts—is a wellspring for him, the source of a remarkable vision. He needs the Bronx because his art is important," she writes.

In *The Politics of Memory* (1996), Kramer collects six pieces, each of which asks a different question about the emergence of the "new Germany." Her piece about Peter Schmidt—an East German teenager whose lack of self-knowledge mirrors his country's anomie—is a good example of how illuminative the theme of marginality can be in Kramer's hands. "Peter says that maybe the problem of being East German, the pity of being East German, is that you are always at your best, and your clearest, standing at a wall or a border or a prison door, reflecting on the other side," she writes.

Kramer became interested in right-wing militias at the time of the Oklahoma City bombing, when she was, once again, returning from a long stay in Europe. "I had been covering the extreme right, among other things, in Europe for a long, long time. I had covered wars, I had covered fighting, I'd written about Le Pen, about neo-Nazis, and the most ghoulish and insane and hateful characters. And I was relatively untouched by that experience. But when it happened in my own home I was heartbroken, and it made me realize just how American I was, how tragic for me that collapse of promise was when it pertained to this country," she says. Kramer conceives of *Lone Patriot* (2002) as taking up where *The Last Cowboy* left off. "How did we go from someone like my father, an immigrant who believed he could be whoever he wanted to be, to a West where the myths of entitlement are established, the sorrow deepens, and the possibility of reinvention diminishes? What do you do when you get to the end of the line, you've reached the other end of the continent and there is nowhere else to go?"

What kinds of subjects are you drawn to?

I'm interested in cultural clashes and implosions. We live in a moment in which the world is suddenly as culturally complicated as the Roman empire. Vast migrations of labor have scooped up people from all over the earth and flung them together in the big cities of the West. Here, of course, we're *all* from somewhere else, we're *all* mixed up in parentage—each of us is a multiethnic world of conflicted and conflicting realities. That, for me, is the postmodern story. The really interesting story. And I like teasing one thread out of that vast story.

How do you find your stories?

I'm attracted to puzzling characters, to people I can look at and say, "If I understand this one person, I will understand something about this country or this moment in history or this experience."

For example, I wrote a profile of Peter Schmidt in the early nineties—he was the young East German political prisoner who'd been "brought West" right before the Wall came down ["Letter from Germany," *The New Yorker*, June 18, 1990]. When I started that story, I was on my way to Berlin and Bonn to talk to politicians for one of those boring "After the Wall, Whither Germany?" pieces, but I'd stopped in Hamburg to pick up a graduate student I had hired to help me. We were having dinner that night, going over schedules, and she casually referred to this odd guy Peter she knew. He had *nothing* to do with anything we'd been discussing. But something clicked. I said, "Tell me about Peter," and the moment she started talking, his story intrigued me and I wanted to meet him. And when I finally did meet him, I just stopped right there, in northern Germany. I canceled all my Berlin plans. Peter was so spiritually becalmed—almost paralyzed by his confusion. I thought that if I could discover what it was about East Germany that had produced Peter, and what it was about West Germany that was incapacitating him now, *that* would be the story I'd come to write.

Do you usually start with an idea?

Sometimes. The idea for *Whose Art Is It?*, my book about the American artist John Ahearn and his South Bronx bronzes, came to me while I was working in Paris in the mid-nineties. In Paris, the very ideas of "identity politics" and "political correctness," ideas that were very much in vogue then in America, were something of a joke. I mean, imagine a Paris artist identifying himself as an *"Afro-French"* artist for a museum show! It would be unheard of. The French aren't obsessed with "naming."

So, in Paris, I heard about all the peculiar debates about correctness raging in America. And when I went back to New York, and was looking for a kind of refresher course on the country—something I often did, coming home—I decided to write about them. I started asking friends and colleagues here if they knew any interesting "correctness" stories, stories that might say something about these negotiations of American identity. But people kept suggesting very abstract, very elite debates that were taking place in and around the academy.

Then, one night I was at a dance performance at BAM—talk about political correctness!—and ran into the mother of one of my daughter's school friends. She turned out to work for the city's Percent-for-Art program. I told her why I was back, what I was trying to do, and she asked, right away, whether I'd heard anything about John Ahearn and his South Bronx bronzes. The details she told me in *ten minutes* of intermission piqued my curiosity more than all the abstraction I'd been hearing for weeks and weeks.

Who do you most like writing about?

The people I write about have to be capable of carrying the narrative. They have to be people I can speak through, people whose voices I can use. I like writing about people who, by most "news" standards, would be considered marginal. I find that the perspective from the margins is usually much more telling—if you're interested in how power works—than any number of conversations with politicians and especially with important ones like presidents and prime ministers. I thought a lot about this when I was exploring people on the margins of established bourgeois life for my book *Unsettling Europe*. I think I must have realized back then the extent to which my fascination with margins had to do with women of my generation being, almost by definition, marginal to power, too. We had looked at the world from our own very marginal perspective. So perhaps it was natural for me, as a writer, to cultivate subjects who were, in one way or another, replicating my own distance from the center.

People at the *center* of power always present you with a well-crafted public self. They are propagandists for themselves. And, as I said, I'm more interested in character than in politics per se. I'm more interested in the context, the setting, of a life. In that sense, I'm probably a novelist manqué.

Is this why you so seldom write about celebrities?

Yes, I've deliberately avoided writing about people you would call celebrities because they leave me no freedom as a writer. There is nothing to create *from*. Because somebody famous is already, almost by definition, a finished product. Obviously, I also like people who have the time to talk with me at some length—which, of course, famous, powerful people usually don't.

Some of your ideas gestate for years. At what point do you know they are going to be stories?

If I'm lucky, from the beginning. But I have often to wait, sometimes for months, or even years, before a story is ripe—which is to say before the time is right to report it. For instance, I wrote one very long piece about symbolic anti-Semitic violence ["The Carpentras Affair," *The New Yorker,* November 6, 2000]. It began with a desecration in an old Jewish cemetery in Carpentras, in the Vaucluse, and it came with a history that had fascinated me from the minute I heard about it. But I didn't start reporting it right away because the town was very closed and hostile, and I decided to give it a year to cool down.

When I returned to Carpentras a year later, I was startled to see the extent to which the town was *still* closed. There was only one man, a local doctor, whom I could really talk to. So I pretty much gave up on it for another year. Without the kind of openness I needed, whatever I wrote was bound to be superficial.

Then one day—out of the blue, really—I got a letter from the doctor saying that he had come across one of my books, in translation, in a local bookstore, and had read it and liked it. He said that if I ever decided to come back to Carpentras, I could stay with him and his wife and family. He offered to introduce me to the town so that I would have the imprimatur I needed—this is of course crucial in any small French town, and especially a town in the south. I *raced* back to Carpentras to report the piece. And I kept going back. The finished story required a lot of waiting: nearly ten years!

Do you prefer long- or short-term projects?

Ideally, I like to work for about two months on a long piece and then *basta*! But that's ideally.

How many pieces do you work on at once?

I am constitutionally unable to work on more than one thing at a time. I certainly *follow* other stories while I'm working on something, but I've never been able to sit down to work on one piece in the morning, and then work on a different piece in the afternoon.

Once you decide to pursue a story, how much research do you do?

A lot of what you'd call my background research usually comes somewhere in the middle of a piece, and often at the end. I try to wait for the moment when I'm fluent in the vocabulary of the event or context or person I'm covering, and then I start doing that "serious" research into what other people have had to say.

How do you begin reporting a piece?

I plunge into the *characters*. I depend tremendously on those initial responses you have when you're really green, impressionable, and ignorant. My first impressions are often my most accurate impressions, because they are uncomplicated by, say, discretion, or friendship, or loathing, or rejection.

Is it best to approach people directly or through mutual acquaintances?

It depends. When I started working on *The Last Cowboy,* I knew that, given the famous male reserve of that West Texas cowboy world, it would be better to walk in the door under the umbrella of someone local, someone who had the cowboys' respect. It was a way to temper—or maybe the word is to "mediate"—my strangeness, my outsiderness, through that person's familiarity.

How do you convince people to talk to you?

Sometimes it's instant. They just start. Sometimes, it can be a long and very involved process. In the case of John Ahearn—John has become my friend, but at first he didn't want to talk to me at all. I understood that. He didn't want to jeopardize his relationship with his neighbors, who were his own subjects, in the South Bronx. Those people who were the source of his art and his energy, the models for his bronzes. When we finally did meet, I was getting ready to go back to Paris to do some work, and that was good—it gave him about five more months to decide.

When I returned to New York a few months later, I started going up to the South Bronx to see him, and then, gradually, to start meeting people in the neighborhood. They were such great, feisty characters. I fell in love with them all. Once John saw that, he said, "Okay, let's talk."

I also had to negotiate for a while with John Pitner, the head of the militia I wrote about in *Lone Patriot*. He was very nervous and cagey and wasn't going to talk to anyone he didn't know well. What finally helped my access to him—to his story—was the very same thing that had held me up to begin with. Pitner and the rest of the militia suddenly got arrested. And it turned out that a lot of the people he knew were something else: an FBI special undercover agent, an informer, an FBI agent posing as a real estate agent. And there I was, doggedly waiting around for him to talk to me—the only new person in his life who had never pretended to be anybody but herself.

How do you decide whom to interview first?

I tend to start with the people central to my story. And, of course, that list changes because every day new names emerge from the day's interviews, and I call those new names. And, also, when it comes to official people—by the time I talk to the police chief, I make sure I've talked to everybody who either loves or hates the police chief.

But what usually happens is that, as I go along, somebody I haven't seen yet becomes absolutely *necessary* to see in order to understand the story. When I can't go *one more day* without that person's input or information, I'll stop everything until I find him. Then, after those central interviews, I'll try to stop and talk to the people who might be more formally important but who are more peripheral to the story I'm telling.

Do you have a special method for interviewing peripheral characters?

Yes, I ask each of them the same questions. It's a kind of Rashamon tactic. I'm interested in what emerges about each person in terms of what he or she adds or subtracts from that basic narrative. I find it is *so* revealing when people lie. *Why* do they lie? *What* do they lie about? A better question might be, "What *don't* they lie about?"

Do you deceive them by pretending to know information you don't?

Being fluent in the vocabulary of any event is, to a great extent, a performance. And everything depends on how quickly you master that vocabulary. The object is to get people to assume that you know *everything*. That way, it's harder for them to write you off or deceive you.

Do you prepare your questions in advance?

No, I don't go into an interview with a list of questions. After I've gotten to know a character quite well, I will sometimes compile a list of those questions I've forgotten to ask. And I'm always making long lists of research questions I need answered.

Do you ever send your questions ahead?

In principle, I will *never* send written questions ahead. Nor will I ever let people vet their quotes. If you give a politician the opportunity to vet a quote, he'll change it. *Point final!* When I come into an interview, I like to psych out the subject. I don't want to give him the opportunity to prepare a "public self." I want to see what he's like when I first enter his office. Whether he is welcoming. Whether he is relaxed. Whether he is sexist or in any way condescending.

I'm interested in people at the moment their "cover" slips, when the seamlessness of their self-presentation slips and you can enter that margin of psychic space between who they are *inside* and who they are *outside*. It's in that space—that negotiated space—that you can find the person. That's fascinating to me, but maybe it's also a fairly cold-blooded pursuit.

I think that's why a lot of conventional journalism, unlike long-form nonfiction, gets blurry. The people writing it are either tired of investigating that "space" between in which image is created, or they are too identified with the power of the person they're writing about to know it's there.

What is your policy about changing names?

I will often ask to change names when my characters are private, unworldly people who don't truly understand what it means to have a journalist appropriate their life. It doesn't matter how often we've discussed what's going to happen—that their names and quotes and stories are going to be published in a magazine in New York—in the end I make the decision that's morally comfortable for me. I'm speaking now of people who've said, "Go ahead, use my name."

Then there are cases in which I'll change a name for reasons of safety. I wrote a piece about an Afghan woman refugee who was tortured, and she was quite terrified of repercussions in Afghanistan, and also, I know, about how inconsistencies in her own story might imperil her application for asylum. So I changed her name ["Letter from Europe: Refugee," *The New Yorker,* January 20, 2003].

Sometimes subjects *feel* themselves in danger, even though they actually aren't. This happened when I wrote about Peter Schmidt. His mother, who had lost *everything* to the Stasi—her husband, her son, her daughter—was terribly scared. She could not believe that the Stasi weren't coming back. Never mind that the Wall had fallen and East Germany had, for all intents and purposes, ceased to exist. She asked me to change her name. And of course I did.

The ultimate question is: What best serves your journalistic purpose? Is it the name? Or the freedom to tell the story without you or your subject worrying about what will happen?

How much of a subject's time do you require for a piece?

There is no set *amount* of time. The rhythm of the interviews determines that. There are some people whom you have to *swallow* very quickly. Peter Schmidt, for example. I did the bulk of my interviews with him in a week of intensive, day and night interviews. I knew that if I let go he'd get scared and retreat psychologically.

The rhythm is the key. If I see someone too soon after the last interview, that person might retreat. Or if I stay an hour too long, or schedule one session too many, that person may become bored or irritable.

I once wrote a story about a spinster in Burgundy who owned this priceless little patch of vineyard. She had been courted by every vintner in the area. She had lived through some amazing things, and had had a remarkable, totally eccentric but somehow totally French life. I stayed in her town for over a month on just one of my visits, because Armande—that was her name—had a certain *rhythm*, which you could call the rhythm of her interest in me. There were times when she'd be delighted to see me, but I also knew, if she got too prickly by the end of the day, that I would have to say not "See you tomorrow" but "See you next week." By "next week," she would miss me.

How do you begin an interview?

If it's a profile, I like to spend at least one visit discussing the occasion for the piece: why I'm there, what puzzles me, what the person I'm interviewing thinks about whatever it is that's happened. Then I make it very clear, very quickly, that I'd like to come back and *really* talk about their life. I want to know *where* they decide to start their story. I take them back as far as they'll go, to as far away as imagination or memory lets them go.

Taking down life histories is really the key to my research. The history may have very little to do with the subject at hand, but it's crucial to the eventual piece. Even if I don't use that information directly, the persona that emerges from this kind of narrative coherence is a priceless guide.

For instance, once, in Morocco, I was interviewing a woman who was ill, and who told me her illness began before she was born, when her grandmother crossed a grating on the street in what was a particularly taboo way. And, obviously, what I realized was that this woman had a notion of causality completely different from mine. She believed that her misfortune had actually started fifty or sixty years earlier.

How much do you reveal about yourself during an interview?

I exchange a great deal of information with people during the first encounters. There's no way to be a blank slate in the kind of intimate conversations I want to have. Nor do I think it is *personally* very decent to be unforthcoming, especially with people with whom I'm in some sort of sympathy.

Are your interviews generally conversational?

Yes. I try to get conversations going and, if I'm lucky, they take on their own shape and form. That way, I can observe how a particular person improvises. I learn more about the person I'm interviewing that way. Although in a *real* conversation I'm a lot more straightforward about my opinions.

So you deceive your interview subjects?

To say that what journalists do isn't in some way ruthless would be to lie. Within fairly strict moral limits, I will use *any* way available to me to get at a story. In other words, if I'm talking to a reactionary, I don't necessarily start arguing from my own liberal bias. But if I get to know that reactionary fairly well, I will probably start arguing, but never to the point where the interview is threatened.

How important is establishing a good rapport with a subject?

It doesn't matter whether it's the president of a country or the concierge of an apartment—*everything* depends on the kind of rapport you have. The rapport needn't necessarily be a *friendly* one. It can be hostile, as it was when I interviewed Le Pen. He was incredibly nasty to me.

Let me put it this way: my most effective persona is the one who "agrees" with you *completely*. I sat there with Le Pen saying, "Oh, that's really *interesting*. I never thought of it *quite* that way . . ." I deliberately come across as credulous.

Are you ever confrontational during an interview?

Yes, but not when I'm reporting in preparation to write a piece of journalism. I've been more confrontational when I've been on fact-finding missions for the Committee to Protect Journalists. These result in reports to the Committee. I am usually traveling with a male colleague, and we badger people. And I've always been amazed at the male confrontational role and how men seem to get away with that.

I think younger women today are *expected* to be as confrontational as their male counterparts. But women of *my* generation were taught to *cajole*. We weren't supposed to argue with a man, to get what information we needed by way of confrontation. I think my inability to be confrontational in a nervous-making situation is a direct result of being a well-brought-up young woman from a Quaker school in Providence, Rhode Island.

Do you *ever* correct your interview subjects?

This was something I had to deal with when I wrote about the militiamen. They were so delusional, so misinformed about so many basic facts about the world, that I couldn't help myself. By the end, I almost *had* to argue with John Pitner. I would take out an encyclopedia and turn to a copy of the U.S. Constitution. I'd say, "Look, *here* is the Thirteenth Amendment, which you say doesn't exist." And he would reply, "No, this encyclopedia was published by the New World Order. I know for a *fact* that the Thirteenth Amendment was never passed." I finally gave up. There is no way to have that kind of conversation with someone who has bought into a conspiracy theory. It was maddening.

Do you conduct interviews face-to-face, by phone, by e-mail?

I don't mind getting basic information over the phone, but I don't even really like to do that. I always try to do even the shortest interviews face-to-face. And I hate having to quote someone I haven't met. It makes it almost impossible to know if they're bullshitting.

Do you tape or take notes?

I usually use my old messy longhand. I am addicted to these very precisely-sized notebooks: lined tablet notebooks that are small enough for me to slip into my handbag, but big enough to write a lot in. Then again, small enough so that the person you're talking to can't look over your shoulder and see what you're writing.

Taking notes is a kind of editing process in itself. I write down only what I must, at some level, be hearing as important or notable. The conversation gets distilled into what *I* think of the person I'm listening to, *as* I'm listening.

There are exceptions to this, of course. The best example I can give you is Allen Ginsberg. I was taking Allen's life history for my book about him, and his *voice,* the way he expressed himself, was so particular that I didn't want to lose it. Even if I was going to quote directly from my written notes, I wanted a record of his absolutely exact phrasing.

How do you know you've done enough interviews for a piece?
When I begin to hear the voices in my head. When I know exactly what a person will say next. When I start repeating my questions. Then it is time to leave.

What is your writing routine?
I wake up at seven thirty, and can't start working until I've had a lot of juice and coffee and completed the crossword puzzle— another form of procrastination. I do the puzzle in ink, with a lot of crossing out. Then I walk the dog. It takes me a long time to get from the bed to my desk. I do my best work when nobody is in the house: the day is mine, the house is mine, the rhythm is mine.

Does it matter where you are when you write?
Absolutely. I have to squirrel myself away in a familiar place. And when I move, whether for the summer or for a trip, it always takes me a while to feel comfortable enough to write. Even if it's a familiar place, I always have to factor that lost between-time into my schedule.

Do certain stories require that you be in certain places?
Yes. I prefer to be *exactly* where my story is *not* taking place. For anything long—I'm not talking about those Europe short letters—I cannot write where I've been reporting. The hardest thing for me is, say, to be in New York while writing about New York. Or in Italy writing about Italy. I've done it, but it is hard. I like to think I'm so sensitive that I have to put an ocean between myself and my subjects.

The truth is that I need to be somewhere else to sort out my perspective, to know where *I* am in relation to the material. If I am writing about Germany, the forests and trees look different there than they do when I'm back in New York. The balance of a story becomes more apparent when I'm at a remove. I'm able to become obsessed with my *own* obsessions, as opposed to the obsessions of the people around me when I'm reporting. It helps me get back into my own head.

What do you do once you've completed your research and interviews?

The first thing I do is to type all my written notes—of which I have far too many—into the computer. That takes a great deal of time. It's a form of procrastination, like the puzzle, but it's also a way to settle my thoughts while I'm typing away on a kind of automatic pilot.

Do you annotate these notes while you type them?

I flag really important sections with asterisks. I have a method, sort of like Michelin restaurant ratings. I rate things in order of importance, using anywhere between one and four stars. But the problem is that by the end I'm convinced that *everything* said was priceless, so I add too many asterisks to too many points. I increase the number of them, and then make every point more important than the one that came before!

Do you make an outline before you start writing?

Not really. I just start working on the opening of the piece and let it talk to me. The outline won't be much more than a list of the topics I want to cover.

What do you do once you've entered your notes?

I immediately go into a *frenzy* of cooking. I cook compulsively whenever I'm laboring over an opening. Maybe because it's in the opening that I try to settle my themes and plant hints about the things I'll take up later. I want all these elements simmering in the reader's mind so that she won't be shocked when she gets to them.

Do you cook any particular dishes?

I make dishes that take a lot of looking after: stirring, watching, changing the heat. My study is right next to the kitchen, so I go into the kitchen and stir the pot and mull over my thoughts. Writing is like cooking in that all the recipes you have in your head get distilled through *you*. So when you finish cooking *your* meal, it is something that nobody else could have cooked. That's so similar to the way I feel about writing that it's become how I get from the information in my head to the voice that, I hope, is me. Early in my career, I used to write by my stove. As a result I spend half my life quite thin and half my life on a diet!

How much do you think about the sound of the language while you write?

I keep the sound of the words in my head when I'm writing the opening section. I think of it as "composing" an opening in a musical sense. I think of the rhythms: *When* I want the reader to pause. *When* I want to flip an idea on its head. I love putting together a sentence that takes off, makes nice little loops, circles its assumptions, qualifies itself, and then ends up surprising me with its finale.

Do you print sections as you write?

No, because if I print out the text the process bogs down. The only way I can gain the necessary momentum is by plowing through. Then, I begin every day by reading over what I've written so far—at least until there's too much there to make that practical.

What do you do once you have a draft?

Once I've edited my draft, I change the file's indentation and font size to create skinny little columns that look *exactly* the same as *The New Yorker*'s columns. It unfamiliarizes the writing for me; I can pretend a stranger has written it. Everything becomes clearer, and I can read myself more—the word is "professionally." I can cut, I can restructure. It gives me that necessary *break* between the me who wrote it and the me who is reading it and saying, "God, how could *anyone* have written this?"

Is the experience of writing a short piece very different from writing a long one, or from writing a book?

When I first started writing the "Letter From Europe," in the 1970s, I wrote at a very fast clip of perhaps one a month. They were never more than three thousand words and that was an easy rhythm for me. And very long pieces are an easy rhythm for me as well.

But where I have problems is with anything between, say, six thousand and twelve thousand words. How do you *build* a character in that space? How do you tell a rich story? It's like learning a whole new stylistic discipline. *The New Yorker* is different. I don't have thirty-five thousand words the way I used to ten years ago. Today I have, perhaps, eight thousand words. The odd thing is that, while the pieces have gotten *shorter,* I have found that it takes much *longer* to write them!

Do you require a certain number of words from yourself per day?

No. I lack the discipline of accepting that it's *over* for the day. Even if the words aren't coming, I will sit there in my study all day long, ruining my life. I *will not* let myself go out and do something enjoyable. I *will not* say, "To hell with this!" and take a walk in Central Park. It's a form of self-chastisement. My dream is to know when work is over, and then to stop.

What do you do once you've written your opening?

After that, I let the story go along, depending on where it takes me and what I'm thinking about. But I *know* where I'm going to *end* the piece. That is my lodestar. That is what keeps me on track. For instance, the Afghan woman I wrote about is someone whose cause I'd fight for, but whom I really don't like. She was seeking asylum status, which—for legal reasons—required a certain amount of self-invention. The problem is, I need to feel I *know* her in order to plead her cause, and yet I knew I couldn't know her in any real way. So I had the moral and professional conundrum of how to draw a portrait of someone who is "unknowable" and not very likeable and at the same time very worthy. That idea, that question, became the subject of the piece.

Do you talk about your pieces while writing them?

It depends. There have been times when I've been *so* excited about something I'm working on, and have talked about it so much, that I've lost the freshness, and have had to put it aside for a while, just to get excited again.

Does your method differ depending on which country you are in?

Yes, there's a huge variety of style in the different countries in which I work, and you have to adjust your reporting techniques to them accordingly. For instance, I recently wrote a piece about counterterrorism in Germany ["Letter from Europe: Private Lives," *The New Yorker,* February 11, 2002]. It was hard to write, but not really difficult to report because it's not a problem to sit down and have a really good conversation with most German politicians. They are very straightforward, well educated, and familiar in an American sort of way. But in France, the politicians are quite *correct,* and they establish a hierarchy immediately. The style of French politicians is to make you feel about two inches tall.

How do you report when you don't speak the language?

The most important thing is to get the right interpreter. I never use professional interpreters. I always work with students because they're easy to be with and unthreatening. They don't have that smack of hierarchy or officialdom. I want somebody who is warm, who can wear jeans and sit on the floor with me. And I want somebody I can bully. I want to know *exactly* what the person I'm interviewing has said. I do *not* want the translator's precis, I do *not* want a summary, I do *not* want a tidying up of language. I want it *word for word.*

When I'm interviewing via a translator, I tend to get *extremely* sensitive to tone, body language, intensity of voice—to any clue I might have to someone's character. Sometimes I simply observe characters, even if I don't understand a word they're saying.

What kind of authorial presence do you strive for?

I prefer not to be a character in my pieces. I like to establish my voice by the way sentences are constructed, the way statements are queried, stylistically, as they are being made. I like to get in between my characters—invisibly—and establish my presence that way.

I put myself in a piece only when it seems to me important to tell the reader where I stand and how I see things. For instance, in the late 1980s, I wrote about a revolutionary Portuguese general, Otelo, who I was immensely attached to ["Letter from Europe: Lisbon, November 19," *The New Yorker*, November 30, 1987]. He got to know my family and we became friends. I wanted my readers to understand the emotional context I was writing in. Otelo was very ideologically unsophisticated, and I wanted to make sure the reader knew that I wasn't looking down on him, or making fun of him, when I described him. So I brought myself into that piece.

Why are so many of your pieces profiles of one kind or another?
I like looking at a larger story through a particular personal lens so that I'm not simply analyzing or asking "Whither the world?" I look for marginal figures who by definition look at the world with the skepticism of a journalist. There is something almost collegial about looking at life through the eyes of another outsider. It gets me into the *juicy* pleasure of writing. Plus, it's not so different from what novelists here do: try to find one protagonist with one story which will be emblematic of the whole American picture. This is a very *American* fantasy.

You once said that long-form nonfiction journalism is a peculiarly American form. Why do you think this is?
I think it comes out of the English-American novel, the great social novels—out of that particular tradition of the novel of social life which is peculiar to England and America.

I've always been mystified by French contemporary nonfiction. The French have had such a great narrative and such a great critical tradition, and seem to have lost them both. Think of the French essay tradition—the essays of Montaigne and Voltaire and Montesquieu—and the fact is that you cannot read a piece of criticism anywhere near that level in France today. The same is true of the narrative tradition.

In England, a lot of what narrative nonfiction does began with Orwell. But in America, the country's history and temperament is such that the big quest was for the "emblematic" American story.

The story of liberty and immigration and settlement and expansion. Which, of course, has created the myth of the holy grail of the great American novel—the conviction that this is a country so vast that nobody has grasped it, but maybe *I* will. American novelists really do believe that there is some story out there that will explain America. Maybe nonfiction writers have inherited that quest.

Do you believe journalism can lead to truth?

I don't know. I dig hard, and because I keep returning to places I know well, maybe I come to believe I understand them. But so much of what a journalist today writes gets cut in the editing process, and those decisions—what do I cut, how to I fill the gap— are often made on the fly, under constraints of space and closing schedules. So I wonder whether you can even talk about "truth." What would have been "truer" would be the whole piece. What gets printed is often a bit skewed because, while it may track better shorter, it lacks that awkwardness of puzzlement or confusion that might have made it more "true."

Do you consider yourself part of the "new," "literary," or any other tradition of journalism?

It isn't something I think about. There certainly *is* something that sets the people like us—the people you're putting in this book—apart from the people who do straight reporting. The literary nonfiction writers I like are distinctive because they are *stylists*. There is no way you can read a piece by Joan Didion and imagine that anybody else wrote it, and the same goes for Tracy Kidder, Bill Finnegan, etc.

On the other hand, the difference between what we do and what novelists do is that we have different parameters. We've accepted a different set of rules, we have a different contract with reality. We are committed to not making anything up. That said, our project is the same as that of anyone who is setting out to write a novel or a short story.

How did you learn to be a reporter?

The person who probably taught me the most about reporting, way back when I was in graduate school studying literature at Columbia, was R. W. Apple, now of *The New York Times*. He lived down the hall from me and was already quite a glamorous figure in that he had a real salary and could buy you dinner. He had worked at *The Wall Street Journal* and was then writing the *Huntley/Brinkley Show.* I went to him for advice. He had hard, cold, journalistic advice. Such as: if you can't figure out how to get that sentence right, throw it away and write a new sentence. That was the *best* advice I ever got. I labored way too much over my sentences.

In many ways, I learned the most about journalism from my husband, who isn't a journalist. He's an anthropologist. Right after we were married, we moved to Morocco to do fieldwork, and while we were there I ended up taking a lot of life histories from women. I became sensitive to the way people tell their stories, by the seemingly unrelated details that connect them. I learned how picking up on those details—noting precisely *where* and *when* people chose to start their own narratives—was what gave any richness to any account of their life then.

What writers and editors have most influenced you?

Mr. Shawn could look at forty pages of mine and say, "The adjective in the middle of page thirty doesn't sound like you." I had great help finding my voice when I was starting out.

When I first got to *The New Yorker,* I was profoundly intimidated by the efficiency of a lot of my colleagues. I shared an office with Edmund Wilson, which was truly terrifying. I was so in awe of Wilson that it was very hard to ask him, "Are you going to be using the office today?" The only person who wasn't flustered was my mother, who used to give him long messages for me. Mary McCarthy was another influence. Almost a mother-figure to me. We used to talk at great length about questions of morality in our work—questions of betrayal, questions of ruthlessness. We talked about how to accept the implications of what we did.

Are you optimistic about the future of long-form nonfiction?

It is a question of venue—of having enough magazines devoted to that form. If nobody can make a living writing the way people like me do, then nobody is going to try. More and more, literary nonfiction exists only in books, not magazines. But it isn't a talent that can be honed in a garret. It needs constant, and often expensive, engagement with the world. It is such a thrilling American form, and has produced so many wonderful voices, that if it goes it will be a tragedy.

BY JANE KRAMER:

Lone Patriot: The Short Career of an American Militiaman, Random House, 2002

The Politics of Memory: Looking for Germany in the New Germany, Random House, 1996

Unter Deutschen, Tiamat, Berlin, 1996

Whose Art Is It?, Duke University Press, 1994

Sondebare Europäen, Die Anderen Bibliothek / Eichborn, Frankfurt, 1993

Eine Amerikanerin in Berlin, Tiamat, Berlin, 1993

Europeans, Farrar, Straus and Giroux, 1988

Unsettling Europe, Random House, 1980

The Last Cowboy, Harper & Row, 1977

Honor to the Bride Like the Pigeon That Guards Its Grain Under the Clove Tree, Farrar, Straus and Giroux, 1970

Allen Ginsberg in America, Random House, 1969

Off Washington Square; A Reporter Looks at Greenwich Village, N.Y., Duell, Sloan & Pierce, 1963

WILLIAM LANGEWIESCHE

Most Americans were traumatized by the terrorist attacks of September 11, shocked by the kind of chaos and destruction they associate with distant lands. *Atlantic Monthly* national correspondent William Langewiesche was not. "After years of traveling through the back corners of the world, I had an unexpected sense not of the strangeness of this scene but of its familiarity. Wading through the debris on the streets, climbing through the newly torn landscapes, breathing in the mixture of smoke and dust, it was as if I had wandered again into the special havoc that failing societies tend to visit upon themselves. This time they had visited it upon us."

Within hours of the attacks, Langewiesche was on the phone with his editor, discussing how he should cover the story. He flew to New York and tried to determine how to get access. At police headquarters, he found that only limited-access press passes were available, and even those were difficult to come by. He and his editor sent two faxes, one to City Hall and one to Kenneth Holden, the commissioner of the little-known Department of Design and Construction. It turned out that not only was Holden an enormous fan—both of the writer and *The Atlantic Monthly*—but he had read several of Langewiesche's books. "He is very interested in how things work, and how people relate to processes," Holden told the *Columbia Journalism Review*. "It seemed like it would be a very good fit." Holden gave Langewiesche unlimited access to the site and all meetings concerning the physical cleanup—making him the only journalist with such privileges.

One year later, *The Atlantic Monthly* published three installments of "American Ground," the longest piece of original reporting (seventy thousand words) the magazine had ever run (the book version appeared in October 2002). In it, Langewiesche chronicles the dangerous and complicated task of "unbuilding" some of the largest structures in the world. With no master plan, no memos or organizational chart, thousands of engineers, construction workers, policemen, and firemen cleared the World Trade Center site of 1.5 million tons of rubble, twisted steel, and human remains. The dismantling, rather than the destruction, of the WTC became his metaphor for national exceptionalism—the peculiarly American combination of resilience and ingenuity.

In writing about the World Trade Center disaster, Langewiesche used the same tools—an unsentimental perspective, prodigious reporting, a stark prose style, a near-omniscient tone—he had employed for his *Atlantic* assignments all across the globe. Langewiesche's sensibility—which he calls "the aerial view"—is a democratic view that looks at mankind "as creatures struggling through life on the face of a planet, not separate from nature, but its most expressive agents." If the WTC disaster was more horrific than the downing of an airplane or a distant war, for Langewiesche they were differences of degree, not kind. Some praised his frank approach, while others accused him of being cold and even callous.

Langewiesche decided to be a writer when he read John McPhee in high school. His father, Wolfgang Langewiesche, was a pilot and the author of *Stick and Rudder,* a 1944 classic on flying techniques. William spent much of his youth in airplanes and first flew alone at age fourteen. He graduated from Stanford University in 1974 with a degree in anthropology and moved to New York, where he worked for *Flying* magazine. Langewiesche didn't like the insularity of the New York magazine world and left it to become a professional pilot, spending the next fifteen years flying cargo planes, air ambulances, air taxis, and corporate jets.

He continued to write magazine articles on the side and in 1990 submitted two pieces about Algeria to *The Atlantic Monthly.* The editors liked his writing and, while they didn't publish those pieces, they gave him an assignment about North Africa, which became his first book, *Sahara Unveiled* (1996).

During the next decade, Langewiesche wrote a series of lengthy, eclectic *Atlantic* articles: "The Shipbreakers," a report from Alang, India, where massive ships are torn apart by hand and turned into scrap metal; "The Million Dollar Nose," a profile of influential wine critic Robert Parker; and a number of pieces that benefited from his knowledge of aviation. In 1998 he wrote about ValueJet 592, which crashed into a Florida swamp and killed 110 people. Using skills that presage his WTC reporting, he persuaded the investigators to allow him into the crash site, even convincing one helicopter pilot to let him fly. His exhaustive investigation in the "The Crash of EgyptAir 990," which showed how a pilot's intentional act led to the deaths of 217 people, won a National Magazine Award in 2001.

If all *American Ground* had done was tell the story of the cleanup project, it would simply have joined the ranks with hundreds of other faithful accounts of the tragic disaster and its aftermath. Instead, Langewiesche used the occasion to pose some uncomfortable, perhaps taboo, questions. He felt that the notions of tragedy and heroism had become part of the default vocabulary for all commentators. Firefighters and others working on the cleanup "though ferociously dedicated to a grim and dangerous task, were simply not involved in heroics," he wrote. By using the word so loosely, it had been divested of meaning. "The image of 'heroes' seeped through their ranks like a low-grade narcotic. It did not intoxicate them, but it skewed their view."

The response to *American Ground* was mixed, with critics like *The New York Times*'s Michiko Kakutani calling it a "weirdly voyeuristic book." In her view, Langewiesche had given too much weight to the engineering project, and not enough to the tragedy itself. Others, like Jeffrey Goldberg, writing in *The New York Times Book Review*, perceived it as "an antidote to the overwhelming saccharinity of the recent September 11 commemorations." For Goldberg, one of the most valuable characteristics of the book was Langewiesche's decision to reject pathos in favor of "truth, unclouded by sentiment." Writing in *The New York Review of Books*, Michael Tomasky echoed Goldberg: "Unlike much of the writing about ground zero, there is a freshness of perspective in those sentences, owing largely to Langewiesche's determination to approach September 11 not as the one great cataclysm of American history but as just another part, albeit a big one, of the long history of human struggle, and of man's attempt to impose order on disorder."

One passage in particular from *American Ground* drew an enormous amount of criticism. In it, Langewiesche describes a scene in which a fire engine is found crushed under the ruins, "filled with dozens of new pairs of jeans from The Gap, a Trade Center store." "It was hard to avoid the conclusion," Langewiesche writes, "that the looting had begun even before the first tower fell, and that while hundreds of doomed firemen had climbed through the wounded buildings, this particular crew had been engaged in something else entirely."

A New York art historian and sculptor, Rhonda Roland Shearer, whose Spring Street studio was near the towers, immediately attacked the book, setting up a Web site to detail alleged errors and establishing an organization to create an alternative history of the disaster. George Black, an independent journalist, wrote a fifty-page report, using maps, satellite data, and aerial photographs to argue that Langewiesche's description couldn't possibly be true.

Langewiesche replied that although he did not himself witness the scene, it was based on the testimony of those who had been present, and was reliable. In the May 2003 issue of *The Atlantic Monthly* he conceded that while "it is clear that the passage has been misinterpreted by many as an accusation . . . some of the misinterpretation may also be due to an unintentionally ambiguous choice of wording." He added that the passage concerning the truck and the jeans would be amended in the paperback version of the book.

In November 2003, Langewiesche returned to the aerial view with an examination of the factors that caused the *Columbia* shuttle to explode over the Southwest. His fifth book, *The Outlaw Sea: A World of Freedom, Chaos, and Crime*, was published in September 2004.

What do you like writing about?

If there's a unifying theme to my work, it is that the "small world" idea is a myth, a serious misreading of our times. It's obvious why it exists—jet travel, the Internet, the globalization of markets, the similarity of hotel rooms. But these are largely superficialities. The real world—of the history-making kind—simply is not defined by the ease and speed with which people can flit around the globe.

So what is the reality?

The reality is that the world remains enormous, and in important ways it is getting larger and more "foreign" all the time. This is because the real size of the world is defined not by physical geography, but by human constructs. From that perspective—I mean the way that individuals experience their surroundings and lives—the world is becoming more complex and varied all the time. And even the apparently unifying penetration of foreign cultures by, say, American television, movies, and advertising, turns out to be pretty superficial.

Can you give me an example of the world's increased complexity?

Sure. Look at the attack on the World Trade Center. On the one hand, these men were able to get at us partly because of the ease with which they could travel—so, "small world," right? On the other hand, what really seemed to matter was their determination to attack, their fundamental hatred of our society, and our own bewilderment and surprise—those were the elements of a really big world. In my own work and travels, I am struck by this all the time. For instance, when I was working on a story about the ship scavengers on the beaches of India and Bangladesh ["The Shipbreakers," *The Atlantic Monthly,* August 2000], it became obvious that the workers on the beach had a completely different viewpoint—a different cosmology, really—from the world I was used to.

I mean this in a very immediate sense. It was not just that they had different political views or ideologies from my own, but that they had a completely different sense of the experience we were sharing at that moment. There were times when it seemed amazing to me that we were capable even of breathing the same air. We were animals of the same species, of course, but our understanding of the room in which we were sitting, or the field in which we were standing, or the bus we were riding in, was completely different.

How has your career as a professional pilot influenced your journalism?

I often take what I've called "the aerial view." It is a somewhat detached view of the present. The aerial view, I write in *Inside the*

Sky [1998], "strips the facades from our constructions, and by raising us above the constraints of the treeline and the highway it imposes a brutal honesty on our perceptions. It lets us see ourselves in context, as creatures struggling through life on the face of a planet, not separate from nature, but its most expressive agents."

How do you come up with story ideas?

I always have a lot of ideas swirling around my head. My problem isn't coming up with ideas; it's that I have trouble keeping ideas at bay. I can't even read a newspaper for pleasure anymore because every article seems to be related to subjects that I have written about, or am writing about, or am thinking of writing about. To maintain my sanity, I typically work on one story at a time and keep a few other stories on the back burner. The most interesting stories tend to be the ones that have long gestation periods.

After the terrorist attacks of September 11, 2001, you were deciding between going to Afghanistan and to the World Trade Center site for The Atlantic. How did you make up your mind?

I ordinarily would have chosen to go someplace exotic, like Afghanistan. But I sensed that I could almost write the story of the American troops in Afghanistan without ever going there. Plus it was premature. When I go somewhere for a story, I need to sit, watch, and think about it for months in order to produce something interesting and different. Now two years later, I think Afghanistan is becoming an interesting story, but it's maybe a bit too early to write.

So why did you choose the World Trade Center site?

It was clear to me that the *unbuilding* of the World Trade Center would be a complex story, from which something deep about America would emerge. There was a commonality of purpose to the work being done there, which made it a perfect metaphor for the nation as a whole. It *was* America. The title *American Ground* was not chosen lightly.

Do you pursue only your own ideas, or will you take ideas from friends and editors?

I'm happy to take ideas from anybody. But they have a way of changing once I start working on them.

For example, I wrote a piece about the wine critic Robert Parker. ["The Million-Dollar Nose," *The Atlantic Monthly*, December 2000.] It was an unusual story for me because I don't really care about wine. I was on the way to India, and a friend in Paris suggested that I write about the weird aristocracy in Bordeaux. But when I got there, I discovered that all these French aristocrats were talking about some American wine critic they hated: Robert Parker.

That planted the seed. When I returned to the U.S. a few months later, I looked Parker up. I was surprised to find that the guy who so antagonized the French winemakers was in some ways a really simple fellow—an American on a consumerist crusade all about "good wine," which of course is a very unimportant matter. But the interesting thing to me was that he was also a social and economic *revolutionary* who was busting up this little Bordeaux cartel with his democratic, un-aristocratic American ideas. For me, the story of Robert Parker was a parable about globalization, international trade, and American influence in the modern era. It didn't end up being anything like the story my friend recommended, or even like the story I initially set out to write.

Okay, once you have an idea, how do you find the story?

Once I have a general idea, I look for the most specific, concrete story I can find with which to explore it. In the case of the wine piece, it was obvious. Given the choice between writing about the Bordeaux aristocracy and about Robert Parker, he was much more specific—a single, pivotal person, whom I could bring to life. In addition, frankly, he had the advantage of being American, and therefore someone *The Atlantic*'s readers could identify with. My natural inclination is to go squat with the natives. But it's tricky to write for American readers about foreign subjects that have no connection to America. And squatting with the Bordeaux aristocracy would have been tedious.

Are there any kinds of stories you are consistently drawn to or repelled by?

I don't like stories about superficial politics—like who's on top in Washington—and I'm not particularly interested in hand-wringing about the future of the world. I think predictions are cheap. I'd rather describe the world as it is.

What are the most important elements you require for a good story? Character? Narrative?

My subjects rarely have an inherent narrative, an obvious beginning, middle, and end. Rather, the narrative tension is usually something I have to create from scratch.

The only stories that have had anything resembling a natural, inherent narrative have been my stories about airplane accidents. You'd think that would make them easier to write. But the narrative is just the starting point. If there isn't much beyond the story of the accident, I'm not interested in writing about it. I use those airline accident pieces to explore much larger questions: the phenomenon of the "normal accident," in the case of "The Lessons of ValuJet 592" [*The Atlantic Monthly*, March 1998], or the relations between the first world and the third world in the case of "The Crash of EgyptAir 990" [*The Atlantic Monthly*, November 2001], or the failings of a bureaucracy and of the national space policy in "Columbia's Last Flight" [*The Atlantic Monthly*, November 2003].

How do you conceive of your role as a writer?

I am my readers' eyes and ears. If I have one job, it's to tell my cherished readers to look beyond the facade, to have the courage to embrace the ugly and the real, and to avoid romanticizing the world. I am their agent on the ground. I put myself into complex, three-dimensional situations—call it reality—in which everything is connected to everything else. There is no inherent narrative. It's just a blob. And writing is the process of choosing the path through that confusion. It is in some ways an arrogant act, of course, because I am saying to the reader, "I'll figure out what's significant and what's not. And I'll build a path through it so you don't have to suffer through the same confusion I did."

How do you transcend the confusion?

I have a visceral emotional experience at the beginning of a story. It's as if I'm rubbing my eyes and staggering around saying, "I can't see, I can't see." I don't know what I'm looking for, or what I'm looking at. Things are happening all around me, but I don't understand them. This may go on for weeks.

So what do you do?

I spend a lot of time walking around when I arrive at the place I'm reporting on. I sometimes spend days and days, just looking around. I try not to jump to conclusions. I'm aware of my limitations. That's the "rubbing my eyes" stage, the "I can't see, I can't see." I talk to a lot of people. I ask questions, and listen. I get around as much as possible on foot. I walk very fast. I walk through the bad as well as the good parts of town. I walk with such purpose that natives often ask *me* for directions. Then I gradually begin to see. I begin to eliminate one element at a time. I begin to be able to distinguish the important from fluff. I begin to understand the motivations of the people I'm talking to. After a while I'm ready to start thinking about a narrative path.

Do you prefer long projects or short ones?

Most of my pieces are long, probably because I find it very hard to tell stories correctly in short form. I don't do the sort of short slick pieces you typically find in magazines. And by the way, I don't "pitch" stories to anyone. That's a term, and an approach, I dislike. I'd rather just go back to flying airplanes.

Then how do you get assignments?

I talk to my editors, whether at Farrar, Straus and Giroux, or at *The Atlantic Monthly.* I talk to my agent. I have longstanding relationships with these people. I tell them, "This is what interests me. What do you think?" It is a conversation that has no beginning or end. Most of our conversations don't result in stories. They are my sounding board.

How do you determine how much time you need for a project? For instance, how did you decide to spend six months at the World Trade Center site, rather than, say, a year?

I rarely know how long I need to stay somewhere when I start reporting. But in the case of the World Trade Center I knew I had to be there *constantly*—from morning to night, every day of the week— while I was reporting the story. It was a fascinating story for the first five months, but I stayed about a month longer than I needed to.

What happened?

Two things. First, I found I could predict a week ahead what would occur from an engineering point of view. Second, I sensed that the culture of the pit was stabilizing, becoming more "normal." The end came one day when a "safety" guy came up to me and said, "You have to put safety glasses on or leave the pit." And I said, "Are you kidding?" And he wasn't. It was becoming a normal, procedure-ridden construction job. That was when the great American experiment was over, and when I bowed out.

How do you pace yourself while reporting such long stories?

It depends. On a story like *American Ground,* I work hard every day from morning to night. But when I'm reporting a story in the third world the pacing is just the opposite. Those societies are often so inefficient that I have down time by the truckload.

What kinds of research do you do?

I read a lot of academic stuff—journals, scholarly books—out of a sense of responsibility. They give me a general grounding. I rarely end up using any of that information in the piece, but it prepares me for thinking. I usually also collect a much bigger stack of stuff to read than I get around to reading. If you do too much preparation, you never get around to doing the job.

How do you report in cultures whose language you don't speak?

I speak enough languages to get by in a surprisingly large part of the world. Otherwise, I use a translator—sometimes formally, often not. The most important thing to realize when reporting a story in a culture where you don't speak the language is that it changes the very premise and scope of what you can do. You can still discover interesting truths, and create a narrative path through the tangle of reality, but you have to do it in a different way than when you speak the language. Oddly enough, the result may be better for it. At least you avoid the pitfall of becoming overly anthropological or academic.

Do you have a reporting method?

I listen to people very carefully. The secret is: *let the guy talk*. You never know where they're going, and it gets really interesting when you let people run on. Every once in a while they say something that makes me want to stop them—"Wait! Tell me more about that!"—but I resist the impulse, because I might lose the jewels that are about to fall from their lips. Instead, I make a mental note to go back to the topic later.

How do you convince people to spend so much time with you?

I'll go with them wherever they're going. I like to be with them when they're doing something. People generally enjoy companion-ship, and they appreciate the opportunity to express themselves. I give them that opportunity.

I also make it a point not to condescend to the people I interview. I do not look down on them, or look up at them, or romanticize them in silly or insulting ways. I look eye to eye at them. Take the ship-breakers in India. European reporters go there full of environmental-ist or humanist zeal, and they ask them, "Why do you work here in this very unhealthy environment? Are you unaware of the poisons and dangers?" Given the setting, it's an insulting question. Well *of course*, they're aware of the dangers! They're making rational, inde-pendent choices. I make it clear to them that I respect their think-ing—or at least that I'm listening to it very carefully.

Do you ever do standard interviews?

I try to avoid standard, sit-down-and-take-notes interviews—you know, preparing questions in advance and making an office appoint-ment to see a powerful man, who sits behind his desk and addresses me as a reporter. Of course I've had that experience. For instance, when I was in Sudan writing a piece on Islamic law, I went to see Hassan al Tarabi, the Islamic radical who was the de facto head of the Sudan ["Tarabi's Law," *The Atlantic Monthly*, August 1994]. To my amusement, I found myself in the role of "the reporter" going to see "the president," who expected me to interview him and dutifully regurgitate whatever lines he chose to feed me. So I came up with some bogus questions and took some random notes—about his office, the weather, his clothes, "This guy's got very white shoes for someone living in Khartoum"—to make him feel I was playing my role. And indeed the setting was interesting. But the truth is I couldn't have cared less about what he was saying.

Do you always identify yourself as a journalist?

If I'm going to quote people, sure. But otherwise, not always—because it would come across as pretentious and irrelevant. I never hide my position. In anything other than brief and casual conversation it always comes out. But let's just say I don't wear a badge saying "Press."

Does this practice ever create problems for you?

No, because I'm very careful not to take advantage of the people I talk to. I never lay traps. I try to be very straightforward. For example, at the World Trade Center site, when I was reporting *American Ground*, I met a southerner who was working on the Fresh Kills part of the operation. We were with a group of five or six other engineers, and I wasn't going to quote from anything anyone was saying. I spent maybe five hours with this man, walking through the pile, talking about the work, having a meal at the Taj Mahal (which was the name for the feeding station). At one point, he started speaking very frankly about the failings of New York City government at the site. And I realized, with surprise, that he did not know I was a reporter. I could not imagine that he would have been talking this way if he had. I didn't want to say anything then—there were all these guys around, and again it would have been pretentious—so I sent a message to him through another man I knew: "Tell him who I am, and tell him that anything he said to me is strictly off the record and will remain that way." I don't want there to be any confusion.

Will you negotiate what is on and off the record?

Yes, I always lay out the ground rules when it is clear that I'll be quoting someone. I tell him he can say what he wants, and that anything off the record will *remain* off the record. I've never had a problem with that.

What were the ground rules for the extraordinary access you had to the World Trade Center site?

The ground rule was that there were no ground rules. Ken Holden, who was basically in charge of the cleanup operation, was a longtime *Atlantic Monthly* reader, and had read several of my books—and he knew that I don't write PR. On the very first day, I told him that giving me complete access would be a risk for him. If the operation screwed up, I would write about it in those terms. He knew the deal. There were no negotiations beyond that. He gave me full access to the site, as well as to all meetings having to do with the cleanup.

Do you prefer approaching people via an introduction or calling them directly?

I think it's easier to be an outsider than an insider. That way the people you write about don't have as many preconceptions about how you'll treat them. Introductions can be a little loaded. But, in the end, it doesn't really make much difference. It's a brutal profession and you sometimes have to be brutal with people—no matter how you've met them.

Do you tape or take notes while reporting?

I do both, depending on the situation. It's a luxury to use a tape recorder. I always ask permission to tape, and if the guy's relaxed and understands that a tape recorder makes the interview process easier and more accurate, it isn't a problem. But there are many situations in which I can't use a tape recorder. If the people I'm interviewing aren't media savvy they get intimidated by it. All of a sudden I'm a "reporter" who's sticking a microphone in their face, and I try to avoid that scenario.

What kinds of notes do you take?

I write sloppy longhand. There are times in the third world when I've deliberately kept it sloppy and cryptic so that government officials can't read it. I don't want my thoughts to be too accessible.

What kind of a notebook do you use?

I never use a ring binder because the pages fall out too easily. I use a small notebook, with a strong binding sewn onto the side. I stick it in the small of my back, just under my belt. That way I can bend over while carrying it. And putting it there also keeps the notebook dry. When it rains, the driest place on your body is usually the small of your back.

I have a system of taking notes: I use only the right side of the page, and use the other side for *taking notes on the notes*—which I do when I'm done with the reporting and I sit down to prepare myself to write the piece.

My note-taking got complicated when I was doing the reporting for *American Ground* because it appeared as a three-part piece in *The Atlantic* first. So I used three different colored pens to indicate which notes pertained to each part. It got pretty confusing.

Do you transcribe your own tapes?

Sometimes, but it's extremely time-consuming, and I now have an assistant who helps. When I've done it myself, I index rather than transcribe the tapes. I take a yellow legal pad, and make an index down the left-hand side, noting the information I cover in the interview, and correlating it with the place it appears on the tape. Once in a while I transcribe an entire passage because I know I want to use it, or a particular phrase is so interesting. But the *ideal* is just to listen to the tapes without transcribing them. That lets me relive the whole interview.

Do you ever do interviews by phone or letter or e-mail?

Never by letter or e-mail. Sometimes by phone, but that works only if I already know the person.

Do you ever confront or argue with your subjects?

Oh sure, although I'm not antagonistic. I argue if I think they're wrong. It's an honest expression of my thoughts.

For example, when I was reporting "The Crash of EgyptAir 990," I wasn't interested in "discovering" the truth during my interviews, because I already knew what the truth of the matter was—that the pilot had deliberately crashed the plane. Rather, I was interested in the *reactions* of the people, particularly in Egypt. And that required a certain amount of pushing and antagonism. They thought I was reporting on the accident, but I was actually reporting on *them*.

What kinds of arguments did you have during that story?

I'd say, "Look, I'm a pilot. So why don't we just dispense with the standard line you've been giving to the press. Spare me." I learned a lot by prodding them. It became obvious to me that not only were they lying, but that they didn't care that I *knew* they were lying. At that point, I had learned what I needed to know. They had an entirely different view of the world, which underscores my original point that the world is a much bigger, stranger place than we are told.

How much time do you like spending with your main subjects?

I stay with someone until I reach the burnout point. I work from early morning to late at night, seven days a week. On any given day, at the point where the good conversations are over, I concoct an excuse and check out. I'm often exhausted by then, and need a break.

Is writing more difficult and/or enjoyable for you than reporting?

I like them equally. Reporting has the great advantage of letting me be physically active and out in the world. The disadvantage of reporting is I'm not actually producing anything yet. I have all this anxiety, but I can't really do anything with it. I never know if the material I'm getting is any good. I'm always wondering whether *this* is finally the story that's going to fail.

So writing has the huge advantage of finally producing something and seeing it all come together. At its best, when the writing is really working, the pieces seem to fall out of the sky and into place.

What is your writing routine?

I take the notebooks I've used while reporting, the transcripts that are made from my interviews, lots of other documents, and a stack of books—and read through them all. This part of the process can take weeks. The notes and the transcripts are where the rich hunting is. I number each page in the notebooks, so I can find the material easily once I start writing. The rest of the stuff I use more as background, so I don't go through it as carefully.

As I take notes on the notes, the structure of the piece begins to become apparent. I start scribbling notes to myself about where each section will go.

Do you make an outline?

Yes, I go from scribbling notes to making an outline. The outlines get very, very detailed. But my outlines don't look like a classic outline.

What do they look like?

I start writing on sheets of standard 8½ by 11 paper, and when I run out of space on a sheet I staple another one to it and keep going. They grow into strange shapes. Sometimes they grow laterally, sometimes they grow vertically. When I'm done I tack the whole thing up on the wall.

And what's in these outlines?

The themes, facts, stories, and characters I'm going to use. The entries are indexed with the page numbers of my notes. An entry in the outline might say, "Rinaldi, 9-1," which would mean a story about Rinaldi in notebook nine, page one. I constantly update the outline as I write. I also deviate from it freely.

How do you start writing?

I often jump the gun and start writing a little too eagerly. I get impatient with the outline and just start writing. Once I'm into the writing process I'm really *working*. I call this phase the "sausage machine": I'm grinding away and the stuff is just coming out the other end.

What do you write on?

I write on a word processor, so the writing that emerges is pretty refined. I think word processing has greatly *improved* writing.

Don't most people believe just the opposite has happened? That word processors have made writers more verbose and less careful?

That's what people say, but it's nonsense. Word processors have improved writing because they allow for easy and continual revisions, and revisions are good. People who criticize word processors either are old-timers, or have some kind of a romantic idea that an evil machine is getting in the way of the pure creative process. As if the pen or the typewriter isn't a machine. To each his own of course. I've got nothing against people who want to write longhand, or for that matter with a quill pen. All that really counts in the end is the quality of the book or article. But people who criticize word processors are barking up the wrong tree.

Do you have to be anywhere in particular to write?

Not really. I don't care about views or setting. The idea that you have to be on a gorgeous Greek island to write is ridiculous. The only view I need is the view of a computer screen. My only other requirement is for lots of desk space to lay out the notes and documents I'm working with. I like big, big desks—so motels or hotels are the worst places for me to write, because their desks are typically miniscule.

How do you pace yourself while you're writing?

I don't. I get up early in the morning, go to work, and crash late at night. It took me five months to write *American Ground*, but it was five months of constant work. From seven a.m. to midnight on many days, with very short breaks.

Do you write straight through a piece, or stop and revise?

I write straight through, start to finish. I have a hard time writing sections out of order—I'm too neurotic, or perfectionistic, and I feel that I'm missing opportunities when I write without knowing every detail of what has come before. The revisions, as I said, are continual. The process is something like a wave on a beach, breaking forward, lapping back.

Do you show your work-in-progress to others?

Sure. And I'm my own biggest fan. I'll call a friend and say, "Let me read you this. It's so damned good I can't believe it!"

Who do you read to?

Sometimes it's people at *The Atlantic*. Sometimes it's a pilot friend of mine. He's not particularly literary, but he's a nice guy and he will listen to my stuff. It is very helpful to me to have someone to read to.

Why?

Because writing has to be readable. It has to be "readable-out-loudable." Sound and rhythm are extremely important. By reading out loud I can see whether it's working. And reading out loud to yourself is strange and unsustainable.

What kind of authorial presence do you strive for?

The presence of someone who can be trusted by the reader to be honest—sometimes even brutally so. Writing is a private conversation with the writer and each individual reader. It is a very intimate communication, which relies on trust. So it is crucial to establish that trust by never tricking the reader, never playing cute, never cajoling, showing off, or wasting the reader's time.

How would you describe the tone of your writing?

Minimalistic, maybe lyrical, unsentimental, unromantic. Above all, I strive for clarity in the prose and thought. A sort of crystalline quality. I believe that the highest art of writing is simplicity. That's probably partly a cultural thing. For instance, I have a hard time reading French writers—I find them far too ornate, and I think they find me not nearly ornate enough.

Have any particular writers influenced your tone?

Nobody I can think of. One thing I can say objectively about my writing is that there is nothing imitative about it—for the simple reason that I don't know whom to imitate. I never took a writing class or studied literature. On the other hand, I certainly have been influenced by other writers—especially in terms of the possibilities offered by narrative nonfiction.

Like whom?

John McPhee. Now, my writing is not at all like his, but he has had a huge influence on the *way* I think about what you can do with writing. I first discovered him in high school and realized with sort of a shock that you could actually do really *good* nonfiction writing. That the market would allow you to do that. That readers would find you.

V. S. Naipaul is another writer who has influenced me. He is a famously nasty man, but also an acute and honest observer of the world. And Joseph Conrad because he was so interested in the world "out there," as well as the people in that world. And then, of course, Graham Greene. If I had to pick one writer who I would even *remotely* one day like to approximate—should I be so lucky—it would be him. Why? Maybe because he lived so long.

But much of what I read I actually don't like very much—I mean strictly from a writing point of view. Certainly there are a lot of writers whom I *don't* want to imitate. A negative influence can be as important as a positive one, I suppose.

Who comes to mind?

Paul Theroux. Although he's written some very good stuff, he's basically a prima donna who is more interested in showing himself off than in exploring the world. When I read him I think, "I *don't* want to write like that."

As I read American Ground, I thought about the other great work of nonfiction about a terrible, man-made disaster: John Hersey's Hiroshima. Did that influence you?

Going into *American Ground,* my goal was to write a very slim book that would stand up as well as *Hiroshima.* I hadn't read it since high school, and when I recently reread it, I thought that structurally the book was surprisingly primitive, and kind of a mess.

Do you think journalistic inquiry can lead a writer to truth?

Yes, although truth is a very complicated thing. Journalism is a lot like writing history. History is this very massive, complex thing, which *seems* a little simpler because the information that is available is reduced with time. But even so, you know that an historian is having to sort through a lot of material and come up with a story about what "really happened," and that two histories of an event might be very different, and yet *both* be "true." Journalism is like that, too. It just happens in the present tense.

Do you think that the kind of long-form nonfiction you write is a peculiarly American form?

It seems to be. Partly because there aren't any magazines like *The New Yorker* or *The Atlantic*—even in England—let alone in continental Europe or Asia. The form has British roots, but it doesn't seem to be practiced as much there today, although I guess *Granta* is an exception.

What do you call the kind of journalism you do?

"Narrative nonfiction" comes close, although in truth it doesn't really have a label—which is why you can never find the stuff in a bookstore. They don't know where to put it, so they try to force it into existing categories. You know, *Inside the Sky* gets filed in "Transportation." And I suppose *American Ground* will end up in "Urban Studies," or something.

What do you think about the prospects for the genre?

They are excellent, unlimited. The other great fallacy of our time is the "short attention span" nonsense. The notion that the American public has such a short attention span that it can only handle nugget-sized pieces of writing is *systematically* disproved again and again and again by *good writing*. It's just an excuse that people come up with to justify their inability to produce, or publish, good writing.

So it amounts to this: don't insult or condescend to the readers, don't waste their time. Engage the readers, and the readers will come along. All of the magazine and book publishers who publish this kind of work are desperate for good work. These are beasts that have to be fed. But they are hungry for *good* stuff, and they are usually fed poorly. There is a feeling on the outside that this world of writing and publishing is some kind of a closed club. That again is nonsense. There are no real barriers to access in this field, no secret passwords for getting in. All that matters is the really hard stuff—which is the quality of the work.

BY WILLIAM LANGEWIESCHE:

The Outlaw Sea: A World of Freedom, Chaos, and Crime, North Point Press/FSG, 2004
American Ground: Unbuilding the World Trade Center, North Point Press/FSG, 2002
Inside the Sky: A Meditation on Flight, Pantheon Books, 1998
Sahara Unveiled: A Journey Across the Desert, Pantheon Books, 1996
Cutting for Sign, Pantheon Books, 1993

ADRIAN NICOLE LEBLANC

There were nights during the decade that Adrian Nicole LeBlanc reported *Random Family*—her 2002 saga of drugs, crime, life, and love in the South Bronx—that she'd grow so fatigued she would simply hand her tape recorder to her interview subject and go home to sleep. "Do whatever you want with it," she'd say. Part desperate measure, part journalistic ploy, the practice provided her with valuable material.

Coco, the book's protagonist, would read her lover's prison letters into the recorder after her children had gone to sleep; others shared secrets they were too shy to discuss with LeBlanc in person; some just goofed around, singing songs and telling jokes that would make LeBlanc smile when she listened to the tape later. "Maybe I secretly wish my characters could tell their own stories. They'd probably do a better job than I do," she says.

Most likely they wouldn't, of course. But in LeBlanc's fantasy one finds the kernel of truth, the feeling of unmediated access she provides the reader. *The New York Times*'s Janet Maslin called *Random Family* "a book that exerts the fascination of a classic unflinching documentary." Combined with what the writer Mark Kramer has called LeBlanc's "relentless neutrality," her up close view of life in the drug-ridden South Bronx can be unnerving, no matter your political outlook.

LeBlanc's technique has led a number of critics to conclude that she is condoning, rather than simply depicting, her characters' behavior. Conservatives criticized her for not being more of a social critic or policy analyst, for failing to chastise her subjects' tendency to have children out of wedlock, subsist on welfare, or dabble in crime. Liberals faulted her for portraying the poor in such a direct, unsentimental light.

A few commentators recoiled at LeBlanc's frankness, assuming that her troubled characters were chosen with sensationalism, rather than realism, as her goal. Writing in *The Washington Post*,

John L. Jackson Jr. called the book "a Jerry Springer-ish account of unwed mothers and the drug dealers who love them." Others, like *The Village Voice*'s Amy Farley, sensed the novelistic complexity of LeBlanc's vision, calling *Random Family* "perhaps the most intimate chronicle of urban life ever published." In the *Los Angeles Times,* Lauren Sandler concurred, calling it "a nonfiction *Middlemarch* of the underclass."

Most readers appreciated how hard LeBlanc had worked to suspend the norms of middle-class judgments that most writers make of the poor, and to simply bear witness to her subjects' lives. As the writer/editor Anne Fadiman told *New York* magazine, "I know of no other writer who dug in as deep. She didn't just report; she burrowed into a world so well that she lost every speck of foreignness." Writing in *Newsday,* Liza Featherstone noted the delicate balance LeBlanc struggled to maintain between comprehension and forgiveness: "She doesn't fail to observe her subjects' mistakes, yet she shows us how little room they have for error."

Adrian Nicole LeBlanc was born in 1963 and grew up in Leominster, Massachusetts, a small factory town near Boston. Her father was a union organizer; her mother worked in a drug rehab center. Her background gave her a strong sense of blue-collar values, which only deepened when she studied sociology at Smith College. LeBlanc got her first taste of literary journalism at Smith in classes she took with the Pulitzer Prize–winning author Tracy Kidder and journalist Mark Kramer (now the director of the Nieman Foundation Program on Narrative Journalism at Harvard University).

LeBlanc published her first piece in the then recently founded magazine *New England Monthly.* Written for Kramer's literary journalism class, it was about a rash of suicides that had taken place in Leominster (eleven suicides in eighteen months). Her descriptions of the drinking and drug use by the town's adolescents (of which she had recently been one) shocked their elders and set off a mini-scandal in the local newspaper.

After receiving a Master of Philosophy and Modern Literature at Oxford University in 1988, LeBlanc became the fiction editor at *Seventeen* magazine. The position was flexible enough that she was able to continue to write for magazines about the marginal figures—prostitutes, drug dealers, gang girls—who had come to fascinate her.

She found the seed for *Random Family* in a tiny clip in *Newsday* announcing the trial of a hugely successful heroin dealer named Boy George (at age eighteen, George was making $1 million per week, accumulating so much cash that he had to store it in garbage bags in an apartment rented solely for that purpose).

While reporting the piece ["Kid Kingpin: The Rise and Fall of a Drug Dealer," *The Village Voice,* December 10, 1991], LeBlanc got to know the girlfriends of the various dealers, and they soon became the main story. LeBlanc was twenty-seven when she got the $40,000 book contract from an editor who had been associated with *New England Monthly.* "Don't worry," he assured the nervous writer, "it will be a small book by a young reporter." Boy George agreed to cooperate, but only if he was convicted. If he was acquitted and LeBlanc revealed anything he had told her, he promised to kill her. (He is serving a life sentence.)

LeBlanc quit her job at *Seventeen* and threw herself into the story. Other than a year during which she held a journalism fellowship at Yale Law School (studying the effects of the draconian Rockefeller drug laws—a topic relevant to the book), she spent the better part of the next twelve years working on the book, going through two agents, two publishers, and five editors. Five years into the project, LeBlanc missed the extension of the extension of the contract deadline, and her first publisher canceled the book. Despite having completed only seventy-five pages, she resold the book to another publisher, which repaid the original publisher, but gave LeBlanc no more money. She realized it was time to bring the project to a close one day when she was interviewing Boy George in jail. "Adrian, this is old shit," he said. "I'm in prison. Get a life!"

Excerpts of *Random Family,* which ran in *The New Yorker* and *The New York Times Magazine,* guaranteed that the book would be widely read. Reviewers marveled at her ability to make even the mundane, gritty facts of life in poverty fascinating. "None of the people she writes about veer definitively toward a newer or better life—they tend toward the same tired grooves—yet she makes their stories riveting," writes Margaret Talbot in *The New York Times Book Review.* But Talbot argues that LeBlanc hasn't questioned her characters' poor choices adequately. "Why does somebody like Coco keep having children, against all evidence that another child will not win her what she wants—a stable partner, a decent house for her kids, some kind of security? LeBlanc doesn't step far enough back from her subjects to pose a question like that quite so baldly. She sees her subjects' faults, but she takes their explanations pretty much straight."

LeBlanc acknowledges that her critics have a point when they fault her for focusing on description, to the exclusion of explanation. However, her unwillingness to diagnose, she explains, results more from her ignorance than her reticence. "I resist understanding what's driving the story until the absolute end. I find it *so excruciating* to come out and say, 'This is what I think it means . . .' Because I feel that, despite all the time I've put into reporting, I still don't know what it *means*." The reviews of *Random Family* convinced her that she needs to do more explaining, although she'll never see herself as a policy advocate. "I'm now realizing that I'm more intellectually responsible for explaining the meaning than I had thought. After all, I am delving into the meaning *anyway*—simply by selecting which scenes to use, which characters to highlight, which incidents to exclude—so I might as well do that part of the writing more clearly."

The New York Times Book Review named *Random Family* one of the ten best books of the year. It was a finalist for the National Book Critics Circle Award and won the Anisfield-Wolf Book Award. LeBlanc's next project is a book about a stand-up comedian.

———

Do you think of what you do as New Journalism?
I think of myself as a reporter. I think the word "journalist" is too fancy.

Do you perceive yourself as part of an historical tradition?
I've been inspired by people who have written about social injustice, such as Jacob Riis, Susan Sheehan, Jonathan Kozol, William Finnegan, Alex Kotlowitz. I'd like to think of myself as being part of that tradition, which is a documentary tradition as well as a literary one.

What do you call the kind of journalism you do?

Some people call it "immersion journalism," but I think of it as reporting with the luxury of time: open-ended time to be present, to revisit conversations and information and scenes, and to think about what I've seen. Imagine reporting as being immersed in water. Once you get under the water you really can't see very much beyond shapes and blurry images. But when you come up again you can see more clearly. When you step out of the water, you are more conscious of the temperature, the quality of air. There are certain feelings and sensations that you can only feel when you're in the water. And, similarly, when you surface, and get *out,* you can think more clearly about what was visible when you were in.

What do you like writing about?

I'm interested in the issues of proximity that exist between insular worlds. This might be one of the reasons I've written about children, whose position requires them to negotiate proximate worlds: family and home, school and friends. Adolescents, too, live in distinct worlds of their own, which are also on the cusp of adulthood. The dynamic between people and these locations, how environments do and don't shape identity, are some of the things that interest me.

Is this notion of "insularity" the reason you've written so much about marginalized, inner-city people?

The worlds I've reported on certainly can *feel* tremendously isolated and insular, but I'm less and less comfortable thinking in terms like "marginalized." Are demarcations quite so clear? Is the "inner city" a knowable place or a dynamic, or a culture, like business or the "world of sports"?

If, say, the world of the South Bronx and the world of the Upper East Side are in remarkably close proximity, why do you choose to write only about the former? There must be something more than proximity involved.

Sure. I feel a sense of purpose in the work I do. The stakes are extremely high in a place like the South Bronx. More personally, my heart goes out to people in the South Bronx more easily than to people on the Upper East Side, whose daily struggles aren't challenging journalistically in ways that interest me.

Virtually all of your journalism has been about people who are poor and involved in drugs and crime. Could you ever see yourself writing about a celebrity?

Not a celebrity per se, but maybe the culture of celebrity. A magazine once asked me whether I'd write a profile of the socialite Hilton sisters, and I thought, "Oh, I'd *love* to do that!"

Why?

I could learn some things. And I suspect that there are lots of connections between the Hilton sisters and what engages me: gender, consumerism and young adulthood, the ways in which people who don't have structured lives spend their time, sibling issues. I think there are actually a lot more connections between the very poor and the very rich.

Why do you write so often about children?

The perspective of children enhances my consciousness; imagining their perspective requires a kind of rigorousness. Say something happens on the street—a fight, or a flirtation, some kind of transaction—and children are watching. I often try to imagine how they make sense of what they see. Children also generally don't edit their reactions the way adults learn to do. "Uncluttered," my dad used to say.

Also, the reader tends to be sympathetic to children. The natural sympathy that the public used to extend to adolescents involved in the criminal justice system has eroded. It's practically a requirement that I have to keep getting younger and younger subjects in order to generate a human connection. It is almost a tactical move on my part.

How do you come up with ideas?

They usually evolve from previous stories or from conversations. Like some of the best information, they arise incidentally. An image or a comment or a gesture will stick with me. I just can't get it out of my mind, so I mull it over, try to see if there's anything there. This can be a slow accumulation of half-thoughts and preliminary interviews that sometimes takes months. I've had some ideas for years.

Do you maintain a big idea file?

Yes. I have lots of idea files. Probably between thirty and forty at any given time. Recently, for example, I made a file I call "protectors" that evolved from meeting children who have disciplinary problems in school, but who act as protectors of their peers on the street. I've another called "sibling violence" because I am struck by the variations in the behavior between siblings on the street and indoors. It's obvious, but also a case of proximity: same kids, same neighborhood, different contexts, different behaviors. The files include stray comments by siblings about each other, their friends, parents commenting on the divisions between their children, a couple of articles about siblings and child development, names of experts on the subject. Are these stories? I don't know. But they're in the files.

Do you also take story ideas from friends or editors?

Some of the best stories I've written have come from editors' suggestions. Their clarity can be an enormous relief. And I tend to learn a lot from those stories because I'm pushed in ways I might not push myself.

How do you know when you've found a genuine story?

I know I've found a good story when I'm absorbed by it almost to the point of obsession.

What obsesses you?

Someone's psychology or situation. Voices obsess me. Sometimes I get hooked simply by the *way* someone says something—phrasing, lilt, what's not said, pauses, what's said repeatedly.

Do any parts of the world interest you more than others?

I have trouble reporting in places that lack signs of workday life— something I find in abundance in places like the South Bronx, or in small cities and towns. My background has given me a genuine— unsentimental—respect for working people.

What is your thought process when considering a project?

I tend to have an intuitive response to a set of circumstances or people, a desire to be around a person or place all the time, to read about it or related ideas. The hunch becomes a filter and I use it to edge into a point of view.

For example, an idea I'm considering came from an interview with a comedian that appeared in a magazine my brother mailed to me. I read it and went to see his show. He was riveting. I put the clip in a file and had well over ten files before I even introduced myself to him. But it was a moment of his performance that stayed with me—particularly his physical enormity onstage, and the diminishment from this larger-than-life onstage persona to the insecure guy I saw in the postshow receiving line. I was struck by the resilience I imagine such work requires. What does it mean to have to constantly prove yourself? What toll does it take? ["On the Bark: Learning to Be a Comedian in Times Square," *The New Yorker,* April 19–26, 2004.]

Comedy is a natural extension of my interests because, like street life, a lot of comedy comes from being smack-up against adversity. And both comedy and street life can foster a kind of freshness and frivolity and recklessness. I'm interested in the question of how a performer gives enough of himself to entertain, and yet protects himself enough to survive.

I'm interested in people who challenge me, who provoke me to seriously reconsider things. I can see that reporting on this comedian is going to be exhausting. But that is exciting to me.

What kinds of people do you *least* and *most* like writing about?
I hate writing about anyone who is familiar with the press or has a "story." I like to write about people who don't necessarily see what their story is, or what my interest might be. I like subjects who really know how to enjoy life or are immersed in whatever they are doing fully. For example, in *Random Family,* even though Boy George and Jessica end up in jail, they both lived their lives to the maximum. Jessica had hard, depressing times in her life, but when she went out to have fun, she really had fun. Perhaps I'm interested in them because in some ways they are so different from me. Not that I'm incapable of enjoying myself, but I tend toward the melancholy. I'm quite serious and often ill at ease. I am hesitant.

How much do you identify with your characters? I often detect a "there, but for the grace of God, go I" theme in your work.

I think that sentiment is true, but that posture is less helpful than understanding the mechanics of it all. I am constantly struck by the element of chance that separates their lives from mine.

Do you think of your work as variations on a theme? As a series of distinct pieces?

Sadly, variations on a theme. It'll be a series of distinct pieces—highly refined variations—if I become strong enough a writer for that kind of stretch.

Are you always aware you're working on a story, or do you sometimes wake up and realize that some part of your life is also something you'll be writing about?

I used to think that my interest signaled the *absence* of a story—that I should have a dispassionate idea of what a story was about. Thankfully, I've smartened up, but I'd say this—my awareness that I've landed in a story is sometimes evidenced by a sense of dread. The dread is an initial resistance to the surrender of time and effort and attention that the best stories demand of me. But there have been days in the field, reporting, that I am so elated or absorbed that I forget the larger mission, which was to write a story. On the other hand, I sometimes worry about thinking too journalistically and constantly wondering, "Will this make a good scene? Should I use that quote?" If there is enough room in my brain to think of those technical questions, I'm obviously not "present" enough in the field.

What kind of research do you do?

Initially, I want to rely on my own intuition while I'm reporting, so I generally stay away from experts, at least at first. I don't want to waste their time, and I'm worried that they will make too much of an impression on me. If I go into the field with an expert's ideas in my head, I may be distracted from really seeing the things that are going on in front of me.

Generally, I gain as much insight into the root causes of the social problems I see—drugs, poverty, race, lack of education, overcrowded housing—from people who are experiencing them, whether or not they consciously impart insight. Some of this is simply practical—their voices and analyses rarely get heard.

In *Random Family,* you write a lot about the technical, financial, and even chemical basis of the drug trade. What kind of research did you do?

For eight years, I had a stack of books on the economics and history of the drug trade sitting in my apartment. I didn't read many of them, although perhaps I should have. Most everything I learned about the drug trade came from conversations I had with Boy George, his supplier, other street dealers, and countless customers. I went to drug trials, and worked as an intern at a drug court. What interested me was less the details of the drug business, but what it *felt like* to be a young Puerto Rican kid from the Bronx who was able to fly to Hawaii with his girlfriend at the drop of a hat. Again, I wanted to know what happened when these different worlds knocked up against each other.

While reporting *Random Family,* you had a journalism fellowship at Yale Law School. What were you doing?

I was formally studying the history of drug policy and the evolution of the federal sentencing guidelines, although very little of that information made it into the book overtly. But such foundations are key. It's a kind of study that appears in places, like the first half of this sentence: "Drug charges couldn't stick to minors, but the lifestyle could." I'd inadvertently landed in the midst of a historical moment in the Bronx—the result of the Rockefeller drug laws, the expansion of the prison industry, and the atrophying of funding of poverty policy—when kids began to be employed as dealers. Understanding the intellectual history of those laws helped me know what I was seeing. If the writing is the building, this kind of research is the scaffolding.

I did become interested in the Yale law students themselves, though. It was fascinating to be in the midst of their socialization as lawyers, witness to their orientation to and preparation for real positions of power in the world. It gave me insight to see young, Ivy League, idealistic law students at the beginning of their careers, who were similar to the people I later met when they were district attorneys and judges and politicians and policy wonks. The exposure to the culture of elite lawyering makes my understanding of the justice system, of its moments of connection and disconnection, ultimately more sophisticated, I think.

What is the first thing you do when you begin reporting a story?

I drive around and observe. Then I work up the courage to walk over and introduce myself to the people I'm reporting on, explaining as much as I understand of what I'm doing, and that I just want to "be" with them, and not necessarily do anything. I draw the parallel with making a movie: "Imagine I'm making a movie about your life. Show me the places that are most important to you: your room, the schoolyard, anywhere you like to be. So that someone who knows nothing would be able to get a sense of your life." We go to the store. We go to the park. We sit on the corner and talk. They sometimes can't believe that this mundane stuff is what I want to see, so it takes a while to convince them that I'm not a failure as a reporter, or a fool.

How do you convince them to spend so much time hanging out with you?

In general, I find people are surprisingly responsive. It helps that I'm sincerely interested. Boredom helps me a lot. Kids are pretty bored, so they are happy to have something to do and someone new to talk to. I've had the problem of being wanted *too much*! I was always being asked to come over, to stop by. Some people actually felt slighted when I spent time with other people.

How do you convince the more reluctant ones?

I tend not to pursue people who are reluctant, unless the reluctance seems like a cryptic plea to be pursued. I might ask if there is anything about their lives they feel is misunderstood. I'll try repeatedly, but I won't push.

Does anyone ever ask, "Why would you want to make a movie about my life?"

I usually hear that from people I'm *not* interviewing, who are envious of those I am. Cesar was one of the few people who questioned my interest in him and his early life. He still tells me, "Adrian, I know a *thousand* dudes like me." It depends on the person, of course, but it can be great when people are wonderfully confident. "Well, *of course* you want to spend time with me and find out what my life is like! Who wouldn't?"

How much do you share about your project and yourself?

I reveal as much about my life as they care to know, which is usually not much. I'm not that interesting. As for the project, I explain the topic of my piece and share my preliminary ideas, which are usually pretty vague. I might say I am writing about poverty, or drugs and people in jail, or what life is like for a young girl with kids. The bittersweet thing to me is how *uninterested* most people are in elaborate detail.

Do you ever arrange activities to see how your characters react?

Rarely, although in a piece about gang girls ["When Manny's Locked Up," *The New York Times Magazine*, August 14, 1994], I took some of the teenagers to a screening of *Mi Vida Loca*, Alison Anders's movie on girl gang members in L.A. I'd interviewed her and she invited me to the screening. I simply wanted to know their impression of the movie. Much to the distress of the PR folks and the attendant critics, the kids hollered and whooped and clapped through the film. One kid tagged a wall. They threw gang signs. It was a *great* experience for me as a journalist because I got to see how they bumped up against another world—one that was, in fact, depicting a version of them. I got to see the fearful responses of subway riders on the ride back, the nervousness of the movie critics watching a film about what gang life means.

What is your reportorial persona?

Tentative, shy, perplexed by what I'm seeing. I often feel directionless, and as a reporter, I'm asking, "Who are *you*? *Help me* figure this out." I'm quite reticent. Once, after the first week of a trial, as I was working up the nerve to speak to some people, one girl *came over to me* and said, "When are you going to come over and talk to us?"

Having said that, once I get going, I'm absolutely *in* the moment when I'm reporting, if all's going well.

How did you pace yourself while reporting and writing *Random Family*?

I got the contract for *Random Family* in late 1992, but didn't really find my focus until 1994–95. The writing took about two years, but the whole process—from the initial contact, through the editing—took from 1989 to 2001. Actually, in some ways, it's ongoing.

I didn't pace myself well during that project. In retrospect, I wonder if I should have moved into an apartment in the South Bronx for a few years and completely submerged myself in the book.

Let's talk about interviewing. Will you negotiate the terms of an interview?

Yes, if explaining qualifies as that. I want the person to know that everything that happens is potential material for my story. When I'm interviewing someone, especially teenagers, I remind them that what they say is on the record because when the conversations get good, this awareness can get lost. They need concrete examples of what the conversation means. I might give them copies of my clips. Or, if we are talking on the phone, I might say, "Do you mind if I write this down?" just to remind them of the process—taking notes on the notepad—that, were I there in person, they would just see.

I tell them that if there is anything they don't want to appear in the story, they have to tell me it is "off the record." But even if something is off the record, I ask them to tell me about it. I won't print it, but the more I know, the more fully I'll understand their experience.

Did the fact that you talked to some of your characters for years ever make the terms of your interviews too confusing to remember?

I'm running into that problem more in the piece I'm writing about that comedian. He thinks and talks so incredibly fast that I have to tape him to keep up. He'll tell me something and follow the comment with, "Oh, that's off the record, or on, or off, or *whatever* . . ." and then just keep on talking! This behavior is central to his personality because *everything* for him is on the flip side of a simple "yes" or "no." That's why he's so funny, but we have to reach an understanding if the project is going to proceed.

Where do you *most* and *least* like interviewing people?

I like to interview people where they are happiest, which can be difficult for me if they're happiest when on a noisy street. Interviewing people in a car is great because it is quiet. It is like my mobile office. I did some of my best interviews with Coco while driving to visit Cesar in prison. The kids would fall asleep in the back and we could talk, uninterrupted, for a few hours while I drove. I also like interviewing people in kitchens, probably because I write a lot about women, and the women I write about have led fairly traditional lives in which kitchens are "their" place. Kitchen tables are a warm, easy place to talk with someone. Lourdes, in *Random Family,* really came alive when she was cooking—which she did very well—in her kitchen.

I hate interviewing outside because the neighborhoods where I've done most of my interviewing are noisy and busy. Also, everybody there is minding each other's business, so I feel as if everybody is watching. I don't like restaurants for the same reasons.

Do you pace your questions while you are interviewing?

My brain isn't wired that way—that would require too much calculation, and with everything else going on, that split-frame of consciousness is exhausting to me. Many of the obvious questions don't occur to me until fairly late in the reporting. Until then, if I have a question, I'll simply ask it.

In the case of *Random Family,* whatever "pacing" I did was unconscious. Looking back, I see that much of the story was fully available to me quite early in the project. The problem was that I perhaps couldn't handle hearing it. I was always finding reasons to leave the South Bronx because it was often simply too much all at once: too many people, too much sadness, too much vitality and activity. It took me a long time to get out of the way. But in the early tapes, I interrupt people at crucial moments in the interview—repeatedly!

Do you tape your interviews?

Yes, but given the kinds of subjects I write about (crime, drugs, etc.), taping can unnerve my subjects because it makes the encounter feel like an interrogation. The people I interview associate a tape recorder with a cop or a lawyer who is asking them questions about a crime.

One technique I've developed to avoid this dynamic is simply to hand my tape recorder over to someone and tell him to use it in whatever way he wants. There were times while reporting *Random Family* when I got so tired that I'd just leave the recorder and go home. They could interview each other, or give me information they thought I should know. Sometimes they joked around, but other times they took it seriously.

Was it effective?

Yes, it was incredibly helpful! I learned a lot of stuff I doubt I would have discovered otherwise. Sometimes Coco would tell me things on tape that she felt embarrassed to tell me in person. Sometimes she'd read Cesar's letters to her from prison into the tape recorder, or get distracted by trying to get her daughters to brush their teeth. She would put the kids to sleep and then talk about how she felt about things—all to the tape recorder. It was great because I'd get her perspective differently. It was her telling me about what she chose to share of her life, not me asking her about what I thought might matter.

Do you transcribe your own tapes?

Yes. It is important for me to hear the dynamic of the exchange, the dance of the interview. Intonation, pauses, the places where people get excited. Perhaps a professional transcriber could capture these, but I've never had the money to try.

In the future, I've promised to be as zealous about the housekeeping tasks as I've been about my reporting. I let my notebooks pile up for months at a time, and as a result I lost a lot of extraordinary material. And it was even worse when it came to the tapes.

How do you know when you're finished reporting?

When I start to feel distracted and impatient with my subjects. Or when I start to feel opinionated, when I'm listening less and thinking more about what *I want to say*. When I find myself retreating into global theories, it's time to stop reporting and think about writing.

Let's talk about writing. Is it more or less enjoyable/painful for you than reporting?

I love to report, and I dread writing. It often feels to me like the whole experience of a story is over for me by the time I have to write. I do eventually reach the point where I love the writing as well.

How do you organize your material before you write?

I go through all my notes—both from taping and writing—which I've already typed into the computer, and open up theme files as I notice them popping up. For *Random Family* I had files on "boyfriends," "housing," "music," "street comments to girls," ".baby 'cuz" (listing all the reasons people gave for having babies), "euphemisms for drug use," etc. I had "atmosphere" files for all the major institutions in which scenes took place (hospitals, welfare offices, homeless shelters, apartment lobbies, courtrooms). And I opened biographical files and portrait files for each person. I also had a massive, hundreds-of-pages-long, annotated chronology.

Once I have most of my theme files, I cut and paste sections from my notes and copy them into the relevant thematic file. Then I read and print the files and reread them, highlighting the most interesting material. So when I write a scene I have a pile of highlighted notes next to me, with all sorts of comments in the margins.

How did you organize all these files?

I had a few hundred files for the book, and I'd print them up and divide them into milk crates that I lined up against the wall. The theme files were organized alphabetically, the biographical and portrait files were organized alphabetically by name, and then the fieldwork was organized chronologically ("George and Jessica meet," "George and Jessica dating," "George in jail," "Jessica in jail," "George and Jessica in jail"). The periods of time I wasn't present for, I organized by the location where the action occurred, chronologically.

How do you start writing?

I find myself feeling crabby and frustrated, which is a sign that I'm either hungry or need to write. I try to start writing, but I'll read books and magazines—anything to keep me from writing. The way I know that I'm really ready to write is that I get incredibly tired and I have to sleep. I make sure to read my notes right before I go to sleep so that I'll wake up with them fresh in my mind. Then I sleep—sometimes fourteen hours straight—and wake up early. That's when I know I'm going to write.

Any particular time of day, or place, you like to write?

I like to write early in the morning, before I'm fully awakened. So I'll try to start writing before I even make a cup of coffee. I'll go straight from bed to my desk and start writing. The resistance to writing is so great that I need to make myself start writing before I fully realize what I'm doing. Then once I get going, I'll pause and make myself some coffee. After a few days of this routine, I can make the transition to a fairly normal writing day, where I can talk to people and have a phone call.

In terms of place, I've had good luck writing at writers' colonies, although it takes me a while to settle down. My dream would be an office I could sleep in, so I could wake up and just start writing.

How important is writing the lead?

I obsess over the first paragraph for days. And it almost always gets cut, or moved around and becomes the end of a section.

Do you write chronologically?

Usually—although this is changing—I write emotionally, from scene to scene, not chronologically. I'll write a scene from 1988, and then a scene from 1996, and then try to figure out the connection between them. It created all kinds of practical problems—new characters would appear in a scene who hadn't been introduced earlier, so I'd have to go back and map things out.

The only thing I know from the start is how a section is going to end. I have a scene, or a sentence, or a quote in my head, and I write toward it. It might be the only thing I'm sure of when I start writing.

For example, one section of *Random Family* ends with the sentence "Her daughter and her man walked through the first hole of spring." It came from a moment I witnessed, of Frankie and Mercedes walking down the street, with Coco watching, that stayed with me for years. I somehow knew a section would end with that image, but I had no idea how to earn it, to get down all that needed to precede it to make the seemingly mundane moment as meaningful as it was in real time to me.

What does "writing emotionally" mean?

Trusting that my responses possess—at least once in a while—useful psychological associations and leaps. The first things I write about are the events or people that stay with me emotionally and interest me the most—what you distill into, say, the story you tell your wife that describes the gist of your day. I try to figure out what it is that moves me about the story enough to tell it, and if I can understand it, I can test its validity, draw from it or discard it, but either way, get myself out of the way.

Do you write through a piece before revising?

I keep writing until I have a rough draft, which is usually a bunch of jumbled, out-of-order scenes, or, really, fragments. I then print them out, and take them away from my house, perhaps to a coffee shop, and read them. After I read each I ask myself, "Okay, what is this bit *about*? Why was I attracted to this scene?" And I write the answers—sometimes just a word or two—in the margins of the scenes. Then I take those marginal comments and put them in an outline.

You make an outline *after* your first draft?

Yes. I generate my outline from my first draft. It's a process of distilling, of trying to figure out my original intentions, and then ordering them. Writing the actual piece really gets going when I sit down with my outline on one side of my desk, and my rough scenes on the other. Then I start spending long hours in front of the computer, writing entirely new stuff, drawing on the scenes and the outline. So I guess my first rough draft is more a formalized version of my notes than a proper first draft.

What would your ideal writing day look like?

I'd get up at around five a.m., work an hour, have a cup of coffee and breakfast, then return to writing a few more hours. Then I'd go swimming and have lunch. Maybe spend an hour rereading what I'd written that morning—not a close edit, but perhaps just making some marginal notes and small changes, and leave off in a place I can easily pick up on the following day.

What kind of authorial presence do you want to have?

Understated, tentative. I'm acutely aware of how little I ultimately understand about the world I'm describing. I'd like to have a presence that is quiet and respectful of the ultimate mystery of the reality I'm writing about.

Your writing is full of microscopic details—your characters' physical appearance, their homes, their lives. Why do you write with this level of detail?

I can't absorb so much of what is going on so much of the time that I cling to the details. Reporting is very disorienting for me, so I use tiny facts to orient myself.

Let's talk about some ethical issues. You immerse yourself so deeply in the lives of your characters. Do you ever worry about getting too close?

I have to get close to bring a reader close, especially if the world I am depicting is unfair and painful, or disturbing, or tremendously sad. What worries me more is the distance we keep from poverty, how comfortable we are knowing so little about the nature of ordinary suffering.

In some cases, my feelings get in the way of the journalism. For example, I probably could have been there the day that Jessica came home from prison after ten years. My editor wished I'd gone to report the homecoming. Part of me felt, "*My God,* this was her first day with her kids after ten years! I would never intrude on that." It might have been great for the narrative, but as a human being, I don't regret respecting Jessica's privacy. The avoidance was also probably selfish. It was also such an emotional moment, much too powerful for me.

What was your policy on whether you would give advice, or nonmonetary assistance, to the characters in Random Family?

That assumes that I possessed advice that was of use or that people looked to me as some kind of authority. The few times I was stupid enough to think I had useful information, I was promptly told that I "sounded like a social worker"—a polite way of telling me to shut up.

But those times when I did try to assist someone in navigating the system in which I had more leverage also turned out to be something of a learning opportunity for *me*. For example, at one point I called Legal Aid about a woman who was being evicted because her son, allegedly, was selling drugs. I was amazed to learn that they don't provide legal counsel for any drug-related evictions—even charges that are not proven.

Do you worry that your presence might influence the story?

I'm sure my presence affected the story, but reporters are far less important than we like to believe. There were times when the very fact of my presence made it impossible for me to use something I would have liked to include. Sometimes one is present in a way that is clunky or where the explanation is distracting or too complex to explain without taking the narrative in an awkward direction.

However, there were times when I thought the situation was too serious for me not to try to help. For example, it was terribly difficult to only bear witness when Mercedes was being faced with expulsion from elementary school. So when I met the school superintendent and told her that I was there as a journalist, I also made it clear that I was also there as a friend of the family.

What guidelines do you use in reconstructing scenes?

Get as much information from as many sources as possible, conduct repeated interviews with them about their memories of the event, and, if possible, have them take me to visit the scene. Ask them to describe how the action took place, who stood where, see if there is corroborating evidence—photographs of sites, letters, other documents. Have sources draw pictures and charts.

Scouting locations is fun. In *Random Family,* Cesar and Coco spend a weekend at a hotel in the Poconos. To verify whether they gave me the right details I drove up to the hotel and took photographs of their room and interviewed the hotel management. I asked, "Were the bedspreads that color? Was the decor the same then?" Then I showed the pictures to Cesar and Coco in order to stir their memories of the weekend.

Do you believe that the kind of journalism you do can lead to truth?

I don't know about truth, but I believe journalism can lead to a moment of real human connection between the reader and a world that they would not otherwise know. And with luck it will be a lasting connection. I always tell the people I write about that I'm writing about their world, but that it will be my story. So the truth will be my truth, not necessarily the truth that they believe.

Are you optimistic about the prospects of long-form nonfiction?

Books seem like the best place to do what I want to do. I've had a positive experience with magazines, but I see that the limitations of magazines are increasing. The understanding of what can be entertaining is narrowing. It is harder and harder to find places that give writers the time and space they need. That has changed a lot in just the last decade.

BY ADRIAN NICOLE LEBLANC:

Random Family: Love, Drugs, Trouble, and Coming of Age in the Bronx, Scribner, 2003

MICHAEL LEWIS

Michael Lewis has a talent for placing himself at the center of a revolution. In the eighties it was Wall Street, "the epicenter of one of those events that help to define an age," he writes in *Liar's Poker* (1989). In the nineties it was Silicon Valley, "one of those places, unlike the Metropolitan Museum of Art, but like Las Vegas, that are unimaginable anywhere but in the United States," he writes in *The New New Thing* (1999). In *Moneyball* (2003), it was the national pastime—and an Oakland Athletics manager who was radically rethinking the game's basic business principles.

This predilection for change—and an ongoing fascination with mavericks—may be a reaction against Lewis's deep roots in the city of New Orleans, where he was born on October 15, 1960. (His great-great-great-grandfather was appointed Judge for the Territory of New Orleans by Thomas Jefferson.)

Lewis studied art history at Princeton University both because he loved the subject and because he was put off by the rampant preprofessionalism he saw among his fellow students. He took his only microeconomics course (pass/fail) in his senior year. He loved it, too. When he received his degree in 1982, he moved to New York City, where he worked for seven months as a stock boy at the prestigious Wildenstein gallery. After a few months apprenticing with a cabinetmaker, he moved to England to pursue a master's degree at the London School of Economics.

In 1984, Lewis was invited by a distant cousin to a dinner given by the Queen Mother at St. James's Palace. He turned up in a rented tuxedo and found himself seated next to the wife of the managing partner of Salomon Brothers International, who, at the end of the meal, assured him her husband would secure him a place in the bank's training program.

Lewis split his time between Salomon Brothers' London and New York offices, eventually earning $275,000 a year trading bonds.

"Wall Street paid top dollar for what I could do, which was nothing," Lewis writes. "I didn't really imagine I was going to work, it was more as if I were going to collect lottery winnings." He left the firm in January 1988 and soon received a $60,000 book contract to write a history of Wall Street. Instead, he wrote a memoir based on the detailed journals he had kept. *Liar's Poker* was an instant bestseller, sold out in bookstores around Wall Street, and circulated in annotated Xeroxes. The book became a cult classic for its vivid descriptions of the money-mad eighties (it "makes the bond-trading business look like a cross between *Animal House* and *Greed Inc.*," wrote *The Washington Post*'s Steve Mufson). "Never before have so many unskilled 24-year-olds made so much money in so little time as we did this decade in New York and London," writes Lewis.

In 1991, he moved to Washington, D.C., to write for *The New Republic*, for which he covered the 1996 presidential campaign. Although his dispatches were a hit, his idiosyncratic approach quickly brought him into mild conflict with his editors. The problem was that Lewis—like most Americans, barely 49 percent of whom bothered to vote—was bored by the major candidates (Bob Dole and Bill Clinton), and preferred focusing on the marginal figures who didn't have a chance at winning. ("Apathy is a perfectly intelligent response to our current politics," he writes.) Lewis found at "the bottom of the political food chain" those things missing at the top—"bravery, adventurousness, engagement, a passionate devotion to ideas and principles." His search for something *real* kept pulling him back to the also-rans: Pat Buchanan, the conservative ideologue, Alan Keyes, the antiabortion moralist, and Morry Taylor, the straight-talking Michigan businessman.

He wasn't attracted to them simply for their oddness (although there was that). Taking a page from his Wall Street days, he looked at the campaign as a marketplace. "You had two large corporations that had long ago given up doing anything innovative or entrepreneurial themselves, and were just watching small entrepreneurs dream up ideas and concepts and put them out there," Lewis explains. "If you want to know where the market's going to go, follow the entrepreneurs and you have some idea where things are headed. The big campaigns gave up trying to influence where we're headed as a nation; if you wanted to know about that, you had to look at guys like Buchanan, Forbes and Keyes." *Trail Fever* (1997), the book version of his *New Republic* dispatches, was well reviewed ("*Trail Fever* gives the reader something voters desperately needed last year—some good laughs," wrote Phil Gailey in *The New York Times Book Review*) but sold poorly.

In 1997, Lewis moved to California with his wife, journalist Tabitha Soren, who had a one-year fellowship at Stanford University. Lewis knew he wanted to write about the Internet boom and used a series of dispatches for the online magazine *Slate* to explore the subject. He was looking for someone who personified the spirit of innovation and anarchic capitalism that ruled the Internet industry, "the Valley's Gatsby," he says. He found that character in Jim Clark, the billionaire founder of three successful companies, including Netscape. For Lewis, Clark is the ultimate anti–Organization Man, the originator of new new things (which Lewis defines as an "idea that is a tiny push away from general acceptance and, when it gets that push, will change the world").

The New New Thing consisted of parallel narratives: the first told the story of Clark's rise from math geek to Internet guru, while the other described his quest to build *Hyperion*, the world's tallest single-masted sailboat, a state-of-the-art $37 million ship outfitted with $30 million of Impressionist art and sixty miles of wires, and controlled by twenty-five computers.

This time, the book's sales matched its extraordinary reviews. "No one has conveyed the atmosphere of the boom better," writes James Fallows in *The New York Review of Books*. "People will read this book years from now to know what the Internet boom was like—as they now read his first book, *Liar's Poker*, to recapture the atmosphere of Wall Street during the bond-trading heyday of the 1980s." Writing in *The New York Times Book Review*, Kurt Anderson praised Lewis's wry sensibility. "Lewis conveys with a rare combination of wisdom and glee both the thrill and absurdity of late-twentieth-century business." The book was sold to the movies, and Lewis wrote a screenplay, *Silicon*, that was never produced.

The idea for *Moneyball* grew out of a simple question: "How did one of the poorest teams in baseball, the Oakland Athletics, win so many games?" The answer, Lewis discovered, had more to do with how a team spends its money than how much money it has—the polar opposite of baseball's conventional wisdom. An extended portrait of Billy Beane, *Moneyball* explains what happens when a baseball organization starts rating players using statistics and computers. The miracle of *Moneyball* is that Lewis has, essentially, written a study of statistics in the guise of a (bestselling) book about baseball ("What next—an inspirational tale about superior database management?" joked *The New Republic*).

The book's influence reached far beyond the baseball diamond. Reviewing *Moneyball* in *The Weekly Standard*, investment banker Mark Gerson suggested that not only was it Lewis's best book so far, but also that "it may be the best business book anyone has written." *Daily Variety*'s Jonathan Bing reported that it was being read closely by Hollywood executives, "casting new light on the talent business, the packaging of films, and the financial-performance statistics that get plugged into almost every facet of studio accounting." The *San Francisco Chronicle*'s David Kipen wrote that "*Moneyball* isn't just about baseball, any more than Lewis' *Liar's Poker* was just about Wall Street, or *The New New Thing* about computers. At its heart lies a universal, almost Newtonian question that has nothing to do with baseball—can talent be created or destroyed, or only altered?"

Moneyball was the first of a two-book deal, the second of which, *Underdogs*, will follow the first five years of the careers of the players drafted by Beane. While Lewis watches them work their way from the minor league to the majors, he is trying his hand as a screenwriter. He is at work on *The Money Shot*, a television pilot for CBS about three women who start a hedge fund. And he is cowriting *Bit Players*, a "fish out of water" movie with Dustin Hoffman, Gene Hackman, and Robert Duvall as Montana rubes whose company is purchased by an unscrupulous Wall Street investment firm, and who travel to New York to regain control.

———

What kinds of subjects get you excited?
I start with either a character or a situation in flux. When I am lucky enough to find a great character who is changing a big situation—as I did with Internet entrepreneur Jim Clark in *The New*

New Thing [2000]—I get a wonderfully odd view of the status quo. Since the status quo is always responding to the people who change it, by looking at a "marginal" figure's conflict with the status quo, I can see a lot about it I wouldn't otherwise see. The people I've gotten excited by tend to be having an argument with the world that they are at the center of—and they can kick the doors down, bringing me along into the center of the action with them.

In the case of Jim Clark, I was fascinated by how someone who only a few years before had been a marginal figure at a marginal company in a marginal industry, could all of a sudden become an agent of change and wreak havoc at the very heart of American industry.

When I covered the 1996 election for *The New Republic* [a version of which was published as *Trail Fever,* 1997], I was consistently attracted to the putatively marginal figures—Morry Taylor, Alan Keyes, Pat Buchanan, Ralph Nader, John McCain—who were saying much more interesting things about the process than the actual contenders, Bill Clinton and Bob Dole. The troublemakers were the ones who provided a truly different perspective on the process, so I went along with them.

In *Moneyball,* I write about how Billy Beane, the manager of the Oakland A's, a financially marginal baseball team, challenged the game's received wisdom about the best way to win. Under Beane, the A's won more games, while spending less money, than any other team in their division.

Your fascination with extremes—Wall Street in the 1980s, Silicon Valley in the 1990s—seems to be a consistent theme in your work. Why?
Probably because I grew up in New Orleans, which is the complete opposite of these worlds. New Orleans is a stable, unchanging world.

How do you come up with story ideas?
I have a bench in my office, on which I keep many piles of paper, each of which is a potential story, or subject. So, for instance, my pile of "financial" ideas is a pile of little ideas for the financial column I write for *Bloomberg News* or other finance-related magazine

pieces. I clip items from newspapers, scribble notes to myself after conversations, etc. When a pile gets so high it might tip over, I go through all the clips.

How do you develop these ideas into stories?

It is different in every case. For example, I only came to write about Jim Clark and Silicon Valley because my wife got a Stanford University journalism fellowship in 1997, which meant that we moved near Silicon Valley. It was *clear* to me that what was going on in the Internet industry there was very weird, just from a financial point of view. It seemed like such a strange episode in the history of capitalism that I wanted to document it.

That's a pretty big topic. How did you find the *specific* story?

I knew I had to learn more about Silicon Valley, so I started writing a series of small pieces for *Slate,* just to familiarize myself with the territory. They were all over the map, but they all took place in Silicon Valley, and they ended up introducing me to all the characters and issues.

How did you settle on Jim Clark as your central character?

As I wrote more about Silicon Valley, I was struck by the fact that virtually *all* the trails led to him. I'd interview people at venture capital firms and they'd all be obsessing about Jim Clark's next move. Kids starting companies told me they were modeling themselves on Jim Clark. Netscape, which Clark founded, created the financial model for the entire industry. I realized that it was Jim Clark's era. He was the perfect representative figure, the very embodiment of the innovative spirit, which is what the Silicon Valley phenomenon was all about. I get excited when I sense that a person's *character* says things about his environment; when the *way he is* tells me something about the world around him.

Then, I was sitting in a diner one afternoon, taking a break from a bike ride, and I realized that I had to *call Jim Clark!* I found his number in the directory and called him on a pay phone. He invited me to come over, so I got on my bike and rode a couple of miles over to his house. I was drenched in sweat when I arrived, but an hour into our conversation I thought, *"My God, there's a lot going on here!"* He was volcanic.

Who do you least like writing about?

I get endless entreaties from people—some of them quite famous—who want me to write about them. Many of these people are, at least in theory, *very* interesting. But they *never* interest me. It may not be their fault. It may simply be that it is necessary for me to feel that *I've* stumbled upon a topic on my own. In order to write a good piece, there has to be a situation in which *I'm* originating the project, whether or not the characters want me to.

Who do you most like writing about?

It is rarely just a character that gets me excited. I'm attracted to some combination of a character and *ideas*. I don't care only about a character, or the situation a character finds himself in. What I care most about is the situation in which I find myself in relation to the character. I need to have an emotional response to somebody I write about. When someone makes me laugh or feel intellectually excited, I'm confident that everything else about the story will take care of itself.

Do you pursue only your own ideas, or will you take suggestions from others?

Since the process of *discovering* an idea is so important to me, I'm not inclined to take stories from editors. The problem with editor-driven stories is that they come in a neat package. The editor already has the piece in mind when he calls you. He knows what he wants you to say.

It used to be that every time an editor from a fancy New York magazine called me with a "great" idea that "everyone here" thinks is "perfect" for me, I'd be so flattered that I'd take the assignment.

For example, after the Ayatollah Khomeini issued his fatwa, *Esquire* wanted me to do what was essentially a hatchet job on Salman Rushdie, who they thought had been given a "free ride." I instantly accepted the assignment and thought, "*Wow,* I'm writing for *Esquire* magazine!" I went off and read all of Rushdie's novels and realized that he was a genius. Then I interviewed some of his most vociferous critics and thought, "These people are off their rockers!" I was lost. I wrote about 385 words of the piece, but it was worse than bad.

Now, I'm lucky enough to have a few very fruitful relationships with editors I talk to all the time. In the course of a conversation, one of us inadvertently comes up with a good idea.

Are you always aware of the fact that you're reporting a story, or do they sometimes grow out of your everyday life?
Moneyball came straight out of my life: watching baseball, reading the sports pages—all the things I waste my time on. I noticed an anomaly: the commissioner of baseball kept complaining that the economics of the game kept poor teams from winning . . . while at the very same time this poor team just down the road, the Oakland A's, *were* winning lots of games. I wrote *Moneyball*—which I originally conceived of as an article—to figure out what was going on.

Do you prefer writing books or articles?
I much prefer books because they give me the time to master my subject and test all my theories. I have to be passionately involved with a subject to write a book, while I can write a magazine piece about a topic I'm not particularly smitten with. But the agonies of actually writing a book are far greater than anything I've ever experienced writing an article.

How many projects do you work on simultaneously?
Too many. At any given moment, I have at least four projects under way. I write short columns for *Bloomberg News* or *Slate*. I'm usually working on a book. I write screenplays, none of which have ever been produced (but which provides my family with health insurance by virtue of my membership in the Screenwriters Guild). And I'm usually at some stage of one of the long articles I write for *The New York Times Magazine*. I don't know whether it is a character flaw, or just comes with the life of a freelance writer.

Do you do most of your research before, during, or after your reporting?
I do most of my research while I'm reporting. For example, when I was reporting *The New New Thing*, I spent three weeks at Stanford University reading their archive on every business and idea in Silicon Valley since the early fifties. And when I was writing *Liar's*

Poker, I spent days in the Princeton library reading all the business memoirs published in the last century in order to get a better sense of the genre I was writing in. I didn't actualy *use* any of the research in either case. But it gave me a feeling of being grounded and confident. I don't think any writer can write until he's persuaded himself— falsely or not—that he has an original view, that he has something worth saying.

Do you prefer to approach a subject as an outsider or an insider?

It's always better if you can get an introduction, because I want them to think of me as something *other* than "a reporter who wants a quote," which is what most people assume when they're approached by a journalist.

How much do you tell a subject about your project?

The only way to develop these relationships of trust—especially since they are relationships of trust that are partly unfounded, since I'm going to write anything I like—is to actually *tell* the person what I'm thinking while I'm taking notes. I develop theories about their character or motives, which are not always flattering. But I bounce the theories off them anyway. I'm not a cipher. I don't make myself a mystery to my subject.

For example, I wrote a profile of Harold Ickes, Clinton's deputy chief of staff, for *The New York Times Magazine* ["Bill Clinton's Garbage Man," September 21, 1997]. Ickes was the guy who took care of all the scandals. His father had been the secretary of the interior under FDR, and wrote millions of words in diaries, both published and unpublished. When I read Ickes Sr.'s diaries, I was struck by the parallels between father and son. The son had a relationship with Clinton much like the father's with Roosevelt. So I opened up my interview by mentioning these parallels. I told him my theory that, unbeknownst to him, he was reliving his father's experience in some strange way. And the conversation just *flowed!* He revealed emotional and factual material I never would have gotten otherwise. Even though he objected to my theory, he objected in useful ways.

Do you have a reporting routine?

I don't have a system. But what I do have is a conviction that if I want to get to the truth of someone's life, I have to insinuate myself into that life as thoroughly as I can.

How do you convince people to allow you to do that?

I make sure my presence isn't obnoxious to them. If I am a chore, I'll become the reporter they let into their lives for a few hours to ask a few superficial questions. And that's not enough access for what I do.

For someone to *want* me around, I have to be *useful* to them. And the best way to be useful to them is to help them think through the problems they are facing. I'm often my subject's sounding board.

For example, when Jim Clark was launching Healtheon, we talked about how he should deal with the investment bankers. The fact that I had worked on Wall Street helped. Clark was also in the process of acquiring about $200 million in paintings, and the fact that I had studied art history in college helped our relationship as well. Whether it was about finance or art, we could have a conversation that might be useful to him.

Moneyball is an even better example. I developed relationships with the players, the coaches, and the front office while I was reporting the book. I could tell the front office things that the players were thinking and saying that *they* hadn't heard. And I could tell the players things that the front office was thinking and saying that *they* hadn't heard. The fact that I was *useful* to all of them made them less resistant to talking to me when I showed up at the ballpark. I had *something to trade.* I didn't have a parasitic relationship with them. I had a symbiotic relationship.

The ideal relationship isn't reporter-subject. It's just two people hanging out together.

How do you initiate such a relationship?

It starts as a casual conversation—without my taking notes and asking interview-like questions. I don't even have a notebook. But at some point the notebook comes out, and then it *stays* out.

We talk informally for a while. I explain exactly why I'm curious, which is pretty vague in the beginning. I think it's *offensive* when a writer knows what he is going to write before he starts reporting. It presumes that the actual contact serves no purpose other than to fuel the writer's theory. So I find it is natural, and also best strategically, *not* to have too much of a theory going into a piece. I take the time to see what someone is like. I ask, "Do you mind if I hang around? There's no way I can do what I do based on one conversation."

When do you tell someone how much time you'll need?

Never! Nobody would ever agree, up front, to the kind of relationship I require. Hey, *I* wouldn't either! If Billy Beane, in our first meeting, said to me, "You can write about me. But you've got to spend the next eight months hanging out with me," I'd have said, *"No Way!"*

It is an organic process. I hang out with someone and think, "Hey, this is interesting." I hang out some more and think, "This is *really* interesting." I hang out some more and think, "This is *it!*"

How would you describe your reportorial stance?

There is a group of writers—George Plimpton, Hunter S. Thompson, Tom Wolfe, Truman Capote—who seem to me the very model of how one should immerse oneself in a subject's life. I read all their books when I was a kid, not because I thought I'd be a writer, but because they gave me pleasure. When I *did* start writing, I thought to myself, "How the hell do you get yourself into a situation where you end up being stomped by Hells Angels, the way Hunter S. Thompson did?" And the answer they gave me is: *you become one of them!* I don't think of myself as a "reporter." *That's* my reportorial stance.

Is there any particular persona you use to motivate people to talk?

I approach my subject in the spirit of the anti-journalist, of the amateur. I try to avoid the rituals of "professional journalism." My goal is to attain the best possible, necessarily imperfect, understanding of this situation. And the best possible way to do that is to *forget* the ordinary rules of journalism, the standard relationships between subjects and writers, and the sorts of questions you're *supposed* to ask.

How do you pace yourself while immersing yourself so deeply?

I'm careful to *under*-stay my welcome. I'll sometimes leave, even when I have a chance to be with someone I'm writing about. I've found that it alleviates a subject's anxiety if I show him that I have a life, too.

But then how do you make sure not to miss important events?

I always do a certain amount of dropping in just to keep the relationship current. And I also hang around because it's fun. And, after a while, it becomes clear which kinds of events I want to see them experience.

For example, I wanted to make sure to see Jim Clark meet with the investment bankers who were trying to persuade him to take Healtheon public with them. I worked very hard, structuring *everything* in our relationship toward that event. I assured him that I wouldn't bother him with all sorts of other requests, but that I just *had* to be there at that meeting.

Do you ever set scenes up in order for you to see a character in specific circumstances?

I'm not opposed to it, but the problem is that most of the people I write about are so extraordinarily *willful* that getting them to do anything I want them to do is difficult.

Do you worry that your close relationships with subjects influence the story too much?

No. I've never influenced anyone I've written about. At some point the subject will inevitably remind me that I'm there at *their* pleasure, which I am.

Do you have any guidelines about what you will and won't do with your subjects?

Some writers have rules about not giving their subjects money, which I would never do because I'm cheap. But most of the people I've written about have plenty of money, so my rule is the opposite: I don't let *them* give *me* anything. In the months I spent reporting on the Oakland A's for *Moneyball*, I *never* accepted a free ticket. It isn't so much that I'm afraid of being corrupted, as that I'm afraid some asshole will accuse me of coloring my opinions because I accepted a gift.

Have you found yourself in potentially compromising situations?

Yes. For example, when my wife and I were having dinner at Jim Clark's house one night, Clark's wife offered to put us on the "friends" list for the Healtheon IPO. The "friends" list is a list of people in and around a company that is about to go public, who can buy shares at the original IPO price. When the price shoots up, they can sell the shares for a huge profit. I wouldn't ever do something like that. It would put me in a position where I couldn't say anything good about him either.

So I guess if I had to formalize my rule it would be: would I be embarrassed to see someone who meant me harm use this incident against me in print? If I would, then I shouldn't do it.

Do you ever do straight interviews?

I do them all the time. But they themselves are rarely immediately useful for the piece I'm writing. I'll almost never get a good quote in a situation in which I'm doing a straight interview with someone in his office. They can be useful in the sense that a straight interview might *lead to* something interesting.

Like what?

A straight interview may lead to Jim Clark's offering, "Come along with me on my helicopter." (Flying with him was a perfect metaphor for him. Everyone who dealt with Clark was a passenger in a helicopter of a man who you weren't sure knew what he was doing.) Or Billy Beane's saying, "Come with me while I scout baseball players." Now, all of a sudden, I have a *scene*! I don't just have quotes, I have dialogue, details, movement.

Will you agree to send questions to someone before an interview?

Being asked to fax my questions ahead is the *surest* sign that I'm not going to have a substantial relationship with that person. If someone asks me to do that, the whole exercise is pointless.

Do you do interviews by e-mail or by phone, or only in person?
Interviews by phone are grossly inferior to interviews in person.
But using the phone is sometimes inevitable. For example, in
Moneyball there is a scene in which Billy Beane almost trades himself to the Boston Red Sox. The negotiations were all taking place
over the phone, and I was talking to Billy three times a day in order
to keep up. There was no other way to follow it. But I would never
rely on the phone if I didn't already know the person.

Where do you like interviewing?
Characters are always so much more interesting when they are
moving through space than they are when they are at rest (especially
when they are behind a desk in their office). Once I've developed a
relationship with a subject, the first question I ask is whether they
have plans to go anywhere, and whether I can come with them.
Even when what they're doing is irrelevant to what I'm writing
about, I just want to participate in something with them.
Billy Beane let me go with him to scout a few minor league baseball teams. Those trips resulted in the deepest, most intimate conversations we had—all of them in his car, driving back and forth
between Oakland and Modesto, where the A's have a team.
I learned this technique in college, during the best job interview I
ever had. I was applying for a job to lead a bunch of high school girls
on a tour of Europe. When I arrived for the interview, the guy who
was supposed to see me was flustered, and apologized. He said he
was in the middle of moving his furniture from one office to another,
and asked if I could help. So we spent the next hour moving his furniture together. It was brilliant on his part. The way he interviewed
people was to make them *do something* with him. He believed he
saw character more clearly that way. I agree.

Do you take notes or tape?
The only time I can remember having to use a tape recorder was
when I was writing about the presidential campaign of Alan Keyes.
I've never heard someone speak so eloquently and quickly. So I
bought a tape recorder. Otherwise, I never tape.

What kinds of notes do you take?

I use my own style of shorthand. I write on yellow legal pads inside leather binders to keep the paper from getting smudged. Then immediately afterward I go to the computer and type them up.

How much will you argue with someone you're interviewing?

One of the few times I've had a heated argument during an interview was with Securities and Exchange Commission chairman Arthur Levitt. I was writing about a teenage stock trader ["Jonathan Ledbed's Extracurricular Activities," *The New York Times Magazine*, February 25, 2001], and so violently disagreed with Levitt that I felt it was better to tell him in person, rather than simply write it in the piece. The truth is that I felt a kind of contempt for Arthur Levitt because of the way he had handled the situation. I felt he was a phony, and I still think he's a phony. He's not a person I'm ever going to have a relationship with.

I sometimes find myself in heated arguments with other of my characters, but they have all been in the context of mutual understanding and respect. But if I've got criticisms, I find it useful to lay them out and see how they respond. It's all good material.

Do you ever assign pseudonyms to your characters?

Almost never. I did it twice in *Moneyball* because in both cases they were private figures who would have been publicly ridiculed by the casual mention of their names. It seemed gratuitous to mess up those people's lives by using their names. In *Liar's Poker* I changed the names of a couple of people I worked with because I didn't want them to get fired, which they would have been. I'm not categorically against pseudonyms, but I don't think that a writer should use them a lot. Once you get loose with names there's a chance you'll get loose with other things too.

Will you negotiate about what is on and off the record?

If I'm in a real relationship with someone, he *has* to be able to declare certain things off the record. What amazes me is how rarely people I write about invoke it. I think that is because if someone believes I'm trying to understand him he will eventually be very open with me. At some point, the ambitions of the writer and the subject converge.

How important are the particulars of your identity—New Orleans, Princeton, investment banking, the Internet, etc.—in your writing?

I'm delightfully self-absorbed and don't at all mind writing about myself, in the right circumstances. So my personality is quite important to my writing. When Tom Wolfe was asked whether one of his theories about human nature applied to himself, Wolfe replied, sharply, "I'm not in the business of developing theories that exempt me." I agree. I think that at some level you always have to be testing what you think about the world against yourself. "Do I contradict that? Does that ring true with me?" The diary form comes very naturally to me.

Is that why you are so often a character in your writing?

"I" is just another tool in my toolbox. I try to be tactical about using myself as a character. I often cut myself out of a draft if I decide it isn't necessary or that my presence is distracting the reader.

For example, I wrote all my *New Republic* pieces about the 1996 presidential campaign in the first person because there was no other way to capture all these disconnected fragments. The only thing that could connect them was a single sensibility, which was the author's sensibility. I haven't been a major character in my last two books— *The New New Thing* and *Moneyball*—although I do pop in every now and then. I do this for a reason. There are times when the reader needs a seat at the table and the "I" gives it to them. The "ordinary fan" needs to be in the ballpark during an Oakland A's game having "ordinary fan" responses. Or he needs to know what it feels like to be up in a helicopter with Jim Clark, who only just learned how to fly and is ignoring his instructor.

The relationship between the reporter and the subject is somewhat claustrophobic and I can let some air in by telling the reader that there are actual human beings interacting with each other. "I" is the screwdriver with which I jimmy the lock open and let some air in.

Do you reconstruct scenes you haven't witnessed?

I place tremendous importance on being there myself because a scene is *never* as good when you learn about it from other people. What *really* makes a scene swing on the page are the little things that nobody but the writer would ever notice. The participants in a scene might help me discover what happened, but they wouldn't be looking at it from the perspective of a writer who wants to render it artfully, which is what I want to do. But if I wasn't there, I'm happy to reconstruct it after talking to everyone who was. If someone tells me he said something, and someone else verifies it, I feel comfortable putting those words in quotes.

What I disapprove of is the way writers like Bob Woodward claim to capture their subjects' inner thoughts. I don't believe it for a second. His characters end up having the capacity to feel only what Bob Woodward feels. And it's always the *same* feeling.

How do you know when you've done enough reporting?

When I can't wait to get to the computer and start writing.

Is writing more pleasurable/painful than reporting?

They both have their difficulties and pleasures. When I start writing, I always have the horrible feeling that I'm doing it for the first time. It never feels easier than it was before. I've always written with the feeling that I'm under some kind of onerous deadline.

But I get tremendous pleasure once I get into the writing. Writing is a very physical act for me. I sweat, my pulse rises. People who've been near me when I write tell me that I cackle to myself.

Do you make an outline before starting to write?

Yes, I write a point-by-point outline for even the shortest piece. When I'm working on a book, I'm outlining the whole time I'm reporting. Three weeks into the project, I'll have one outline. As I learn more, I trash it and write a new one. It is an endless process.

What do these outlines look like?

I have a computer file called "Outline" in which I save my successive drafts. I outline chapter by chapter, each outline consisting of an ordered list of the information, scenes, characters, and details I

want to include. As I accumulate more material, I drop it into different chapters, rewriting the outline of each chapter as I go.

How do you begin writing?
Fitfully. I'll write something, but it won't be the beginning or the
middle or the end—I'm just getting an idea out on the page. Then, as
the words accumulate, I start thinking about how they need to be
organized.

What is in front of you when you begin to write?
Nothing, except for the computer screen. I write from memory, as
if I were writing a novel. When I finish a day's writing I go back and
check the text against my notes to make sure the facts and quotes
are right, and that I haven't inadvertently made anything up. The
quotes are almost always accurate because by that point I've gone
over the material so many times in my head.

Do you pay much attention to the sound of your words?
I do, but I'm *anti*poetical. I don't like being pretty for the sake of
being pretty. I'm put off by florid prose, or prose that gets in the way
of the meaning. I find elegance in sparseness.

How many drafts do you do?
I probably do twenty drafts of each chapter. I write something
over and *over*. It's like *Groundhog Day*. My writing process is sweaty
and inelegant. The most common pleasant thing people say to me
about my writing is that it looks "effortless" or "easy." It is the opposite of effortless. There must be some compulsion in me to want to
make it look easy because an awful lot of what I do literarily is
designed to make it look like I didn't do a lot of reporting or work.

Isn't that the WASP cliché, never to show effort?
It is no longer a cliché to be a WASP cliché.

Is there any time of day you like to write?
I've always written best very early in the morning and very late at
night. I write very little in the middle of the day. If I do any work in
the middle of the day, it is editing what I've written that morning.

What would your ideal writing day look like?

Left to my own devices, with no family, I'd start writing at seven p.m. and stop at four a.m. That is the way I used to write. I liked to get ahead of everybody. I'd think to myself, "I'm starting tomorrow's workday, *tonight!*" Late nights are wonderfully tranquil. No phone calls, no interruptions. I like the feeling of knowing that nobody is trying to reach me.

Is there anywhere you need to be in order to write?

No, I've written in every conceivable circumstance. I like writing in my office, which is an old redwood cabin about a hundred yards from my house in Berkeley. It has a kitchen, a little bedroom, a bathroom, and a living room, which I use as a study. But I've written in awful enough situations that I know that the quality of the prose doesn't depend on the circumstances in which it is composed. I don't believe the muse visits you. I believe that *you* visit the muse. If you wait for that "perfect moment" you're not going to be very productive.

Do you talk about your projects as you work on them?

I don't like to because I worry that it will sap my energy. So I lie. I've gotten very good at killing someone's interest in what I'm working on by making it sound *so* tedious that there is no follow-up question.

Do you show your work-in-progress to anyone?

Yes, but very selectively. I send my editor at W.W. Norton, Star Lawrence, a few chapters at a time, just to make sure I'm not going off the rails. I might show my wife something I've written that day if I think she might get some pleasure from it, or might have something to say about it.

What kind of authorial presence do you strive for?

It varies from piece to piece, and book to book, but the worm's-eye view is generally much more interesting to me than the God's-eye view. I use my presence to lure the reader into adopting my point of view. Adopting a personal, intimate authorial presence enables me to include elements—small observations, insights—that are difficult to get into a piece if the author is detached and impersonal.

How do you conceive of yourself as a writer?

I don't think of myself as a "journalist." I don't have anything in common with, say, a business reporter at *The New York Times*. Not the spirit in which I operate, not my ambition. *Nothing.*

I have *huge* literary ambitions. When I bother to write a book, I hope it is a book that might one day be thought a "classic." I have grandiose notions of what my writing might be and that's what gets me excited.

You've flirted with the idea of writing a novel, and have said that you might one day find a situation which would best be rendered through fiction.

I might write a novel, but I don't have a lot of anxiety about the form. I don't think that novelists are somehow more like "artists" than I am. I think the distinction between "fiction" and "nonfiction" is overblown. I reject the notion that there is some limit to the importance or universality of what I write *because* it is "nonfiction." My themes and subjects can go mano a mano with those of any novelist, and do fine.

Whereas journalists once felt humbled by the novel, we now live in an age in which the *novelist* lives in a state of anxiety about nonfiction. You see it most clearly with films in the lust to be able to put at the end of the film, "This is a true story." And in the scramble for the "real world," whether that is in "reality television" or any other form.

I compare what I do to "travel writing." I make my characters move through space, I explore new worlds and depict them for my readers. "Travel writer" isn't a bad description of what I do.

What writers have influenced you the most?

Mark Twain influenced my choice of tone—to the extent that a writer can choose a tone. Orwell has been a great influence on me because of the way he disguises complexity as simplicity. He is so plainspoken and direct, except that there is nothing actually "plain" about his writing. Wolfe's zeal for reporting has inspired me, and when it comes to tone, Wolfe is a kind of poet. The *noises* he can make on the page are extraordinary. But I'd be a moron to try to imitate him. It would be like trying to imitate Arcimboldo, the seventeenth-century Italian painter who made portraits out of vegetables. You can only do something like that *once*.

Do you believe the kind of writing you do can yield truth?

Truth is a very loaded word. If I limit my ambition to capturing the subjective truth of an experience, to getting across exactly what it was like to be that person in that situation, then I'm doing pretty well.

I reject the idea of the "objective journalist." The notion that you can be so detached that who you are doesn't affect how you see things is *worse* than bad. It is the enemy of good writing. The best I can do is to purify my vision and then leave it to the reader to decide what it is worth. The ultimate goal of writing is to give pleasure, not to deliver objective truth.

Do you think long-form nonfiction is a peculiarly American form?

It has certainly flourished here like nowhere else, although English travel writing is the unacknowledged model for a lot of what we do.

There are other reasons Americans have dominated the form. Americans are lucky enough to be living in a place which, in relative historical terms, is *breathtakingly* important, not just militarily and politically, but also culturally. The stories we tell about life in America have a universal appeal that stories from no other place have. There is a market for it. This may be superficial, but it's true. An American writer can write about something American and *feel* as if there isn't anywhere on earth where people won't be interested— even if there are actually *plenty* of places on earth that aren't interested. It is a level of confidence that no other nationality has at the moment.

Do you consider yourself a New Journalist in Tom Wolfe's sense?

I very much identify with Wolfe's view of journalism. But I never thought that the New Journalists were all that new. What they had, that nobody else at the time had, was a brio and energy. I *completely* identify with that.

But the *technique* of the New Journalists was never that new. I've been reading Dickens's *Bleak House* and have been struck by how similar it is to what I do. The beginning of *Bleak House* reads like a screenplay, and his introduction—in which he says that readers will complain about how implausible the book is, but that all you have to do is look at society to see that he's right—could have been written by an American literary journalist anytime after about 1970. It begins, "London. Michaelmas term lately over, and the Lord Chancellor sitting in Lincoln's Inn Hall. Implacable November weather. As much mud in the streets as if the waters had but newly retired from the face of the earth, and it would not be wonderful to meet a Megalosaurus, forty feet long or so, waddling like an elephantine lizard up Holborn Hill." Sound familiar? The New Journalism isn't "new"! It's a sensible English tradition that, like so much else, Americans took hold of and ran renegade with.

What do you think about the prospects for the kind of writing you do?

They've never been better. I wouldn't trade this time and place in history to do what I do, with another time and place. The market for it is bigger and bigger every year. The material is as rich as it's ever been. The ability to get inside people's lives, at all places in the social order, is easier than it's ever been. An awful lot of the top of society was, not so long ago, completely inaccessible. And I don't think that is true any longer.

And there are so many different vehicles for chronicling these worlds. I don't think the book is in danger. We shouldn't think so much about the fate of the genre—because all the genres are viable—but just of the quality of the individual work. All the nonfiction genres are viable and will flourish. I wouldn't worry about the novel either. There is still a good market for a good novel, like Jonathan Franzen's

The Corrections. The only genre I worry about is poetry—though worry is probably the wrong word.

I certainly don't worry so much about the fate of long-form nonfiction in magazines. It is true that there are fewer magazines to publish it in than there were twenty years ago, but I wouldn't be surprised if there are more of them twenty years from now. The problem isn't with outlets or the market. The problem is with the quality of the stuff that is being written. If people want to read it, you can get it published.

BY MICHAEL LEWIS:

Moneyball: The Art of Winning an Unfair Game, W.W. Norton, 2003
Next: The Future Just Happened, W.W. Norton, 2001
The New New Thing: A Silicon Valley Story, W.W. Norton, 1999
Trail Fever: Spin Doctors, Rented Strangers, Thumb Wrestlers, Toe Suckers, Grizzly Bears, and Other Creatures on the Road to the White House, Knopf, 1997
(Published in paperback as *Losers: The Road to Everyplace but the White House,* Vintage Books, 2000)
Pacific Rift, W.W. Norton, 1992
The Money Culture, W.W. Norton, 1991
Liar's Poker: Rising Through the Wreckage on Wall Street, W.W. Norton, 1989

SUSAN ORLEAN

New Yorker writer Susan Orlean is known for her quirky stories about "ordinary" people who are not normally in the public eye or consciousness, but in whose very ordinariness Orlean finds something extraordinary. These include a profile of a ten-year-old boy, a woman in suburban New Jersey who keeps tigers, and a New York taxi driver who also happens to be the king of the Ashanti. "An ordinary life examined closely reveals itself to be exquisite and exceptional, somehow managing to be both heroic and plain," she writes in the introduction to *The Bullfighter Checks Her Makeup: My Encounters with Extraordinary People* (2001). "I really believed that anything at all was worth writing about if you cared about it enough, and that the best and only necessary justification for writing any particular story was that I cared about it. The challenge was to write these stories in a way that got other people as interested in them as I was."

Susan Orlean was born on October 31, 1955, in Cleveland, Ohio. Her father was a real estate developer and her mother worked in a bank. Orlean studied literature and history at the University of Michigan at Ann Arbor, where she wrote poetry. "The poetry I wrote was not wildly different from the kinds of things I write about today. Not super-abstract, somewhat narrative and descriptive. It taught me to appreciate compact, concise writing. Writing poetry was a good exercise for learning about the economy of word choice," she says.

Orlean got hooked on nonfiction when, as a young girl, she loved reading *Life* magazine. At the time, the magazine published pieces offering "slice of life" stories about what it was like to be a country doctor or a policeman. "There was this notion in *Life* that subjects like these were genuine 'stories.' The idea of writing about something real was enormously appealing to me," she says.

Her interest in literary journalism grew while she was in college and her best friend gave her a subscription to *The New Yorker* for

Christmas. In one issue, she read a piece by Mark Singer that pro-filed three brothers who were all building superintendents in New York City. "A bell went off in my head. I read Mark's piece and thought: 'This is what I want to do,'" she says. From then on, Orlean dreamed of writing for The New Yorker, but had no idea how one went about doing so. "Then, even more than now, The New Yorker was the Kremlin. You didn't even know who worked there, or who wrote the stories, or anything," she told The Yale Literary Magazine.

After college, Orlean moved to Portland, Oregon, to be with a boyfriend who was starting law school there. Her first job was writing for a tiny monthly magazine called Paper Rose. Her second job was with the Portland alternative newsweekly, Willamette Week, where the editor (who had worked for The Wall Street Journal) became a mentor, teaching her the basics of journalism. Orlean wrote music reviews and features about everything from Hmong refugees to the eruption of Mount St. Helens. She wrote her first freelance piece for The Village Voice about the New Age community founded by Bhagwan Shree Rajneesh in Oregon. One day Orlean got a call from Rolling Stone writer Michael Gilmore, who had previously written for Willamette Week. He liked her work and asked her to contribute to Rolling Stone, where she pro-filed musicians and actors.

In 1982, Orlean moved to Boston and became staff writer at the alternative newsweekly The Boston Phoenix, moving later to The Boston Globe, which made her a columnist. Her first book, Red Sox and Bluefish: And Other Things that Make New England New England (1987), collects her pieces from the Globe.

While still in Boston, she also started writing Saturday Night (1990), a book that chronicles how people across the United States spend their Saturday evenings: dancing, bowling, dating, drinking, and even murdering. Beyond its ostensible subject, it was an opportunity for Orlean to report on ordinary people. "Observing different kinds of people in different parts of America who live in different sorts of circumstances at leisure on Saturday night seemed like a perfect opportunity to observe them in their most natural and self-selected setting—like studying an elephant romping around in the Ngorongoro Crater as opposed to studying an elephant carrying an advertising sandwich-board in front of a used-car lot in Miami," she writes in the book's introduction. *Saturday Night* was well received, *Publishers Weekly* writing that "tight, clean prose and thoughtful observations make this series of essays about the Saturday night experience hum with all the vitality and activity of its subject."

Orlean moved to New York in 1986, where she wrote for *Rolling Stone* and *Vogue*. Soon after she arrived, she heard that *The New Yorker*'s new editor, Robert Gottlieb, was looking for writers for the "Talk of the Town" section. Her first "Talk" piece was about how Benetton teaches its employees to fold sweaters. "Some of my ideas were a little outside of *The New Yorker* mold, which Gottlieb liked. He liked the populism of what I was interested in," she says. Orlean became a staff writer in 1992.

In 1994, she read a newspaper article on the theft of two hundred rare orchids from the Fakahatchee Strand Preserve State Park in Florida. The orchid thief was John Laroche, a horticultural consultant who once ran an extensive nursery for the Seminole tribe, with dreams of making a fortune by cloning the rare ghost orchid *Polyrrhiza lindenii*. Orlean interviewed Laroche after sitting through his trial, and the result was "Orchid Fever," which appeared in *The New Yorker* on January 23, 1995. Orlean expanded her research and returned to the Florida swampland to pen *The Orchid Thief: A True Story of Beauty and Obsession* (1998). *The Wall Street Journal*'s Frances Taliaferro called the book "a swashbuckling piece of reporting that celebrates some virtues that made America great. Here are visionary passions and fierce obsessions; heroic feats accomplished in exotic settings; outsize characters, entrepreneurs at the edge of the frontier, adventurers."

The Orchid Thief was the springboard for the movie *Adaptation*, directed by Spike Jonze (*Being John Malkovich*) with a screenplay by Charlie Kaufman (who, in an odd twist, appears in the movie as a character played by Nicolas Cage). Orlean is played by Meryl Streep and Chris Cooper portrays Laroche (in a role that earned him an Oscar). *Adaptation* was the second movie developed from one of Orlean's pieces; the first was *Blue Crush*, which was developed from her article about teenage surfer girls in Maui.

Orlean and her husband, John Gillespie, an investment banker, live in New York and Boston. They have a red-and-white Welsh springer spaniel named Cooper, with whom Orlean wrote *Throw Me a Bone: 50 Healthy, Canine Taste-Tested Recipes for Snacks, Meals, and Treats* (2003). She was a 2004 Nieman Fellow at Harvard University, and her second collection, *My Kind of Place: Travel Stories from a Woman Who's Been Everywhere* was published in 2004. She is currently writing a biography of Rin Tin Tin.

————

What kinds of subjects are you drawn to?

I'm not an "investigative reporter," in that I don't look for the "secret story" or try to discover the machinations behind something. I love stumbling on an idea, or something, and thinking, "Oh my God, this has been here in front of me all along!" My stories tend to fall into two categories: the part of daily life you've never stopped to think about, and the fully realized subculture that I don't know anything about.

An example of the first kind of story is a piece I wrote about a supermarket. One day I was in the supermarket talking to the manager and thought, "How do supermarkets work?" ["All Mixed Up," *The New Yorker,* June 22, 1992.] It seemed like a complex universe, functioning like a little United Nations (which actually turned out to be the way supermarkets *do* function). It was a great common denominator. We've all been there a million times, it is part of the way the world works, but we've never thought about it and how it functions.

An example of the second kind of story I write is the profile I did about a gospel group ["Popular Chronicles: Devotion Road, *The New Yorker,* February 20–27, 1995]. It was astonishing for me to glimpse a world that was so fully developed—with its own stars, sagas, myths, history, millions of devotees—that I, in my narrow life, had no idea existed. In that kind of story I'm more the traveler or explorer, as opposed to looking at my own life.

I have a kind of missionary zeal to tell my readers that the world is a more complex place than they ever thought, to make them curious about things they'd never ordinarily be curious about. I have the ability to say, "The guy next door, the cab driver you thought was a nobody, is actually a fascinating character! Come with me, and I'll show you . . ." My readers don't have the time to look into these things, but I do.

Are there any particular subjects or themes you find yourself returning to?

I don't really have a beat. There's almost *nothing* that I can't imagine becoming interested in. And maybe *that's* my beat.

I'm very curious about people's passionate attachments. I don't really care *what* they are attached to. As I write in *The Orchid Thief,* "I suppose I do have one unembarassing passion. I want to know what it feels like to care about something passionately." I'm curious about the things that people make the focal point of their lives. It is often something I don't personally have any attraction to, which only makes me *more* curious about what might evince such an emotion in someone else. I'm interested in how people, myself included, fit themselves into the strange experience of life.

What do you require for an idea to become a story?

My requirements for a story are purely emotional, intuitive, and visceral. The only questions I pose of a topic are, "Am I curious about this? Is there something here that I genuinely *wonder* about?" Do *I* get excited and passionate about somebody else's passion?

It is only in hindsight that I truly understand what has drawn me to a story. I tend to bridle when people say things like, "Oh, *you* like to write about eccentrics." Well, no, I don't. I don't think, "Gee, let's find an eccentric to write about." I'm constantly cutting *against* the grain on the expectation of what is supposed to be "my" kind of story.

For example, a few years ago someone asked me whether I'd consider profiling Al Gore for *The New Yorker,* and I thought, "Oh! That would be really cool!" This is nothing like what people think of as "my" kind of story, which was part of the attraction, of course.

How do you gauge your level of enthusiasm for a story?

I find myself talking about it to everyone I know. If I'm *not* talking about it, and am *not* able to convey my excitement, something isn't working. I use the same litmus test when I return from reporting: I like to talk about what I've found. It is a useful way to figure out what

I'm *really* thinking. It is the most unadulterated, unmannered version of the excitement I have for a piece.

Do you talk to anyone, or only certain people?

Mostly to my husband, but also to certain friends. Or I'll listen to myself talking to a group of people at a dinner party. It should be that kind of talk. Sometimes I try out various anecdotes on my audience to see if they work, fiddling with them at different tellings. Writing is all about engaging people, seducing them to be interested in a story they ordinarily wouldn't care about. And there is no better way to do that than talking it through in front of an audience.

The kinds of stories you write must be difficult to explain to an editor. How do you manage to get the assignments you do?

I hate writing proposals, or even talking about a story beyond saying, "I want to do a story about a kids' clown," or some such thing. I feel like a two-word proposal is about as far as I'm usually able to get. This is partly because I feel like proposals are so phony. At that point in the process, I *don't know* what the story is. If you already know enough at the start to describe precisely what your story is about, then the story probably isn't that interesting.

At this point in my career what I'm "selling" to my editor is my sensibility, more than anything else. The editor will either say, "All right, I see your point," or "Well, if *you* think it is interesting, I believe in you." My editor's job is often to help me filter my own ideas and enthusiasms, to ask, "Are you *sure* that's the story you want to write?"

What is your filtering process?

As much as I say that I can get interested in anything, I also have quite a "commitment problem." I get excited about ideas and then I get nervous and think, "Nahh, it's not going to sustain me." I worry things through a lot. And a lot of stories just don't go past that phase of worrying.

What gets an idea past your worrying phase?

I need to feel that a subject keeps expanding, rather than contracting. Each time I look, there needs to be more and more there.

In *The Orchid Thief,* I write, "Sometimes this kind of story turns out to be something more, something glimpsed in life that expands like one of those Japanese paper balls." Something can look very small on the surface, and I have to make sure it doesn't remain small. Sometimes small things are just small.

What is the ratio of stories you become excited by to stories you actually write?

That's hard to say. There are a bunch of stories I love but that I just don't have time to do. For example, I heard about a community of bread fanatics. They are a group of people who have been growing a sourdough starter for over one hundred years. They call it the "mother dough," and all have pieces of it. I found a guy who had collected sourdough cultures from around the world. But the timing just didn't work out. And it tends to be that if I get a head of steam up for a story, and if the timing doesn't work out, I don't usually return to it. I probably won't end up doing it.

Then there are a number of stories that *sound* good, and then when I think about it a little more, they just don't hang together. The main character isn't as interesting as I thought, or it turns out that there has been a lot of previous media coverage, which usually kills my interest. For example, I was thinking of profiling the oldest active female stockbroker in New York (she was eighty-nine). I called her to talk and she said, "I'll send you the tapes of all my television appearances. I've been on CNN, CNBC . . ." And I realized that this story just wasn't for me. She was very "camera-ready," and that didn't appeal to me. I'm happier when someone resists me a little than when they are too eager and have their press agent at the ready.

Many of your stories come directly from your life. Do you just stumble on a new insight into something you've always done and write about it, or is there a break between your life and the job of reporting one of these stories?

There is a real break. For example, one day I was having my hair done and was listening to the conversation at the hair salon. I thought, "Boy, this would make a great story. To write about the interaction that people have at a hair salon." Now I could have gone to a different hair salon, but I already knew this place. I knew that the guy who cuts my hair is such a great character, and there were certain things about that salon, such as its size, that seemed perfect for the story ["Popular Chronicles: Short Cuts," *The New Yorker*, February 13, 1995]. But then I came back later with my reporter's hat and interviewed people. I rarely write memoirlike stories. I always write as a reporter.

Do you only like writing stories you've come up with, or will you take suggestions from editors or friends?

I like it when people bring me ideas, but I almost never do them. First of all, people tend to bring me the kinds of stories *they* think are "such Susan Orlean" stories. It's a little like having someone dress me! I have fairly individual and eccentric taste. People think they know my taste, but it usually doesn't fit me. People sometimes confuse my taste with a kind of kitschy approach to popular culture and Americana. And I'm not interested in that.

So where do you get your story ideas?

From reading widely. I try to read fairly specialized publications for people with specific interests: dog magazines, hunting magazines, etc. There is nothing affected or twee or darling about them. This is the real world, and these magazines are the way the real world communicates to itself within these very specialized worlds. For me, reading these magazines is like hearing the slang of a subculture that is *really* used. It's thrilling. Reading magazines like these is one of the best ways to jog my mind.

Are there any parts of the world or country that you find inherently more or less interesting?

No, I'm fairly ecumenical. Sometimes it is exhausting. I'll think, "Gee, there's a great story to write about the annual donkey market in Morocco." And then the next minute I'll think, "I just heard about this incredibly crazy town in Patagonia where they just found a dinosaur skeleton they are reassembling to try to create a tourist culture." And then I'll think, "You know, it would be really cool to cover a Rainbow People convention in 2003."

It's not that I'm restless and need to travel all the time. In fact, if someone told me that for all my stories I had to be in New York City, I'd be fine.

Do you think of domestic stories in a different way from your international ones?

They are different because the international stories *begin* with an exotic overlay (exotic, at least, to an American readership). The assumption is that the story is about a culture which is somehow *different*.

Domestic stories are the inverse. We all think of ourselves as living in one country, and yet there are all sorts of surprising and mysterious worlds within the country. These worlds are new to my readers, so the *appearance* of familiarity is the surprise that's waiting for them. Whereas stories in other countries assume that difference.

Is there a reason why you haven't written much about celebrities?

Yes. When I write about a celebrity they control the experience so much more than when I am writing about a noncelebrity. I enjoy immersing myself in a story, and with a celebrity I usually don't have that opportunity. I did a fair amount of celebrity writing when I was starting out, and I just got tired of it. I certainly got tired of the feeling that I wasn't really getting the story I wanted to get, whether because of access or other issues. I'm over being sick of it, so I could imagine writing about celebrities now. But it would have to be on more favorable terms.

What kinds of people do you most and least like writing about?

I most like writing about people who come to ignore me. Who aren't playing to the camera. A good example of that is the ten-year-old boy, Colin Duffy, I wrote about for *Esquire* ["The American Man, Age Ten," December 1992]. He didn't care about me at all.

The people I'm least excited about writing about are the ones who are most like me. I'm more interested in writing about people who aren't like me.

Do you see your writing as a series of distinct pieces, or as all being part of an overarching project?

A lot of what I write about is a quest about—to be perfectly blunt—"the meaning of life," as clichéd as that may sound. I want to understand what in life has meaning for someone. As a cultural relativist, I'm curious to see how that meaning varies from situation to situation, from region to region. My whole book *Saturday Night* is a meditation on that theme by looking at a similar template in several different situations. In contrast, in *The Orchid Thief,* I took a single thing and burrowed deep down into it. But they were using the same intellectual architecture, which was to ask, "How is it that people make their lives work?"

Do you prefer writing long or short pieces?

I like mixing them up. I like the flexibility of getting excited about something and knowing that it can be a short "Talk of the Town" piece, and doesn't *have* to be a ten-thousand-word piece.

How many projects do you work on at once?

One. I sometimes balance more than one, but I absolutely hate it. When I'm working on a piece, it's best for me to be *living* in it in order to have the mental associations and inspirations all be about that one piece.

How much research do you do before you start a piece?

None. All I need to know is that I *want* to know about something. If I'm going to write about someone who knows a lot about something, I'd rather learn about it from him. I say to a subject, "I know nothing about gospel music or orchids, and this is your life's passion. Teach me." I don't want to be competitive or have "smart" questions for someone. I have no ego when I'm reporting.

And a lot of times I'm writing about people who already feel a bit defensive or intimidated by the fact that I am a writer from New York, usually writing for *The New Yorker.* So it would be the worst thing to start whipping out facts and trying to show them how much I know about their field. It would be counterproductive. Instead, I say, "Here I am. I'm ready to listen to you."

I'm such a blabbermouth that, if I know too much, I'm not sure I'll listen as well as when I'm out of my depth and floundering. *My* vulnerability is important to reporting, too. It can be quite uncomfortable to have orchid growers yapping at me in Latin, and having to say that I don't understand. It is crucial for me to stay receptive and impressionable, to keep worrying. It is like a stubborn sore; it is a little painful, but it keeps me more open.

I usually start doing my book learning once I've picked up a little knowledge and understand better what I have to know.

Where did you learn how to be a reporter?

I had done no reporting at all when I was graduated from college. The only thing I'd done in college, aside from academic writing, was poetry and one book review.

After college, I went to Oregon and was hired as a reporter at a little publication called *Paper Rose*. We were taught nothing, so I made it up as I went along. At my second job I had an editor who had worked at *The Wall Street Journal* and was much more of an instructor/editor. He taught me a lot about how you report, as well as the ethical and legal aspects of reporting. That was a very important experience for me.

Do you have a reporting routine?

The beginning of the reporting phase is very hard. It's often very upsetting. I keep wondering, "What am I *doing*? What's this *about*? What's the *story* here? Maybe this isn't such a good idea?" I feel quite lost.

I'll call the local newspaper and introduce myself, and ask whether anyone wants to have a drink. I'll wander around and poke into stores and coffee shops and chat with storekeepers. I like to visit the junk stores to see what kinds of objects people here have cast away. I drive around a lot just looking. I try to get a kind of street sense of what I'm writing about. A lot of times I'm looking for one person who will introduce me to the next level, the level that isn't as obvious.

For example, when I was writing about Midland, Texas, where George W. Bush has his ranch, I wandered into a downtown coffee shop and struck up a conversation with a guy who, miraculously enough, turned out to be a retired oil guy ["Letter from Texas: A Place Called Midland," *The New Yorker*, October 16–23, 2000]. He drove me around and showed me stuff. I called the oil reporter at the local paper. I was trying to peel apart the town and get a feel for it. My question was, "What is it about this town that Bush makes such a big deal about being from?"

Is the way you report in a foreign country very different from the way you report in the U.S.?

Not speaking the language changes everything. The lucky accident of overhearing a conversation, the chance meeting—that's all missing. Even though I speak French, I'm not able to pick things up easily. I've written a number of stories from Spanish-speaking countries, where I rely on an interpreter, which is frustrating.

Why frustrating?

Well, when I hire an interpreter I always try to get someone who is interesting, or who has some connection or interest in the story. Since I don't do many standard, sit-down interviews, I need someone who can kind of *act as me*. I want someone who will explain that world to me, and not simply translate. But sometimes I just have to get someone from an agency.

My problem is that when I know the precise question I want to ask, I *probably* already know the answer as well. I pose questions in order to prod someone, to learn the things I wouldn't even know to ask about. And I can't do that when I'm doing it all through an interpreter.

How do you pace yourself when you're reporting a long piece?

It's hard because no amount of time seems like the *right* amount of time. I don't know what I'm going to need, so I always try to give myself more time than I anticipate needing.

Reporting always has a lot of downtime for me. I always try to set up a few things before I get there, if only to keep my existential nausea at bay. If I've set up a few interviews it's a little less distressing. Cell phones have made a huge difference in the way I pace my reporting. I used to sit around in my hotel room watching CNN, waiting for people to return my calls.

*How much of a distance do you think is important to main-
tain with someone you're reporting on?*

I don't feel I need to keep much of a distance. If I can get invited
into someone's home, all the better. The more I find out that isn't
exactly on topic, the better. All of that enriches and enlarges my
sense of the person and the story.

*So many of your subjects are not public figures. Do you worry
about the impact of your reporting on your subjects?*

A journalist, by definition, invades and stirs up people's lives. We
don't wreck or change them substantially, but the fact is that we are
invaders. I don't think a lot about the effect my work has on someone's life. It is hard for writers to imagine their work out in the world.
It is good to stay humble and not be overimpressed with the power
of your readership and reach. It is always a surprise to me when a
piece does have an effect. For anyone who is a public, press-savvy
character, the impact will be almost zero. And for the kinds of private people I tend to write about, few people in their worlds read
The New Yorker, so it isn't usually a problem.

*How do you prefer to approach someone once you've decided
you want to interview him? Is it more advantageous to be an
outsider or an insider?*

I almost always just go in as the outsider, unless it is someone
well-known who has to be approached through others. But going
direct is the most natural approach for me. Obtaining an introduction would probably be helpful, but I prefer to go straight to the
source and lay myself out in front of them. It is the honest thing to
do. If someone resists that approach I usually give up.

How do you convince people to spend so much time with you?

One thing I do is to make it absolutely clear from the outset that
they don't need to *do* anything during a lot of the time I want to
spend with them. They don't need to perform, they don't even need
to be talking to me. So much of what works for me is observational.
So if someone is doing an errand or going about their ordinary workday it is ideal for me to tag along and shadow them. The more I do that,
the more people realize that they don't have to perform. And the more

comfortable they become, the more time they give me. I emphasize to them that I just want to hang out with them—regardless of what they are doing.

What if someone objects, "I'm just doing dumb stuff. You don't want to do that with me."

This is often the toughest part of what I have to do in order to convince people to give me their time. I have to make them understand that "dumb stuff is my kind of stuff." That I'm happy to be an enthusiastic piece of wallpaper.

It is sometimes very difficult to see people just doing what they ordinarily do, without my influencing what they do. I had a lot of trouble with this when I was writing my first book, *Saturday Night*, which was about what people across the country do on their Saturday nights. If what they were doing was boring and unexceptional, then *that* was what I wanted to see. I was constantly dissuading people from throwing a party, or planning some fantastic event for my sake—which was exactly what I *didn't* want.

It has been a real education for me when the shoe is on the other foot, when a reporter tells me he just wants to come by and watch me work. And, just like everyone, I'll say, "But it's so boring. There's nothing to see. You don't want to watch me do that." Part of it is that I don't want anyone to know how much time I waste while I'm "working."

When—if ever—do you tell someone how much time and access you'll need?

I try to avoid talking about how much time I'll need because it scares people. So I try to be vague, to make my request very inexact. I say something like, "I'm coming down next week and will be there for a few days, so anytime you've got would be great." I get really distressed when someone says something like, "I can see you from 11:00 to 11:45." I reconsider the story if I run into that. But that only tends to happen with celebrities or so-called "important people."

When it is someone who is less well-known, I'm pretty sure that once I get down there and they see who I am and how I conduct my time with them, that I'll be able to get more of it.

Is there anyplace in particular you like to conduct interviews?

I try to meet people in an environment where we can make small talk and relax. When I see someone at home I'm essentially running a lint brush over their life. I'm able to pick up a thousand little threads of who they are and how they lead their life. I need to understand the context of their life in order to understand them. Now someone's home isn't always the relevant context. If I were interviewing a Wall Street power-player, a hot restaurant might be as much their "home" as anything else. The thing I try to avoid is meeting someone in a place with which they have no connection. For example, I interviewed Hillary Clinton at the photo studio where the magazine was taking her picture. It was awful. There was nothing there of her. It was completely sterile. But I couldn't think of where else I could ask to interview her. Her schedule was pretty busy.

I try to interview people in places that feel natural for them. For instance, I got Laroche to take me to orchid shows because that was where he was most himself. But I'd rather have the person I'm writing about decide where to take me. It feels more natural that way. I once wrote about the artist Frank Stella, and we went to a squash tournament together. He is an avid squash player, so it was natural for him to go to a squash tournament. But it was also a chance to write about him in a completely surprising—but natural—environment. I love stumbling on something like that, rather than, say, going to an art museum with him.

How do you start an interview?

With small talk. Chitchat. I conduct an interview like a conversation. Which means I have to go back and fill in all the questions I forgot to ask. But I like the interview process to be organic and take on a life of its own.

Do you ever prepare questions?

No. Being vulnerable is an important part of the dynamic between me and a subject. People tend to be distrustful of writers from places like New York. You have to make clear that you're not arrogant, that you're not here to make fun of them, but that you are open and genuinely want to learn from them. It is important for the person you're interviewing to feel a bit more powerful than he might otherwise feel. It evens out the relationship somewhat.

Do you take notes or tape-record your interviews?

I take notes in a sloppy "medium-hand," which is a combination of longhand and shorthand. I'm not a great note-taker. I've always got my notebook at the ready, but I often walk away from a long interview with very few notes.

Why don't you tape your interviews?

So much of the time I spend with people is spent just blabbing. I talk about a lot of stuff that isn't at all relevant to the story, just so I can get a sense of who they are. I can spend hours talking to a subject about something like makeup. Do I really want to transcribe hours and hours of tape of that?

Do you adopt any particular persona in order to motivate people to talk?

If you asked the people I write about to characterize me, I think they'd say I was a little younger than I am, and a little bit more shy than I am. A little more naive than I am. People sometimes have the impulse to mother me, which I don't discourage. I don't play dumb or helpless, but I try not to come off as slick and sophisticated. It is useful, but the fact is that this is often the way I feel: far from home, nervous about the story, somewhat exposed.

Laroche had this kind of a protective relationship with me: "What's a little girl like you doing out here?" He was always acting exasperated at my goofiness, joking about how many times he had to tell me the name of a particular flower.

Will you agree to various ground rules (off the record, anonymous quotes, etc.)?

I begin with the assumption that everything is on the record. The only time I bring it up is if someone gets a little touchy about a topic. Then I offer the option of telling me something off the record in order to encourage someone to open up. I make sure that people know that fact-checking will be done, and I take pains to explain the process. I want them to know that they will have an opportunity to correct any factual errors I make. But I never let anyone look at the story before it is printed.

How much do you reveal about yourself and your piece during an interview?

I don't encourage people to ask me a lot of questions about myself, although I don't stonewall, or refuse to answer when someone does ask. But if I'm doing my job right, they aren't going to be spending much time thinking about me. I'll be focusing more on them.

I don't use my own life experiences as a way to lubricate the conversation, as a way of creating empathy ("Boy, I can really understand what you're feeling because I once . . ."). It is partly because for most of the people I write about I just wouldn't have a parallel in my life. I'm an enthusiastic listener and a nonjudgmental observer, and *that* is how I create empathy.

How important is timing—when you speak to which character—in the interview process?

Timing isn't usually a big issue with my pieces. I usually start with the main character and stay with him. I don't tend to work my way to the main person. I go for broke. I'll wait to the end of our interviews to ask awkward questions. Mostly because I'm so chicken. Sometimes, if the questions are extremely awkward and personal, I'll do the last interviews on the phone. I feel that it allows for a little bit of dignity and safety if the person isn't sitting right there in front of me.

For example, I once had to ask someone about incest in his family. It was the hardest question I've ever had to ask, so I waited until we were on the phone. It was terribly uncomfortable, but I felt it was fairer to him to ask it over the phone.

Do you reconstruct scenes or only write scenes you have yourself witnessed? How do you go about reporting in order to reconstruct a scene?

If I have to reconstruct a scene I make sure that the construction shows. I describe it as a scene that I make clear I didn't observe. I'm not comfortable at all—in fact I'm repulsed—when a writer writes a scene as if he were there—when there was no possible way for him to have been. The worst is when a writer claims to have reconstructed a character's thoughts. There are other ways of writing intimate, powerful portraits. The idea of my writing, "He thought to himself . . ." just feels inauthentic. To me it is a cardinal rule. You just don't write that way. The belief that the writer can see through brick walls, or into people's minds, strikes me as the unfortunate outgrowth of "New Journalism." That's what fiction is for. We have no shortage of opportunities to write stories from the inside out.

You don't have to hit the reader over the head, but you can quite naturally write a scene that you weren't able to observe, making it clear to the reader that you are reconstructing it for them. I don't think readers have trouble with that. It doesn't destroy the narrative as long as you are careful to explain what you are doing.

How do you know when the interviewing phase is done?

When my attention span becomes shorter. In the beginning of a story my learning curve is so steep that everything the person says is new and fascinating. Then it slows down naturally as I become more familiar with the person and his story. Finally, I feel an intuitive shift from listening to the process of writing the story in my head. Making connections, sketching scenes, creating the story. That's when I need to start writing.

What do you do in order to prepare to write?

The first thing I do is type up my notes into a computer. I organize each interview as a separate file. Then I'll make another file of general observations I've made during reporting. Then I print those all up, read them, and highlight the useful passages. Then I spread all the pages out around me and start working on the lead.

How do you start writing?

I like to do something physical before I start writing, whether that is running or playing squash. Then, when I sit down, I always feel that I don't have anything to write. That I haven't gathered enough information and don't have a story.

Where do you write?

Either at home or at *The New Yorker*. It doesn't matter to me too much where I am. But, wherever I am, I have to have my notes with me. Even if I'm not looking at them, I can't write if I don't have my notes with me.

What is your writing routine?

I get up, have my coffee and read the paper, and usually start writing at around eleven or so. I usually print out what I've written at night before I stop, so I start the day by reading that. Once I've read it, I call the piece up on the screen and begin polishing. I think of this process like the stretching exercises I do before running.

I hate going out to lunch because that is exactly when I am usually getting up a head of steam. So I usually just grab a sandwich and eat at my desk. I get up from my desk and walk around a lot while I write. Rather than taking a break because I *can't* get anything done, I take a break whenever I write something that I feel really good about. I used to write far into the night, but I do that less now. It is hard for me to stop for dinner and then go back to work. So I often stop writing around eight p.m. I like to read what I've written that day one last time before I stop. I try to end knowing what I'm going to write next.

What kind of authorial presence do strive for?

I want to be the tour guide. It's important to me to acknowledge being present in a piece, although I like to think I don't put myself front and center. I want to tell the story in a conversational tone, which requires that I occasionally make my presence felt.

I also want to be the conductor, in a musical sense. I'm very conscious of controlling the rhythm and the musical aspect of a piece. I want to know that people are being drawn into something hypnotically descriptive, or staccato. I want to manage the reader through the experience of reading me.

How would you describe your tone?

Intimate. I like to be droll, to lull my readers and then surprise or startle them. I like using plain words in a way that gives them a renewed power in their plainness. I like reinventing a cliché, or using it in a bold way.

Do you pay a lot of attention to the sound of your words?

Yes, sometimes to a fault. There are times when I simply want a sentence to end on a downbeat, and will spend an hour figuring out how I can do it, even though it goes against the logic of the section. I can't stand it if an editor changes the *rhythm* of one of my sentences. I'm more ornery about those kinds of changes than I am about changes to the content of a piece. That's why I prefer doing my own cutting. Cutting often improves a piece, but it can wreak havoc with the tone.

What writers have influenced you in your choice of tone?

Definitely Joseph Mitchell and Joan Didion. John McPhee is another. And a lot of fiction: Faulkner, Fitzgerald.

Do you think that the kind of journalism you do can lead to truth?

Absolutely. I think we've all learned that facts without a human sensibility filtering them are not necessarily truer than the somewhat more subjective version of reality that you get in literary journalism. It can be true the way a painting can be true. It is an emotional and factual truth. It's a richer version of experience than mere factual reporting would necessarily provide.

Do you think literary journalism is a peculiarly American form?

Yes. I was just interviewed by a German newspaper and the reporter told me that German writers had only recently started doing literary journalism.

I think Americans are uniquely curious about the American experience. Maybe it is because we are such a large country with such a diverse culture. We're a country that is constantly being reinvented, and it's been a part of our culture to wonder about who we are, and what makes us work. And maybe it is in that quest that this kind of reportage has thrived. European journalism is, perhaps, more argumentative, but American journalism, perhaps, has a greater wish to explore and understand the reality of our national experience. It may be that we have more *need* for it.

When *Saturday Night* came out, the only foreign sale it had was to Japan. A lot of other countries were interested, but they didn't understand it. They didn't know what it was. *The Orchid Thief* has sold to many, many different countries, partly because orchids are a hobby around the world. But I also think that this kind of journalism has become more familiar in more cultures than it was a decade ago.

Do you consider yourself a New Journalist in the sense that Tom Wolfe defined it in his famous essay?

Yes. I think his definition is probably as good a one as has ever been conjured. I feel completely free to use any formal technique (other than untruths) whatsoever.

Do you see yourself as part of a historic tradition?

Certainly because I work at *The New Yorker,* I feel part of the tradition of the writers who have written for it. The magazine has played such a large part in supporting the tradition, starting with Liebling, E. B. White, and all the other early contributors, continuing on to writers like Alec Wilkinson and Mark Singer today.

What is your view of the prospects for this kind of literary nonfiction?

I think it is a good time for the form. We've passed through this spasm of people feeling that print is dead. The curiosity about the world, and the appetite for books that explore it in a literary way, is stronger than ever. If you look at the books that have sold well in the last five years, a remarkable number of them have been works of literary nonfiction. *Seabiscuit, The Orchid Thief.* These were completely unlikely books to become bestsellers.

Books may play a larger role in the future of the form than they did in the past. They may be a better vehicle because they don't rely on advertisers. Books give you much more freedom, more of a chance to be unconventional. The book rises or falls on its own ability to appeal to an audience, rather than a magazine's need to sell itself to an advertiser.

Newspapers have gotten much more magazine-like. Newspaper feature pieces are a lot longer than they were ten to fifteen years ago. I get asked to speak to the staffs of newspapers a lot. They are very interested in how to make their writing better. They still don't get a lot of space, but there is a real desire to incorporate some of the tone and intimacy of this kind of writing in a newspaper, and maybe *that* is where the literary journalists of the future will come from.

BY SUSAN ORLEAN:

My Kind of Place: Travel Stories from a Woman Who's Been Everywhere, Random House, 2004

The Bullfighter Checks Her Makeup: My Encounters with Extraordinary People, Random House, 2001

The Orchid Thief, Random House, 1998

Saturday Night, Knopf, 1990

Red Sox and Bluefish, Faber & Faber, 1987

RICHARD PRESTON

Richard Preston may be the only literary journalist who has had an asteroid named after him. Discovered by Carolyn and Eugene Shoemaker—the astronomers who were the subject of *First Light* (1987), Preston's first book—Asteroid Preston measures between three and five miles across. In a scenario that could come from one of his own books, Asteroid Preston will likely collide with Mars or the Earth during the next hundred thousand years.

Preston has developed a genre of literary journalism that lends scientific subjects—virology, astronomy, gene theory—the drama and excitement more often associated with great travel or adventure writing. His characters aren't caricatures; they are neither heroic scientists, nor anonymous technicians. "The people I write about are 'ordinary' Americans, who worry about whether they're putting the right fertilizer on the lawn . . . but *also* worry about things we know nothing about." Preston's characters are pioneers, extending the boundaries of knowledge in much the way that the early American explorers did. "The field of science right now is like the Louisiana Purchase was for Lewis and Clark. It's huge, wide-open territory," he says.

In "The Fabric of Fact" (1983), Preston's unpublished English dissertation, he makes much of the distinction between the scientist and the writer—the professions he was to straddle just a few years later. Early nineteenth-century America, Preston writes, was an age "in love with facts," regardless of whether they sprang from a researcher's microscope or an adventurer's journals. The difference between the scientific and literary sensibility was what they did with those facts. "While science struggled to fit all of these facts into a fabric of knowledge, writers struggled to embody facts . . . into a fabric of imaginative literature."

Preston was born in Cambridge, Massachusetts, on August 5, 1954. A mediocre high school student, he was rejected by every college to which he applied. He so desperately wanted to attend Pomona College in California that he called the dean—collect—to ask whether he ever changed his mind. Even after the dean told him he didn't, Preston called once a week for the next few months. His perseverance eventually paid off and he was admitted to Pomona in time for the second semester.

In 1977, Preston was graduated summa cum laude with a degree in English. He went to Princeton for graduate school, where he met his wife, Michelle, also a graduate student in the English department. In 1979, he persuaded John McPhee to allow him to take his "Literature of Fact" writing course, which was then open only to undergraduates. "McPhee taught us precision in shaping words and sentences. He taught us absolute respect for facts." The class is a famous incubator for literary journalists, and two-thirds of McPhee's students are reputed to have become professional writers or editors.

Preston realized that he preferred journalism to academia and took a year off from Princeton after passing his master's exams to see whether he could survive as a freelance writer. He spent the year living in a basement apartment in Boston, writing science stories for *Blair & Ketchum's Country Journal*. While he enjoyed the work, he went steadily broke. After consulting with McPhee and his dissertation advisor, William Howard, Preston decided to return to graduate school to work on his writing with the aid of a Princeton stipend.

After receiving his degree, Preston supplemented his freelance income by writing fund-raising letters for Princeton's development office. In 1985, he received an advance from Atlantic Monthly Press and spent much of the next year observing the astronomers at Caltech's seven-story-tall Hale telescope (also known as "the Big Eye") for his first book, *First Light*. The assignment gave him the opportunity to put the saturation reporting techniques he had learned from McPhee into practice. "Eventually the astronomers seemed to forget I was there, and so I became like Jane Goodall among the chimpanzees. I was able to watch them without causing a disturbance, while they fed on Oreo cookies or looked at galaxies on television screens, oblivious to the presence of a reporter scribbling in a corner," he writes.

First Light was praised for covering a difficult technical subject without either distorting or oversimpifying the facts. "Preston's narrative—a blend of anecdote, history, scientific theory, and technical explanation—brings the heavens down to earth," writes Ruth Johnstone in *The Christian Science Monitor.* The book won the 1988 American Institute of Physics Science Writing Award and has since become a cult classic among science writers.

His next book, *American Steel* (1991), grew out of a small article Preston read in *Forbes* about the Nucor Corporation's search for a new way to pour sheet steel. He was surprised to hear that someone in the moribund U.S. steel industry was innovating, and intrigued by the story of the small company going up against its much larger rivals, building a new steel mill in the middle of a cornfield outside Crawfordsville, Indiana.

"As a meditation on how high-tech business is done these days, as a window on the American response to foreign competition, as an initiation into the romance of heavy industry, as an exuberant celebration of the way that everyday people talk while they do important things, *American Steel* is very hard to beat," writes David Warsh in *The New York Times Book Review.* The book placed Preston in good literary company. "In the best tradition of John McPhee and Tracy Kidder, Preston captures the feel of the project through direct observation of people at work," writes Mark Reutter in *The Washington Post.*

In the early 1990s, Preston became convinced that the AIDS epidemic was only the tip of the iceberg—that other deadly viruses would soon begin emerging from once-remote forests and work their way around the world. He began interviewing scientists with the goal of finding the story through which to describe this danger. During a conversation with a virologist at Rockefeller University, Preston grew frustrated. "So far, all I've heard is a lot of scientists wringing their hands and talking about what *might* happen. But I want to know whether anything *has* happened yet," he complained.

The virologist told Preston of an outbreak of Ebola among monkeys in Reston, Virginia, that had received almost no press coverage. Fearing the virus might infect the community, the government seized the building and killed the infected monkeys. Ebola Reston turned out to be a Level 4 virus, a relative of Ebola Zaire, one of the most virulent viruses ever. Preston reconstructed the events, tracking the virus from a cave in Uganda to Virginia, in "Crisis In the Hot Zone" (*The New Yorker,* October 26, 1992).

Expanded into a book in 1994, *The Hot Zone* became an international bestseller. Stephen King called it "one of the most horrifying things I've ever read in my life."

The book's sales were matched by positive reviews. Reviewing *The Hot Zone* in *The New York Times,* Michiko Kakutani wrote: "Having immersed himself in the world of virus hunters and biohazard specialists, much the way Tom Wolfe immersed himself in the world of astronauts and test pilots to write *The Right Stuff,* Mr. Preston acts as the reader's guide to this mysterious realm, explicating its technology and expertise, even as he's conjuring up its dangers."

Preston continued his exploration in two further volumes of what he calls his "dark biology" series. The first was a novel, *The Cobra Event* (1997), which was sold to the movies for $3 million. After reading it, president Bill Clinton convened a group of experts to discuss the book's implications, and revised the federal budget in order to bolster the country's defenses against biological weapons. *The Demon in the Freezer* (2002), about smallpox and other deadly viruses, was developed from a *New Yorker* article of the same title, which won the 2000 National Magazine Award for public interest writing.

Calling Preston "our troubadour of troubling microbes," National Institutes of Health director Harold Varmus wrote that Preston "has probably done more than any other writer to establish a nationwide imperative to think about infectious agents as global threats and potential weapons." *The Economist* praised the way Preston's intimate approach to science "probes deep into the motives, fears and personal lives of the men and women who choose this risky business."

Most recently, Preston learned little-known tree-climbing techniques in order to write about a botanist who studies the ecology of the California Redwood forest canopy, thirty-five stories above ground.

———

What kinds of ideas are you drawn to?

Ever since childhood, I've been fascinated by science and nature. Science has everything: an enormous amount of human passion, conflict, and the wonder of nature itself. It isn't about facts, it's about what we don't know. I write about science to remind my readers that the world of nature—and the universe we live in—are bigger and far more complex than we'll ever know.

How does this fascination emerge in your writing?

I have an apocalyptic streak as a writer. In my books there are always immense forces swirling around the human stories I tell—themes that dwarf the human species. For example, *First Light* [1987] was about nature on the largest possible scale: the universe itself. *American Steel* [1991] is about the human effort to control a virtually uncontrollable material—molten steel. The first time I saw hot steel being poured, I was absolutely entranced: the sound, fury, and violence was awesome, especially when contrasted with the precision with which the steel workers worked. It was just the kind of collision of forces that I wanted to write about. In my "dark biology" series—*The Hot Zone* [1994], *The Cobra Event* [1997], and *The Demon in the Freezer* [2002]—I explore the microscopic world within, the *other* infinity, which is the extremely small, yet powerful, world of viruses.

My current project is about a botanist who studies the ecology of the forest canopy by climbing some of the tallest trees on earth. So I guess I've swung back to the macroscopic scale, the middle world.

Where did you learn how to be a reporter?

I had a lot of literary interests at Pomona College. Then I got a PhD in English at Princeton, not knowing whether I wanted to be an academic or a "writer." In college, I read John McPhee's book *Coming Into the Country,* in which there is a long, beautiful passage about how grizzly bears forage. It was so gorgeous that it made the hair on the back of my neck stand up. I had to pace my room to clear out my head. So when I learned that McPhee taught a Princeton writing course called "The Literature of Fact," I had to take it, even though it was for undergraduates.

McPhee taught us to shape words and sentences precisely. He

taught us absolute respect for facts, and to go to extreme lengths to make sure we got everything right. Here's something amazing: something like two-thirds of the students who have taken that course have become professional writers or editors. We call ourselves McPhinos. As in neutrinos, the small, nearly massless particles that stream out of a nuclear reaction.

Do you consider yourself—and your writing—a part of the New Journalism as Tom Wolfe defined it?

Yes, I consciously identify with the movement. I was very influenced by Wolfe's famous essay, in which he argues that a nonfiction writer can make his voice sound a lot more like his subject by employing his "downstage voice" to mimic him. I was in graduate school when I read that, and I thought, "He's exactly right!" That's what I try to do in my writing.

The average so-called "science writer" has only one voice. It is the voice of the professor lecturing in front of a class about a "gee whiz" subject. It is Carl Sagan's voice, bless his soul. It is pure expository writing with no shift in narrative, no shift in point of view, no modulation, no delicacy in the way the voice moves around. But those are all the devices I *love*. So my work is very indebted to the New Journalism.

How do you come up with ideas?

I troll through magazines and newspapers, but it would be an exaggeration to say that I have a method. I develop a lot of stories that don't go anywhere. It is an intense winnowing process during which I probably pursue five stories for every one I actually write. I tend to go a long time between books, with a great sense of uncertainty about what I'm going to do.

Do you ever troll through the Internet for ideas?

No. I find the Internet virtually useless in that respect. The problem with the Internet is that you can read Web page after Web page and never get the sense that you are either hearing the straight story, or learning something *new*. So much of it seems to be incomplete, half-baked, or just repackaged information.

When I'm coming up with ideas, I need to talk to the top experts in a field, people who are deeply immersed in an area. I zero in on that person because he or she can tell me, in a nutshell, what is really new and exciting in the field. You can spend years trolling the Internet without ever getting information of such high quality, yet you can get it in half an hour by making human contact with someone who knows it.

How do you develop an *idea* into a story?

I start with a subject, but there is a vast difference between a subject and a story. When I consider whether an idea will make a good story, I think about the expectations that all readers have. Aristotle described these expectations in his *Poetics:* A story must have a beginning, middle, and an end. It has a protagonist, a climax, and conflict. Any good story begins with a conflict or an unresolved situation that is either crying out for an ending or is inherently unresolvable.

Where did you come up with your book ideas?

First Light came about because I wanted to break in to *The New Yorker* by selling a profile to the then editor, William Shawn. I learned of the Princeton astronomer James Gunn through an article in the *Princeton Alumni Magazine.* Gunn built these telescopes by hand—often from junk parts—through which he was able to probe the edge of the universe. On my first visit to the Palomar observatory (in California), the people I met were so fascinating and passionate I realized that the story was a book, rather than just a profile. When Shawn rejected my proposal for a profile of Gunn, I had no choice but to write a book.

After *First Light,* I saw a small article in *Forbes* magazine that said, "What Ken Iverson is doing at Nucor is going to revolutionize the world steel industry . . ." My reaction was, "Wait a minute, I thought the American steel industry was *dogmeat.* I've got to find out about this." So I called Nucor and talked with Ken Iverson (who, although he was president of a Fortune 500 company, answered his own phone). He told me about his new steel mills, and invited me to tour them with him.

What do you actually do when you are winnowing ideas down into those that might make good stories?

I call people up and tell them that I'm *exploring* the idea of writing about a certain topic and I'd love to hear their thoughts. I ask them to bring me up-to-date on their area of expertise, and to introduce me to others in the field. I do all my preliminary interviews on the telephone. I put on my headset and ask for permission to take notes, which I do on my computer.

During this process, I'm also testing *my* passion for the topic. Given all the frustrations of journalism, you have to be somewhat out of your mind to embark on any book. So the *only* good reason is that you are obsessed with the story and the subject.

Do you ever stumble on the fact that a story has been in front of you all along?

I've never simply stumbled on a story that turns out to have been in front of me. I *wish* I could do it that way, but the opposite is actually the case. I've had a number of great stories sitting in front of me—stories that *other* journalists recognized were great, and wrote themselves.

For example, Sylvia Nasser wrote *A Beautiful Mind*, a wonderful book about the Nobel Prize–winning economist, John Nash. Now I was aware of John Nash during the time I was a graduate student at Princeton, and I even had a number of encounters with him. It's a story I could have tackled if I had been as alert as Sylvia is. Duh.

Another example is Jonathan Harr's *A Civil Action*, which was about an enormous lawsuit against W. R. Grace. My *father* was a managing partner at the law firm that defended Grace, and I spent my high school years listening to him talk about what a fascinating case it was. But it never occurred to me to write a book about it—duh again.

Do you prefer long-term pieces or short ones?

I like doing both. I used to write a lot of "Talk of the Town" pieces for *The New Yorker.* They were deeply satisfying because I could go in, do it quickly, and get out. In October 1987, I was at the New York Stock Exchange when the market crashed. I wrote a "Talk" piece about a monk in orange robes whom I found praying in the visitors' gallery. He told me, "Our master teaches us that we are to pray in the most dangerous places, and right now the New York Stock Exchange is the most dangerous place anywhere. As the Dow goes down, I can feel my dharma going up."

You've written fiction and nonfiction. When you have an idea for a story, how do you decide in which genre to render it?

I decided to write *The Cobra Event* as a novel in order to solve a very specific journalistic problem. I became interested in biological weapons while writing *The Hot Zone,* and I realized that there was something very important about them that the scientific community was trying its damnedest to ignore. But the weapons experts I needed to talk to wouldn't go on the record because their positions in the government were too sensitive.

But once I decided to write a *novel* about biological weapons, they were delighted to tell me everything I needed to know, from how FBI agents dress and get along with their families, to the scientific work they did on bioterrorism. These conversations pretty much ended, however, when a high-ranking FBI official became aware of my research for the novel and sent a memo out forbidding all agents from talking to me on the grounds that I was "an endangerment to national security." Eventually, I found FBI sources who were willing to meet with me and talk. They felt that the threat of bioterrorism needed to be aired. I ended up visiting the FBI facilities at Quantico, Virginia, including a secret facility that I ended up describing in *The Cobra Event.*

Then, in the fall of 2001, when the anthrax attacks began, all of my best sources for *The Cobra Event* were pulled into the investigation. It became apparent to me that I had to revisit this story in the form of *nonfiction.* I needed to find out how the kinds of bioterrorism scenarios I'd written about in fiction played out in reality.

What was the main difference between fiction and reality?

The novel ended with the crime of bioterrorism being solved. The real crime has so far proved impossible to solve. As of now, the perpetrator(s) of the 2001 anthrax attacks have not been found. When I was at Quantico, I hung out in the Quantico Café with a group of agents and scientists—it's a place where they can have a beer and decompress in the evenings—and listened to them describe how they would use forensic science to solve a crime of bioterrorism. One of them, a scientist named Randall Murch, who was then the deputy head of the FBI labs, ended up predicting that science might not be able to solve a bioterrorist crime—that it would be solved by old-fashioned, gumshoe detective work. Murch turned out to be right.

Is writing fiction a different experience than writing nonfiction?

Oddly enough, I've discovered that you can get away with more in *nonfiction* than in fiction. For instance, one of the things I did in *The Hot Zone* that a novelist couldn't get away with was changing the narrative point of view. The book begins with a very remote, cool third-person narration. Then I move to very close interior monologues. And then I pull back and tell the story from the perspective of each main character, using a kind of cubist/Rashomon technique. Finally, I end the book in the first person. Now if a *novelist* were to do this, the novel would be labeled "experimental fiction," and it would be noncommercial. But to date, not one critic has ever mentioned the changes in perspective I made in *The Hot Zone*, which was a bestseller.

What's the moral of the story?

The moral is that the rules for fiction and nonfiction are different, and the expectations the reader has for each genre are different as well. When we read nonfiction we take it for granted that the author is telling a story in the "natural," or "normal," way. We don't really think about the narrative or rhetorical forms the writer is using. But the only reason that nonfiction writing feels "normal" is that the writer has successfully manipulated so many different forms. It is artfully designed in order to achieve a "natural" effect.

When I studied with McPhee, I realized that one could do *literary* writing in nonfiction; that all the techniques available to the novelist are also available to the nonfiction writer. And there are some techniques available to the nonfiction writer that the novelist can't touch. So it's not just that you can make a simulacrum of a novel by writing literary nonfiction; you can actually exceed the power of the novel.

In what respect?

It has to do with the implied contract between the reader and the writer. The nonfiction writer is assuring the reader that what he or she is about to read is the repeatable result of an experiment, that it is the verifiable truth, or at least the closest I can get to it. We may never know the ultimate truth, but this piece of nonfiction is my best stab at it. And in exchange, the reader agrees *not* to invoke the "willing suspension of disbelief"—the essential clause in the contract between the reader and the writer of fiction. With nonfiction, the reader can believe that the facts are true, even though he may sometimes feel *as if* he is reading fiction. Nonfiction's combination of narrative literary form and truth makes for, at times, a more powerful experience than the novel.

What kinds of people do you most like writing about?

People who are driven to achieve, who are so obsessed with their work that they don't even notice I'm in the room. I like writing about people who are very intelligent and who perceive things that the rest of us don't. But at the same time, the people I write about are "ordinary" Americans, who worry about whether they're putting the right fertilizer on the lawn, and about how their kids are doing in school. What draws me to them is that they are *also* worrying about things we know nothing about, like deadly viruses, or asteroids that are going to smash into the earth.

What kinds of people do you least like writing about?

I don't like writing about people who think they are so important that they *should* be interviewed. When someone says, "I don't know why you're talking to me. I'm not very interesting"—a little green light goes on in my head and I get much more interested.

Your books are often on very technical scientific topics. What kind of research do you do?

I love coming into a world that I know nothing about and not only taking notes, but also participating in whatever activity it is that constitutes that world. The physical process is very important in my writing. For example, I'm writing a piece about a scientist who studies the ecosystem of the tops of trees. So I've spent the last year learning professional tree-climbing techniques, using ropes and gear, and I have fallen completely in love with it. If you come around to my house looking for me these days, you are likely to find me sixty feet off the ground in a tree.

The only way I can describe something is if I've experienced it myself. For *The Hot Zone,* I asked the commander of the army's USAMRIID lab at Fort Detrick whether I could put on a space suit and handle Ebola virus myself. He said that was impossible, but later on, two scientists sort of quietly escorted me into one of the Level 4 Ebola labs, where there was live Ebola virus. When we were in the staging area, I put on a pressurized space suit and picked up my pencil and reporter's notebook to go into the hot zone. And one of them said, "Where do you think you're going with that pencil and notebook?" I explained that I had to take notes. She replied, "You're welcome to bring your notes into Level 4, but they won't come out. The only way your notes will come out is if they're burned to a crisp in a sterilizer first." She gave me a sheet of Teflon-like paper to write on, and, after we had passed through the air lock into Level 4, she gave me a special pen (it never leaves the Level 4 hot zone). I met some monkeys that had survived Ebola. On the way out, they took the notes I had taken on the Teflon-like paper, crunched them up, stuffed them into a vat of decontaminants, and scrubbed them clean. Amazingly, the writing survived. This was long before 9/11. Today, I doubt a journalist would be allowed into the army's Ebola labs.

Once, while writing a profile of Craig Venter, the head of CEL-ERA Genomics ["The Genome Warrior," *The New Yorker,* June 5, 2000], I asked a Nobel Prize–winning chemist named Hamilton Smith, "What does DNA really look like? How do you handle it?" He took out a vial of human DNA (which ultimately turned out to be Craig Venter's own DNA) and pulled out a little mucuslike strand with a toothpick for me to look at. I wanted to know *everything* about DNA: how it tasted, what it smelled like. So I ordered some calf DNA from a lab supply company. It arrived in powder form and I put it on my tongue. It was faintly salty, and a bit sweet. I used that detail in the article, and I think it helped make the whole idea of DNA more concrete for readers.

Beyond experiencing your subject, how do you learn about it?

By talking to the top people in the field. I essentially attach myself to them as a temporary graduate student. I'll never be a properly credentialed expert, but there are certain areas in which I will know enough to be on a par with, say, a graduate student who hasn't yet passed his general exams.

Do you read anything?

Yes. I always ask the experts for a list of books and articles, which I then immerse myself in. Their lists are essential. If I were just to walk into the Princeton library and start doing research on, say, modern virology, I'd be completely lost.

How do you know when you've done enough research to write on a subject?

John McPhee used to say to us, "You only know you've done enough research on a story when you meet yourself coming in the opposite direction." It is a metaphoric way of saying that you never quite get to the bottom of a story. But if you pursue it long enough, you find yourself getting the same answers from different people. Or you find an expert telling you that you really need to speak with Dr. so-and-so—and you've already interviewed him!

Once you've come up with an idea, refined it into a story, and done some research, how do you begin reporting?

As quickly as I can, I try to experience the world of the person I'm writing about. This goes for reporting that will end up in fiction or nonfiction.

For example, *The Cobra Event* has an important autopsy scene, so I knew I had to learn what it felt like for a doctor to cut open a cadaver. A doctor I know in Princeton agreed to call me the next time there was an autopsy, and one Saturday morning he called to say that there was an autopsy scheduled in thirty minutes. I rushed over to the hospital and watched the whole thing: the assistant cutting and opening the body, the pathologist using a bread knife to slice organ samples. When the pathologist cut the skull and lifted the brain out, she handed it to me. It was a soft, gelatinous blob. And the smell during the autopsy was *profound*. The contents of the large intestine stink, and the freshly cut human flesh smelled, I must say, a little like raw pork. Experiencing that autopsy myself made the scene in *The Cobra Event* incredibly real and accurate.

How would you describe your reportorial stance?

I'm gentle and nonconfrontational. I'm generally admiring and I'm always respectful. My goal is to capture this human being, to "immortalize" the person in prose. For many of the people I'm writing about, this may be the only time in their entire life that their work will be handled with respect and detail by an author who knows what he is doing. I take that responsibility very seriously.

How do you conceive of your role as a reporter?

I go back to the historian Thucydides, who was originally an Athenian general during the early stages of the Peloponnesian War. General Thucydides lost a battle to the Spartans and was nearly executed for it. He fled to Sparta, where he interviewed Spartan generals about the war. In the opening passages of *Peloponnesian War* he writes something like, "Believing that these events were important and worthy of narration, I chose to write them down, not just for this time but for future ages . . ." He identified events of his day as worthy of being immortalized in the form of narrative history. In a way, I'm writing history. The people I've written about are all going to die, but there will always be a record of what they achieved. The little threads of human existence are like feeder-streams in the great watershed of history.

Once you're ready to begin interviewing, how do you decide who to talk to?

I suppose I think about the people I'll interview in the same way a playwright thinks about how his characters will fit together onstage. It's like a play by Pirandello, in which the actors take over the drama and act on their own—except that it's real, *not* a play, and they *do* act on their own.

As for the kinds of characters I look for, I like polymaths, people who have hugely diverse, eclectic minds. For example, James Gunn can build complicated telescopes and instruments from spare parts and do Einstein's equations of general relativity in his sleep. Or characters like Eugene Shoemaker, who is a *geologist* who looks at the sky! I love paradox. Or Ken Iverson in *American Steel,* who is a CEO of a Fortune 500 company whose office is in a shabby mall, who flies coach, and who answers his own phone because his secretary is too busy!

I look for characters who embody the paradoxical interaction between the public figure, who has very important public responsibilities, and the private person who is dealing with the mundane reality of American life.

How do you begin an interview?

I tell the story of how I found the person I'm interviewing, who else I've talked to, who recommended whom, how his name came up, etc.

For example, when I interviewed D. A. Henderson, the chief eradicator of smallpox, I started by saying, "I'm very interested in your work. Everybody says that you were an important figure in the global eradication of smallpox when you ran that effort at the World Health Organization. One reason I want to interview you is that I want to find out where the world stands today. Is smallpox gone for sure? Does it exist in laboratories? And, if so, how much of a threat is smallpox, and what are we going to do about it?" And that launched him off. I hardly had to say another word.

How much do you tell someone you're interviewing about the specifics of your project?

I rarely operate under concealment. Although I sometimes don't reveal the *full* scope of my project. But that's only in situations in which there is a boiling controversy, or where people have secrets that they want to conceal.

For example, when I was profiling Craig Venter, his relationship with the Human Genome Project (run by Francis Collins and James Watson) was bitter, contentious, and rivalrous. But *neither* side was willing to admit that publicly even though it was as obvious as the sun. To the contrary, Francis Collins was giving me all this pablum about how it was "good" to have Craig Venter working on the same project, how it was "good" to have a competitor. Meanwhile, behind the scenes, they were all cutting each other's throats and doing everything they could to interrupt the other group's work, to surge ahead in what was, essentially, a "scientific race." I called it a race in my article, thereby infuriating *everybody*.

So when I interviewed James Watson, who rarely grants interviews, I couldn't very well say, "I'm really interested in Craig Venter, Dr. Watson. What do you think about *him*?" So, instead, I said, "I'm very interested in the Human Genome Project. What can you tell me about it?" What I said was all *true* . . . it just wasn't the *whole* story. Toward the end of the interview, when I had the information I needed, I started asking questions about Craig Venter, whom Watson had once called "the Hitler of the Human Genome"!

Do you prepare questions for an interview?

I don't usually write down any questions beforehand. I try not to come into an interview with any preconceived notions about what the person is going to say, or where it's going to lead. The interview is an organic process. I let the interviewee take over the interview and decide, essentially, what questions will be asked. This is extremely time-consuming and can turn what should be a one-hour interview into a six-hour interview. People generally want to talk about *everything*. It's a little bit like fishing. I'm there with a line in the water, pulling something out once in a while. It sometimes takes a long time to catch a big fish.

Wouldn't it be more efficient to direct the interview with your questions?

Perhaps, but then I'd probably learn less about the person. If they're *really* interested in something, there is a reason for it. So then *I* become interested in it, and want to know *why* they are interested in it. That's generally how my interviews work.

Sometimes these nondirected interviews can be extremely valuable in other ways as well. For example, when I was interviewing people at Fort Detrick for *The New Yorker* article "The Demon in the Freezer" [July 7, 1999], I ran across this very odd character named Steven J. Hatfill. He ended up talking a lot about bioterrorism and his own research, and not much about smallpox. He told me that he had worked for the U.S. Special Forces in Rhodesia, doing work he "couldn't talk about," and that he had two CVs: one classified, the other open. I spent two hours with the man and found him terribly charming and likable, if a bit of a big-mouth. I never transcribed his interview onto the computer because it wasn't relevant to the story I was writing. Later, when his name came up as a so-called "person of interest" to the FBI during the anthrax investigation, I was able to retrieve my notes, transcribe them, and put the interview into my book, *The Demon in the Freezer*. As far as I know, that was the only full interview with Steven Hatfill that a journalist has been able to obtain. And the only reason I got it was because I did it as a casual, nondirected interview more than a year before the FBI started focusing on Hatfill.

Where do you *most* and *least* like conducting interviews?

It's never very productive to sit in a biologist's office and talk. I want to see the person in the lab, out in the field doing research. That way I get to tag along and be introduced to everyone in that person's world.

How confrontational will you become during an interview?

I'm like an interrogator, although a *nice* interrogator. I'm good at wearing people down. I can interview someone forever. I have the stamina of a member of the Soviet Politburo. I never get tired. I just keep asking the same question over and over again, in a slightly different form, until I get an answer.

But I rarely become confrontational, and that is partly a function of the people I choose to interview. I generally don't interview scum. That's not to say that conducting interviews with scumbags isn't a very important part of journalism, nor is it to say that I haven't done it myself. But even when I *do* interview scumbags, I try to make it a nonconfrontational, genteel, and often friendly interview. Then, later, when I'm putting the piece together, I try to keep my encounter with the bastard tonally neutral. I just describe what they said and did, and let that speak for itself.

John McPhee points out that people get angry when you get facts about them wrong. But they generally don't get angry if you describe them accurately. So if a person is a jerk, and you describe him as he really is, he'll recognize himself and may not quarrel with it.

What about interviews with admirable people who are lying to you? How confrontational will you become then?

I've learned a few tricks from interviewing FBI agents. FBI agents are trained in interviewing techniques. When you're interviewing an agent, he will quickly turn the interview around: "What's your book all about? Who have you talked with?" That sort of thing. It's all done very nicely. They've told me that they deal very calmly with suspects who appear to be lying. They just point out contradictions between the evidence and the suspect's statements. So if I think a nice guy is misrepresenting what happened, I'll say, "But there's evidence it happened differently. What do you say about that?"

How much do you reveal about yourself during an interview?

A lot. It helps build rapport. I tell them about my struggles as a writer. I'll say, "This book is driving me *crazy*! I'm having all sorts of problems." It turns the interview into a participatory experience. I enjoy it when a subject gets interested in the literary aspects of the composition. Some of the scientists I write about see it as another "problem" they can solve. They make suggestions about how I should write the piece. Some are terrible, some quite good.

How do you convince subjects to give you so much time?

I show a real commitment to learning about them. For example, in order to convince Steven Sillett, the tree-climbing scientist I'm writing about now, to let me climb redwood trees with him, I got basic training in professional tree-climbing techniques, and I spent months practicing in trees around my house. I carefully observed the gear that Sillett uses—he is a major gearhead—and I duplicated his gear for myself. I'm probably still not that good a climber, but I showed him just how far I'd go in order to follow him around.

Although I come to most interviews cold, I'm very knowledgeable about the culture of science. So when I come into someone's lab and begin asking questions, they pick up pretty quickly that, although I don't yet know much about their work, I'm scientifically literate. I make it very clear early in the interview process that I'm going to have to come back to this person because I don't know enough to know where I'm going wrong. "Only you can tell me," I tell him.

Writing about science and scientists is tricky because scientists often say terribly nuanced things. It's important to them that a writer understand that their findings are not written in stone, that they are just tentative *results*. A writer needs to be able to introduce the element of uncertainty, which is difficult. If you read *The New York Times* reporting on science, it can be of the ilk: "Great New Discovery Will Change the World." Scientists *hate* that kind of hyperbole.

How, and at what point, do you tell your subjects how much time and access you'll need from them?

I warn them right up front, but they are still never prepared. I say, "I want to spend some time with you." I take whatever they will give me at first. As the first interview winds down, I ask, "What's your schedule like? Do you have another hour, or two, or three?" Sometimes interviews go on *all day*. I just tag along and ask more questions.

The other thing I try to prepare them for is the fact-checking process I do, which is *in addition* to the fact-checking *The New Yorker* does. I warn them that after all our interviews are done, I'm going to call them on the phone, and we could end up spending hours and hours going over details. I tell them that it will drive them crazy, and might even require an all-nighter. I don't want to scare them away, but I want them to know how I work.

Do you tape or take notes?

I take fast, longhand notes.

What kind of notebook do you use?

I use a small (four-by-seven-inch), spiral-bound notebook that I get at the drugstore. I always use the kind with the spirals on the side. It is just small enough so that I can usually slip it into my shirt pocket. I am careful to make my note-taking conspicuous, so the person I'm interviewing is sure to know they are being interviewed. If I'm socializing with someone I've just finished interviewing and they start to relax, have a drink, and tell me more interesting stuff, I pull out my notebook and ask whether I can write it down. They usually say yes. Or if the circumstances are such that I either don't have my notes, or there is some reason I don't want to pull them out, I am ethically bound to pose those questions again at a later date, when it is clear that I *am* interviewing the person. But I never take notes or interview surreptitiously.

What do you write with?

I use a mechanical drafting pencil. I push the eraser to make the lead come out. I use HB lead, a medium-hard lead that has a very low friction coefficient, so it moves very fast over the paper. Also, the mark it makes is rather light, so my interview subject can't see what I'm writing.

Does taking notes distract the person you're interviewing?

No. In fact, I've found that a notebook disarms someone *more* than a tape recorder. The presence of a tape recorder sometimes makes someone feel as if their words might be turned into legal evidence, whereas a notebook doesn't seem as threatening.

I have an interviewing trick that uses this misperception to my advantage. When someone says something really explosive, I put a bored expression on my face and stop writing. I listen to them in a very noncommittal, distracted way, and make sure not to react to what I'm being told. I do this until my short-term memory register is beginning to fill up, and then I change the subject and ask a question I *know* will elicit a long, boring answer. At *that* point, I begin writing like mad in my notebook to get it all down.

Is that why you don't use a tape recorder?

That, and the fact that this is the way I was trained in McPhee's class. The disadvantages of a tape recorder are many. First of all, I'm a mechanical idiot and tape recorders always seem to break on me. Second, a tape recorder cannot capture a scene. A scene is kinesthetic: it has sound, smell, sight, and emotional environment all around it. The way a person is dressed, the way he's behaving, the weather, the natural environment—none of that is captured by a tape recorder. Whereas in a notebook, you can take down all these kinds of details.

Third, when I'm interviewing a person it is often in an environment where a tape recorder is simply not going to work: three hundred feet above the ground in a tree, or in a space suit handing deadly viruses. When I was writing *First Light,* I found that the best time to interview one of the astronomers was in the middle of the night when he would pace around the catwalk on the Hale telescope. He would only open up to me in the moonless, pitch-black darkness. It was way too dark for me to take any notes, but I'd listen intently and remember what he was saying. Then I'd sit down immediately after our conversation and write down the important remarks.

But wouldn't that be the perfect situation for a tape recorder?
Perhaps, although then there is the hassle of transcribing all those tapes. With a notebook, I do a lot of transcribing and editing *while* the interview is taking place. I don't miss the really important things people say. And people tend to repeat the really important points. If it is important to them they will usually say it more than once.

How do you know when the interview phase of the piece is done and you're ready to begin writing?
It's *never* done. I conduct what I call "fact-checking interviews" up until literally the moment before the article or book goes to press. The people in the production department hate me because I'm always making changes at the very last second. And if they won't let me make changes I tell them that it is a *legal* issue, which always scares them. I say, "I've been doing more fact-checking. I've encountered new information, and if I can't put it in the book we're all going to be sued!"

Tell me more about these fact-checking interviews.
Fact-checking is a crucial part of my writing. Starting with *First Light,* I got into the habit of calling my subjects on the phone while the piece was in draft form. I find that I can't often get a passage right until I've read it aloud to a real expert. I sometimes spend hours and hours on the phone with an expert. My phone bills have been known to top $1500. I never show written material to my subjects, but I always read it to them over the phone.

If you are willing to read passages of your writing, and even your subject's quotes back to them, why not just send them the text itself?
Because if they read it on the page, they get upset or want to make all sorts of changes. But if they hear the flow out loud on the

phone—and I'll read it as many times as they want to hear it—they help me make it more accurate. I'll ask, "Is this correct? Have I got the letter correct, but missed the spirit?" If so, we'll work on it until we are both satisfied.

I write about a lot of scientists, and the problem is that they are so used to dealing with peer-reviewed, or collaborative, writing that they even want to rewrite *my* piece! I've often had a scientist say, "Just send me the draft and I'll work on it for you." They'd want to change their quotes and make everything muddy and indistinct. So I will only read select passages to them over the phone. Then *I* make the changes.

The other great thing about fact-checking is that it helps me establish a whole new level of trust, especially with scientists. By taking the time to fact-check, I'm demonstrating unequivocally that all I care about is *everything being right*. I'm putting my ego aside and telling the scientist that I'm not interested in my "take" on the story—in fact, I'm not really interested in *his* "take" either—I just want to get it right.

A kind of friendship often develops from the process, and they begin telling me things they would *never* have said during earlier interviews. So the so-called "fact-checking interview" is *actually* another interview. It's often when the most important and interesting material flows forth.

Every journalist wants to be accurate, but why is accuracy such an obsession for you?
Getting the facts right is crucial. If a technical or scientific reader encounters a howling error it blows the entire piece's credibility. And even an ordinary reader senses when a piece has been fact-checked. It's tight, like when you slam the doors on a new car and nothing rattles.

How do you pace yourself while reporting long projects?
I don't pace myself well. I get a lot of support from my wife and children, who have learned to adapt to my sudden absences. When I do these long narrative pieces—whether it is a steel mill or the Palomar observatory— I can only be there for short periods of time. So on each trip I pick up where I left off and try to re-create the events I missed.

The result is what I call my "leap and linger" technique. My writing has a structure that is similar to a ballad. There is usually a lyrical passage about one event, and then I move way ahead in time. Then there is another lyrical passage about an event, and so on. I'll focus in on one event—often something that I've witnessed—and make it stand in for other, larger events in the story that I don't tell the reader as much about, often because I *wasn't* there to see them. Then I move forward in time to another event, or an interview with a key character.

What rules do you use when reconstructing scenes you haven't witnessed?

My rules are to try to talk to as many participants as possible, and then to cross-correlate what they say. There will always be disagreements about what actually happened, particularly if it is contentious, which is the kind of thing I want most to write about. When I have conflicting accounts, I'll go back to one character and say, "Well, so-and-so remembers it differently. This is what *he* said. What do *you* think?" And he will either agree with the other person's account or try to convince me that his account is actually correct.

What do you do if the accounts are diametrically opposed to each other?

I have to sort through it with the understanding that it is kind of like a lawsuit, and there will be no final version of events. When I render the scene on the page, I'll often note that "So-and-so doesn't remember it that way. He remembers . . ." And just let it sit there.

Do you worry about keeping a distance from your characters?

Ultimately, the success of the piece will depend on how well I maintain my neutrality. Keeping a professional distance is important, but is very difficult for me. I have to keep telling myself that *every* human being has a dark side, that nobody is perfect. I usually like, and even identify with, the people I write about, so I have to be very careful not to become their advocate. I sometimes find myself defending a character, when all I should be doing is describing his actions. I'm better at pulling back during the writing and editing of a book than I am during the reporting.

What kinds of ethical ground rules do you set when reporting?

The first is that I won't exchange money with a subject. The second is that I won't ever have a contractual relationship with a subject, such as a "life story agreement," according to which I get the exclusive right to tell his life story in exchange for paying a subject.

When it comes to movie rights, the situation is somewhat different. In that case, I've had to make agreements with people I've written about or else each studio will make an agreement with a different character in the story, and then they all fight over who gets to make the movie. But agreements of this kind are typically made after the book is published.

What kinds of negotiations will you engage in about the material you can, and can't, use?

I generally let people have their privacy as *they* define it. Often during an interview, someone will say, "I don't want you to write about it, but I'm going to tell you something." Now, according to the standard rules of journalism, since he didn't say it was "off the record," I'm justified in using it. But I don't do that. Rather, I'll engage him in a discussion about it. I might say, "I think the information you've told me is important to the story for the following reasons . . ." If I can't convince them, then I won't use it. I'll explain the "on the record" vs. "off the record" distinction so that everything is clear in the future.

What is your policy about using pseudonyms?

I am willing to change someone's name if it's necessary to protect that person's career or personal security. I always note in the text if a name has been changed. It is always best to get somebody to talk under their real name. But when I'm talking to government employees about something like bioterrorism, they have good professional reasons why I can't use their names.

Is writing more difficult for you than reporting, or vice versa?

Writing is *far* more difficult than reporting. I love reporting. In fact, I love reporting so much that, if left to my own devices, I'd never get around to the writing.

How do you organize your material in preparation to write?

The first thing I do is read through all the interviews on the screen of my computer. I underline, highlight, and put asterisks to mark the sections I want to use.

Since I interview most of my subjects several times, I draw connections between things they told me during one encounter and things they told me during others. If I make changes to my notes in electronic form, I make sure to put brackets around any changes—quotes, thoughts, observations—that I am recalling or making at a time that isn't contemporaneous with the interview notes themselves. That way I can distinguish contemporaneous material from the material I add later, and can reflect these distinctions in the text.

Do you have a method for writing?

Yes, I do have a regular method, but it is painful, if not chaotic. I'm not proud of it. It seems to work, but I hate it. I wish I could write like Charles Dickens, who drafted his serial novels chapter by chapter, the words just flowing from his pen. That's not the way it is with me.

Do you make an outline?

I always write a little outline—not more than a few lines on a piece of paper—and then depart from it immediately. I think of my outline as an *anti*-template, the structure that I am guaranteed not to use, since it's my useless outline! But nevertheless, I feel compelled to write one. In addition to the written outline, I have a scene-by-scene outline in my mind.

My writing is scene-based, so I use an outline to figure out the *sequence* of the scenes. Blending complex scientific information in with a story about human beings is difficult. It's like hanging laundry on a line. The facts are the laundry, and the line is the line of the story. If you hang too much laundry on the line, the line will be dragged to the ground by the weight. I've got to be careful to keep myself from freighting the narrative with too much information.

What does your typical writing day look like?

I wake up at six thirty, have breakfast, and drive my children to school. I come home and go straight into my office. I treat writing as an eight-to-six job. It normally takes me an hour or two to get myself together to the point where I'm ready to write. I answer e-mail and anything else I can do *not* to write. Eventually I get to the point where I figure that I had better start writing or else I'm going to lose the entire day. I've found that it really pays to stop when I'm done for the day. Even if I've only written five hundred words, I can *feel* when I begin to burn out. So I just quit.

Is there anywhere in particular you need to be to write?
I prefer a bare office. Nothing too luxurious. My office needs to feel like a place where work gets done, not where you go to relax. It has to be fairly quiet, and I can't have a phone around.

Any particular time of day you write best?
I tend to be hottest after lunch, from about one to three in the afternoon.

So how do you begin writing?
I begin by writing a lead, which I can spend weeks on. At first, it is too complicated, wooden, dull, windy, aimless. There have been times when I've rewritten a lead anywhere from thirty to forty times. I write the lead and throw it out. I write a slightly longer lead and throw that out. Eventually I decide it sucks and move on to the middle phase of the piece.

Do you write straight through from start to finish, or do you write discrete sections?
A little of both. I skip around a lot at first, drafting a whole bunch of scenes, some of which are very quick collections of barely grammatical sentences. The idea is just to ram them down on the paper as fast as possible in whatever order they come out. Then, as I keep sketching out scenes, I begin rearranging them into a narrative. Finally, when the structure is more or less the way I want it, I write the ending quickly. Then I go back to the beginning and revise from start to finish until I get it the way I want it.

Do you revise as you go along, or only once you have a full draft?

I revise sequentially. I print out the manuscript every day and edit. I worry it half to death, although I know I should just leave it alone and get it done. It is a circular motion in which I keep returning to the beginning and rewriting, advancing the book bit by bit.

How do you pace yourself when you write?

I keep track of how many words I write each day. It varies anywhere from six hundred to two thousand words. I know my first draft is pretty much done when my daily word counts begin decreasing. I'll write *negative* five hundred words one day, *negative* seven hundred and fifty words the next. One of my strengths as a writer is that I have the strength to "kill my darlings."

What do you do once you have a complete first draft?

I print the whole thing out and read it. I've usually convinced myself that it is more polished than it really is. So it's quite a shock when I finally read it on paper. I think, "Oh my God! I have no talent. I must have had a silent stroke, I've lost my ability with words. I'm a *fraud*! Just look at this stuff." My first drafts are *terrible,* and I don't show them to anybody—especially not to my editors. I made the mistake, a long time ago, of believing that editors can take draft material and make it better. They cannot. When I have shown my drafts to editors, they tend to panic.

How do you move from a terrible first draft to a finished manuscript?

I love revising. I find it much more satisfying than writing, because at that point I *know* I have something that is going to be really good, and I can concentrate on writing it well. Toward the end of the revising period on a book, I often work twelve- to fifteen-hour days. I go into a fury of revision.

Do you discuss your work-in-progress, or do you prefer not to talk about your work?

It depends on the project. With the tree-climbing piece, I'm talking my way through it with everybody. With the piece I wrote about smallpox, I didn't talk about it with anybody.

What makes the difference between talking about and not talking about a piece?

Some subjects are hard to explain. Tree climbing is pretty easy to explain. Viruses are not. When it's hard to explain, I tend to keep it to myself. It's a bad experience to be all excited about a piece of writing and start telling people about it, and to get blank stares in return.

What kind of tone do you strive for in your writing?

I try to maintain a cool, understated tone. "Litotes" is the Latin term of rhetoric for the understated, simple voice, which is often grammatically simple as well. I've been very influenced by Latin authors, especially Tacitus, and I used to read a lot of Latin. You can find the Tacitean style in most of what I write. I write simple, direct, declaratory sentences, often in the form "subject-object-verb." I sometimes repeat the principal noun in two or three sentences in a row, the way it is done in the Bible.

Or in The New Yorker?

Yes, it is a kind of style one finds a lot in the *The New Yorker.* Then I love to follow up a simple description with a flight of fancy, a sentence that is almost too lush or too gorgeous. As in *The Hot Zone,* when I write, "They were the face of Nature herself, the obscene goddess revealed naked. This life form thing was breathtakingly beautiful. As he stared at it, he found himself being pulled out of the human world where moral boundaries blur and finally dissolve completely."

What kind of authorial presence do you strive for?

I have a somewhat self-deprecating, humorous, mild-mannered persona. But one has to be very careful not to overuse the personal pronoun, the "I." You need a little bit of an "I" to provide a validating consciousness for the events you're describing, but it has to be done subtly. Journalists go astray when they dwell on themselves. It is an occupational hazard for the literary journalist because the form has roots in the tradition of travel writing, in which the "I" is necessary to keep the narrative moving forward. There is usually a lot more of "me" in the first draft than the final manuscript. I spend a lot of time during revision taking out references to myself.

Do you think that literary nonfiction can yield truth?

There are many different kinds of truth. Academic literary criticism often takes the easy way out by saying, in effect, "It's all text, it's all just non-referential, fictive constructions." And, therefore, literary nonfiction is no different than the novel.

But the truth is that nonfiction writing, at least as I practice it, isn't like that at all. It borrows heavily from the scientific method, which is based on the requirement that a successful experiment have "repeatable" results. Journalists understand this because our work has to be subject to fact-checking and independent verification, which is exactly what a scientist expects when he reports his results. If a piece is accurate and has been properly reported, another journalist should be able to conduct the same interviews and arrive at a fairly similar result.

There is another form of truth, which is emotional and cultural truth. That's the truth that one encounters in Fielding's preface to *Tom Jones*, in which he argues that even though Tom Jones never really existed, his story is "true" because it tells the human truth. It is the true description of the human condition and human emotions.

Similarly, when we read a work of nonfiction, we recognize the human truth in the characters. If I've done my work well as a writer, then we recognize the human truth in *The Hot Zone* when Nancy Jacks thinks she's going to die of Ebola virus and is annoyed that she forgot to go to the bank that day! That's a human truth. She was dealing with these very practical issues in the same way that anyone in these extraordinary circumstances would do. I conveyed her thoughts via an interior monologue. It rang absolutely true when she first described her thoughts to me. But then I went over it again and again until I was finally sure that this was—to the best of her recollection—what she thought at that moment. I'd write the passage out and read it to her out loud on the phone.

Is literary nonfiction is a peculiarly American form?

Yes, it is a characteristic American literary form. I was entranced by it while writing my dissertation, "The Fabric of Fact: The Beginning of American Literary Journalism" (1983), on writers like Thoreau, Melville, and Twain.

We're a pragmatic society. Benjamin Franklin, the archetypal American scientist, was an empiricist, not a theorist. It's like jazz; we're always testing a new riff, performing a series of reiterated empirical experiments to find out where we want to take the music.

And, like jazz, nonfiction writing is grounded in American experience. It is grounded in "facts," which Americans have always been really big on. It is something I even see in the art of Thomas Eakins. There is a cool, blue, American light in Eakins's paintings that takes the reality of American life and turns it into a passage of wonder about human existence that is just transcendent in its power. I'm thinking especially of his painting *The Gross Clinic*. And, as in Eakins's *The Gross Clinic,* we also have these deeper poetic truths that we can weave with the facts to make a work of art. Dr. Gross was a real guy, he really performed this experiment, this was a real patient, many of the faces in the crowd are portraits of people who were really there. Yet, at the same time, it has been organized by an artistic consciousness as a *purely artificial work of art.*

Are you optimistic about the future of literary journalism?

Yes, although the genre is much more subdued today than it was when Wolfe and Capote were first writing. It has become much more commercially important. There's just a lot more money in nonfiction than there ever was before. That may have had a smoothing effect on it; it might have made it a bit more commercial and self-conscious. A book like Jon Krakauer's *Into Thin Air* is a very good, straightforward piece of writing that became a huge bestseller. *Into Thin Air* doesn't contain much in the way of literary experiment, whereas *The Right Stuff* and *In Cold Blood* were enormous literary experiments.

We're in the post–New Journalism era. Truman Capote's and Tom Wolfe's achievements have been *achieved.* I think the real question is, "Where's the literary experiment today? Who's on the cutting edge of literary nonfiction? What's next?" I don't know.

BY RICHARD PRESTON:

The Boat of Dreams: A Christmas Story, Touchstone Books, 2003
The Demon in the Freezer, Random House, 2003
The Cobra Event, Random House, 1997
The Hot Zone, Random House, 1994
American Steel, Simon & Schuster, 1991
First Light, Atlantic Monthly Press, 1987

RON ROSENBAUM

As a child growing up in sleepy Bay Shore, Long Island, Ron Rosenbaum devoured Hardy Boy mysteries by the shelfful. He was enamored of the brothers' lives—packed as they were with skulduggery, adventure, and storybook endings—and vowed that he, too, would one day solve mysteries. As an investigative journalist, Rosenbaum has had more success than most in translating his youthful fantasies into reality. Only one element has failed to come to fruition: unlike the Hardy Boys', Rosenbaum's mysteries aren't neatly solved.

A self-described "buff buff," an "investigator of investigations," Rosenbaum's goal is less to answer questions than to pose them anew. The mysteries he writes about include such weighty questions as the source of Hitler's evil, the true story of the Kennedy assassination, and the identity of Watergate's "Deep Throat." It might be more accurate to say that he investigates enigmas rather than mysteries, primal puzzles that confound one generation after another, curiosities whose complexity grows in direct proportion to the number of seekers who engage them. It is not only among recognized authorities but also among heretical outsiders that Rosenbaum finds his best material. His pieces often take the form of a quest, our protagonist investigating the story of the story, filled with the twists and turns—false steps, dead ends, red herrings—he experienced along the way.

"Are we any better off, any closer to the truth, as a result of all our re-investigations?" he asks in the introduction to his collection *Travels with Dr. Death and Other Unusual Investigations* (1991). "In fact, my nonpessimist side would argue that we have both more truth and more uncertainty. Or to put it another way, more truths, if not the truth."

Rosenbaum's respect for the truth, his keen sense of its elusiveness, only fuels his search. His voice—one of the most distinct and enjoyable in contemporary journalism—is the product of his total commitment to the truth. Reviewing *The Secret Parts of Fortune* (2000) in *The New York Times Book Review,* Luc Sante characterized Rosenbaum's voice as "a masterly concoction, a blend of boy reporter, Ancient Mariner, lounge lizard and grandpa by the fireside. He is a showman, and that allows him to put over dryly complex exposition, minute textual analysis, even (as in the Dead Sea Scrolls business) fearsomely recondite arguments with ease and flair."

Ron Rosenbaum was born in Manhattan on November 27, 1946. He attended Yale University, graduating Phi Beta Kappa in 1968 and winning a Carnegie Fellowship to attend their graduate program in English Literature. Once the bastion of the New Criticism—the school of thought that preached that the meaning of all literature was to be found through keen examination of the text—Yale provided Rosenbaum the critical scholarly skills (close reading, a sensitivity to ambiguity) he would later put to good use in his journalism.

Yale also provided material for two of Rosenbaum's most famous pieces. The first was about Skull and Bones, the secret society whose members—both presidents Bush among them—have been some of the most powerful figures in American political life ["The Last Secrets of Skull and Bones," *Esquire,* September 1977]. The second looked at the university's practice, from the 1940s through 1960s, of taking nude photographs of all freshmen, which became part of a bizarre eugenic study ["The Great Ivy League Nude Posture Photo Scandal," *The New York Times Magazine,* January 15, 1995].

Rosenbaum's first job in journalism was covering the 1968 Democratic convention for the *Suffolk Sun.* The following summer he got a job as an assistant editor at the *Fire Island News.* His writing attracted the attention of *Voice* writer Nat Hentoff and of Rhoda Wolf, who recommended him to her husband Dan Wolf, the editor of *The Village Voice.* Rosenbaum soon became known as "the Dostoyevsky of the *Voice.*" In Kevin McAuliffe's history of the *Voice, The Great American Newspaper,* he describes Rosenbaum: "He could write fast, and long, driving himself to stay awake for extended periods of time to finish something, and with such seemingly easy force, that they were dazzled by him." When *New York* magazine bought the *Voice* in 1974, many feared that the downtown weekly's independent character would suffer under the leadership of Clay Felker, *New York's* founder. Rosenbaum announced his resignation in 1975—by shredding his paycheck in front of Felker.

After leaving the *Voice,* Rosenbaum wrote *Murder at Elaine's* (1978), a murder mystery—serialized in *High Times*—filled with veiled references to New York's literary and journalistic world. Rosenbaum also continued writing for *Esquire* and began writing for *Harper's* and for *MORE,* the journalism review of which he was executive editor. A collection of his pieces from this period, *Rebirth of the Salesman: Tales of the Song & Dance 70's,* was published in 1979.

In 1984, Rosenbaum began writing for the newly founded *Manhattan, inc.,* a monthly New York magazine that chronicled the excesses of the eighties. Rosenbaum was initially hesitant to join the magazine—after all, his usual beat was obsessive outsiders— but was persuaded by editor Jane Amsterdam, who argued that, for better or worse, the decade was being defined by a new cast of characters with a new set of values. "This should be exciting to you as a writer," she said, "because it's a realm that's previously been written about mainly by bottom-line-minded business magazines." Rosenbaum wrote many of the magazine's most memorable pieces: "The Shame of the Super Rich," in which Felix and Elizabeth Rohatyn accused fellow socialites of ignoring the poor; "Trump: The Ultimate Deal," in which Donald Trump argues that he is uniquely qualified to make a deal with the Soviet Union to rid the world of nuclear weapons. His *Manhattan, inc.* pieces were collected in *Manhattan Passions: True Tales of Power, Wealth, and Excess* (1987), which *Business Week's* Bruce Nussbaum called "*The Great Gatsby* of the 'Easy Eighties.'"

Rosenbaum quit *Manhattan, inc.* after Amsterdam resigned in 1987, and spent the next few years writing primarily for *Vanity Fair* and *The New York Times Magazine.* He also continued to work on a decade-long project. In 1983, Rosenbaum found himself talking with a group of Jewish militants who were discussing an attack on neo-Nazi groups with pipe bombs. Rosenbaum argued that such vigilante-style justice was dangerous and futile. One of the men challenged Rosenbaum's reasoning. "Wouldn't assassinating Hitler in the 1920s have been a good idea?" he asked. Rosenbaum was intrigued by the question. *Would* the Second World War and the Holocaust have occurred if Hitler had been eliminated? He began a historical novel about an attempt by Jews to assassinate Hitler, but a few years into his research, he realized that the question had the makings of a larger, nonfiction book.

Explaining Hitler (1998) is Rosenbaum's most ambitious book so far. In it, he admits that he admits that he thought, like many of the Hitler explainers, that if one could only find an essential clue (the "lost safe-deposit box"), the mystery of Hitler's evil might be solved. He eventually realized that the search itself—the investigation of the investigators—was a more engaging story. The book consists of a series of encounters with various "Hitler explainers"— historians, scholars, artists, and autodidacts—who have dedicated their lives to trying to understand Hitler. Rosenbaum uses these encounters as a vehicle for his own ruminations on Hitler, and on the nature of evil itself. The result is an extremely contemporary book that uses Hitler as a way to address the most profound questions of Western philosophy. Hitler explanations, he writes, "are cultural self-portraits: the shapes we project onto the inky Rorschach of Hitler's are often cultural self-portraits in the negative. What we talk about when we talk about Hitler is also who we are and who we are not."

Writing in *The New York Review of Books,* John Gross praised Rosenbaum's idiosyncratic approach. "It is both thoughtful and deeply felt, and in some ways its personal, freewheeling qualities enable Rosenbaum to get closer to the demonic element in Hitler than he would have done if he had been a professional historian." Other reviewers, like *The Washington Post*'s Marc Fisher, understood that Rosenbaum's investigation was as much about us as it was about Hitler. "What's most remarkable about *Explaining Hitler* is how new it feels, because Rosenbaum has considered every major stream of fact, near-fact and utter fiction about the Nazi dictator, and shown how the history of Hitler is the history of the postwar mind . . . With words and ideas that surprise, amuse and even elevate the reader, Rosenbaum has helped to restore Hitler to the historical record and remind us that the histories we write are as much stories of ourselves as of our past."

For his next book, Rosenbaum turned the question he poses of Hitler—Was he an "exceptional" figure in history?—to Shakespeare, another figure who has long fascinated him. Was the playwright simply a remarkable human being, or was he in a category of one, a genius who developed an insight into the nature of humanity that was uniquely his? He's spent the past five years with Shakespeare scholars and directors, exploring the questions they pursue. Ron Rosenbaum's investigation of the investigators continues.

———

What kinds of subjects are you drawn to?
In the mid-eighties, a magazine editor suggested to me that I get angry when I come across people who act as if they've "figured it all out." I think he was right. I struggle so hard to figure things out—and find so many questions *un*answerable—that I'm *allergic* to people who overstate their claims of certitude.

I resent—and am fascinated by—people's overconfidence in their theories, whether they are about the Kennedy assassination, about the spy Kim Philby, about what made Hitler tick. Time after time, I'd find each debate dominated by people who were convinced of their own truth, when in fact there were a half-dozen conflicting truths. So I like to investigate the factual basis for their confidence, and then try to see what the agendas behind these theories are. Those are the kinds of subjects I'm attracted to.

How do you then find your stories?
I often stumble on what I call a "tip of the iceberg" fragment. Elizabeth Kübler-Ross's "Death and Dying" cult is a good example ["Turn On, Tune In, Drop Dead," *Harper's,* September 1982]. I had always been skeptical about her five stages of dying. One day I came across a wire-service clip about how Kübler-Ross and her disciples had been deceived by this second-rate, fake psychic medium named Jay Barham, who convinced them that he could channel afterlife entities. He'd actually have them materialize, come to their rooms, and sometimes sleep with them. Of course, the "materialized entities" were all Barham himself, often wearing a turban and nothing else. And here was Kübler-Ross, America's official philosopher of death, falling for this obvious fraud. That made me want to write about her.

Another "tip-of-the-iceberg" example came from a small, wire-service clip on an inside page of *The New York Times* about an air force major who was fired from his Minuteman missile capsule duties for asking a simple question: "When I receive the launch order, which will result in my massacring millions of people, how do I know that the order comes from a sane person?"

I thought that was a pretty good question. After all, how *do* we define "sanity" in a system which requires us to destroy half the planet once we see missiles coming to destroy our half of the planet. The story kept getting larger and larger, taking me into the debate on nuclear strategy, and into the way nuclear nightmares had infiltrated the culture—the genre of pop-fiction I called "nuke porn." Then I discovered that the serious literature on nuclear strategy was in fact a kind of "nuke porn" itself ["The Subterranean World of the Bomb," *Harper's*, March 1978].

Do you always generate your own ideas?
I'm happy if someone comes to me with a great story idea. But most of my favorite stories come from my own ideas.

A homicide detective in your story "Crack Murder" describes a "good murder" as one that elicits his best work. What is the journalism equivalent of a "good murder"?
I first came across the notion of a "good murder" when I was doing a story for *MORE*, the journalism review where I was executive editor, about Pat Doyle, the legendary *Daily News* police reporter who claimed to have covered something like 15,000 murders ["The World's Greatest Police Reporter," *MORE*, July 1976]. I was interested in the way that tabloid stories have deeper dimensions, higher levels, passions—the *same* elements that inspire great art. After all, isn't *Anna Karenina* on one level an adultery-suicide tabloid story?

Doyle's definition of a "good murder" was one with a "twist of fate": a couple shot on their wedding day, a shoot-out at a funeral home, some kind of cosmic irony—although *he'd* never use that phrase.

When I talked about Doyle with *Esquire* editor Harold Hayes, who was consulting for *MORE,* he said something that surprised me. "You know what *really* interests you about Pat Doyle?" he asked me. "John Milton," he answered. "In the epigraph to *Paradise Lost* Milton says he is going to attempt to justify the ways of God to man. And that is what Pat Doyle is doing, too." And Hayes was right. What Doyle was trying to figure out was why it was that *this guy* is murdered, when the guy standing next to him isn't. Why fate plays out in such odd and seemingly random ways.

So for me, the journalistic equivalent of a "good murder" is a story that raises dramatic questions beyond "Who did it?" It forces me to ask questions about *why* it happened. Questions of "theodicy," also known as "the problem of evil." How we reconcile evil oftentimes with the notion of a moral order in the universe. Where was God?

The "problem of evil" is a big theme in your work, whether you're writing about Hitler or nuclear war. Is this conscious?

I *am* very interested in metaphysical questions, but I don't like to write about them in the abstract.

After I left Yale, I rejected abstraction. When I became a journalist I wanted to get out there with cops and criminals, to have real adventures and untangle real mysteries. Perhaps abstract questions were lurking beneath the narrative I was crafting, but I certainly didn't want to call the reader's attention to them.

There were some stories in which I think I took this strategy too far. When I was writing about the Super Bowl for *New Times,* I arrived at the Houston Astrodome a few days early and discovered that it was hosting a convention of bull-semen entrepreneurs. Very expensive, very rare, breeding stock bull semen, preserved in nitrogen-cooled canisters. The works.

So I devoted about *one-third* of my first draft to recounting my wanderings through the bull-semen exhibition. But I didn't relate it *at all* to the Super Bowl, which was the *subject* of the piece. So when my editor, John Larsen, said, "Can't we cut some of this long section on the bull semen?" I protested, "No, no, you don't understand! It's a *metaphor* for the commodification of masculinity," or something like that. And he paused, and said, "Well, if that's the case, Ron, why don't you just come right out and *say* that?"

He definitely had a point! But I was so determined to immerse myself in the particular that I was reluctant to direct the reader to any of the ideas in my pieces. It was sometimes a coy little game on my part. I would cover my tracks so *completely* that the reader would miss the ideas entirely! I eventually became more comfortable writing about ideas explicitly.

How much research do you do while preparing for a story?

I love to gather documents. When I was doing the nuclear war story, I found volumes and volumes of these amazing congressional hearings on command-and-control that had been overlooked, but were really important. It turned out there were a lot of holes in the command-and-control system. I knew I was on the right track when I discovered that the key witness was an academic named Professor *Quester*!

I make copious notes on my reading. Then take notes on my notes. And then more notes from them as I refine my questions: who is the key person, what are the key questions, etc.

How do you keep from being overwhelmed?

I'm helped by the fact that the emphasis of my education was on "close reading" of literature, mostly seventeenth-century metaphysical poetry. I found that the ability to read these poems was the most practical skill I had as a journalist. Being able to go through a document and spot what one of the New Critics once called "conspicuous irrelevance."

For instance, if you are reading an exquisite poem and suddenly come upon an awkward phrase or word? What's behind this awkwardness? Maybe the awkwardness is a kind of *node* in which are embedded fascinating resonances, conflicts in the mind of the poet, etc.

Close reading is particularly handy for reading documents like trial transcripts, wiretaps, or transcripts of my own interviews. You see someone suddenly swerve toward or away from something. You learn a lot more from an interview when you read the transcript. When you're *doing* the interview there is too much going on: thinking of your next questions, trying to listen and respond, worrying whether your tape recorder is on. But when you can read it as a text you *see* things you didn't *hear* the first time around.

How do you decide whom to interview?

I often begin from the outside and work in. I start with the heretics. They are usually angrier, more outspoken, less inhibited. They are more willing to talk about the competing agendas, hostilities, and crosscurrents of any given debate. Their freedom comes from being marginal. This doesn't mean that they don't have as much, or more, of the truth as those who are in the mainstream. They just have less to lose and so are more willing to talk.

For my story about the Dead Sea Scrolls, I started my reporting with a scholar named Robert Eisenman, who was brilliant and had his own heretical theory about the Scrolls ["The Riddle of the Scrolls," *Vanity Fair*, May 1991]. I didn't necessarily *believe* everything he had to say about who "The Righteous Teacher" and the "Wicked Priest" in the Scrolls really were, but he helped me orient myself in the debate because he had a lot to say about the people at the *center* of Scroll scholarship.

How do you prepare for interviews?

I try to absorb everything I've learned from the documents. I write down, longhand, pages and pages of questions. Then I do a close reading of my questions, and refine and restructure them—*revision* is a theme in every step of the writing process.

Do you memorize your questions?

No, I bring them along so that I can refer to them. And people respect you more if they see that you are prepared. I take the approach of the "earnest nerd." That comes naturally to me, but I also think it is useful and practical. People want to feel that you respect them enough to have done your homework, rather than being scattershot and casual. The *worst* thing you can do is to come in and pretend that you are more sophisticated, or know more, than they do. Instead, the notion that you want to learn from them will ultimately make for a better interview.

Do you do all interviews face-to-face?

While the conventional wisdom is that it is always better to do an interview face-to-face, I've often found that people are actually *more* forthcoming over the phone because they are not distracted by looking at you to see how you are reacting to what they say. Over the phone they are speaking in the comfort of their home or office. I wouldn't ever do all the interviews for a piece by phone, but there are times when they are better.

How do you convince people to talk to you?

Often I'll bring along a copy of something I've written that is related to the story I'm working on. People are curious about who you are, what got you interested in the story. That helps to get the conversation going.

You did a series of "investigative lunch" pieces for Manhattan, inc. Why lunch?

I was writing about a lot of eighties figures, and I found that they would often become more expansive and revealing in a lunch setting. Their peers are stopping by the table, they are "posing" as themselves and showing off their public persona. Restaurants in the eighties were like stages, so a lunchtime interview was equivalent to talking with an actor on the set.

Do you tape or take notes?

I'm a *terrible* note-taker, and always find the tape recorder the best way to reproduce interviews accurately.

Do you transcribe your interviews yourself?

It all depends who is *paying* for it. If a magazine will pay for this expensive process, I'll do that, although there is a downside. If someone else transcribes it, you often end up depending on the typescript rather than listening to the tape and the tone of voice. It is often useful to listen to an interview a second time. The problem is I find it very difficult to listen to the sound of my voice. *Painful* sometimes: the awkwardness, my sometimes transparent calculation. But it helps to capture the significant pauses, the tone of voice, etc. In the best of all possible worlds I'd get it transcribed and *then* listen to it.

Do you ever try to trick your subjects into revealing information?

I'm not good at that kind of thing. I find that often the *opposite* method works better for me: when people see me fumbling and stumbling awkwardly, as I often am, shuffling multiple pages of questions, they feel sorry for me and want to help me out. They'll tell me *anything* at that point.

You often take great pains to let the reader know you've actually visited the "scene of the crime." Why is this so important?

I think it is important to bring the reader as close as possible to the subject. It is another legacy of my English training. I had a great seminar teacher, a practicing Catholic, who emphasized the importance to a lot of the seventeenth-century poets we were reading of the Spiritual Exercises of Saint Ignatius Loyola. One aspect he emphasized was what is called "composition of place." Loyola held that in order to bring oneself closer to God, the person praying should imagine himself at the foot of the cross while Jesus was being crucified. To actually *be there* at that moment. The more you can see the world through the eyes of your subject, the more real it becomes. And it is also a valuable storytelling aid.

Do you reconstruct scenes, or do you only describe events you've witnessed?

When I first started writing, I tried to present seamless narratives. I'd use court transcripts, actual witnesses, observations from investigators. But I always found that there were, inevitably, a lot of conflicting points of view that made it difficult to reconstruct a truly seamless narrative. So I began to question that technique. Now you can *still* construct narratives where you *use* the fact that there are a number of different, conflicting points of view on a particular point. It is often from the seams of the narrative that the really interesting questions emerge: *Why* do these people's stories conflict? *What* are their agendas?

How do you start writing a piece?

I'm always looking for the lead. Whether it is a lead scene or a lead phrase, I start thinking of it the moment I start the story. For me, the lead is the most important element. A good lead embodies much of what the story is about—its tone, its focus, its mood. Once I sense that this is a great lead I can really start writing. It is a heuristic: a great lead really *leads* you toward something. Many journalism school types argue for an opening anecdote, a neatly contained scene (and that's often a good way to do it), but there are other kinds of good leads that break this form.

Has writing always been easy for you?

No, I used to be a *very* agonized writer. I was agonized by the fact that I didn't know how to get the best out of myself. I had so many ideas about storytelling, so why was the process so difficult?

I'd sit around struggling to find a lead. I wouldn't put anything on paper until I could think of a perfect next sentence or paragraph. Then I'd stay up all night because I thought that would be the way to get the most out of myself, or at least prove that I was really suffering for my art. Freud said that the whole point of psychoanalysis was to move you from neurotic suffering to ordinary unhappiness. For me it was to move from neurotic suffering to ordinary hard work.

What changed?

I finally found a method that channeled all of my energy and ambition for a story into actual *work,* rather than just wishing that I would come up with something good. I changed my life around and started writing early in the morning. And I learned this method of what I call "writing by rewriting."

How does it work?

Once I get the lead, I write a few paragraphs longhand, and then type them up. I then take the paragraphs I typed up *out* of the typewriter, put them to the *left* of the typewriter, put a *new* sheet in, and mechanically—almost—start *retyping.* And in the process of retyping, I discover that I make these *small* improvements each time through. And then the small improvements give me the confidence to go further, and trigger new ideas, new phrases. Then I take out the slightly improved version, put *that* to the left of the typewriter, put a new sheet in, and then start from the top.

That sounds pretty mechanical.

But it's *not* mechanical. It is a way of channeling my energy into labor, but the labor pays off in cumulative small improvements that eventually lead to a finished piece. It taps into a way of thinking that works for me. I don't do my best thinking abstractly, staring into space, but through active, concrete rewriting.

What do you write on?
An Olympia Report Deluxe typewriter.

Why don't you write on a computer?
When I teach, my students always ask me that. And I tell them that they are free to use a computer *as long as they print out their text and rewrite it from the top.* The seduction of the computer is that it is too easy to tinker within paragraphs and make everything *look* good. But all the tinkering and shifting paragraphs around doesn't give you the benefit of starting from the beginning and incorporating the changes you've made from one draft into your rewrite.

Do you make outlines?
Eventually, after four or five redrafts of an opening I feel good about what I'm doing. Then I scribble out a mini-outline of where I'm going to go next. Then I go a little further—rewriting all the way.

How many drafts do you go through?
Many before I show it to anyone. I then fax off my messy type-scripts—if I can afford it—to someone who word processes it and makes nice-looking digital files. Then I do more work on the copy the word processor makes and fax *that* version back. Certainly for the beginning sections, I go through at least ten to fifteen drafts.

Do you discuss your work-in-progress with people?
I find that it helps a lot to talk to friends or editors immediately after I return from a reporting trip. It puts me in a storytelling *mode*. Even though I'm less preoccupied with producing a seamless narrative than I used to be, I do feel that narrative energy is crucial to distinguish a *story* from a research report. When you are telling a story to a live human being you get a sense, immediately, of what people respond to. It gets you outside of your own head. And often people ask questions that I haven't thought of—questions that force me to look at the reporting in a new way.

Do you have to be in any particular location to write?

I get writing done in two kinds of places. Particularly when I am starting a piece, I find it helps to write in coffee shops. First, for the caffeine, obviously. Then there's some truth to what Roland Barthes (not a favorite of mine otherwise) once wrote about writing in cafés: adopting the pose of the writer in public in some way helps you to actually start getting writing done. There you are in the coffee shop: "What am I supposed to be doing? Am I just a *poseur*? No, I'm a *writer*! I'd better get some writing done."

The beginnings of stories, the beginnings of *sections* of stories, are easier to write in a coffee shop. I write longhand, with a Mont Blanc fountain pen on narrow-lined, large yellow legal pads. I don't know if it is exactly liberating. But it is more playful, more sensual, than the mechanical typewriter. It is more provisional. You can doodle around, sketch some stuff out, see a half-formed thought. It is just such a *pleasure* to write with that pen!

Do you write the entire piece in the coffee shop?

Once I've gotten a piece under way, I'm happiest being back in my apartment with my typewriter.

Is there any time of day you prefer to write?

I am an insanely early riser. I was up at three a.m. today! My brain chemistry is better then. I'm much sharper in the morning. Also, I am more isolated from the world at that time in the morning. Friends, editors, *creditors* are not going to call you at four a.m., for the most part. You've got this entire block of time when you can indulge in the pleasure of solitude, without any threat to break your concentration.

What does your ideal day look like?

I wake up at four a.m., make some strong coffee—Ethiopian lately. I drink two or three cups to shock me awake. Then I might do a little tai chi, which is a little meditative—although I do it in a really *sacrilegious* way, since I'm often watching tapes of *Mystery Science Theater 3000* at the same time. I hate to be *alone* with my thoughts.

Does exercise help?

I used to get a lot of good ideas while running. But I found that the endorphins made me so blissfully *content* that I didn't have the *edge* required to get the writing done afterward.

How does the rest of your day progress?

After the tai chi, and some more coffee, I sit down and write. And lately I've found it such a pleasure to sit down and work. I think it was Hemingway who suggested that at the end of the day you should stop writing a little before you've exhausted your idea, so that when you pick up the next morning you are already in the middle of something. That strategy works for me.

Do you require quiet in order to work?

I go back and forth. I'm slightly ashamed to admit it, but I often have the television on while I write. It sounds like such a horrid *violation* of the writer's solitude. But I have a theory of "competing concentration." If there is too much quiet, it is too easy for your thoughts to kind of drift off to some other topic. But if you have something that you have to focus *against*—sometimes music, sometimes even television—it forces you to concentrate on the *work*. Because you are deliberately shutting something out, as opposed to if there is just silence, then you are in danger of opening something up.

I would warn anyone reading this: don't try this at home. I'm not advocating it. But occasionally it works for me.

Why do so many of your pieces take the form of a quest?

I've always been attracted to mysteries of one sort or another. I was deeply influenced as a kid when I came across a cache of my father's old Hardy Boys mysteries. I read about *fifty* of them, all at once. I think it is a genetic, deep-seated impulse. I love stories, I love mysteries.

What kind of an authorial presence do you strive for?

I like to use a mixture of first person and third person within the same story. I also like to write stories that are divided by sections so that I can move back and forth from first-person speculation, to documentary investigation, to philosophical conjecture. It was in my nuclear war piece that I first realized this was a good way of putting an enormous variety of subject matter and different kinds of investigations into one piece. Each section required a different tone from the others, so switching around allowed me to do that.

Does one perspective bring you closer to truth than another?
Not necessarily. Sometimes being there can distort your perspective; sometimes it gives you unique insights.

But I do object to the way journalism schools insist on the third person as a somehow more truthful or objective way of writing. It seems like such an *obvious* misconception to me. Because the third person often turns disjunctions and discrepancies and conflicting versions into the *illusion*—the false *simulacrum*—of omniscience. When, in fact, omniscience is not to be had by any person. Putting your cards on the table as the narrator—your doubts, your hesitations, your conflicting thoughts and impressions—is often more honest than third-person writing.

Is this why you sometimes address the audience directly?
I got that device from Henry Fielding. I *love* the way eighteenth-century novelists buttonhole the reader, grabbing his attention by badgering, charming, or insulting him. And I think readers like it, too. Even though you are establishing a relationship with an imaginary reader, at least you are trying to establish a relationship. It's fun. And as a writer you feel less alone in the story because you are making the reader into another *character* in the story.

Do you consider yourself a "literary journalist"?
I have some problems with the term. It sounds self-consciously highfalutin. And it is misleading because it suggests that literary journalism is about rhetorical flourishes and elevated wordplay. That it requires a consciously elevated style.

A better way to put it is that literary journalism is journalism that asks the same questions that literature asks. Questions about God and man, fate, human nature, etc. And these questions don't have to be asked in a particularly ornate style.

You've often criticized "peg-driven" journalism. Why?

The "peg" is a sort of false reason for doing a story: "Let's do a story about X because there is a movie coming out that focuses on this theme." Or because it is "hot," or some such blather. I'm not against a story having relevance. But I think of relevance in a somewhat broader sense than peg journalism. Relevance defined in a way that isn't necessarily immediately apparent, or determined by the latest buzz or celebrity focus. I think the best stories are the ones that create their own peg. The stories after which the reader says, "Wow, I never knew about this whole world. I'm so glad I learned about it."

When I called the peg "the self-destruction of magazine journalism," I meant that it has led some editors and journalists to write about only the most contemporary, surface phenomena. Then magazine journalism becomes nothing more than a game with editors trying to guess what is going to be hot in thirty days, or two months. Rather than saying, "This is really *exciting* to me. It *speaks* to me. I didn't know anything about it, and now I want to know more."

Who are your literary/intellectual heroes?

Certainly Murray Kempton, who I first read when I was a junior in high school. I read *Part of Our Time,* which was just a revelation to me: that you could write about people in history in a way that was filled with conflict and ambiguity, and was exciting and had all the shadings and layers of great fiction. I learn so much when I pick up anything by him.

Others are writers in the past who wrote speculatively about metaphysical questions. The Roman poet Lucretius wrote a fascinating epic called *On the Nature of Things.* The seventeenth-century writer Robert Burton, whose *The Anatomy of Melancholy* was a wonderful send-up of scholarly certainty. Burton played with the conflicting truths of two thousand years of writing on subjects like love, melancholy, God, etc.

Another is John Keats, whose idea of "negative capability" has been a tremendous influence on me. He believed that one should be able to accept uncertainty. Fitzgerald's rendition of Keats's "negative capability" is that one must be able to hold two conflicting ideas in one's mind without necessarily deciding that one must be the truth and the other must be a lie. The idea is that the conflicts *themselves* are interesting and an essential part of the whole. As Keats put it, "To dwell in uncertainty without an irritable reaching for certainty." I *love* that phrase "irritable reaching" because that is what we all do: we are constantly reaching to find a satisfying, consoling resolution.

The more work I do, the less often I find satisfying resolutions. But that doesn't make the conflicts any *less* interesting, it makes them *more* interesting.

BY RON ROSENBAUM:

Those Who Forget the Past: The Question of Anti-Semitism, Random House, 2004 (editor)
The Secret Parts of Fortune, Random House, 2000
Explaining Hitler, Random House, 1998
Travels with Dr. Death and Other Unusual Investigations, Viking, 1991
Manhattan Passions: True Tales of Power, Wealth, and Excess, Beech Tree Books, 1987
Rebirth of the Salesman: Tales of the Song & Dance 70's, Dell, 1979
Murder at Elaine's: A Satire, Stonehill, 1978

ERIC SCHLOSSER

Taken together, Eric Schlosser's three books—on fast food, the underground economy, and prisons—form a haunting triptych, "an alternative history of the United States," he says, that undercuts the optimism of the age of consumerist capitalism.

Eric Schlosser was born in New York City on August 17, 1959. His father, Herbert Schlosser, is an NBC executive who was president of the network in the early seventies. His mother has worked with the Martha Graham Dance Company for many years and is now on their board.

Schlosser attended the Dalton School and then studied history at Princeton University. His senior thesis was on Princeton's policies toward academic freedom during the McCarthy era. Schlosser edited the university humor magazine, wrote plays for the Triangle Club, and studied literary journalism with John McPhee (Richard Preston was in the same class).

After Princeton, Schlosser spent three years studying British imperial history at Oriel College, Oxford. He was particularly interested in the moment at which, in the late nineteenth/early twentieth century, the British and American empires intersected—one falling apart and the other on the rise. "The Boer War was the point when the British empire began to crumble, and then World War I did it in. We secretly provided military and economic aid to England, which was the beginning of our 'special relationship.' That was when the people in both countries who believed in empire got together," he says. Schlosser abandoned his plans for an academic career, but channeled his Oxford research into a play, *Americans,* which he wrote in 1985, and which was eventually performed in 2003.

Schlosser floundered after Oxford, writing plays and a novel while living in Vermont. He returned to New York in 1992 to work as a script reader and story editor for Tribeca Productions, the movie company run by Robert De Niro. Schlosser tried his hand at screenwriting with a script about Asian gangs in New York's Chinatown, before pitching his first piece of journalism to *The Atlantic Monthly*. The magazine passed on his proposal to write a story about homosexuals in the military, but liked his writing and gave him another assignment: a story about the New York City bomb squad after the 1993 World Trade Center bombing ["The Bomb Squad," *The Atlantic Monthly*, January 1994]. A few months after the story ran, he received a call from William Whitworth, then the magazine's top editor. "He was curious about whether there were people serving long prison sentences for marijuana possession. There had been a sea change in drug laws and the new mandatory sentences hadn't really been written about at the time," he says. "Reefer Madness" [*The Atlantic Monthly*, August 1994], his second story for *The Atlantic Monthly*, gave him the confidence to leave Tribeca Productions and become a full-time journalist.

A long, exhaustively reported *Atlantic* article about the migrant workforce that picked strawberries in California ["In the Strawberry Fields," November 1995] attracted the attention of Will Dana, an editor at *Rolling Stone* magazine, who asked Schlosser whether he'd be interested in using the same methods to examine the fast-food industry. "He called me up and said, 'We want you to do for fast food what you did for strawberries, to reveal the world behind this commodity that we all eat.'"

Schlosser was wary at first. He didn't want to take a sneering, condescending attitude toward fast food. After all, he—and virtually everyone he knew—ate it. As Schlosser began reading about the industry, its power and scope amazed him. He found that some of the best sources of information were industry trade journals with names like *Food Engineering*, *Chemical Market Reporter*, and *Food Chemical News*.

After working on "Fast Food Nation" for a year, it was published in a three-part series in *Rolling Stone* in 1998. Despite the article's length, Schlosser felt he had only scratched the surface and decided to expand the article into a book on the subject. Houghton Mifflin executive editor Eamon Dolan made a preemptive offer for the book. As the publisher of Rachel Carson's *Silent*

Spring, Dolan was eager to publish a work of "activist journalism in the best tradition."

Schlosser was right—the size of the fast-food industry is staggering. McDonald's has twenty-eight thousand restaurants, is the world's largest owner of retail property, and is America's largest purchaser of beef, pork, and potatoes. McDonald's famed golden arches "are now more widely recognized than the Christian cross," he writes. Although written one hundred years later, Schlosser's searing portrayal of the industry is disturbingly similar to Upton Sinclair's *The Jungle* (1906): nightmare working conditions, union busting, unsanitary practices. *Fast Food Nation*'s reviews put Schlosser in the company of Sinclair, Lincoln Steffens, and Ida Tarbell. "This is a fine piece of muckraking, alarming without being alarmist," wrote Rob Walker in *The New York Times Book Review.* The book's literary qualities were recognized as well. "Schlosser is part essayist, part investigative journalist. His eye is sharp, his profiles perceptive, his prose thoughtful but spare; this is John McPhee behind the counter with an editor," wrote Nicols Fox in *The Washington Post.* Schlosser has been approached by people who want to turn the book into a movie, and even a Broadway musical. "I'd rather have it never be made than run the risk of their watering it down and turning it into something icky," he says.

Reefer Madness (2003), Schlosser's next book, wove three pieces together into a meditation on America's underground economy. "If the market does indeed embody the sum of all human wishes, then the secret ones are just as important as the ones that are openly displayed. Like the yin and yang, the mainstream and the underground are ultimately two sides of the same thing. To know a country you must see it whole," he wrote in the introduction.

Again, Schlosser's information was fascinating. Revenues from pornography match Hollywood domestic box office receipts and exceed sales of rock music. Twenty years after the "War on Drugs" began, marijuana may be worth as much as $19 billion a year, making it the nation's most lucrative cash crop (ahead of corn, wheat, and tobacco).

America, Schlosser's 1985 play about the price of American empire, took on new meaning after September 11, 2001, and was performed in London in the fall of 2003. The play is about the anarchist Leon Czolgosz, who assassinated president William McKinley at the 1901 Pan American Exposition to protest America's colonial war in the Philippines. Czolgosz saw himself as a patriot who wanted to warn his countrymen. In the current era of anti-American terrorism, one of his speeches felt prescient. "You are going to be punished for what your government is doing right now, or your children will pay for your outrageous vanity. And when this great nation of ours goes down in flames, when our cities are in ruins . . . don't say nobody warned you. When it comes, you deserve it, and I told you so," he says. The play received respectable reviews. "This is a rare thing: a big political play that seizes the crucial political arguments of our time and runs with them. Whatever you think of its creator's philosophy, only the comatose will fail to be provoked and stimulated; this is a political triple espresso," wrote Johann Hari in *The Independent*.

Schlosser now lives in northern California with his wife, who is a painter, and their two children. Visits to fast-food restaurants are forbidden in the Schlosser family. "My ideal life would be to write journalism, plays, and novels," he says. His book about prisons is scheduled for publication in 2006.

What kinds of ideas or topics get you excited?
Subjects that are timely and that aren't being adequately reported in the mainstream media. I'm especially interested in stories that concern social justice—although not defined in any narrow, left-wing way. There have been periods in our history when journalism was concerned with exposing injustice, and I think we're entering one of those periods now. I guess what I'm doing is an old-fashioned kind of journalism.

How does your interest in social justice manifest itself in particular stories?
One example would be the story about marijuana I wrote for *The Atlantic* ["Reefer Madness," August/September 1994]. The idea for

the piece came from the editor at the time, Bill Whitworth. He asked me if there were any people serving long prison sentences for marijuana crimes. I said that I had no idea, and he said, "Why don't you find out?" So I did some research and found that there are people in the United States serving life sentences, without parole, for nonviolent marijuana crimes. Well, that's when it became an interesting story for me.

Interesting in what way?

Interesting on two levels. First, I consider myself pretty well-informed—and I had no idea people were getting life sentences for marijuana. So I had this glimpse of a reality that was hidden from us and that wasn't being discussed by the mainstream media. Second, there was the injustice of it. I mean, it is insane for someone to get a life sentence, without parole, for their first nonviolent marijuana crime. Especially when the inmate in the next cell gets off with five years for killing someone.

How do you come up with ideas?

They're often inspired by something in the news. I got the idea to write about farmworkers after I heard Pete Wilson, who was governor of California, say that illegal immigrants were welfare cheats who came to the U.S. in order to live off of American taxpayers. My gut told me that what he said wasn't true. I'd spent some time in California, and the illegals I'd seen there were working very, very hard, cleaning people's houses, mowing their lawns, taking care of their kids. Some instinct told me that Wilson was lying.

I started reading about the whole subject of illegal immigration, and farmworkers seemed like an extreme example of Wilson's "big lie." Most of them were illegals, and their hard work and low wages were in fact *propping up* California's largest industry. And the growers who were exploiting these illegal immigrants happened to be some of Governor Wilson's biggest campaign contributors. In the article I barely mentioned Pete Wilson, but I tried to show this other, hidden reality. The people who were routinely being depicted as welfare cheats were actually integral to the state's economy.

How do you then work from a general idea—fast food, illegal immigrants, marijuana—to a specific story?

Once I settle on an idea for a piece, I go to the library. I have a vague sense of the story and start reading broadly on the subject.

In the case of *Fast Food Nation*—an idea that came from Will Dana, an editor at *Rolling Stone*—the assignment was to write about fast food in much the same way as I'd written about illegal farm-workers in California. To go beneath the surface and find what was really happening. To be honest, I wasn't that interested in fast food when Will brought it up. I was reluctant to accept the assignment. So I went to the library and started reading. What I quickly learned was pretty amazing. And I was amazed by how little I knew about the subject, how little most of us knew at the time. And yet we all ate fast food.

What made fast food a good story from your perspective?

The enormous size and power of the industry, the impact it's had on agriculture, on popular culture. And then there was the fact that the fast-food industry is the largest employer of minimum wage labor in the U.S.—and one of the biggest opponents of any increase in the minimum wage. But what really got me hooked was reading about the changes in meatpacking and realizing that the new class of meatpacking workers were recent immigrants from Mexico and ille-gal immigrants, just like the migrants I'd met in the strawberry fields of California. I thought things were terrible in the strawberry fields, but the working conditions in these slaughterhouses were much, much worse. So I saw the fast-food story, among other things, as a way to depict the rise of this migrant industrial workforce. We've had migrant farmworkers for generations. Migrant industrial workers—that's a new thing, and a very disturbing one.

What elements do you require for a story?

Most of the time, it's just a good subject. I find an interesting subject first, then look for a way to write about it. What I learn dictates how I tell the story. One exception was my pornography piece ["The Business of Pornography," *U.S. News & World Report*, February 10, 1997]. It began when I found an incredible story, the story of the man who founded the industry. I had some ambivalent feelings about pornography, because the moral issues it raised were so complex. On the one hand, I didn't think that pornographers should be locked away in prison for creating sexually explicit material. On the other hand, most of the porn was so terrible and degrading that I couldn't imagine championing it. What really got me hooked was the story of Ruben Sternman, which I thought was a quintessential American tale, an extraordinary rise and fall. Again, I was amazed that I'd never heard of the guy, and neither had any of my friends.

You are unusual in that so little of your journalism is narrative driven. Why do you make this choice?

The idea of finding a great story and writing it from A to Z is really appealing. I love great stories. But sometimes a narrative isn't the best way to structure a piece. Sometimes it's too easy and too obvious. Today there's an enormous amount of pressure from book and magazine editors to turn everything into a strong narrative. Often it's best *not* to have a narrative. *Fast Food Nation* doesn't have a conventional narrative, although I think it has an inner logic, an argument, working its way throughout the book. By choosing to not have a narrative, I may have made the book more difficult for some readers. There's no single protagonist or story to follow. But I didn't want to structure *Fast Food Nation* as a narrative, I didn't want it to be about my "shocking" discovery of how fast food is produced, or my "journey in the world of fast food." It may sound pretentious, but the protagonist of that book is the U.S.A., the "nation" in the title. So following me around, or anyone else, wouldn't have achieved what I was aiming for. The problem when you avoid a conventional narrative is that it makes everything much more difficult. Without a narrative you run the risk of writing something really boring and bad.

But narrative doesn't mean that you have to write about yourself. Why do you resist even those narrative stories that don't focus on the author?

Hey, I like good stories. I started out writing plays and fiction and screenplays. *The Perfect Storm* is one of my favorite nonfiction books, and that's one hell of a good story. But when people tell me I have to do something one way, my instinct is to figure out a different way. There's no single way to approach a subject. And a narrative is just one approach. All that matters to me is that the reader keeps turning the page.

As you consider subjects, do you find any parts of the country either more or less interesting?

Other than a piece I wrote about the New York Police Department bomb squad ["The Bomb Squad," *The Atlantic Monthly,* January 1994], I've pretty much avoided big cities. *Fast Food Nation* started out in Los Angeles, but most of that was historical stuff that was unfamiliar, at least to me. For the most part, I'm interested in the America that lies in between New York and L.A., and outside of Washington, D.C. That's where you find the stories that are being ignored by the mainstream media. Also, I grew up in New York City and Los Angeles, and I've spent time in Washington, so I'm not as curious about those places. I like to get out of familiar surroundings and meet new people.

What kinds of people do you most and least like writing about?

I've pretty much avoided writing about celebrities and major politicians. I have no interest in them, and the mainstream media is so obsessed with them that I don't need to do it. I'm more interested in writing about someone that I've never heard of. And I try to write about people on the margins, give them a voice.

Do you think of your collected work as variations on one theme, a few themes, or as isolated pieces?

Somehow they're connected, but I'd like to think there's more than one theme there. One piece often leads to another. The marijuana article led to my prison piece, and later to the book I'm writing about prisons. Visiting a hippie biker locked up in a maximum security prison for his first pot offense got the ball rolling. Writing about migrant farmworkers eventually led to *Fast Food Nation,* and then various articles about agriculture and food.

How many stories do you like to work on simultaneously?

I'm always collecting information on things. I always have three or four stories in the works, but one of them usually takes up 70 percent of my mind. The rest help me take a break from that big one.

What is your process for coming up with ideas?

The starting point for me is always books. I buy a lot of books, probably too many. Even if I haven't read them yet, I'm like a chipmunk gathering acorns for the winter—I'm always gathering books for the next big project. I also clip things out of newspapers and magazines, or download off strange Web sites.

Where do these clips come from?

They could come from anything from *The New York Times* and *The Wall Street Journal* to airline magazines. I also get a lot of information from trade journals. I couldn't have written *Fast Food Nation* without meatpacking industry journals, flavor industry journals, publications like that. Right now I'm delving into the trade journals of the prison industry, which are a great source of information.

Do you like working on long-term stories only, or do you sometimes like to write stories where you are in and out in a fairly short period of time?

I've mainly done long-term, intensely reported stories. But I'd like to do some more short pieces. It would be good for me as a writer. I didn't come to this profession through daily journalism, so I don't have much experience of writing something on short notice.

What is your research routine?

I begin most of my projects in the main reading room of the New York Public Library. My research process is to start reading secondary sources. Then I move to academic journal articles. Then I move to trade journals. I don't call anyone up until I've done an enormous amount of reading on the subject. And then the first people I call are usually people whose academic or trade journal articles I've already read. I don't want to talk to anybody until I feel I know a fair amount about a subject. I find that the conversations are much more interesting that way.

Do you do a lot of research before embarking on a project to find out what else has been written?

I use Lexis/Nexis intensively, but I don't use it to do an exhaustive search for everything that has been written on a topic. If a lot has already been written about a subject, I instinctively want to avoid it entirely—unless there is a way to do it that feels new. I use Lexis/Nexis to find wonderful, obscure information that would be next-to-impossible to find otherwise. Search engines are good for finding stuff you don't know exists.

When you get to the place you're reporting, what is the first thing you do?

I usually show up in a town having made one appointment to see someone—say, a meatpacking worker, an academic, a union organizer. That person usually leads me to another, who leads me to another, and so on. I put a lot of faith in random conversations at bars. Once I show up in town there's a lot of serendipity involved.

How would you describe your reportorial persona?

I try to be very straight with people about what I'm doing, what I'm interested in, and why I want to talk to them. I give people every opportunity to talk to me or to tell me to get lost. If they don't want to talk to me, 99 percent of the time it doesn't matter, because there is someone else who does.

You won't try to strong-arm someone into talking to you?

The only people I get pushy with are corporate executives and government officials—you know, the people in power. It irritated me that nobody at McDonald's would talk to me for *Fast Food Nation*. But if I'm writing about working conditions in a meatpacking plant, and a worker doesn't want to talk to me, that's fine. Because it's the worker who *does* want to talk that I want to meet. Most of what I've written hasn't been dependent on any one crucial source, which is a relief.

Once you've come up with an idea and done some research, how do you approach the people you interview?

It depends on the story. It helped to have an introduction when I was writing about the porn industry. But I have no qualms about calling someone on the phone and simply introducing myself.

Do you call, send an e-mail, write a letter?

I don't like to introduce myself via e-mail. I usually call, or write a letter and fax it. The letter is pretty straightforward: I say who I am, what I'm writing about, and why I want to talk to them.

How do you convince people to give you so much of their time?

A lot of the people I write about see talking to me as an opportunity to be heard. We have mutual interests. I'm trying to tell their story, and they want their story to be told accurately, truthfully, and fairly. So talking to me usually isn't an inconvenience for them.

If it were Madonna, and I was number 488 of her 500 weekly interview requests, then getting more than a half hour might be a stretch. But if you've lost a child to murder, or have been wrongly imprisoned, or have been injured at a meatpacking plant and want other people to know what is happening, then talking to a reporter doesn't feel like much of an inconvenience. I try hard to treat the people I interview as people, not objects, and try not to take more of their time than I need. I guess sometimes, though, they may regard me as a pain in the ass. You should ask them.

Do you prepare for your interviews?

I may write down a few key questions on my notepad, but most of the questions are in my head.

Do you ever send questions ahead?

I really prefer not to. Big companies often ask you to do that, and I'll do it if that's the only way to get the interview. But once the interview starts, I'll do everything in my power to go beyond those questions.

Where do you prefer, and most dislike, interviewing people?

I don't like interviewing people on the phone. The most interesting conversations usually take place face-to-face. An exception was a piece I wrote about people who've lost a family member to murder

["A Grief Like No Other," *The Atlantic Monthly,* September 1997]. The subject was so upsetting that some people found it much more comfortable to speak to me by phone. But a phone interview is always easier to do if I've already met the person.

Where do you most like conducting interviews?
As long as it's a comfortable place to hang out and talk, I don't really care.

How do you begin an interview?
Most of the interviews I do aren't standard journalistic interviews— you know, Mike Wallace confronting the greedy polluter getting out of his car. Most of my interviews are just conversations. I often just show up without a pad or tape recorder. After the conversation, if something someone has said strikes me as worthy of quoting, I'll get back in touch with them, remind them of what they said, and see if they want to be quoted. Or I'll come back with a tape recorder and notepad and conduct the interview in a more formal way. But the vast majority of my interviews are off the record and done so that I can find out what's going on. I don't care if I get a juicy quote or not. I just want to learn.

How much do you reveal about yourself during an interview?
It depends. I try not to push my story on anyone, but I don't go undercover either. I'm trying to treat people as people, so it is per- fectly natural to share some details about my life.

How much will you negotiate with a subject about what is on or off the record?
A lot of the people I write about have very good reasons to be wary of journalists. Pot growers, pornographers, illegal immigrants—the stakes are very high for them. The key thing is to make them trust that I'm not going to screw them over. And I don't screw them over. I'm pretty good at keeping secrets. The only way to make them trust me is to hang out with them, show them other things I've written, show them the kind of work I do. Ultimately the work speaks for itself. People either trust me—or they don't talk to me.

I'm glad to talk totally off the record, if I really want to know about the subject. If someone doesn't want to be quoted because he or she will get in trouble, I'll offer to let them use a pseudonym. I try very hard not to twist anyone's arm. I don't want to have to live with having twisted somebody's arm and then feeling awful if something bad happens to that person because of something he or she said to me. So far I've kept my promises and never revealed a source. May that always be the case.

Do you ever confront or argue with a subject when you know they are operating with false information, or lying to you?

Absolutely. So much of what I do, so much of my work, is done for its own sake, and not just to put together a book or article. So, if I'm interviewing a prominent antidrug campaigner, I'm going to record their views, but I'm also going to argue with them about drug policy. I don't want to miss an opportunity like that. How can you pass up an interesting conversation? I try to be very clear about what I agree with and disagree with. So that there's no illusion about where we stand. I try not to personalize things, not to insult people, but I don't lie to anyone.

How do you start an interview?

The first few times I meet someone we'll just talk. Often I won't take notes or record the conversation. I want to have as natural a conversation as I can with people.

Do you tape, take notes, both?

I like to tape as much as possible. If I'm only taking notes, I'll always get back in touch with someone to make sure that the quote I've written down matches what they said. I feel very strongly about making sure that quotes are accurate.

Does taping make your subject uncomfortable?

Well, the drug dealers I interviewed didn't want me to tape them. But most people tend to be reassured by the presence of a tape recorder. People who haven't been interviewed a lot often watch you very closely while you're taking notes. They're nervous that you're not getting their words down right. They like the fact that a tape recorder won't miss anything.

Do you transcribe your own tapes?

It depends. Sometimes the magazine will pay for someone to transcribe them, and I *love* when that happens. More often I'll listen to the tapes and take notes on the gist of what was said. Then later on I'll transcribe direct quotes that I think are significant.

How do you start writing?

When I'm done with my research I'll have notes from my reading, transcripts from interviews, books that are dog-eared—all sitting in boxes in my office. The first thing I do is write an outline. And maybe halfway through the outline I'll write the opening paragraphs.

What kind of an outline is it?

It is fairly detailed—from beginning to end. I work chapter by chapter: the outline tells me where I start and finish each chapter, the information I want in each, the people and scenes I want to include. I spend a few weeks writing the outline, and that's perhaps the hardest part of the process. It's the part where I'm really tearing out what little hair I have left. I have boxes and boxes of material in front of me, and I know that 90 percent of it will never be used. The writing doesn't begin in any meaningful way until the outline is completely done. I need to know where I'm going and why.

What do you write on?

I used to write only on legal pads with dark, black ink. But now I write about two-thirds on the computer and the rest by hand. Sometimes writing by hand is the quickest way to get something out, because I don't see it as clearly. Writing on a computer is sometimes too clear, too stark, and the flaws become too readily apparent. I'll often write some of the most important stuff, like the introduction and conclusion, by hand.

How many drafts do you typically go through?
I generally go through two or three drafts.

What does your ideal writing day look like?
My ideal writing time would be between around eleven thirty at night and three in the morning. But because there are other people in my life, that schedule isn't sustainable. I love the stillness of the world during those hours. The critic in me falls asleep around midnight, and the writer in me loves to stay up late. Late at night the writing feels clean and pure. If I get up early enough in the morning, say five or five thirty, I can get some of that feeling. The critic in me sleeps late.

What is the relationship between the "critic" and the "writer"?
Keeping the critic at bay is essential, but having the critic around is important too. The writer is always saying, "Yes!" and the critic is saying, "No, uh-uh." Often the writer is wrong, and the page you wrote, loved, and then threw away deserved to be thrown away. At the same time, when you can't write a word, it's because the damn critic is just being too tough. Ultimately the critic has to shut up so that I can get the writing out into the world. It may not be the most beautiful, perfect prose, but at least it gets out there. If I only listened to the critic, I'd be doomed. I'm not Flaubert, and I can't spend a week on a sentence.

So what does a typical day look like?
I get up at about five or so and try to get to my desk as quickly as possible. Then I just start writing and see how long I can go for. I'll take a break around ten, then get back to work, and by lunchtime I'm usually petering out. After lunch I usually read over what I've written that day and do some editing to make sure that it fits with what I wrote the day before. I try to quit at around three and go for a run or a hike—something physically active. Then I rejoin the human race.

Do you print out as you go along?
I print out a lot because of my innate distrust of technology. I do most of my revising on the hard copy.

Do you show your work-in-progress to anybody?

I try not to show anything to anyone until the last word has been written. I showed the first half of *Fast Food Nation* to Eamon Dolan, my editor at Houghton Mifflin, because it was my first book and I was nervous. But I told him that I didn't want any detailed comments or criticism. All I got back from him was, "Great, keep going." On the one hand, that was enough. But since it was Eamon, I wasn't sure if he was kidding. Anyway, I'll never do that again. The most important thing for me is to finish. I don't want anyone else's feedback until I'm done.

Do you talk about your work-in-progress?

I try to talk about it as little as possible. I don't want to dissipate the energy. It feels cleaner that way. Later, people can judge the written work by the work, and not by what I've said about it.

How would you describe your attitude toward being edited?

You can ask any editor I've worked with and they will tell you that I am just a little lamb. I just do whatever they want me to do, without any fight or argument.

Really?

No. That's a total lie. I wouldn't say that I'm a *complete* pain in the ass—but maybe one of my editors would. I care about every semicolon, every word, and every comma. So with my editors, there's always a give-and-take of listening and ignoring. I try to be open enough to hear what is true in their criticism, but I block out comments that I know will screw things up. I've been lucky to work with some great editors: Bill Whitworth, Cullen Murphy, James Fallows, Corby Kummer, Will Dana, Eamon Dolan. It really helps to have brilliant people making suggestions about your work. My editors have been invaluable in telling me when things need to be cut. I tend to go on at too great a length. A three-thousand-word piece becomes a thirty-thousand-word piece. It's always a struggle because—for example, when I was writing about fast food, I was trying to put myself out on a limb and write about the subject in a way that wasn't dry and prosaic. On the other hand, it started to sprawl so far and wide, I had to pull myself back from some of the tangents, so that there wouldn't be a chapter on eating habits in ancient Mesopotamia.

Do you enjoy writing more than reporting, or vice versa?

Enjoy might be the wrong word for a lot of the reporting I've done. A lot of it is grim stuff. I don't really enjoy going to prisons. But I'd say that the reporting almost always feels like time well spent. It's uncomplicated in a way that writing isn't. Reporting is reading books, thinking, visiting new places, meeting people—it all makes sense in a way that writing doesn't. Reporting—even if I hate it—provides all sorts of new experiences, broadens my outlook. Writing is more stressful, more of a challenge. Putting what you've seen and what you know into words is hard. The words never come close enough to the knowledge and the experience.

What kind of authorial presence do you strive for?

I want to be present, but out of the way. I try to stay in the background. The facts and evidence should speak for themselves. I want my writing to be calm and straightforward. When I first started writing, I was much more "clever," and my sentences were much more ornate. The writing called attention to itself and to its "smartness." I try to get rid of those things now. The critic in me hacks away at that stuff. Writing something simple and true is the hardest thing.

How would you describe your tone?

I try to be calm. Whitman said the ideal poet "judges not as the judge judges but as the sun falling around a helpless thing." That's a worthy aim. Not putting your style or literary flourishes before the thing itself. That's what I'm trying to do.

Do you think the kind of journalism you do can lead to truth?

I think it can lead people to find their own truths. I don't pretend that anything I've written is the truth. It's just my honest view of things. I'm not trying to write agitprop, telling people exactly what to think. I'm just trying to make them think. That's enough for me.

Do you think there is something peculiarly American about this kind of long-form nonfiction?

Yes. I was just talking with a British editor about the dearth of long-form nonfiction in the UK. She said there is a real hunger for it over there, but the Brits don't have the kinds of magazines that support it. The long-form nonfiction that's successful there tends to be written by Americans.

Who are your literary heroes or influences?

In nonfiction: John McPhee, Cary McWilliams, George Orwell, Hunter Thompson. Among my contemporaries I really admire the work of Sebastian Junger, Ted Conover, William Finnegan, and John Seabrook, among others.

Where did you learn to be a reporter?

In John McPhee's class. I would not be a writer had I not taken that class. McPhee is the master. Studying with him was like studying with the world's greatest woodworker, a master craftsman with integrity in every detail. He taught us to care about every word, every punctuation mark. He taught us to immerse ourselves completely in a subject—but tell the reader only what's necessary. He taught us the importance of what you leave out. "Your writing should be like an iceberg," he said. What you put on the page is like the tip of the iceberg. Everything else is there, beneath the surface, even if the reader can't see it.

Perhaps the two most important things I learned from McPhee— and anyone can learn them just by reading his work—is that nonfiction can be the equal of fiction, and that your integrity ultimately is the most important element of your work.

What do you think of the prospects for this kind of writing?

I'm optimistic. The success of *Fast Food Nation* has been incredibly gratifying, and I hope it paves the way for other writers to do similar kinds of investigations. Right now nonfiction writers are getting involved with the events of the day in a way that fiction writers aren't. There is a sense of engagement with the big issues, of writers taking real risks. But, having said that, you never know when the next Zola or Steinbeck or Dos Passos is going to come along and write fiction that is equally connected to the moment.

BY ERIC SCHLOSSER:

Reefer Madness, Houghton Mifflin, 2003
Fast Food Nation, Houghton Mifflin, 2001

GAY TALESE

om Wolfe once dubbed Gay Talese the founder of the New Journalism, but Talese himself has always been uneasy with the label. It isn't difficult to understand why. His style doesn't have the rhetorical braggadocio of Tom Wolfe's or Hunter S. Thompson's. Wolfe's and Thompson's principal contributions were amped-up, flamboyant adventures—producing a distorted, if amusing, view of the world—while Talese's legacy is more purely journalistic. There is nothing surreal about the reality Talese presents—whether he is looking at the life of a Mafia capo, a bridge builder, a baseball legend, or a sexually liberated adulterer.

Talese represents a parallel tradition within the New Journalism. His legacy is twofold. First, he is the indefatigable reporter whose books and articles are the product of extensive research. He can take years with his subjects, attempting to become their companion, to "travel through time with them until he sees what they see." For Talese, accuracy is the highest goal. Second, he is the poet of the commonplace, the writer who demonstrated that one could write great literary nonfiction about the "ordinary"— whether ordinary people who discover themselves in extraordinary circumstances, or the ordinary lives of extraordinary people.

If the aim of most New Journalism is to write so vividly and report in such intense bursts that a scene leaps from the page, Talese goes in the other direction. He slowly drills down through the mundane subterranean reality of human existence to its "fictional" core. "I believe that if you go deep enough into characters they become so real that their stories *feel* like make-believe. They *feel* like fiction. I want to evoke the fictional current that flows beneath the stream of reality," he says.

Talese was born in 1932 to Catherine DePaolo and Joseph Talese, an Italian tailor who immigrated to America and settled in

Ocean City, New Jersey. Journalism provided the perfect role for the inhibited immigrant's son. "For individuals who were as shy and curious as myself, journalism was an ideal preoccupation, a vehicle that transcended the limitations of reticence. It also provided excuses for inquiring into other people's lives, asking them leading questions and expecting reasonable answers," he writes in "Origins of a Nonfiction Writer." [In *Writing Creative Nonfiction: The Literature of Reality,* by Gay Talese and Barbara Lounsberry, New York: HarperCollins, 1996.]

He got his start in journalism during his sophomore year in high school when the assistant coach of the baseball team asked him to call in the account of the games to the local paper. He soon developed this into a series of articles, and finally a regular column. A below-average student, Talese was rejected from nearly every college he applied to. He attended the University of Alabama, where he was the sports editor of *The Crimson White.*

In 1953, determined to break into professional journalism, Talese headed to New York, where he was hired as a copy boy by *The New York Times,* but worked for only a few months before going into the army. Other than his two years in the army (where he worked in the Office of Public Information, writing a column called "Fort Knox Confidential" for *Inside the Turret,* the base newspaper, before being transferred to Germany), the *Times* was the only full-time job Talese has ever held. After leaving the army, he was made a reporter first in sports, and later in general news. He wrote two books in his nine years at the *Times—New York: A Serendipiter's Journey* (1961) and *The Bridge* (1964), about the building of the Verrazano-Narrows Bridge. In his review of *A Serendipiter's Journey,* the *Times's* book reviewer, Orville Prescott, divined Talese's journalistic sensibility. "Mr. Talese, a young reporter on this newspaper, has ignored everybody important and everything well known to concentrate on the curious, the unnoticed, the overlooked and the forgotten."

At magazines like *Esquire,* Talese found he could experiment more frequently and at greater length than at the *Times.* He wrote a series of pieces for *Esquire*—now famous profiles, collected in *Fame and Obscurity* (1970), of Frank Sinatra, Joe DiMaggio, and

Floyd Patterson, and several articles about the *Times* itself. His 1966 article "The Kingdoms, the Powers, and the Glories of *The New York Times*" convinced him that a larger book, a "human history," might be written about this immensely powerful institution.

The *Kingdom and the Power* (1969) received only a $10,000 advance from the World Publishing Company and was a surprise hit, becoming Talese's first bestseller and inspiring hundreds of so-called "media books." Although savaged by the *Times's* daily reviewer, it was well reviewed in *The New York Times Book Review* by media critic Ben Bagdikian. "Seldom has anyone been so successful in making a newspaper come alive as a human institution. It is a story that many ambitious newspapers would wish their best writers to produce—about someone else," he wrote.

Honor Thy Father (1971), Talese's second bestseller, originated in 1965 when he was a *Times* reporter covering the indictment of Bill Bonanno, the son of Mafia boss Joe Bonanno, who had disappeared. After observing him from across the corridor, Talese approached Bonanno and his lawyer. "Someday—not now, not tomorrow—but someday, I would like to know from this young man what it is like to be this young man," he said.

Talese's father had always been angered by the number of Italians involved in organized crime as well as the media's portrayal of them, so to write about it would be to confront a familial taboo. But Talese decided that the life of the Bonanno son— Talese's doppelganger, in some respects—would allow him to tell the story of the *inner life* of the Mafia. "When the average American citizen thought about the Mafia, he usually contemplated scenes of action and violence, of dramatic intrigue and million-dollar schemes," he wrote in *Honor Thy Father*, "totally ignoring the dominant mood of Mafia existence; a routine of endless waiting, tedium, hiding, excessive smoking, overeating, lack of physical exercise, reclining in rooms behind drawn shades being bored to death while trying to stay alive."

One of the most remarkable aspects of the book was Talese's reporting. His "fly on the wall" approach was put to the test by the fact that during the six years Talese followed Bonanno, there were long periods when his father was in hiding and Bonanno Jr. was the target of Mafia hitmen. Bonanno Jr. would often show up at Talese's house surrounded by armed bodyguards.

Some critics accused Talese of being too sympathetic to the Mafia. "The flaw in *Honor Thy Father* seems to me to be that Gay Talese has become so seduced by his subject and its 'hero,' that he conveys the impression that being a mobster is much the same as being a sportsman, film star or any other kind of public 'personality,'" wrote Colin MacInnes in *The New York Times Book Review*. It is a sign of the closeness Talese felt to his subject that he used part of the income from the book to set up trust funds for Bonanno's four children (as well as his own daughters).

Nothing in Talese's past prepared him for the reaction to his next book, *Thy Neighbor's Wife* (1980). The book, which combined with movie rights earned him $4 million, was a gossip columnist's dream: while reporting it Talese managed two massage parlors, and lived at a nudist commune in California. As with his book on the Mafia, some critics were so taken by the subject matter that they overlooked Talese's extraordinary reporting. All the characters in the book—most of them middle-class, anonymous folk—agreed to Talese's strict real-names only rule. He was criticized for his excessively heterosexual, male perspective and for ignoring such topics as feminism, homosexuality, and contraception.

For his next book, Talese considered several "respectable" Italian American subjects—DiMaggio, Sinatra, Lee Iacocca—before deciding on a multivolume autobiography. In 1991, Knopf agreed to pay Talese $7 million for his next three books. Part memoir, part history, and part historical fiction, *Unto the Sons* (1992), the first volume, traces Talese's family name back to the fourteenth century.

If one of Talese's contributions to the New Journalism is the idea of watching change over time—returning again and again to his subjects, as opposed to simply reporting on a single event or person in the present—his current project may be its greatest test. In the second volume of the trilogy, scheduled for release in 2005, Talese is revisiting all *his* stories—the Verrazano Bridge, *The New York Times*, the Mafia, American sexuality. As he told the New York *Daily News*: "I was supposed to do this sequel to *Unto the Sons,* but since it had to be my story, I never could find out what my story was, because I could never find out as a journalist who I was, because I was raised in this notion of being outside the story. My story is always escaping to other people."

———

Do you consider yourself part of a journalistic tradition, whether "literary" journalism, New Journalism, or "the literature of reality"?

No, that's all bullshit. Tom Wolfe, in a complimentary way, labeled me as a New Journalist, which I never really liked. The problem is that when you are writing nonfiction you have to place yourself into a category or else Barnes & Noble doesn't know where to shelve your book. So we have all these Barnes & Noble notations like "current biography." I don't fit into any of those. I just want to write about people in a way that is a short story with real names.

What subjects are you drawn to?

The subjects that involve me are those that have, literally, *involved* me. I write about stories that are connected to my life. Although on first impression they might appear to be nonfiction that features *other people's* experiences, the reason I'm drawn to them in the first place is that I see *myself* in them.

I've always worked this way. My first book, *A Serendipiter's Journey,* came from the observations I'd make while walking around the city. *The Overreachers* came out of my curiosity about odd characters who build bridges. *The Kingdom and the Power* is about odd people I worked with at *The New York Times. Honor Thy Father* is about an Italian Mafia son with a background quite like my own. *Thy Neighbor's Wife* came out of my restrictive, Catholic upbringing. *Unto the Sons* is a book about my father's family. And the current book I'm working on is about the difficulty I've had writing for the past ten years.

What kinds of people do you like writing about?

People with whom I have an emotional affiliation. We spend so much time together that we have a kind of an *affair.* I get so close to them that I can write about them as I would write about my kin or my spouse, or a long-lost lover.

I'm curious about how ordinary people live through periods of tumult, the clash between tradition and change, whether it is the sexual revolution or a revolution of cultural values. I want to explore these changes through characters who *don't* have recognizable names, who *aren't* major figures.

Is this why—other than Sinatra, DiMaggio, Peter O'Toole, Floyd Patterson, and Joe Louis—you've written about so few celebrities?

Yes. I don't write about celebrities unless their celebrity is *secondary* to the piece. For instance, although Sinatra was certainly the celebrity *of all time* when I wrote about him, I wrote about him turning fifty: about his voice not working, his loneliness. It was more about midlife crisis than celebrity.

The problem if you write about a celebrity is that the relevance of your piece depends on their *remaining* a celebrity. Celebrity pieces necessarily date quickly. That's why I never wrote about politics. A political figure is *really* going to date you. Whether it's George McGovern, Jimmy Carter, or Bill Clinton—those pieces don't keep well. I'm more curious about things that aren't *"news."*

And how do you find these stories "that aren't news"?

By observing. One of the main stories in my current book came to me while I was watching a women's soccer game on television in July 1999 between the U.S. and China at the Rose Bowl. Toward the end of the game, a Chinese player missed a kick and lost the game for China. I thought *that* was *interesting.* Here's Lu Ying, a twenty-five-year-old from China being watched by millions of people around the world. Furthermore, I know from my reading about the Cultural Revolution that it is unlikely her mother was ever an athlete, and certainly not a "soccer mom" as we conceive of them.

Such a woman surely *can't* be accustomed to having an enormous international audience. After missing the crucial kick, she got on a plane in L.A. and flew back to China. That is a *long* flight to spend thinking about your failure. I saw her in the same way I saw Floyd

Patterson. As someone who overcame losing and humiliation. They get knocked down and they come back. Lu Ying becomes the midfielder who misses the kick and loses the game for China—but she lives on. She's a hero. *That's* a great story.

How do you decide a "non-news" idea like that will make a good journalistic story?

My writing is scene-driven, so I look for promising scenes. When I wrote *The Bridge*, I tried to visualize the Verrazano Bridge and the men who are dangling in the sky, as a picture. The opening scene of *The Kingdom and the Power* is of a managing editor in an office. The opening scene of *Honor Thy Father* is a doorman watching, but not really seeing, a disturbance in the street. *Thy Neighbor's Wife* opens with a scene of a boy looking at a nude woman at a magazine stand in Chicago. In *Unto the Sons*, I open with a scene of me on the beach. These could all be films. I guess I'm essentially trying to write a picture.

I was once at Francis Coppola's house in Napa while he was filming *Tucker*, his movie about the automobile maker. He showed me the scenes he planned on three-by-five cards. That's the same way I've always organized my books and articles. If you look at "Frank Sinatra Has a Cold" [*Esquire*, April 1966], it's scene, scene, scene. The first scene in a bar, the second in a nightclub, the third scene in the NBC studio. Just like a movie.

Not many of the Italian Americans of my generation have become writers, but a lot of them have used their visual skills to make films. Coppola, Scorsese, etc. They are *popular, commercial* filmmakers. Not Fellini. No, the Italian American artist is entrepreneurial and therefore uses the most commercial aspect of his past experience: the gangster world. While the Mafia isn't their *actual* life experience, it's what *sells*, whether it's *The Sopranos* or *The Godfather*.

And how do you decide whom to interview?

I'm never quite sure at first. I just go to where I think the story is. If the story is the building of the Verrazano Bridge, there is nothing that has been built when I begin. So I start with the engineer, who has the concept of the bridge in his mind. He's balancing all sorts of physical forces, including the curvature of the earth. He's creating theater, a work of art with a proscenium arch that spans time, a stage for thousands of actors. When I wrote about *The New York Times*, the building itself was the *theater*. I don't know who the characters are at the beginning, I don't know the story, but I do know the stage of the theater. I find the characters by simply showing up at the "theater." As I spend more time in there, they emerge. It's almost as if I *imagine* them, and then, they mysteriously *appear*.

Do you have a routine for interviews?

Although I can't *start* the process being someone's *companion*, that is my ultimate goal. I need to stay with someone long enough for me to observe their life change in some significant way. I want to travel through time with them, to put myself in a position to see what they see. Then I want to put myself in a situation that is in the *forefront* of the action.

How do you convince people to talk to you?

It's sometimes a long process. I've got to *sell* myself. If I have any talent, it's for getting my foot in the door. This comes from having an authentic interest in people and treating them respectfully. I do not abuse them. There isn't a single person—whether I've written about him favorably or unfavorably—whom I couldn't see again.

For instance, I went to China after I saw Lu Ying play soccer on television. I knew that if I could get through to the Nike or Adidas office I might be able to find Lu Ying, because those were the companies that equipped the team. I eventually got through to Patrick Wong, the director of Nike, and I took him to lunch. He became the most important man in China for me. It turns out that he had a brother in Brooklyn and we developed a kinship. *He is my guy,* my Chinese brother. You need somebody like that for any story. I sold myself and my story to him. Sure, I was in Beijing, but this was the guy who really got me in to China.

I told him that I wanted to find out what it was like for someone like Lu Ying to experience that kind of defeat. I explained that I thought she was a lot like China herself: overcoming adversity, disappointment. We all know disappointment. You can't always win the race. Even Michael Jordan misses more than he makes. It's a universal theme. And he started to get it.

Do you set ground rules for on and off the record before an interview?

I don't start off that way because the kinds of interviews I do are not one-night stands. The person I'm interviewing has got to understand that we're embarking on a long-term relationship, where nothing will *have* to be off the record. Sure, I'll agree to some conditions, and I'll live up to them. But if they say that something is off the record, I simply won't talk to them. I insist that *all* quotes be attached to real names.

When I was writing *Thy Neighbor's Wife* I had one character, named John Bolero, who was originally on the record and then later decided he wanted to go off the record. When he told me this I immediately flew out to L.A. to talk with him and his wife. I told them, "You can't do this. The point is that you're stepping forward and declaring *yourself,* you're not lying about yourself anymore. You're in the forefront of something new!" I finally talked him into going back on the record. I had to make him understand that what we were doing, as partners, was *so important,* that he had to live up to our agreement.

What is your policy about changing a character's name?

I'm not only appalled by, I am uninterested in anybody who writes nonfiction without using real names. I don't care *whom* you're writing about. If I'm reading a magazine and see a name that is not real I put the magazine down.

How do you convince people to give you so much access?

The first thing I do is explain *why* the person is so important to me. I tell him that there is something important about him, and whatever that is, it hasn't been explored at all. I have to convince him that what I'm doing is worthwhile.

Okay, that might get you a whole afternoon. How do you convince them to give you days, weeks, months?

I'll tell you how it happened in China. After several meals with

Mr. Wong of Nike, I got permission to see where the Chinese women were practicing for the Sydney Olympics. I watched, shook hands with them, and had my picture taken with them. And then a bureaucrat from the sports ministry said, "Thank you, Mr. Talese. You got what you wanted. Now you're done." And I said, "*What?* I didn't get *anything!* I want to see her again." He said that she was too busy, and I went back to my hotel feeling very frustrated.

That next day I told Patrick Wong, "You know, I just realized that Lu Ying's *not* the story. Her *mother* is the story! You see, in America we have 'soccer moms,' who are privileged women who drive their kids to soccer practice in SUVs. But in China the mothers of these soccer players don't have cars, or any of the privilege of suburban lives. They've come from terrible poverty." I explained that the heroes were *not* the soccer players seen by millions of people on television. No, the real, unheralded people were those girls' *mothers!*

My strategy was to avoid where the women were practicing— since that was official—and to get the story through the mothers. By focusing on the soccer moms, I hoped that the pressure would be off me and I could get the story I really wanted.

Eventually I was allowed to give Yu Ling's mother my pitch while we sat in my hotel's lobby. I told her how I thought her life had influenced her daughter, how she was typical of mothers in China today, who came out of poverty, out of the Cultural Revolution, and *yet* were able to allow their daughters the *freedom* of playing soccer. She seemed interested, so we made another appointment to talk in the lobby four days later. This time we talked a bit more freely and I asked her whether I could see her home. She agreed and a week later my interpreter and I went to the *hutan* she lives in. It was a building with about twenty-five people in it, and the entire family lived in this tiny place. I saw where Lu Ying slept, and it had a picture of Michael Jordan above her bed. Her little soccer shoes lined up against the wall. It was *great!*

And while we were talking I met an old lady who was the *mother of the mother*—Lu Ying's *grandmother!* And the grandmother had bound feet. She had come out of prerevolutionary China. And I thought to myself, "Wait a minute. This is a *generational* story about a grandmother, a mother, and Lu Ying." I kept coming back and coming back.

So the answer to your question about how I get the kind of access I need is that I do it *one step at a time*. I'm gradually selling myself every step of the way. It's all about hanging around and meeting people.

Do you ever do interviews via e-mail or phone?

I don't have e-mail, so I don't use that. I use the phone to make appointments, but I do all my interviewing in person. I go everywhere in person. I want to *see* the people I interview, and I want them to see *me*. It's all visual.

Do you take notes while hanging out?

I'm always scribbling down things I find interesting. But I'm discreet. I don't use notepads because they're too bulky. Instead, I cut up strips of the cardboard shirt-boards that come with your shirts from the laundry and take my notes on those. I'm always carrying around a pen and a few of these. [Talese takes a few long, slender pieces of cardboard from his coat pocket.]

How do you do interviews in places, like China, where you can't speak the language?

The linguistic barrier isn't really a problem because, no matter where you are, most of what people say isn't really that interesting. Because what people *say* isn't necessarily what they really *believe*. And what they say to you *today* isn't what they are going to say to you *later on*—when you know them well. In the beginning, the interview is all but meaningless. All I'm trying to do is to see people in their setting.

Language isn't even all that important when I'm reporting a story in a country where I *can* speak it. I didn't want to *interview* Sinatra for "Frank Sinatra Has a Cold." I got more from watching him, and the reaction of others to him, than I would have had we talked. When I wrote recently about Muhammad Ali's trip to Cuba in *Esquire,* I never talked to him, because he can't really talk clearly. The reporting I do is more visual than verbal. My reporting is less about talking to people than what I've called "the fine art of hanging out."

How much thought do you give to an interview's setting?

A lot. I like to be in the place where the person works. Or I like to do interviews someplace where I can see the person interact with others. I don't care too much *who* it is: your wife, your girlfriend, or a belly dancer you're involved with. I like to have some dialogue. Again, I think of it in terms of the camera: what works visually. I want to move around and give the reader a number of different things to look at. I don't want to have a series of headshots, like in a documentary. I want interaction, conversation, conflict.

In the book you're writing now, you have a scene at a urologist convention in Las Vegas in which a female urologist and John Bobbit watch a porno movie in your hotel room so she can test whether his penis works.

Yes, it is a wonderful scene in which the urologist, Suzanne Frye, one of the only female urologists in America, is holding John's erect penis and talking about its "blood flow."

Did you set that scene up?

Yes, I arranged it because I wanted to have a *character* in the piece other than John Bobbit and his penis—his penis is actually a character, too. I sometimes see that there is a story there, and that I need to have an actor and an actress play the roles in that story. I play the director.

Where do you most like interviewing people?

I love interviewing people in restaurants because people are very unself-conscious in there. And you can eavesdrop on other conversations. Airplanes are also a *wonderful* place for an interview. I once flew with Joe DiMaggio from San Francisco to spring training in Fort Lauderdale. We sat together for six hours and talked about Truman Capote. You're next to each other. There are people around. There are drinks and food. It's conducive to talking.

Is writing more difficult for you than reporting?

Writing is very hard for me. I *love* reporting and I'm a natural reporter. But I'm so dissatisfied with what I write. I'm filled with that Catholic sense of failure, of inadequacy, of *unworthiness*. I'm not good enough, I could be better—this is the mantra I keep repeating.

What does your daily schedule look like?

I get up by at least eight. I sleep in the same room as my wife, but I do not talk to her in the morning. Our marital bedroom has nothing of mine in it: no clothes, not a toothbrush, nothing. It is really my wife's bedroom, with her dresser, her desk, her manuscripts, her clothes. It belongs to her. I just sleep there.

So I leave the marital bedroom and go upstairs to the fourth floor, which is where I have my clothes. I wash up and put on a jacket and a tie. I go to the corner and buy a *New York Times*, although I don't read it then. But if I don't buy it in the morning it gets sold out and I *hate* that. Then I go down to my office, which I enter through an entirely separate door to our house.

I make my breakfast there in my little kitchen, usually coffee and a bran muffin, and take it to my desk. By now it is perhaps eight thirty. I don't have a phone or e-mail in my office, so I'm not disturbed by anything. At twelve thirty I make myself a small sandwich. Eating kills my concentration, so around one thirty I go to the gym.

At the gym I ride a bicycle and read the *Times* and then do some other exercises. That kills an hour or two. I return around three, and at four I go upstairs to the house for the first time since I left at eight that morning. I work at my desk on the fourth floor answering phone messages, looking at the mail, paying bills. I come back down to my office at five and look over what I've written that day. I try to further it along until eight in the evening.

Then I go out. I like to go out. *Every* night. I *love* restaurants. Not necessarily good restaurants, but *any* kind of restaurant. I try to be home around midnight or slightly earlier. I usually catch the end of *The Charlie Rose Show.*

On weekends I go to my home in Ocean City, where my ninety-five-year-old mother lives. I have an identical office set up there and I'll get up tomorrow morning and repeat the process again. I do this seven days a week.

And what is your routine for actually writing?

I start with a yellow lined pad and a pencil. The first thing I do is try to print a sentence. Note that I say *try* to print a sentence, and *print,* not write. I use big, block letters. Then I look it over, change it, rewrite, and try to do another. It sometimes takes me a couple of days before I have five to six *sentences* in large block letters. This is the beginning of my piece.

When I have about four to five *pages* of block-lettered sentences I type them up, triple-space, on an electric typewriter. Then I edit and rewrite those sentences again and again, until I have a *single* typed page I'm happy with.

I then take the typed page and *pin* it to the wall with dressmaker pins. I have panels of Styrofoam on the wall that hold the pages. Then I go through the whole process again and write another page, and pin *it* to the wall next to the first one. It's like laundry on a clothesline. I have four to five feet of Styrofoam, so I can pin up as many as thirty-five pages in three rows.

Why pin them to the wall?

It helps me get a different perspective: I can see how the scenes move, how the language works, how the sentences flow. I get lost when I rewrite and I want to have another look at it. I want to look at it fresh, as if somebody *else* wrote it. I used to pin the pages up on the wall and then sit on a chair across the room looking at them through *binoculars*. But the office I have now is too narrow for that.

So what do you now do to achieve that different perspective?

I came up with another system. Instead of using binoculars, I create two bound copies of the book-in-progress. The first binder is regular size. The second binder has the identical numbered pages as the first, but I *reduce* each of them in a Xerox machine by 67 percent. Same binders, same numbered pages, but one is small enough to make each page very different. It creates the same distorting effect as looking at pages through binoculars.

Do you use this method only for large projects?

No, I use it for everything. Fifty words, five hundred words, five thousand words—it makes no difference. *Everything.* That's why I can't take on magazine pieces or book reviews. Hell, I can't write a *caption* quickly. An editor will call with an assignment and tell me, "Oh, just knock it out!" But I can't knock *anything* out! If I'm assigned a book review I've just blown a *month and a half* out of my schedule. Sure, I'll *make* the deadline. But I always just *barely* make it—something I learned writing for the *Times.*

Do you require a certain number of words from yourself per day?

No, I don't work that way. I once heard Tom Wolfe say that his standard is twelve pages a day. *Twelve pages a day!?!?* That knocked me out! That amazed me! I just do the best I can do every day. I don't care if it takes me a *month* to write a sentence. All that matters is to get to the point where I can say, "I can't do any better. *Gay Talese* can't do any better. Maybe *Philip Roth* can do better, maybe *Leo Tolstoy* can do better, but *I* can't do it any better." Then I move on to the next one.

Do you do a lot of rewrites as you go along?

Very little. When one of my pages is done, it is *done.* I don't tear stuff apart and move material around at the end. It is too tightly woven for me to be able to move stuff around. It isn't a draft, it is a finished piece.

I'm like a tailor, stitching, stitching, stitching. I don't write in big sweeps. I write a little at a time and build it up incrementally. I try to go in a straight line, but I keep making turns, taking detours. But I don't *see* that I've taken a turn until I'm some distance down the road. I'm like a blind man driving a truck through a tunnel with no lights. I can't go fast because the lights are dim, and the tunnel is narrow. Sometimes I take a turn and go somewhere. But then I have to make my way *back* to the road.

How many projects do you work on at once?

I can only do one thing at a time. I've been working on my current book since my last book was published ten years ago in 1992. I haven't had a major byline for a decade. The only long piece I've written was about Muhammad Ali visiting Castro in Cuba. Six magazines turned that down before *Esquire* published it ["Boxing Fidel," September 1996].

I'm not the kind of guy who can write book reviews, op-ed pieces, even magazine pieces. Because I want to really concentrate on what I'm doing. I don't want to take time away from my book. But look at all these people who prove I'm wrong. Updike can do ten novels in the time it's taken me to do nothing. I wish I were superhuman like him, but I'm not.

What kind of tone do you strive for?

I strive for an *understated* tone, a *graceful* tone that makes it all look easy. Like DiMaggio running for a fly ball from center field and always getting there just in time. I'm not saying I *achieve* that, but that is what I strive for.

My tone comes from my favorite writers, who all have wonderful voices: Guy de Maupassant was the first fiction writer I read in English. There is John Fowles, William Styron (who wrote part of *The Confessions of Nat Turner* when he lived here with me), John O'Hara, and Irwin Shaw. The *dialogue* of O'Hara, and how few words he needed to set up a situation. The early Irwin Shaw, like "The Girls in Their Summer Dresses," where he wrote so beautifully. And I grew up reading Fitzgerald and Hemingway.

Before Thy Neighbor's Wife *you rarely appeared in your pieces. Why?*

If I'm going to be in a piece, I'd better have a good reason to be there. Before *Thy Neighbor's Wife,* the material didn't warrant my being there. A book like *Honor Thy Father* is about Bill Bonanno, who I identified with. We were the same age, had the same background. There wasn't a reason for me to be in the piece because he was there. *He* could be me.

Which is why it is all the more startling when you describe yourself, in the third person, at the end of Thy Neighbor's Wife *("Talese began to see the masseuse as a kind of unlicensed therapist").*

I did that because I didn't think I could use the first person in that book. I wanted to maintain the feeling of detachment, because so much of the sex I was writing about was detached sex. I considered not bringing myself into it, but I wanted to end up at the nudist camp near my home in Ocean City. A lot of people thought it was a bit showy.

You have a signature technique you use to connect the characters in your books. For instance, you trace the knife Lorena Bobbit used to cut her husband's penis off to Ikea, where she bought it. Then you find the woman who sold it to her. Thy Neighbor's Wife opens with a boy looking at a naked model in a magazine. You then trace both their lives. Why do you do this?

I want to convey the wonderment of reality. I believe that if you go deep enough into characters they become so real that their stories feel like make-believe. They feel like fiction. I want to evoke the fictional current that flows beneath the stream of reality.

Do you think journalism can lead to truth?

No, I believe that the editorial choices about what appears in newspapers and magazines are so subjective that you almost never get the whole truth. The editor's fingerprints are on what he chooses to publish. The cast of characters in *The Kingdom and the Power,* if nothing else, shows you that there *ain't* no such thing as "objective journalism." There is no such thing as absolute truth. Reporters can find anything they want to find. Every reporter brings the totality of his battle scars to the event. A reporter never gets *it.* He gets what he is *capable* of getting, what he *wants* to get.

But what about truth in your own writing?

I have a Calabrian point of view that comes from being a descendent of a historically invaded people. We suffer from seeing too many sides at once. I see many, many different points of view. So my point of view is a point of view *that sees many sides*! So where is the *truth* in that?

BY GAY TALESE:

The Gay Talese Reader: Portraits & Encounters, Walker & Company, 2003
Writing Creative Nonfiction: The Literature of Reality (with Barbara Lounsberry),
    HarperCollins, 1996
Unto the Sons, Knopf, 1992
Thy Neighbor's Wife, Doubleday, 1980
Honor Thy Father, World, 1971
Fame and Obscurity: Portraits by Gay Talese, World, 1970
The Kingdom and the Power, World, 1969
The Overreachers, Harper & Row, 1965
The Bridge, Harper & Row, 1964; Walker & Company, 2003
New York: A Serendipiter's Journey, Harper & Row, 1961

CALVIN TRILLIN

In 1979, Calvin Trillin was in Knoxville, Tennessee, to write about a high school girl who had died in a car crash. One night, she had brought the family car home past her curfew. Without going into the house, she got into another car with some friends and drove off again. Her father, a strict disciplinarian, was enraged and jumped into his own car to give chase. A few miles down the road, her car crashed and she was killed. Trillin couldn't get the story out of his mind. He wondered: What must the father feel like? Who was this girl? When a reporter for the local newspaper asked why Trillin had come all the way from New York to write about an insignificant, if tragic, death, the best answer he could muster was, "It sounded interesting."

In a career spanning nearly half a century—forty-two years of it at *The New Yorker*—Calvin Trillin has perfected the art of turning merely "interesting" events into vivid, suspenseful stories. *The Boston Globe* once called Trillin "the bard of American idiosyncrasy," and it is true that his interests are almost absurdly broad. He has written about everything from murders to the Chinatown chicken that beats all opponents at tic-tac-toe. In doing so, he has employed virtually every literary form imaginable (article, essay, book, novel, poem, live performance). Remarkably, Trillin is as successful a humorist as he is a reporter. He wears two hats: "the fedora with the press card and the jester's hat with the balls dangling on it," he says.

Calvin Trillin was born in Kansas City, Missouri, on December 5, 1935. His father, Abe Trillin (originally Trillinsky), was a Ukrainian Jewish immigrant who ran grocery stores and, later, a restaurant. The Trillins weren't a particularly religious family, although they made sure that Calvin went to Hebrew school and had a bar mitzvah. "I don't think anybody in Kansas City could have passed as an Orthodox Jew in New York. We were sort of farm club Jews," he told *Newsday*'s Dan Cryer.

Inspired by reading *Stover at Yale,* a 1911 novel about the WASPish exploits of Dink Stover, Abe wanted his son to attend the great eastern university. Trillin entered Yale in 1953, he recalls in *Remembering Denny* (1993), a "'brown-shoe freshman" who had been selected by Yale "to be buffed up a bit and sent out into the world prepared to prove their high-school classmates right in voting them most likely to succeed."

Trillin studied English and was the chairman of the *Yale Daily News.* He got a temporary job with *Time* upon graduating in 1957, working in the magazine's London and Paris bureaus. After almost two years in the army, most of it spent on New York's Governor's Island, he was offered a reporter's position in *Time*'s Atlanta bureau, where he covered the early days of the civil rights movement. Trillin's first *New Yorker* assignment after landing a position there—"An Education in Georgia," a three-part series—grew out of this experience. An expanded version of the article was published in book form in 1964. Reviewing it in *The New York Times,* Claude Sitton, the paper's Atlanta bureau chief, judged that it came "closer to the essential social truths of the problem than do some works of greater scope."

In 1967, Trillin began writing *The New Yorker*'s "U.S. Journal," a three-thousand-word report, each from a different part of the country, that appeared in *The New Yorker* every three weeks for the next fifteen years. Trillin is typically modest about his prodigious output: "Magazine writers would say to me, 'How do you keep up the pace?' Newspaper reporters would say, 'So, what else do you do?'" Trillin's "U.S. Journal" pieces often had the spare, enigmatic feel of a short story by Gogol or Chekhov. "If Truman Capote invented the nonfiction novel, as he claimed, and Norman Mailer devised variations on it, Trillin has perfected the nonfiction short story; moreover his craftsmanship can contend with that of either Capote or Mailer at their best," wrote *Kirkus Reviews* of Trillin's collection *American Stories* (1991). "What makes *Killings* literature, is the way he pictures the lives that were interrupted by the murders. They glare—not so much with publicity as with incompleteness," wrote *The New York Times*'s Anatole Broyard of his 1984 collection. Some critics, however, felt that Trillin produced these stories so quickly that they were sometimes superficial, presenting stereotypes rather than carefully drawn characters. "There is a story here, obviously, but Trillin cannot afford to try to find out what it is," Roger Sale wrote in *The New York Review of Books* about a 1971 collection.

It was while producing the "U.S. Journal" that Trillin developed a reputation for writing about food. Reviewing *Third Helpings* (1983), a collection of Trillin's food writings in which he spearheads the (unsuccessful) campaign to have the national Thanksgiving Day dish changed from turkey to spaghetti carbonara, *New York Times* food editor Craig Claiborne dubbed Trillin "the Walt Whitman of Eats," noting his democratic taste and enthusiasm. For Trillin, food was never really the subject of these pieces. "Writing about food has been a way of writing about the country without writing about politics or the entertainment industry. I realized when I started writing about food that it was a way of writing about the country in a lighter way. I actually write about *eating* rather than *food*. I write as a reporter rather than as an expert or a food critic," he says. Molly Haskell, reviewing *Travels with Alice* (1989) in *The New York Times,* called Trillin "a comic Magellan, squeezing through the straits between official culture and down-home tastes." In 1994, Trillin was inducted into the James Beard Foundation's Cookbook Hall of Fame. He furthered his reputation in the foodie establishment when his recipe "for scrambled eggs that stick to the pan every time," the only thing he knew how to cook, was chosen for *In the Kitchen with Miss Piggy* (1996).

In addition to his *New Yorker* work, Trillin has written a column in *The Nation* since 1978 (it was nationally syndicated in 1985). It was at *The Nation*—where he was paid in the "high two figures" by his friend, the "Wily and Parsimonious Victor S. Navasky"— that Trillin blossomed as a humorist. In addition to his reported pieces for *The New Yorker,* which also contained moments of comedy, Trillin wrote poems, "Notes & Comments," and many "casuals," as they were called then, including a series about "Barnett Frummer," which was republished as a book in 1969. "I always thought of writing humor as some sort of little, weird thing that I could do in the way some people could play the piano," he told *The Paris Review*'s George Plimpton. "The difficult thing for me is being serious. It's a genetic thing—being funny—like being able to wiggle your ears." In recent years, Trillin has contributed a poem a week to *The Nation* (collected in *Deadline Poet*, 1994), and his book of poems about the Bush Administration [*Obliviously On He Sails: The Bush Administration in Rhyme*, 2004], many of which run only two rhyming lines. Trillin says the motivation for his brevity is simple: the magazine pays him one hundred dollars per poem, no matter the length. "When you want to get the buzz of working for top dollar in your field, write a two-line poem," he advised *The Washington Post*'s Philip Kennicott.

Trillin's writing style tends to be informal and open, peppered with anecdotes about himself, his wife, Alice, and their two daughters, Abigail and Sarah. But until *Remembering Denny*, his work had also been somewhat reticent and impersonal—a characteristic critics often attributed to his Midwestern upbringing. *Remembering Denny* is a memoir about the most promising member of Trillin's class at Yale, who committed suicide in the early 1990s. In the manuscript's first draft, Trillin was a typically remote figure, hardly appearing in any significant way. His wife advised him to rework it so that it read less like an unconventional biography of Denny than a memoir about Trillin and his generation. The result was an uncharacteristically personal book and Trillin's first bestseller. It was extremely well reviewed, with James Fallows calling it "the best of Trillin's many books" in *The Washington Monthly*. Some took exception to the way Trillin used the occasion of Denny's death for his own purposes. Writing in *The New Republic*, Michael Lind excoriated Trillin for pioneering "a new genre of therapeutic-liberal gossip: the vicarious confession. Perhaps other well-adjusted celebrity authors will be emboldened to muse upon the misfortunes of their own obscure, screwed-up and recently buried acquaintances."

In 1996 Trillin continued to write more personally, publishing *Messages from My Father*, a memoir of the gruff, stubborn Abe Trillin, a man whose favorite epithet was "May you have an injury that is not covered by workman's compensation." In 2001, Trillin published *Tepper Isn't Going Out*, perhaps the first novel on the topic of parking. (Another novel, *Floater* [1980], was about a perennially dissatisfied writer who works at a *Time*-like magazine).

In late 2001, Alice Trillin, the foil for much of Trillin's best humor, died of cardiac arrest from damage caused to her heart by radiation that was used to treat her lung cancer twenty-five years before. Herself a graceful, witty writer, she once penned a memorable review of *Alice, Let's Eat* in *The Nation*, in which she rebelled against her husband's characterization of her as a steadfastly "sensible" spoilsport. "I'm not against quests for the perfect ham hock or the perfect barbecue," she writes. "But I think that anyone starting out on such a quest should be aware that his guide is someone who will travel all the way to a place called Horse Cave, Kentucky because he likes the way the name Horse Cave, Kentucky sounds when he drops it to me over the phone."

What kinds of stories are you drawn to?

If we're talking about relatively serious nonfiction, like the "U.S. Journal" series I wrote for *The New Yorker* for fifteen years, I look for stories that have a narrative line. I also seem to be attracted by stories that have to do with one element in society rubbing up against another, whether the difference is class or race or something else. I'm drawn to stories that have a distinct sense of "place." I sometimes read mystery novels on airplanes. What interests me about a good mystery is not the whodunit aspect, but the sense of *place* that good mystery writers communicate. If you read Raymond Chandler or Ross MacDonald, for instance, you come away with a real feeling for a certain part of California. If you've read a Tony Hillerman mystery, you have some idea of what life on the Navajo reservation is like.

In the introduction to Killings, *you describe how you explained your presence at a relatively minor trial to the people there: "The best I could manage was 'It sounded interesting.'"*

Yes, sometimes I'm attracted to a story out of pure curiosity. For example, I once wrote a story about a high school girl from Tennessee who brought the family car home past curfew on a school night, and then, without even coming inside, got right into another car with some friends and left again ["U.S. Journal: Knoxville, Tennessee—It's Just Too Late," *The New Yorker*, March 12, 1979]. Her father was a strict man—a junior high school principal. When he saw this, he jumped into his own car and chased the car she was in. Her car crashed, and she was killed. I found that I couldn't get that story out of my mind. What must he feel like? Who was this girl? Who were her friends? I wanted to know a lot more about it.

I sometimes think of your pieces as intricate puzzles.

Well, they aren't the kind of puzzles that are *solved*. They are puzzles in the sense that I'm putting things together. What TV news shows like *60 Minutes* realized early on is that ambiguity is their enemy. They need to put on a case. Either the guy is innocent, or he is guilty. Or he's innocent, but everybody *thinks* he's guilty—or vice versa. I look for the opposite. I find ambiguity interesting.

How do you come up with story ideas?

When I was writing a "U.S. Journal" story every three weeks, from 1967 to 1982—this was, of course, long before Lexis/Nexis or the Internet—I would go to the out-of-town newsstand in Times Square and buy piles of newspapers. Ninety percent of them were totally useless to me, of course, because they ran the same AP stories. Also, I started writing "U.S. Journal" around the time a weekly alternative press began to evolve, so I subscribed to a number of papers like the *Seattle Weekly* and the *Chicago Reader* and *Maine Times*.

Did you discriminate, or just buy any out-of-town newspapers?

Sometimes I concentrated on some section of the country I thought I'd been neglecting. Also, I liked certain papers, like *The Des Moines Register,* which ran state maps next to stories about Iowa. That helped me because I could read through the paper quickly, stopping only at stories with maps next to them.

Will you write stories suggested by others, or only those you come up with yourself?

I don't care where story ideas come from. One story about a scoutmaster in Oregon who molested some of the boys he befriended and was killed by one of them came from the daughter of someone who lived in that town. She lived hundreds of miles away, but she happened to be a *New Yorker* reader. I would never have heard about it otherwise.

Do you ever have a subject and look for a story through which to write about it?

Almost never. Although when snowmobiles became popular, I thought to myself, "I really ought to write something about snowmobiles, and maybe I could do that by going to a derby in a part of the country that has been affected by them." So I wrote about a snowmobile derby in Brainerd, Minnesota. I still remember a quote from a guy there. He said, "It used to be in the winter that all you could hear around here was the creaking of the Grain Belt beer sign in the wind."

Are there any kinds of stories you especially like or dislike writing?

I don't like doing stories about what groups of people "believe"—what amounts to public opinion. They are mostly crap because there is no way you can really know. I've always thought that when a reporter writes an article about how people feel it is likely to be true in inverse proportion to the number of people he's talking about. If he's talking about "the mood of the nation," he's almost certainly wrong. When it's one-to-one, he has a chance of getting it right, so you could almost believe a statement that begins, "The mood of the taxi driver on the way in from the airport was . . ."

There are some kinds of stories that I simply couldn't do. Like those stories where a reporter just stays with someone for weeks or months. I *admire* some of those pieces, but I couldn't do them myself. I don't have the stamina or the attention span.

You've written novels, poetry, and journalism. How do you decide which form an idea will take?

The ideas usually come attached to a particular form. For example, take a subject like the mysterious disappearance of pigeons in Trafalgar Square. I knew immediately that for me this was a column and not a long reporting piece. I wouldn't go to London for a week and write three thousand words for *The New Yorker* on the disappearance of pigeons from Trafalgar Square. I do write what we call "deadline poetry" for *The Nation*, but that works better when the subject of the poem is pretty familiar. It's awkward if you have to inform people, in verse, that pigeons are disappearing from Trafalgar Square and then comment on it.

Occasionally an idea will morph from one form into another. I once read in a Canadian paper about a guy who bought jewelry for cash and had a TV ad presenting him as "Cash Man." He was a pudgy little guy who in the ad would jump out of a phone booth wearing a weird spandex costume, like Superman. One day he was sued for copyright infringement by the company that owned Superman. At first, I thought about writing a *New Yorker* piece about it—I'd done a couple of pieces over the years on disputes about trademarks or service marks—but it ended up as a column for *Brill's Content*.

Do you think about writing humorous pieces differently from the way you think about writing non-humorous pieces?

If you're talking about lighter reporting pieces—as opposed to essays—the narrative is usually one I have to create myself, such as writing about Buffalo and its food specialty in a sort of mock-scholarly piece called "An Attempt to Compile a Short History of the Buffalo Chicken Wing."

Are you always aware when you're working on a story, or are there times when a story simply emerges from your everyday life?

There are times I discover stories in my life. For example, one year I was having trouble sticking to the "U.S. Journal" schedule because I couldn't leave New York on Halloween, when our family always marched in the Greenwich Village Halloween Parade. There was no way I was going to miss the parade. Halloween was my Christmas, my Yom Kippur. Then I realized that this was the story—the Halloween Parade and how it had become such a momentous event for my family.

Do you keep a list of possible story ideas?

Not exactly a list. I tear things out of newspapers and magazines and throw them in a file that would be called, if it had a label,

"Something I might want to write about one day." When I'm desperate, I look through the file—often a painful experience. I think, "Oh God, not *that* thing! Why didn't I throw that out years ago?"

You don't organize them?

I don't have the patience. Also, I've seen how people get hung up on activities that supposedly make writing easier or more organized. They get hung up on various technical innovations, for instance transcribing interviews from a tape recorder or mastering every intricacy of the Internet. Maybe these innovations help them write, but they can also be used to help them *not* write.

Are certain parts of the country inherently more or less interesting to you?

Not geographically, but certain *types* of places interest me more than others. A summer community, for instance, is often interesting to me because the bones of class divisions show through better there.

I like doing pieces in cities I'm familiar with—New Orleans, for instance, which I've been writing about for forty years or so. In someplace like that I can at least feel confident that I have some understanding of the context of the story.

Food has been a consistent topic in your writing. Why?

When I started writing "U.S. Journal" in 1967, I was in a new city every three weeks. I didn't want to eat the balsa wood food in the motel restaurant and I wanted to avoid eating at the restaurant the town boosters recommended—the place I started to call "La Maison de la Casa House, Continental Cuisine." I often found myself looking for someplace else to eat, out of self-defense.

But how did you start writing about it?

It started out as sort of a joke—and, in a way, it remained a joke. When I first moved to New York, I noticed that if you met somebody who was from Kansas City, you'd talk about missing something like Winstead's hamburgers or Arthur Bryant's barbecue. But that wasn't the kind of food people wrote about in those days. They tended to concentrate on attempts at haute cuisine—what Americans sometimes call "fine dining"—and not bother with what you might call vernacular food, the food connected to the people who live in a place.

In about 1971, I wrote an article for *Playboy* about taking a gourmet tour of Kansas City, eating hamburgers and fried chicken and barbecue. The magazine had been holding a piece by Roy Andreas de Groot, who was a Belgian count and a serious gourmet, called, "Have I Found the Best Restaurant in the World?" It was about some three-star restaurant in France. When my Kansas City piece came in, they decided to run it right after his and to title it "No." My article began, "The best restaurants in the world are, of course, in Kansas City. Not all of them. Only the top four or five."

Your food writings have always struck me as an excuse to write about something else.

Yes. That's exactly how I see it. I realized when I started writing about food that it was a way of writing about the country in a lighter way. I didn't have to write about a controversy or a murder every three weeks. Writing about food was a sort of comic relief—not so much for the reader but for me.

I actually write about *eating* rather than *food*. I write as a reporter rather than as an expert or a food critic. For example, I once learned that people in Cincinnati considered chili a Cincinnati dish made by Greeks. I was interested in that and in the fact that people in Cincinnati could argue into the night about whether Skyline chili is better than Empress chili. I wasn't interested in whether Skyline chili actually *is* better than Empress chili; I wasn't writing a restaurant guide or a "Best of Cincinnati" section for a local magazine.

Another example: I once took my then nine-year-old daughter Sarah, who was a picky eater at the time, to the St. John River Catfish Festival in central Florida to see whether she'd eat catfish. That was the faux narrative—the question of whether or not Sarah would eat catfish. But the story was more about the people living in central Florida, who think of themselves as "crackers" and resent people from flashier parts of Florida, and, by the way, prefer wild catfish to farm-raised catfish because the farm-raised doesn't have the requisite muddy taste.

Murder is another topic you return to often. Why?

A murder story often has a strong narrative line. Also, when someone is killed, a lot of stones get overturned that don't ordinarily get overturned. Murders are also great for reporters because there is likely to be a court hearing with a transcript. I used to say that I'd go anywhere there was a transcript—which isn't quite true, but almost. My absolute *favorite* thing is when there is also a transcript from a defendant's *previous* trial. That way I have both a transcript to read and a trial to attend. The advantage of attending a murder trial is that it gathers together most of the relevant people in one place. I often find all my characters milling around in the hall outside the courtroom.

Why is it that you've so seldom written about famous people?

From the start, I was always more interested in writing about people who weren't normally in the newspaper. I think that's one reason I was so engaged by reporting in the South, when I was in the *Time* bureau in Atlanta in the early sixties. I remember, for instance, covering a sort of wildcat sit-in in a coffee shop. The guy who owned the coffee shop was a Greek immigrant, and you could tell that he had a lot of sympathy with these black students. But he knew that if he served them he could lose his business. That's a situation that seemed to me a lot more interesting than, say, who was going to run for governor.

Do you do most of your research before, during, or after your reporting?

I do most of my research during and after the reporting. I usually know very little about a piece when I start, so it is difficult for me to know what kind of research it will require. I might read a chapter of a book about a city or region I'll be reporting in, but not much more than that.

When I have downtime during my reporting, I visit the local library. There are a few libraries around the country that still have vertical files, with clips organized by subject. So I might find an entire file of clips on, say "water rights" or "race relations" in the town. I sometimes find some amazing information in those files.

But you don't feel the need to prepare much before you start a story?

With a few exceptions, most of my pieces haven't required much specialized knowledge. I once did a piece about the Critical Legal Studies movement at Harvard Law School that practically killed me, because I had a lot of trouble understanding what they wrote ["A Reporter at Large: Harvard Law," *The New Yorker,* March 26, 1984]. And when I first got to *The New Yorker,* I did a long piece about rapid eye movement (REM) sleep. I found that if I turned around and walked in the other direction every time I saw the phrase "central nervous system," I could sometimes understand what was going on, but it was difficult ["A Reporter at Large: A Third State of Existence," September 18, 1965].

Of course, reporters are *always* working in someone else's field of expertise. You obviously can't become a law professor or a scientist in order to write a story. So you have to trust your instincts. It's partly a matter of deciding which people actually know something about the subject.

How did you learn to be a reporter?

Well, "learned" may be too strong. My daughters used to say, when some telephone number had to be found or some research had to be done, "Let Daddy do it—he's practically a trained reporter." I worked on the paper in college, and then I had a temporary job with *Time* magazine between college and the army. After I left the army, I went to the South, to Atlanta, Georgia, for *Time.* In those days, *Time* divided the responsibility for stories between reporters out in the field, and writers in New York. They used to say that being a reporter in the field for *Time* was a very good job unless you read the magazine. You got to cover good stories, but your reporting often didn't have much relation to what was published.

Looking back on it, I think it was valuable for me to work for a year on essentially the same subject. Virtually all my reporting was on race. I was unmarried, and young, and reporting was pretty close to all I did. I was off somewhere in the South reporting during the week, and then I'd go to a mass meeting or two in Atlanta every weekend. I actually got to the point where I *knew something* about the subject, which is very helpful to a young reporter. It takes a leap of faith to write. The natural question is, "Why would anybody care what *I* think?" After a while, I realized that I at least knew an awful lot more about the story than the editors in New York did. I think that year gave me a lot of confidence.

I'm not sure that you ever really get *better* at reporting. You might get better at the process of putting the story together, or writing it up. But I sometimes feel I make the same mistakes I made when I was starting out.

Describe your reporting routine. What is the first thing you do when you arrive at one of the little towns you write about?

I try to find my rental car in the motel parking lot. I always forget what color it is, especially when I pick it up at night. I have to wait for all the salesmen to leave. My car is the one that is still there.

Okay—and what do you do after you find your car?

I've usually called ahead to make sure that I can use the local newspaper's morgue. So I'll go to the newspaper's offices and read the clips—or, more likely, xerox the clips. I sometimes look up the reporter who had been covering the story. For example, several years ago I did a *New Yorker* piece on the papers of the Mississippi State Sovereignty Commission, an anti-integration agency that spied on a variety of people during the sixties. There was an argument over whether to release its papers or whether that would just smear people all over again. A reporter for *The Clarion-Ledger,* Jerry Mitchell, who specialized in old civil-rights-era cases, had done some original work on the papers— including the revelation that *The Clarion-Ledger* itself had cooperated with the Commission. So I looked for him when I got there, partly because he had become part of the story as well as a source.

How do you get people to talk to you?

I try to be as straightforward as possible. When a person is deciding whether to talk to me, or how much to tell me, an awful lot of his decision depends on whether he trusts me. So being a bully, or a con-man, is actually counterproductive.

I'm not very high pressure about getting people to talk. I try to reassure them that I don't have any ax to grind and tell them that whether they talk to me is entirely up to them. It seems to me insulting to assume that someone *has* to talk to me. If they don't know much about the magazine, I tell them a bit about the kind of publication it is and isn't—that *The New Yorker* doesn't do tabloid headlines, for instance.

I believe that if you just talk to enough people, you're probably going to find out what happened. That's partly because everyone has a different notion of what part of the story is secret. If you have the luxury to stay in town long enough—and not every reporter has that luxury—you're not likely to leave feeling that there are big gaps in the story you've missed.

Do you negotiate ground rules in order to encourage someone to talk to you?

Sure. I'm more interested in information than in using someone's name. A local newspaper reporter is normally under some pressure to get people's names in his story. But I write for a magazine with a national circulation. Most of our readers would only be confused by the inclusion of a lot of names of people in a town they've never been to. So talking to someone "not for attribution" isn't usually a problem for me. Occasionally, I'll agree in advance not to use the person's name on any quote unless I clear it first. There have also been times when I've assured people who don't want to talk about a certain aspect of a situation—an aspect that's under litigation, for instance—that I won't ask them questions about it.

What guidelines do you use in reconstructing scenes?

Generally, I reconstruct scenes as long as, in the parlance of *The New Yorker,* it's "on" somebody. In other words, unless what happened is absolutely indisputable, I usually try to indicate where I got the information. For example, I'll write, "And then, as the *police* later pieced the case together . . ."

Do you have any ethical guidelines about what you will and won't do while reporting?

Yes. If I'm asked to break one of them, I usually say that *The New Yorker* has strict rules that would prevent me from doing that. As far as I know, *The New Yorker* has no rules at all, or certainly didn't when

I began, but I just find it easier to present it that way. Some people, when they're deciding whether to talk to me, ask if they can see the article before it comes out. *The New Yorker* has a strict rule against that. It also has a rule against paying people for interviews, although it is happy to pick up the check if somebody is being interviewed over lunch—even over lunch at a pretty nice restaurant. It has a very strict rule against accepting gifts from someone involved in a story—even trivial gifts.

How much do you share the information you've learned "so far" as you interview people?

It depends on the story. I recently wrote a profile of *The New York Times* reporter R. W. "Johnny" Apple ["Profiles: Newshound," *The New Yorker*, September 29, 2003]. In the trade, Apple stories are so common that they're almost a subcategory of the journalistic anecdote. So I'd often trade Apple stories with the people I interviewed. It was a way of having a conversation. For the same reason, I often say things in interviews that aren't necessarily interrogatory. Obviously, I don't pass on confidential information from someone else involved in the story. But I do often use interviews to toss out theories about the situation—both as a way of testing the theories and as a way of getting another view.

Do you prepare questions before an interview?

Not really. Sometimes I have a list of specific things I really need to know. Occasionally the list indicates that I need to know something from a particular person. But that is as specific as it gets.

Do you ever do interviews on the phone, by e-mail, by letter?

Yes. But I prefer face-to-face interviews because it's more natural than talking to someone on the phone.

Where do you most and least like doing interviews?

I don't care where they take place. The less formal, the better. My goal is always to make the interview as much like a conversation as possible.

Do you ever stage scenes?

If you mean suggest that someone do something so that I can observe him doing it, no. I'll sometimes ask if he's going to be doing anything relevant to what I'm writing about—in which case I'd like to go along—but it has to be something he'd be doing anyway.

Do you take notes or tape your interviews?

I take notes. And in some cases I use a tape recorder. But if I use a tape recorder, I also take notes.

Why both?

Because I don't want to have to transcribe interviews. If I take notes while I tape, I can consult my notes to learn where a quote is on the tape. Then I can look it up and get the exact quote.

In what circumstances do you tape?

I've taped interviews when I've done stories about, say, science, because I know so little about the subject that I didn't trust myself to get the information correct in my notes. And I sometimes use a tape recorder when I know in advance that the person I'm going to interview speaks so rapidly that I'll never get it all down in a notebook.

What kinds of notebooks do you use?

I use a little bitty spiral notebook that fits into my shirt pocket. I write phone numbers and names from one end, and when I flip it around, the pages from the other end are where I write down my appointments.

I also use a long, skinny reporter's notebook to take notes during interviews. When I was in the South, *The New York Times* Atlanta bureau chief, Claude Sitton, convinced a stationer in Richmond, Virginia, to design us special reporter's notebooks, which were shorter than the standard notebooks. That way, we could put them in our pockets without being instantly identified as a Yankee reporter who needed to get hit upside of the head with a stick. We called it the "Claude Sitton Memorial Notebook." When I have both notebooks and a tape recorder, I feel like a Transit Authority patrolman: every pocket is stuffed with something.

How confrontational will you become during an interview?

I don't argue about the rights and wrongs of the situation. Or, if I do, I might say, "To be a devil's advocate, this is the way so-and-so might see it . . ." But I don't see the point of getting into an argument with someone I'm interviewing. In the middle sixties, an English politician who'd managed to win an election in the Midlands through race-baiting threw me out of his house in the middle of an interview. When a friend of mine on one of the London papers told a colleague about that, the colleague said something like, "I thought Trillin was a better reporter than that." When I thought about that, I decided the colleague had a pretty good point: I missed whatever the politician would have said after the moment he decided to throw me out.

Do you care in what order you interview people?

I try to save the most important people for last. I like to have talked to a lot of people, and learned more about the central characters, before I talk to them.

You wrote roughly one "U.S. Journal" every three weeks for fifteen years. How did you manage that?

I don't know whether Mr. Shawn had it in his mind that I would be quite as rigid about handing them in when he asked me to write the "U.S. Journal" stories. But that was the only way for me to do it. I had to keep on a schedule and feel that it would be downright *embarrassing* for me not to hand in a story at the end of three weeks. Otherwise I might have worked on one story forever.

I'd usually leave New York on a Sunday night. I'd get on the plane, have a drink or two, and think about the story. I usually knew very little about the story. I didn't do much preparation aside from making sure that the central characters would be in town, and calling the local paper to see whether I could use the clips.

That night or the next morning, when I woke up at my motel, I'd call home and say to my wife, "You know what this story is really about? It's about such and such." By the time I called her I'd have some pretty well-polished theories about the story, particularly if it had been a long plane ride. A week or so later, when she read the first draft of the piece, she would say, "Remember that thing you told me

about the story when you first got there? Well, it isn't in the piece."
And I'd have to explain to her that my original idea had evaporated
once I started reporting. Which is to say that if I have an idea about a
story at the beginning, I am usually wrong.

Is writing more enjoyable for you than reporting, or vice versa?
They're intertwined—partly because writing is a lot easier when
I've done a thorough job of reporting. It's a fairly simple formula:
specific writing is obviously better than general writing. If I don't
know enough to be specific, then it is hard to write. That is one of
the reasons that even the most brilliant editor can't turn terrible
copy into brilliant copy. He can only make it okay, because he
doesn't have enough specific information about the story.

There are parts of both activities that I like and don't like.

The thing I don't like about reporting is calling strangers on the
telephone, which may seem like a rather serious handicap for a
reporter. But once I arrive someplace and get myself out into the
reporting, I'm okay. What I like most about reporting is that I am
constantly satisfying my curiosity. If things are going well, there are
two or three times in a week when I'll stop and think, "*Now* I understand what's going on!" And then the next time I'll think to myself,
"*No,* what I thought yesterday isn't right. *Now* I *really* understand
what's going on!" If I don't have *any* of those moments, or if I have
only one of them, then I'm likely to have a problem with the piece.

What does the perfect writing day look like for you?
I get everything done in the morning and spend the rest of the day
in Chinatown.

Okay, what does a less-than-perfect writing day look like?
My writing routine has changed a bit since I started using a computer. But the basic method is the same; I just use different technology. When I used a typewriter, the first day I was back from reporting
I'd write a sort of *pre*draft draft, which used to be called around the
house the "Vomit Out." I'd write it without bothering to look at any
of my notes. I used to write it on canary yellow paper to distinguish it
from later drafts. It usually started out in reasonable English, but as
I got into it the language would deteriorate.

What is the point of the "Vomit Out" draft?

For one thing, it got me started. Also it gave me an inventory of what I needed to include in the piece. It might also give me some rough idea of what wouldn't work—that the piece would have to be in the first person rather than the third person, for instance, or that starting with the trial wouldn't allow me to plant certain facts I needed to plant about the crime.

When I used to write at *The New Yorker* more, I was always afraid the cleaning women would find my "Vomit Out." Then one cleaning woman would read it out loud to the others. "Just listen to *this!*" she'd say. "And this guy calls himself a *writer!*" Then they'd all laugh and slap their brooms against the desks like hockey players.

Do you ever use an outline?

I've never made an outline. I learned how to in high school, but I never made one after that. At times, I suppose I've scrawled on a piece of paper eight or ten words about what follows what, but it's not a formal outline.

Doesn't your "Vomit Out" draft function as a de facto outline?

Not really. I sometimes don't even look at it. Sometimes I find it at the end of the week, after I've finished the piece. But it gets my brain working.

You type out everything from the first to the final draft?

Yes. Before computers, I wrote by putting things through the typewriter over and over again. My head has been connected to a typewriter since eighth grade. The Kansas City schools ran out of money that year and closed in April, so my father sent me to the Sarachon-Hooley Secretarial School to learn how to type. For a while, I was so tied to the typewriter that I'd do a note that had to be written in longhand by typing it out first, and then copying it in longhand.

Do you write straight through from start to finish before you revise?

Yes. When I first got to *The New Yorker,* a writer I admired told me that he wrote in finished paragraphs—that is, he didn't move on to the next paragraph until he had the one he was working on the way he would hand it in. If *I* did that, I'd still be working on the first paragraph of my first piece.

What do you do once you've finished the "Vomit Out" draft?

I take the piles of notes and documents I've collected while reporting and try to put them into some kind of order. Particularly after Xerox shops became common, I'd sometimes come home with a staggering number of documents. More than any other technological development, the copy machine really changed the way I report.

How do you organize your reporting material?

If there's a lot, I divide it up into subject folders, which I stack in those wire file-holders that enable me to see all the folders at once. Then I read through the notes I typed up while I was reporting. Finally, I take out a legal pad and make a one- to two-page list of the things I want to make *sure* to get into the piece: quotes I especially like, especially good facts or details.

On the second day, when I was writing three-thousand-word "U.S. Journal" pieces, I'd write half of the rough draft on regular, white copy paper.

On the third day I'd write another fifteen hundred words—the second half of the piece. My actual rough draft—the draft after that embarrassing "Vomit Out"—would normally be fairly close to the way the piece ended up, at least in structure. At that point, I would show it to my wife. She was my first and only reader before I handed the piece in.

Do you cross out things as you go along, or do you do all your revising at the end?

Now that I write on a computer, I delete any sentences or paragraphs that aren't working. When I composed on the typewriter and wrote a paragraph I didn't like, I'd rip that part of the page off and throw it out. Then I'd staple the remaining part of the page, with the good material, onto the existing page. It was a sort of messy cut-and-paste method, in which I used a straightedge and a stapler. So I'd end up with these strips of paper stapled to form a page. Some pages had a *lot* of staples on them.

What did you do next?

On the fourth day I'd write what I called the "Yellow Draft." I used the same kind of paper as for the "Vomit Out" draft, but the "Yellow Draft" was the draft I liked best. The structure was usually more or less worked out, and I was working mainly on improving the sentences. I'd put the stapled-together first draft on the desk, start from the beginning, and retype the whole thing, making changes as I went along.

On the fifth day I'd get a pack of carbon paper and type up the piece again. That way I'd have two copies—one for me and one for my editor. That's the version I handed in.

How do you pace yourself when you are writing?

Sometimes I set a word goal for myself. I summon up what I call "The Committee on National Goals," which is a phrase from the Eisenhower Administration. I think of them as a bunch of serious old guys, sitting together on high, like a federal appeals court. They are very intransigent and they don't want to hear any excuses from the likes of me. It doesn't matter if I'm not feeling well, or I have a lot of other things to do. No excuses.

Reporting and writing pretty much fit into the time you allot for them. When I worked at *Time,* I'd spend all day writing a story early in the week. Then, if a story broke on Saturday, just before we went to press, I'd sit down and write it in an hour. It's the same with reporting. Sometimes, I'll decide that a story should take, say, a week or ten days to report. And it does. I could spend a month reporting the same story. Or I could spend four days. The texture of the story would differ, but I'd be able to write it.

You're a prolific writer, yet you appear regularly in only a few publications (The New Yorker, The Nation, Gourmet). How did you come to that decision?

I realized early on that I didn't need to have a piece in every magazine at the barbershop. I figured that I'd rather write mainly for *The New Yorker,* which pays as well as anybody, and then go to the park with my girls when they came home from school. I sort of accidentally came to an understanding of "enoughness" when it came to writing. So when I got through writing what I'd decided I had to write that day, I'd quit.

How important is the lead?

The first sentence sets the tone of the piece. Sometimes I just start by describing what happened: "This started with a bad left turn." It depends what mood I'm aiming for. I think about my lead a lot while I'm reporting.

What kind of authorial presence do you strive for?

It depends on the piece. For something like a piece about a murder, I just try to get out of the way of the narrative. Putting myself in the piece would seem to me a way of inserting lumps in what I'm trying to make a smooth narrative. If a reporting piece of mine is in the first person, it's usually a lighter piece. For pieces about eating, it's almost a persona—the cheerful glutton.

Some have described your tone as understated and Midwestern.

I don't know whether my tone is Midwestern. I was brought up in the Midwest, and my father—although he was at least technically an immigrant; he came to St. Joseph, Missouri, from the Ukraine when he was about two—sounded like Harry Truman. When I did the Johnny Carson show a lot, I used to think that it was easy for us to talk because our speech rhythms were the same. Also, I would see the same things as funny that Carson did. When I watched him interview other people I noticed that he would often make the remark that I would have made—if, of course, I'd been able to think of it as fast as he did.

It is hard for a writer to describe his tone. I *do* know when I'm sounding right, sounding like myself. I don't mean that you sound the same on paper as in conversation—although compared to some writers, my writing is probably fairly close to my conversation.

What writers have influenced you?

Joseph Mitchell is someone whose writing I admire, although I wouldn't say that he influenced my writing style. I first read Mitchell when I was at *Time*, and I was really impressed. I thought, "*Jesus*, this is the sort of thing you can do in nonfiction writing." He writes in a simple way, and he manages to get all the marks of writing off of the piece. It seemed to just appear on the page. You couldn't imagine him laboring over it—although he obviously did.

The other thing I admire about him is that he wrote about these people head-on. He'd never condescend. He had this wonderful sentence in the introduction to *McSorley's Wonderful Saloon*: "It has become fashionable to call the sort of people written about in this book 'the little people.' I find that term repugnant. They are as big as you are, whoever you are." Mitchell is the only writer I know who could have gotten away with writing that.

Do you believe journalism can lead to truth?

Well, I believe you have to do your best to tell the truth. For me, the truth has to do with what actually happened and with your best efforts to understand what actually happened.

I don't think you can stray from what actually happened and claim that you're seeking some higher truth. For instance, you can't justify an invented quote or a doctored quote by claiming, say, "That's a fair approximation of what farmers in that region in that economy would say." Maybe it is and maybe it isn't, but a farmer didn't say it. Almost always, when people talk about getting to a "higher truth" by using facts that aren't literally true, it means that they find the *actual* truth awkward. It messes up their transition to the next paragraph. Or it messes up their theory. The real farmer's quote isn't quite as neatly turned—maybe because he's a farmer, not a writer. Using facts that aren't true isn't getting closer to the truth. It's getting further from the truth.

Do you think of yourself as a New Journalist?

No. I think of a New Journalist as someone who feels he doesn't have to tell the truth, or as someone who believes he can get inside people's heads and know their thoughts.

What if you spend a tremendous amount of time with someone, and he tells you, "At that moment, I was thinking . . ."?

Sometimes it's obvious what he was thinking—the bear came at him and he was frightened—but in most cases, I would still probably write that he *says* that's what he was thinking. In the heyday of

New Journalism, by the way, the reporter sometimes hadn't even interviewed the person whose thoughts were given.

So what do you call the kind of writing you do?

The New Yorker calls the kinds of pieces I write "fact" pieces. I don't think that—except in quality—what I'm doing is any different from what Mitchell or Liebling did.

Do you see yourself as part of a historical literary tradition?

Yes, except maybe for the word "literary." That's partly because I write for a magazine that has always allowed reporters to write narratives without regard to, say, whether the people involved are important people or whether what happened is illustrative of some national trend.

Years ago, after the publication of a long story I'd written on the Zulu Social Aid and Pleasure Club ["A Reporter at Large: The Zulus," *The New Yorker*, June 20, 1964], the only black Mardi Gras club in New Orleans that had a parade permit for Mardi Gras day, my mother told me that it was well written, which is the way she began her comments on any piece I'd done. Then she said, "I think it's wonderful that you can write such a lengthy article about such a nothing subject."

BY CALVIN TRILLIN:

Obliviously On He Sails: The Bush Administration in Rhyme, Random House, 2004
Feeding a Yen: Savoring Local Specialities, from Kansas City to Cuzco, Random House, 2003
Tepper Isn't Going Out: A Novel, Random House, 2001
Family Man, Farrar, Straus and Giroux, 1998
Messages from My Father, Farrar, Straus and Giroux, 1996
Too Soon to Tell, Farrar, Straus and Giroux, 1995
The Tummy Trilogy, Farrar, Straus and Giroux, 1994
Deadline Poet: My Life as a Doggerelist, Farrar, Straus and Giroux, 1994
Remembering Denny, Farrar, Straus and Giroux, 1993
American Stories, Ticknor and Fields, 1991
Enough's Enough: And Other Rules of Life, Ticknor and Fields, 1990
Travels with Alice, Ticknor and Fields, 1989
If You Can't Say Something Nice, Ticknor and Fields, 1987
With All Disrespect: More Uncivil Liberties, Ticknor and Fields, 1985

Killings, Ticknor and Fields, 1984
Third Helpings, Ticknor and Fields, 1983
Uncivil Liberties, Ticknor and Fields, 1982
Floater, Ticknor and Fields, 1980
Alice, Let's Eat: Further Adventures of a Happy Eater, Vintage Books, 1979
Runestruck, Little, Brown, 1977
American Fried: Adventures of a Happy Eater, Doubleday, 1974
U.S. Journal, Dutton, 1971
Barnett Frummer Is an Unbloomed Flower, Viking, 1969
An Education in Georgia, Viking, 1964

LAWRENCE WESCHLER

Bookstores never know where to put Lawrence Weschler's books. *Mr. Wilson's Cabinet of Wonder* (1995), his portrait of the curator of the Museum of Jurassic Technology, is likely to be found in "Psychedelics." *Boggs: A Comedy of Values* (1999), a profile of a performance artist who draws images of money, in "Economics." *A Miracle, A Universe* (1990), which examines the role of torture in the military dictatorships of Brazil and Uruguay, may be in the "Latin America" section. That the confusion stems as much from Weschler's remarkable breadth as a writer as it does a bookstore's parochialism gives him little comfort.

Where does Weschler *want* his work collected? *Calamities of Exile* (1998), his book about three expatriates from three totalitarian regimes—Czech dissident Jan Kavan, Iraqi architect Kanan Makiya, and South African poet Breyten Breytenbach—offers a clue. The volume's subtitle, *Three Nonfiction Novellas*, is a designation (literature? journalism?) that simultaneously clarifies and complicates the question of just what kind of writing he does. For his part, Weschler has settled on the term "writerly nonfiction."

This ambiguity goes to the heart of his work. Weschler is a storyteller—a master of narrative, no matter the subject, or genre. "Every narrative voice—but especially every nonfiction voice—is itself a fiction, and the world of writing and reading is divided between those who know this and those who either don't or else deny it," begins the prospectus for "The Fiction of Nonfiction," the course he has taught at Princeton, Sarah Lawrence, and NYU. "Human beings have glands that secrete all sorts of things. But the human *mind* secretes *stories*. We live narratives. That is the only way we know how to experience anything, and it is our glory."

Weschler's characters tend to be marginal—not in their importance, but in the sense that they provide him with an off-center perspective that enables him to tackle preposterously large subjects (art, torture, the nature of money). His best characters are those whose narratives are interrupted (whether by exile or chance), but whose passion and wonder are recharged by being destabilized. "In all my writing, I guess, I have been concerned with people and places that were just moseying down the street one day, minding their own business, when suddenly and almost spontaneously they caught on fire, they became obsessed, they became intensely focused and intensely alive—ending up, by day's end, somewhere altogether different from where they'd imagined they were setting out that morning," he writes in the introduction to *A Wanderer in the Perfect City* (1998).

Weschler was born on February 13, 1952, and raised in Van Nuys, California. His father was a professor and industrial psychologist, and his grandparents were Viennese Jews who emigrated at the beginning of the Second World War. Ernst Toch, Weschler's grandfather, a composer, was awarded the Pulitzer Prize for his Third Symphony in 1956.

Weschler attended Cowell College of the University of California at Santa Cruz. It was the university's intellectual heyday, and he took full advantage of it, studying Latin with Norman O. Brown (*Love's Body, Life Against Death*), political theory with Sheldon Wolin (*Politics and Vision*), literature with Harry Berger, and philosophy with the phenomenologist Maurice Natanson. "My teachers taught me how to ask questions. And not only how to ask questions, but also the glory of the questioning stance," he says.

After university, Weschler freelanced for the *L.A. Reader* and *L.A. Weekly* while working as an editor and interviewer for UCLA's Oral History Program. His biography of the artist Robert Irwin (*Seeing is Forgetting the Name of the Thing One Sees*, 1982) grew out of interviews Weschler was editing for the program, and in many ways established the tone and method of Weschler's career. In words that could describe himself, Weschler calls Irwin "a master of irony and a devotee of serious play. He has an extraordinary tolerance for ambiguity: he asks questions that seem by their very nature unanswerable, but he maintains his interest because the questions are legitimate—and are themselves probably more interesting than any answer they might summon. In short, he is an artist who one day got hooked on his own curiosity and decided to live it."

With no introduction or connections to *The New Yorker*, Weschler sent the manuscript of the Irwin book to Calvin Tompkins, the magazine's art critic, who passed it to William Shawn, then the magazine's editor. Shawn agreed to publish a portion of the book, and so began Weschler's most important literary relationship. Shawn was "the most curious man in the world," Weschler writes of the late editor in the *Columbia Journalism Review*. "'Go,' he tells [his writers], 'take however long you need but then write me back what it is like there, what the people are saying and feeling, how they spend their lives, what they worry about—write me all that, make it complete, and make it vivid, as vivid as if I'd been able to go there myself.'"

In 1981, Weschler became a staff writer at the magazine, where he divided his time between long, foreign political pieces, and more lighthearted cultural ones. In particular, Weschler wrote frequently about Poland from 1980 to 1982 (collected in *The Passion of Poland*, 1984) and filed annual reports on the rebirth of the Solidarity movement and the transition from communism to capitalism in resurgent Poland from 1988 to 1992.

One of his most powerful books is *A Miracle, A Universe: Settling Accounts with Torturers* (1990), which examines the role of torture in the military dictatorships of Brazil and Uruguay. Weschler wanted to pose a fundamental question: "How do you at once honor, bear witness, and do justice to the victims of the past in *a living way*, but in a way that still allows room for the living?" To answer it, he told several stories, the first about a group of Brazilian human rights activists who stole millions of pages of official documents, containing detailed accounts of torture by the torturers themselves, and published them in a bestselling exposé that was translated and published in the U.S. as *Torture in Brazil*. In another, Weschler told how the citizens of Uruguay forced the government to hold a referendum on whether to grant amnesty to the previous military dictatorship, which had maintained power through wholesale torture. Describing the book's narrative drive, Isabel Fonseca in *The Times Literary Supplement* wrote that it has "the pace of a thriller without diminishing its weight of testimony."

The first of his books not to originate in *The New Yorker* (parts were published in *Harper's*), *Mr. Wilson's Cabinet of Wonder* explores the Museum of Jurassic Technology, a tiny L.A. storefront where one encounters the kinds of bizarre exhibits—the Cameroonian stink ant, horns sprouted from human heads, bats embedded in lead—that were long ago deaccessioned from the great museums of the world. Like the "wonder-cabinets" of Renaissance Europe, curator David Wilson's museum is less a reflection of the world than a delightful escape from it. *New York Times* critic Michiko Kakutani called the book "a thoughtful meditation on the role of museums (and the place of wonder) in our society today" and praised Weschler's "sympathetic radar for human idiosyncrasy and obsession." Weschler's first bestseller, *Mr. Wilson*, was a finalist for both the Pulitzer Prize and the National Book Critics Circle Award.

Weschler first wrote about J. S. G. Boggs in 1987, as the once-soaring stock and art markets were collapsing. "Where did all the money *go*?" he wondered. In several pieces over the next decade (collected in book form in 1999), Boggs proved the perfect marginal character through whom to explore this question. Boggs is a performance artist and monetary draftsman who exchanges original renderings of paper currency for goods and services. He will go into a bar, order a drink, and present a drawing of, say, the back of a five-dollar bill in payment. If it is accepted, he asks for a receipt and change, which he then sells to his collectors, who track down the original drawing and try to buy it. The complete transaction—drawing, change, receipt—constitutes Boggs's art. One Boggs transaction was auctioned for $420,000, and others have been acquired by the British Museum, the Art Institute of Chicago, the Museum of Modern Art, and the Smithsonian. *The Atlantic Monthly*'s Toby Lester picked up on the parallels between author and subject: "Weschler always seems to be, as he says of Boggs, 'engaged in philosophical disruptions, in provoking brief, momentary tears in the ordinarily seamless fabric of taken-for-granted mundanity.'"

In 2001, Weschler became the director of the New York Institute for the Humanities at NYU. His most recent book, *Vermeer in Bosnia* (2004), is a collection of his work from the past twenty years. His next book, to be published in 2005, is a collaboration with *McSweeney's* tentatively called *Everything That Rises: A Book of Convergences.*

———

Despite the variety of your subjects, your work feels like a whole. Is this conscious?

Yes, I'm very conscious that I am building an overarching structure. It reminds me of the Borges story in which a person writes and writes his whole life, and at the end realizes that what he's written is his own face.

The problem is that not everybody *sees* the continuity, and bookstores frequently don't know what sections to put my books in. I just heard that a Barnes & Noble in Ann Arbor put *Mr. Wilson's Cabinet of Wonder,* my book about David Wilson's Museum of Jurassic Technology, in the "Psychedelics" section! *Boggs,* my portrait of an artist who draws money, sometimes ends up in "Economics." *A Miracle, A Universe,* my book about torture victims settling accounts with their torturers, is put in the "Latin America" section.

It is very frustrating because I believe there is a kind of writerly nonfiction—a tradition to which I aspire to be a part—which ought in the bookstore to be in *alphabetical* order in the "Literature" section.

Is that why you subtitled your book Calamities of Exile a "nonfiction novella"?

Yes. You can't realistically expect anything from Barnes & Noble, but even when I talk to the managers of independent bookstores, which tend to like my work, there is a lot of resistance to my suggestion that all writerly nonfiction be categorized as "Literature." They say, "But if we do it with your books, then we have to do it with everybody." And I tell them, no, they just have to make a judgment: are you dealing with a writerly project? This would require a real change of mind-set on the part of bookstores. There are a few writers who sometimes end up in the "Literature" section, like McPhee, Trillin, P. J. O'Rourke. Interestingly enough, there *is* a bookstore where this kind of thing is done. It's called Amazon.com!

You sometimes refer to your articles as "passion pieces." What makes you passionate?

I'm obsessed with a narrow range of huge issues: Passion. Grace. Exile. Blockage.

In the case of passion, the overarching theme is something I describe as "Inhaling the Spore." In *Mr. Wilson's Cabinet of Wonder*, the first image is of ants foraging for food on the rainforest floor, who every once in a while accidentally inhale the spore of a fungus. The spore lodges in their brain and they start to behave oddly. They leave the forest floor for the first time in their lives, climb up the tendrils of surrounding vines, and eventually impale their mandibles on the stalk of the vine and wait to die. They die because the fungus has actually been eating away their entire nervous system, and two weeks after their death, a horn, laden with spores, erupts from out of their heads. The spores then rain down onto the forest floor and the whole process starts again.

All of which is an allegory for what interests me. I'm fascinated by moments when people "inhale spores." When it happens to individuals, it can be fairly comic. When it happens to larger polities—Poland, South Africa, Uruguay, Brazil—it can be immense, magisterial, and also sometimes comic, by the way.

In all my writing, I have been concerned with people and places that were just moseying down the street one day, minding their own business, when suddenly and almost spontaneously they caught fire, they became obsessed, they became intensely focused and intensely alive—ending up, by day's end, somewhere altogether different from where they'd imagined they were setting out that morning. I'm interested both in what happens when a person catches fire, and also—in the political context—what becomes necessary to douse that fire. So I'm also interested in repression and torture and that whole drama.

What about "grace"?

Grace comes into play in those situations in which you work and work and work at something . . . that then happens *all by itself*! It would not have happened without all the prior work, but the prior work didn't *cause* it to happen. The prior work was preparation for receptivity. But then there is something beyond that which is gratis, for free. That is "grace."

For example, one saw it when one spoke to the Polish activists of Solidarity. They beat their heads against the wall from 1968 through 1980, month after month, year after year. Nothing happened, nothing happened, nothing happened . . . and then, in August 1980, *everything just happened*. And in a sense they felt that everything they had done up to that point had *nothing* to do with what happened.

Why are you drawn to the theme of "exile"?

All my grandparents were Viennese Jews who were cast into exile on account of the Nazis, their lives broken in various ways. My grandfather, Ernest Toch, was a composer, and when he was forced to leave Germany, the "all-clear" telegram he sent my grandmother to let her know he was okay read, "I have my pencil"—as if that was all he was going to need. Of course, what he *didn't* have when he came to California was the context, the resonance. He went through a terrible blockage for the first fifteen years he was in America, and then came out the other end of it with an incredible resurgence of energy. He wrote a series of symphonies, the third of which won the Pulitzer Prize in 1956. That symphony has a motto from Goethe, "Of course I am a pilgrim, a wanderer on this earth. But can you say that you are anything more?" Which is to say that the individual exile of the wandering Jew is something of a universal condition.

Are some kinds of passion more interesting to you than others?

I'm interested in all the different variations passion can take. It isn't an ethically positive or ethically neutral fascination. For instance, I'm fascinated by *fascist* aesthetics. When you think about Hitler, for example, you are dealing with someone who—even *before* he is an anti-Semite—is an aesthete of some kind. It is key to understanding Hitler to know that he was a painter, and not even a *failed* painter exactly. What drove him crazy was that he could paint a house that actually *looked like a house,* damn it, and why was it that all this abstract *crap* was being shown in the museum! And from there he noticed that much of the "crap" was sponsored by those "cosmopolitan" Jews. If anything, one could argue that Hitler's hatred of Jews comes from modern art, rather than the other way around.

So the "passion" you're fascinated by isn't always of "the guy fighting the good fight" persuasion?

Not necessarily, although it can be, and those situations often make for some of the more fun stories. Another way of putting it is that what really interests me are "Socratic" individuals. People like the artist Robert Irwin, Boggs, David Wilson—these are people whose métier is to upend your certainties. Like the ant, they've inhaled the spore. I in turn inhale *their* spore and shed it, which is how the reader gets it.

How do you find story ideas?

Well, by now it has all become sort of self-projecting: I'm known as someone who has patience with this sort of thing. I am also open to the notion that the best stuff is stuff that nobody's ever heard of. Sometimes the people I write about *turn out* to be "the next big thing," but that isn't what attracts me to them initially.

This must make you unpopular with most magazine editors.

It has. In fact, Tina Brown, when she was editor of *The New Yorker*, rejected the piece that ended up as the book *Mr. Wilson's Cabinet of Wonder.*

I turned in twelve thousand words, which comprised the first half of the book. Tina gave it back to me without even looking at it and told me to cut it to five thousand words. I told her that there *was* no five-thousand-word piece here; there was a five-hundred-word "Talk of the Town" piece, or a ten-thousand-word piece, but its structure wouldn't work at five thousand words.

And Tina said, "Ren, I couldn't run ten thousand words on Mr. Wilson's Museum of Jurassic Technology if I *wanted* to because it's not *hot*," which she pronounced *hōt*. I replied, "Well, Tina, that's true. It isn't hot, it's *cool*. But if you run the ten thousand words, it *will* be hot." And in a kind of ecstasy of self-knowledge, she shot back, "I don't run ten thousand words on a place that *will* be hot. I run ten thousand words on a place that *is* hot." In fairness, Tina is not the villain in this story. She is simply the symptom of a wider problem.

Is this why you've so seldom written about celebrities?

There is nothing wrong with writing about famous people. Celebrities are often very interesting, but you don't want to talk to them at the moment of their celebritydom. The problem with "celebrity journalism" is that any profile of a celebrity at the moment of his celebrity is a profile of the *condition of celebritydom*. There is a certain philosophy of magazine editing, which is that you describe which fancy restaurant you took the celebrity to, the logic being that the fancier the restaurant the fancier the scoops you'll get.

Another metaphor for the problem of celebrity journalism is flash photography. All flash photographs are bad. The flash from the camera distorts the photo. And all flash photographs are the same: everybody's skin looks the same. And everybody has those same little red dots in their eyes. Celebritydom distorts and obscures whatever *might* be interesting about the celebrity subject.

Before stories started coming to you, how did you find ideas?

There is a range of issues I keep in the back of my mind that I'm always looking for a way to write about. There was a time when I wanted to write about torture and our complicity in torture. And I also wanted to write about the intersection of art and money. You can write about both of those things head-on, but it's boring. So, for instance, I wrote about Boggs in 1987, at the height of the insanity of the art market. But *Boggs* wasn't a story *about* the insanity of the art market.

Anyway, I make a point of keeping up with the literature on these subjects and look for a story, a narrative, a tale, an individual to tell the story through. John McPhee's metaphor for this process is "looking for a ship." I spend much of my life "looking for ships."

How do you know when you have a good story?

A good Geiger counter is what I call the "pillow of air." For instance, I call Ira Glass's radio program, *This American Life*, "pillow-of-air radio." I use the term to describe that experience of turning on the show and sitting down to balance your checkbook while you listen, and forty-five minutes later you realize that you haven't moved your pen. And what you also notice is that your mouth has been open and the air in it has become completely still. There is a pillow of air lodged in your mouth that hasn't moved for two or three minutes. You simply *forget to breathe!* You lose yourself to the experience. It is better than anything else in the world. It is intuitive, but it is *literally* physical.

If I find myself in a "pillow of air" relationship to a story, that's a pretty good indication it is a good story.

Once you've had a "pillow of air" experience, how do you tell the story?

Triangulation is the key. I generally don't try to hit something head-on. I hit it from as many different sides as possible. For example, to get at the question of why we believe in money, I hit it from the side of art, from the side of this guy Boggs, etc. And I try to keep all these different angles going throughout the piece. I'm not particularly interested in interviewing Milosevic when I write about Serbia, or Walesa when I write about Poland. I'm much more interested in taking the temperature of the whole scene, in the bubbling that is crossing over borders.

In addition to approaching subjects from varied angles, your pieces often have a moment where you suddenly stop and take the reader in an entirely different direction.

I call that the "trapdoor." I like to build up the velocity of the story, and at the climactic moment, the moment when I *really* begin to hot things up, I take the reader through a trapdoor. He isn't expecting it, and I use the occasion to introduce him to some new material— other characters, a bit of history, some philosophy. At the moment when the piece has really gotten going, I'm liable to tell the reader, "Now, to understand what is going to happen next, let's step back for a second and take a look at this . . ."

How are "triangulation" and "trapdoors" related?

Well, because I've taken the reader through the trapdoor at the *height* of the piece, he is just *dying* to get back to the main story. The trapdoor may, for example, introduce the reader to a more conventional history at that point. But because this information is being imparted in the context of the skewed, highly interpretive— although not inaccurate—pedestal I've put it on, via triangulation, it will *itself* be skewed. It isn't straight explication, and the reader may not even realize that it is, so to say, "good for him." All I'm saying to the reader at the point I take him through the trapdoor is, "This story I'm telling you is really cool and fun. And in order to make it even *more* fun, you need to know the following things . . ."

Do you prefer pursuing stories you've come up with, or stories that come from an editor?

I tend to pursue my own projects and then try to find someone who will run them. This has to do with the fact that I tend to have the structure of the overarching body of my work in mind whenever I embark upon a new piece. I write each piece, each paragraph, in the context of the larger whole of my work.

Maintaining my independence has always been important to me. Tina wanted to lavish huge amounts of money on me if I would only just sign a contract and become a staff writer. But that would have meant that if she assigned me to do a David Geffen profile, I'd have had to do it. And I couldn't do that. No matter who the editor of the magazine was, I was always paid by the piece and by the word.

Many of your stories gestate for years. Are you aware from the start that you are working on a story? Or are you just living your life when the story sneaks up on you?

Usually I'll know fairly early on whether something is a story. Because I'll hear myself keep telling the story to others. It's like that great W. H. Auden line, "How can I know what I think until I hear what I say?"

Do you work on several stories at once?

At any given moment I'm keeping track of seven or eight stories. One day I'd like to write a story about all the great pieces that got away—stories I *thought* I was doing, but it turned out that I wasn't.

Can you give me an example of a story that "got away"?

The Australian dream case was one of my favorites. About twenty years ago, someone had the idea of giving acrylics to the Aborigines, who had previously been doing all these marvelous paintings in the sand. In terms of aboriginal culture, these paintings were called "dreamings." And the dreamings were thought to be inherited: you were allowed to do a dream because it had been your father's dream. But there were certain dreamings that were more popular on the market than other dreamings. And sure enough, some guy came along and poached another guy's dream! And this ended up in an Australian lawsuit. Just imagine a court case that begins, "Hey, buddy. *You stole my dream!*"

This is a perfect example of "triangulation." The story raises an amazing set of questions: about aboriginal culture, about the comedy that is involved in *every* legal case, about the comedy of capitalism and art, about the comedy of our cultural cross-ambitions. After all, what does that aboriginal thing, hanging next to a Frank Stella painting on the wall in a Park Avenue living room, *signify*? That's a pretty interesting juxtaposition, but it has absolutely *nothing* to do with aboriginal culture. The story had a million angles. Damn.

How many assigned projects do you have under way at any given time?

You wouldn't want to know the state of my business affairs! I tend to be working on a lot simultaneously. Some of them are stories, some are conferences, some are shows or collections. There is a lot of cross-pollination: stories become conferences, conferences emerge from stories. I have many roles. I'm director of the NYU Institute for Humanities. I'm the chair of the Soros (now Sundance) Documentary Fund, so every six weeks I receive a pile of videos I have to watch. I do those convergence pieces for *McSweeney's.* I'm interested in *narrative,* and I don't care so much what form the narrative takes.

Do you do most of your research for a story before, during, or after your reporting?

I do some research before I go anywhere, and a lot while I'm there. Some of the best reportage I've done has been when I arrived raw, went away and did a lot of reading, and then came back. That happened when I was writing about Brazil and Uruguay.

Any *kind* of research you particularly rely on?

One thing I've done when I'm doing research for American stories about events in the last century is to get back issues of *The New*

Yorker from the period and study all the cartoons. There are lots of cartoons from earlier periods that I won't get *at all,* and I figure that if I can get to the point where I *do* understand them, then I'll have understood something about the collective unconscious of the time. In order to understand the spirit of an era or country, you have to understand its humor.

Any other research sources?

I know a lot of people in the human rights world, so I often start there. I do a lot of reading and talk to experts in the field. I also read a lot of poetry and novels.

Why poetry and novels?

To understand the sensibility, the cultural moment of the place and people I'm reporting on. To get a sense right from the start of what the *question* might be.

What do you mean by "the question"?

The question, by the way, is a *fiction.* The question is a point of access to the complexity of what *is.*

With *Boggs* the question turned out to be, "Where does all the money *go* when there is a financial bust?" This turned out to be a really good question. And a question that keeps on repeating itself. We just lost $7 trillion dollars in the economy. *Where did it go?* The answer: *It was never there!* It was a mass-phantasm.

In the case of *A Miracle, A Universe,* the question was, "How do you at once honor, bear witness, and do justice to the victims of the past in *a living way,* but in a way that still allows room for the living?" How to honor the living *and* the dead, which can be contradictory impulses.

Do you have a reporting routine?

When I do foreign reporting I make sure I have an open return ticket. I practice what is sometimes pejoratively referred to as "para-chute journalism." I show up with a certain set of vague questions. I arrange a lot of interviews and start taking notes like crazy.

Invariably, in the first few days, I hit a wall and feel hopeless. Nobody is returning my calls, I don't understand *anything* about the situation . . . But things start to pick up and I reach a kind of poised,

Zen-like state in which, although I still don't understand the story, I let it lead me in whatever direction it takes.

So these first few days are a waste?

No, this is the "quarrying stage." All the time I spend gathering material and doing interviews during my first few weeks is actually about trying to figure out the *question.* One of the most helpful things that anyone ever told me was said by a marine biologist in college named Todd Newberry. I was writing an essay for him on some enormous, unwieldy topic and was floundering badly. And he said, "When you are dealing with a huge, amorphous topic, it is sort of like when you are walking down the beach and come upon a dead walrus and you are curious why it died." (Bracketing the fact that I *don't* walk down beaches, *don't* come upon walruses, and wouldn't give a *damn* why they died!) He continued,

> You can do one of two things. You can pick up that piece of drift-wood over there and start bashing the walrus, but all you'll do is make a mess of the walrus and of yourself. Or you can take that driftwood over to that boulder and sit down, pick up that stone, and start sharpening it. It will take you hours and hours, probably all afternoon to sharpen the driftwood. But at the end of the process you'll have a blade. And you can then use that blade to do an autopsy and you'll figure out what happened in five minutes.

The moral of Todd's story is that when you're confronting a huge, amorphous topic, don't ask huge, amorphous questions. Spend 95 percent of your time *honing* the question. In the early stages of my reporting I often approach an interview with a battery of questions the size of a huge block. "Does this question work? How about that one?" Certain questions don't elicit a response, so I shave them off.

How long does it take to formulate the correct question?

Forty or so interviews during the two to three weeks I'm there. Or I discover precisely *which* of the questions I've been asking all along actually do open things up.

Then, since I've taken good notes during my quarrying period, I can take my finely honed question and interrogate my previous interviews. And as I reread them I start noticing things I hadn't noticed before. But it takes about forty interviews of sharpening the knife before I can cut open the walrus and discover what killed him.

What happens next?

At this point, I understand about 95 percent of what is going on. But I know that if I stay there even one more day I'll get a bit of information that will *completely* shake my faith in anything I do know and I'll be back down to 5 percent confidence in what I know. And it would take me six months to get back to 95 percent—a *different* 95 percent. So at that point I literally haul off to the hotel and stay there, alone, until the next flight leaves—which is why I always travel with that open return ticket.

That 95 percent certainty is your certainty that you've gotten the story?

No, let's be clear about this. There *isn't* a "the" story. I'm a very big advocate of first-person journalism—which is to say the use of an "I" narrator—not out of megalomania, but out of modesty. In fact, I would argue that those stories that *don't* have the first person are the ones that are megalomaniacal.

For example, *The New York Times* is megalomaniacal. They use the voice that says, "This is how it *is*. This is all the news that's fit to print." Thank God the *Times* at least has signed bylines now. But even so you get this totally mind-warping convention of, "In the remotest tundra of Siberia, Mr. so-and-so said to *a reporter* . . ." What's going on here? Were there *three* of you in the room?

The "I" doesn't have to show up every five sentences; in fact it is better if it doesn't. But there had better be an individual voice that says, "This is just one person's view, based on one series of experiences."

Do you have a routine for conducting interviews?

I don't have specific questions other than "What's it *like* to be here?" Not "What is it?" but "What is it like?" An interesting analogy is with my friend Dr. Oliver Sacks, who describes himself as a "clinical ontologist." By this he means that he is somebody for whom the diagnostic question is "How *are* you? How *do* you *be*? What is it *like* to be you?" And the key word of that question is "like," as in, "What is it *like* to be a Bosnian right now?"

How would you characterize your reportorial stance?

An interview with me is a conversation. I see myself as an equal. I am not in the supplicant mode. I have the chutzpah to imagine that I am a fellow human being. And have had experiences that are potentially *as* interesting as theirs, and that might be interesting to them. I'll often do half the talking during an interview. I'll interrupt their nurtured habit of just talking about themselves. I'll often break in and say, "Oh, that reminds me of something I once did . . ." I am open to free-floating associations. They've never been confronted with a question like these, and it opens them up and makes them *think*.

This can have wonderfully *wild* consequences. For instance, when I was doing the Breytenbach reporting in South Africa ["Profile: An Afrikaner Dante," *The New Yorker,* November 8, 1993], a key interview I had was with Alex Boraine, a white member of parliament who had quit government to protest apartheid. And he said to me, "We've got a terrible problem here in South Africa, which nobody has *ever* faced before. We've got to try to create a democracy, but we've got all these repressive security forces and torture victims left over from the previous regime. And how do we reconcile the two?" Because of the cultural boycott, people like Boraine had *no* idea that *everybody* had been grappling with this issue!

I told him about my work on Uruguay and Brazil and Poland, where these exact same issues were being faced, and our discussion culminated in a conference that took place in Cape Town several months later. I helped them invite Adam Michnik from Poland, and Jose Zalaquett from Chile, and that was the conference that led to South Africa's Truth and Reconciliation Commission!

A lot of your stories are reported from countries where you don't speak the language. How does this alter your procedures?

Well, you are obviously at a loss if you are in a place where you don't speak the language—but being at a loss is part of what the story is about. So I get a good translator. The most fruitful way to report in a foreign culture is to have someone translate while you are simultaneously taking notes. That way one can establish great eye contact, while at the same time taking notes. The delay gives one time to get things down.

You can also use a translator to play the "good cop" to your "bad cop." Things that you would never say yourself you can have your translator say, and then blame on you. They can be brasher than *they* really are, and you can be brasher than *you* really are. I tell them to blame it on me, to say, "I'm so sorry, *I* would *never* ask you something like this, but this stupid American wants to know about . . ."

What kinds of translators do you prefer?

I'll answer that question with two stories. When I first went to Poland in May 1981 I didn't intend to do a story. I just went with a friend of mine from high school because it seemed like a cool place to escape from Reagan's America. It was totally exciting, and one day we realized that we needed a translator. We were sitting on the curb outside of the Victoria Hotel, the fanciest hotel in Warsaw, and we looked up and saw a huge banner reading, "International Conference of Translators." So we hired one, but it turned out to be oddly disastrous. We got this lovely woman named Grace who was very spirited and had good English. She was also very pretty, which helped because Polish men are just sexist up the wazoo; show them a little bit of leg and they'll tell you *anything!*

When I got back, William Shawn couldn't run the piece I wrote for a while, so I went back to Poland in September for the Solidarity conference. And I used Grace again. But Grace was not a politically sophisticated person. There was a key moment during an interview at the Solidarity conference with Karol Modzelewrki, one of the leading intellectual advisors to Solidarity. I asked him, "You seem to have a problem here. You keep talking about 'self-governance,' but what if the self-governing enterprise needs to go bankrupt? How does a self-governing enterprise effectively put itself out of business?" Grace listened to my question and said, "I'm not going to ask that question. It's rude! It's very easy for you Americans to come in here with your clever questions, but this is our *life*." I was stunned, but she persisted in refusing to ask him the question.

Now that exchange—with my *translator!*—turned out to be more valuable than any answer *he* could have given me. Because it meant that at a certain point in history, average, decent, patriotic Poles like Grace couldn't conceive of a certain kind of issue. That was much more interesting than what any *expert* could have told me about self-governance.

Here is a second story to illustrate the role of a translator. In Bosnia, I had a very good interpreter who was a medical student. One of the things that happens in these disaster-ridden countries is that you can get top-notch translators because the economy has collapsed. He had a car and he was Serb. He was a "right-thinking" Serb in that he thought it was all insane, but even so he occasionally drifted into his Serb version of events. So there were certain Muslims who wouldn't talk to me with him. But the flip side of it was that there were others who would talk to me *only* because I was with a Serb.

One key moment for me occurred after the war was over when we were at a truck stop in Pale, the Bosnia-Serb alternate capital, overlooking Sarajevo. I had a copy of a cartoonlike "I Survived the Siege" map of the area that had all the mountains on it, with all the locations of the snipers, and all the different monuments to those who were killed. We were standing around talking to Serb truckers when one of them sees my map and starts pointing out sections. He said, "Oh yeah, *this* was a great place to shoot from because from there you could look down the street and hit anyone who crossed your path!" And at this point they *all* started yucking it up, telling jokes about Muslims in Sarajevo. So I told my Serb interpreter to laugh *harder* than any of them to keep them going, and at one point this first guy mimed picking up his rifle and firing—*blam, blam, blam*—into the map. It was an amazing scene, and was made possible *only* because I had an interpreter who could join in with them.

So an interpreter is as much a coconspirator as he is a medium?

Yes, and he is also a triangulation person. I'm always asking for my interpreter's opinion of the things we have just heard. "Did that make sense to you?" And a translator will tell me, "What you don't understand is that . . ." (To which I sometimes reply, "No, what *you guys* don't understand is that this is the twenty-first century, and the rest of the world is going to leave you behind if you keep acting like this!")

How do you typically begin an interview?

I start with the first thing that comes to mind, and usually with a free association that has to do with a story that *I want to tell him.* ("Did you see that *monkey?* It reminds me of a monkey I once saw in Japan . . .") I want to establish myself as interesting. And I actually *am* interesting by virtue of the wealth of experiences I've had.

For example, when I was writing about Roman Polanski, we had a long conversation about fatherhood, which turned out to be a very important issue for him ["Profile: Artist in Exile, Roman Polanski," *The New Yorker,* December 5, 1994]. He had a child who at that moment happened to be the exact same age as he had been when the war started, and that opened *all kinds* of wild stuff. But that discussion started in the context of my talking about what it was like for *my* daughter to be that age. It was a huge challenge to write about Polanski. He was in the middle of making a movie version of *Death and the Maiden,* which happens to be based on the situation of people I actually know in South America. So I told him about that, and *that* caught his attention. Which is the point about such free association. I want him to know right away that this is not going to be a standard interview, that it can be as interesting as he wants to make it.

Do you tape your interviews?

Sometimes. Although when people ask to tape-record me, I tell them that it is okay, as long as they don't quote me *verbatim.* I tend not to use tape recorders, and when I *do* use them, I am certainly not religious about the transcripts. I use them as an *aide-mémoire,* perhaps.

But isn't the point of using a tape recorder to record the exact words a subject uses?

Actually, the tape recorder *falsifies* the situation in two ways. First of all its presence falsifies the encounter. As any writer knows, the moment you turn the tape recorder off you get all the *really good* stuff. And that is even true in those cases where it seems that it no longer matters, that the person is completely relaxed about the thing's presence.

The second way in which a tape recorder falsifies the record is that the transcript is an entirely false record of what has taken place between a subject and a journalist. For what is actually taking place is a *series* of communication events, which really makes it a *symphonic* interaction. These include your expression, my response to your expression (seeing you are bored, interested, excited), my voice going up, my voice going down, your voice going up, your voice going down . . . And *none* of that is conveyed in the flat transcript. The words themselves don't approximate what actually took place *between* us. Phrased differently, what took place between us was a *narrative*, a story, and a transcript is not a story.

But doesn't a transcript still give you a fairly accurate sense of what took place during one of these communication events?

Well, that is like saying you can look at someone's medical chart and have a sense of how they are. No, by looking at a medical chart you learn a lot of abstract information about them, but you don't know *how they are*. The real challenge in writing is to re-create the life of the situation.

I can make two statements, one of which will probably get me in a lot of trouble with the Columbia Journalism School purists. First, I have *never* had a quote challenged. Second, I have *never* quoted any of my subjects verbatim, or at any rate never made a point of doing so.

The challenge is to record as fairly as possible what people *meant* to say, what people even *remember* having said—which is almost invariably not what they said! What they said is almost invariably not what they *meant* to say!

For starters, what they said is out of grammatical order. It's filled with half-thoughts, stops and starts, "um"s and "er"s, pauses and garbled sentences. That is how we *all* talk.

A lot of your interview subjects are quite reticent. How do you convince them to give you so much time?

I take what I can get at first, and by the end they usually want to give me more. They realize that it is fun. They think the interview is going to be the standard interview, and when they realize it isn't going to be, they loosen up. I have no hesitation about saying, "Oh, you're going to the movies? Can I come along? Let's go together." Or: "I'm going to this art show. Want to come along?"

Do you prepare written questions for interviews?

Occasionally. But it isn't a map for what will happen. It is more like a painter planning the canvas: you know that *eventually* you want to have a house over here on this side, three palm trees over here, etc. So I come to an interview with a scene in mind, or a few topics I want to cover. By the end of our time together I want to make sure that I've laid in these palm trees. It doesn't matter when I plant them as long as they get planted.

Do you ever stage scenes? For example, would you invite Boggs, the artist who draws money, on a trip to the mint?

Sure. And beyond that, I notice how whatever does happen can be *turned into* a scene. So whether or not you go with Boggs to the mint, it turns out that Boggs in front of the candy machine is a scene, too.

Do you observe any rules or guidelines for constructing scenes?

There is Flaubert's rule that you need three particular things in the room for the room to become three-dimensional in the reader's mind. So that if we establish this box of Kleenex, that bottle, and that lamp—not in one sentence, but over a few paragraphs—the room will pop into three-dimensional space. And you can have people move around convincingly. "He reached to the left of the box . . . He moved across from the lamp."

It is very important that conversations take place in *places*. That they *take place*. This is another problem with the traditional, pyramid-style journalism that uses free-floating quotes that just kind of hang there. They pop out of nowhere.

Given that you spend so much time talking to your subjects in so many different places, how do you keep all this information straight?

I'm going to say another thing that may scandalize the Columbia Journalism School purists. My warrant is that *every single place* I describe as having been at with somebody, we were at. And that *every single thing* I quote them as saying is the sort of thing they said. I just don't promise you that they said it at that exact place.

But this is true to life, isn't it? For example, if I talked to your class about a particular topic, and we then continued that conversation together at a coffee house afterward, I wouldn't object if you quoted my thoughts on that topic as being uttered in one or the other location. That in fact is true to life. If I were to say right now, "Remember that thing I said to your class?" I wouldn't want you to write, "He was talking about such and such a topic, which he first addressed to a class, and then repeated to me later in such and such a place." The funny thing is when the subject of one of my profiles reads his quotes later, he almost always remembers its having happened the way I've written it!

Will you negotiate about what is on or off the record?

I'll do whatever works. In the case of most of my profiles, I have the subject read it before it is published. I don't guarantee I'll change anything, but I want their feedback. And I want the subject to know that this is what I *wrote*, as opposed to what may later get *published* in a magazine.

Are there any places you particularly like or dislike doing interviews?

It is different with different people. I loved doing art walks when I was writing about David Hockney. I go for lots of walks in the park with subjects when I'm writing in a repressive situation that makes interviewing someone at his home too risky.

Do you adopt any particular persona during an interview?

I'm the well-meaning, intelligent, playful reporter. It is the voice of naive curiosity. I always admit that I am, at some level, a fraud: I'm an interloper wherever I am. I'm *not* an authority on Bosnia, I'm *not* an authority on the art world. I'm a person of reasonable intelligence trying to make sense of something.

There is an extraordinary moment in *A Miracle, A Universe*, during an interview with a Uruguayan general named Hugo Medina. He admits having tortured people, or having knowledge of torture, although he uses the euphemism of interrogating someone "energetically." You write, "He was silent for a

moment, his smile steady. For him, this was clearly a game of cat and mouse. His smile horrified me, but presently I realized that I'd begun smiling back . . . He swallowed me whole." Do you ever confront subjects with their lies?

The interview had reached a crisis, and unless I had smiled, it would have been over. But in the end *I* swallowed *him* whole: I wrote the piece.

I'm not generally a confrontational reporter. I'm even willing to engage the humanity of a scamp. General Medina was a very complicated character. He's no simple monster. He was actually something of a hero; he was the military man who led the transition back to a sort of democracy. Your writing needs to be as complicated as the situation you are writing about.

How do you know when you've done enough interviews?

Well, first of all there is that moment I described earlier when I know I have to leave or my 95 percent certainty will fall apart. Second, it is when I anticipate their answers to the questions I'm asking.

Once you've done your research and reporting, how do you begin to write?

I sit down with my notebooks, which are narrow, spiral pads. I go through them with a red felt-tipped pen, underlining the things I think I want to use. I then take out a pile of blank sheets of paper and I start to index all my notes.

Why index them?

Well, the organizing principle is, "How would I find this piece of information or quote if I want to use it later on?" I don't want to be stuck when I'm writing the piece because I can't find a certain crucial piece of information.

I start with Roman numeral one, page one, and record whatever happens to be on that page. The index will run for pages and pages—the Breytenbach index ran to over three hundred pages—all of which I put into a loose-leaf notebook.

Is your index as detailed as the index at the back of a book?

More so. I'll have a heading of "Bosnia," and then subheadings: "Serb-Muslim relations," "Drunk on History" . . . It gets very detailed. It is generally the case that if you pick a random sentence from any one of my books and ask me where it is in my notes, I can go back to my file and find it for you in two minutes.

I also make a separate index of my note*books:* "Notebook number one has the following topics in it . . . Notebook number one has the following interviewees in it . . ."And I make a list I call "Nifty Riffs," of things I want to make *sure* I include in the piece. That can run to five or six pages as well.

You do this on a computer, right?

No, I do it all by hand, which I don't recommend. It is a *totally* insane process that takes weeks and weeks. It is *stupefyingly* boring. And by the end two things have happened. First, I know the material by heart. And second, the information bores me silly. I'm bored with the material in a way that I will never stop being bored with it. I'll never be interested in the material in the way I was when I was coming up with it.

At that point I have what I call "Double South Pole Writer's Block," which is a situation when my eyes are magnetized south, and the blank page is magnetized south, and *everything else in the universe* is magnetized north. I find myself wondering things like, "*Gosh,* videotape cassettes! How *do* they work?" I am *physically* unable to sit still in the chair, I can't focus on anything. This goes on for weeks.

How do you get out of this state?

The most important thing is to not allow myself to hate myself. When I first started journalism, I just *despised* myself during these periods. I'd think, "I'm lazy, I'm a fuckup, I'm an evil person. Other people are working and I'm doing nothing." It is very important to teach yourself that this malaise is *part* of the process.

Having said that, it doesn't mean you won't panic anyway. And it may well be that the panic turns out to be part of what gets you going again later on. You can't *completely* help hating yourself, I've found. But if you can't get over that self-loathing at all, it is best to stop being a writer. Because nothing is worth that kind of self-hatred.

Are there any activities that help at this point?

Two things. One is that I read a lot of novels. Writers like Larry McMurtry and Walter Mosley are especially good. I'm sort of like a bicyclist riding behind a truck: I want to get into the "slipstream" of that other narrator's narrative. To get the feel of narrative, to be on the road, to remember what it feels like to tell a story.

The second thing I do is play with blocks. I have a very large collection of wooden blocks. Some of them are of my own invention, and some of them are just rectangular.

These blocks belong to your daughter?

No, my daughter is not allowed to play with these blocks. They are *mine*.

And what do you do with these blocks?

Well, my wife, who is an important human rights monitor, and my daughter, who has been off at school, will come home and see the elaborate cathedral I've built on the kitchen table. And they'll say, "We see *you've* been very busy today." And I have! Because although I'm not thinking about the material *at all*, I *am* thinking about structure and rhythm.

My thinking about narrative is essentially musical. What music and narrative have in common is a sequential exposition of material across time in a formful manner. My composer grandfather notwithstanding, I am myself completely musically illiterate. But I use a lot of musical terms when I edit. I'll say, "This is badly syncopated. How about a rest here? This paragraph should be in a minor key. This sentence crescendos three beats too early."

I think a lot about where paragraphs break. And about the play between long sentences and short sentences. That is very important to me. So when editors come along and chop one of my long, archy, curving sentences up it fucks up everything.

As much as I'm interested in the structure of a piece, in the end I want it to have "organic" form. The way a tree is formed by the sap flowing through it. Because the narrative is a story about human beings. Anyway, the blocks, too, are about the sequential exposition of material—across space, if not time. And as with music, in an architectonic manner.

And how do these block structures get translated into writing?

I'll be playing with my blocks and find myself thinking, "Hmm, I suppose if I put this part of the story in *front* of that rather than after it . . . *That* might be interesting." And gradually I start to find formal issues of sequencing. Then I start to notice rhymes that I hadn't noticed before.

For instance, when I was writing about Breytenbach there was a key moment in his story when he is being arrested at the airport and passes by a window in which he sees himself. I thought about what it might have been like to see himself at that moment. And then I remembered that in one of his poems he had a line about "South Africa is like the mirror at midnight when you looked in it and a train whistle blew in the distance, and your face was frozen there for all eternity, a horrible face but one's own." And I thought, hmm, if I put *that* quote next to *that* scene . . .

Now *this* gets really interesting! *This* is fun! And at a certain point everything flips around: I'm suddenly magnetized north rather than south, and everything else in the universe except the blank paper before me is north. I'm at my desk, and wouldn't even notice if the house was burning down around me. And yet, I'm not interested in the material, I'm interested in the *form*. And the thing that is *totally* mind-blowing is that elements I put side by side for purely formal reasons turn out to be true about the real world. And this is because beauty is truth, and truth is beauty. It is the same kind of satisfaction that a mathematician gets out of an elegant proof.

Do you make an outline?

I tape large one-by-three-foot blank sheets together to create a kind of a blotter. I doodle and sketch a lot on the blotter. I make little diagrams to connect things. The point is to lay out and visualize the structures I've been thinking through when I was playing with the blocks. But that is generally speaking as specific as it gets.

Is that when you start writing?

Yes. I spend an enormous amount of time on my first paragraphs. I only recently realized this, but I almost always tell the entire story in the first paragraph. For instance, the Breytenbach piece starts with such a long sentence that *The New Yorker* cut it to shreds when they published it.

And once you've finished the first paragraph?

At that point I write fast. I'm often told that my work even *reads* fast. It *used* to be that I wrote FD=FC (first draft equals final copy), but I don't do that anymore. I always tell my students that great line, "Revision isn't cleaning up after the party, revision *is* the party." Although in my case I do most of the revision in my head before I start writing.

I tend to write longhand and then transfer it to the computer. I may eventually continue writing on the computer, but in the beginning there is a physical connection between voice and writing by hand. It is the same as singing, in that voice is always the result of form and structure. Indeed, tone or voice is what you get when, larynxlike, you breathe through structure.

Is there any particular *place* you need to be in order to write?

Not so much a particular place, as at a particular *time*. I go into a different time zone from my family. There are all these distractions during the day, and I tend to start writing at around eleven p.m. I'm very tired when I start, but I get a second wind and write until four or five in the morning. Then sleep late, am groggy all day, and then go through the process again. I'll in effect be "gone" for two weeks. Then I come out the other end.

And you repeat this sequence every day until you finish?

Yes. On any given early morning, I try to stop before the end of a section. I like to leave myself with two more paragraphs that I *know* how to write so that I have something easy to do the next evening. That helps me get going again. And I often start each new session by reading from the beginning.

Has writing gotten easier over the years?

No. Every time is like the first time. All the secrets I'm telling you I forget *completely*!

Do you show other people your work-in-progress?

I show stuff to my wife. I'm not at all secretive. In fact, I tell the story over and over again. And my wife goes comatose with boredom at dinner parties because she's heard the story twenty times before.

Are you ever worried you'll become bored by the material by talking about it so much?

No, because each time I tell it I'm trying out different cadences and rhetorical strategies. I watch the eyes of the people I'm telling it to so that I can see which sections are most interesting to them. I slow down and speed up according to what their eyes tell me.

Where did you learn to be a reporter?

I had a wonderful education at UC Santa Cruz during its glory days. My teachers taught me how to ask questions. And not only how to ask questions, but also the glory of the questioning stance.

Incidentally, out of two hundred students in my graduating class at Cowell College, of UCSC, two others—Bill Finnegan and Noelle Oxenhandler—also became *New Yorker* writers.

You have a very recognizable writing voice. Playful, casual, curious. What writers have influenced you?

I admire Joseph Mitchell enormously, as well as Trillin, McPhee, Ian Frazier, and Susan Sheehan.

How would you describe the project that is common to these writers?

Well, the class I teach is called "The Fiction of Nonfiction." The whole premise is that every narrative voice—but especially every nonfiction voice—is itself a fiction, and the world of writing and reading is divided between those who know this and those who either don't or else deny it, which is roughly contiguous with the division between writing that is worth reading and writing that's not. It is in stories, in the flow of narrative, somehow, that we are, as Auden puts it, "entired," that we overcome our sense of exile.

Do you think this kind of writing can yield truth?

I am interested in the fictive elements of nonfiction writing. I take for *granted*, not so much objective truth (which, of course, doesn't exist), but things like fairness, accuracy, and reportorial rigor. But that's just the beginning. What's *really* interesting to me is irony, voice, freedom, form—all things that are literally *made up*. So I believe that writing can lead to provisional truth, *human* truth.

What do you call this tradition?

Well, I don't like the terms "creative nonfiction" (I don't know what that means) or "literary nonfiction." I call it "writerly nonfiction." Which is to say, writing as if reading mattered and reading as if writing mattered. It is individual, personal, provisional grappling with the sort of themes that start out looking little and become big. That start out seeming inconsequential and end up being about the most important thing in the world. And are carried along by voice, love of language, and love of structure.

What are the prospects for writerly nonfiction?

Not good. I tell my students, "Nothing in this class will be of the slightest practical value to you. It's *over*. And it's *worse* than that because by the time I finish with you this is *all* you'll want to do. But it's over." And they all laugh, and I say, "You're laughing now, but I guarantee that before the semester finishes four or five of you will be in my office crying hot tears because this is all you want to do."

Having said that, I am still trying to "save civilization," twelve people at a time. As Ian Frazier does in his world and Bill Finnegan does in his world. We do it through our writing and through our teaching. We insist that even though it's over, it *can't possibly* be over, because it is too important. There is a hankering that is out there. It is the hankering not to be addressed as a Pavlovian dog, which is what everything in this culture tries to enforce upon us. And this is especially true of media culture. The task of writing is a "high" task. It is bearing witness, attending to the world.

Writers have a moral duty to be witnesses to violence, to be stewards of the planet, to be concerned about global warming, about Afghani rape, etc. But what they have a *unique* responsibility to is to human storytelling. To the ethical importance of addressing you as a quirky individual, and not as a consumer.

You can do this through books, but they are read by only ten thousand people and I'm not interested in that. I'm interested in general interest magazines that are potentially exposed to hundreds of thousands of people. And that sort of venue for this sort of address may disappear in our time.

Do you detect any hopeful signs?

There is *McSweeney's,* for example, which is evidence that there is a huge potential readership, in that case largely made up of twenty-five-year-olds, the ones who everyone says don't know how to read, the ones with no attention span! So the challenge is to create more magazines like that, and to make this rebirth happen. Which is what I'm trying to do.

BY LAWRENCE WESCHLER:

Vermeer in Bosnia: Cultural Comedies and Political Tragedies, Pantheon, 2004
Robert Irwin: Getty Garden, Getty Publications, 2001
Boggs: A Comedy of Values, University of Chicago Press, 1999
Calamities of Exile: Three Nonfiction Novellas, University of Chicago Press, 1998
A Wanderer in the Perfect City: Selected Passion Pieces, Ruminator Books, 1998
Mr. Wilson's Cabinet of Wonder, Pantheon Books, 1995
A Miracle, A Universe: Settling Accounts With Torturers, Pantheon Books, 1990
Shapinsky's Karma, Boggs's Bills, and Other True-Life Tales, North Point Press/FSG, 1988
David Hockney's Cameraworks, Knopf, 1984
The Passion of Poland: From Solidarity Through the State of War, Pantheon Books, 1984
Solidarity: Poland in the Season of Its Passion, Simon & Schuster, 1982
Seeing Is Forgetting the Name of the Thing One Sees: A Biography of California Artist Robert Irwin, University of California Press, 1982

LAWRENCE WRIGHT

Many journalists felt a new sense of professional relevance after the September 11, 2001, terrorist attacks, none more so than Lawrence Wright. Wright lived in Cairo from 1969 to 1971, speaks some Arabic, and has spent much of his career writing about the vicissitudes of religious faith. Watching the attacks on television, Wright hoped that it wasn't a Middle East terrorist strike. "I was nagged by the likelihood that a culture I was very fond of had declared war on a culture that I was a part of," he says. Wright is currently working on a book that many believe will be the most comprehensive account of the events leading up to that day. "I felt I was born to write this book."

Wright's advantage over others covering the story lies in his familiarity with Arabic culture and language, but also in his sensitivity to the role of belief in everyday life. "Spiritual matters are far more influential in people's lives than, for instance, politics, the mainstay of the journalist's craft," he writes in the preface to *Saints & Sinners* (1993). For Wright, religion isn't an oddity or irrational sentiment, but a subterranean force that informs and pervades all our actions. He likens religion to a subway system: "Aboveground, people go about their business, perhaps unaware of the intricate commotion going on in the world below their feet." Extending the metaphor, one might conceive of Wright's journalistic terrain as a map of the system, charting the twists, turns, and intersections of the various lines ("the Jewish line, the Catholic, the Muslim, to name a few of the multiple possibilities") running beneath our ostensibly secular world.

Lawrence George Wright was born in Oklahoma City on August 2, 1947. He was raised in Dallas, Texas, where his father was the chairman of Lakewood Bank & Trust. Once a week, Wright's mother, a voracious reader, would escort her three sons to the public library to select books to read. All three grew up to be writers.

At Tulane University, Wright got to know Walker Percy, the writer whose novels (*The Moviegoer, Love Among the Ruins*) are extended meditations on philosophy and religious belief. "He demystified the writing thing for me," he says. Wright was graduated in 1969 and nearly enlisted in the Marines before applying for conscientious-objector status. Instead of going to Vietnam, Wright spent the next year in Cairo, teaching English and studying Arabic. Life was difficult for an American in Egypt during that period, but Wright and his wife made many Egyptian friends and developed lifelong passions for the region.

Wright's first job in journalism was as a reporter for the *Race Relations Reporter* in Nashville, Tennessee, in 1971. In 1972, he worked for *Southern Voices*, a publication of the Southern Regional Council in Atlanta, Georgia, and began freelancing for national magazines.

His first book, *City Children, Country Summer* (1979), chronicled a summer with the Fresh Air Fund, an organization that sends inner-city children to live with farm families. In 1980, Wright's work attracted the attention of William Broyles, the editor of *Texas Monthly*. He moved to Austin in 1980 to work for the magazine, and became a contributor to *Rolling Stone*. Between them, the two magazines published most of the profiles of religious figures (Walker Railey, Jimmy Swaggart, Madalyn Murray O'Hair, Anton LaVey, Will Campbell, and Matthew Fox) Wright collected in *Saints & Sinners*. Harvard religious scholar Harvey Cox called it "a nuanced, finely written and immensely insightful book which may tell us more about American religion and culture than any single volume I've picked up in a long time."

Wright's second book was a memoir of growing up in Dallas at the time of the Kennedy assassination, through the Vietnam War, up to the renomination of Ronald Reagan at the 1984 Republican convention. *In the New World: Growing Up with America, 1960–1984* (1988) avoided the solipsism of most memoirs, placing the author's life in the context of his times, rather than the other way around. He describes the book as "the story of an extraordinary generation as witnessed by one rather ordinary member of it." Writing in *The New York Times Book Review*, Steven D. Stark called it "*The Sorrows of Young Werther* circa 1988 in the Sun Belt," and judged that it "succeeds in capturing the times in ways other works of prose have not." The *Times*'s daily critic, Christopher Lehman-Haupt, agreed: "Even on the most hackneyed subjects he offers fresh angles of vision."

In 1992, Wright became a staff writer for *The New Yorker*, where he published his most famous piece, "Remembering Satan" [May 17–24, 1993], the story of Paul Ingram, the chief civil deputy of the Thurston County sheriff's department in Washington state, who was charged with sexually abusing his two daughters. Ingram couldn't remember any abuse, but didn't deny the charges. "There must be a dark side of me that I don't know about," he said as he tried to summon up the repressed memories of his acts. Encouraged by the police and a psychologist, Ingram began producing detailed memories of sexual abuse. Eventually an authority on cults and mind control concluded that Ingram had fabricated his confession and wasn't guilty of anything other than eagerness to please authorities. But when Ingram filed a motion to withdraw his guilty plea it was too late to stop the legal process. He was sentenced to twenty years in prison. "Whatever the value of repression as a scientific concept or a therapeutic tool, unquestioned belief in it has become as dangerous as the belief in witches," Wright writes. "One idea is modern and the other an artifact of what we like to think of as a credulous age, but the consequences are depressingly the same."

The story, which won the National Magazine Award for reporting, as well as the John Bartlow Martin Award for Public Interest Magazine Journalism, became a cautionary tale about the dangers of the widely discredited "recovered memory" movement. "Mr. Wright has taken a sensationalistic story, the sort of story routinely embraced by supermarket tabloids, and turned it into a thoughtful and gripping book," writes Michiko Kakutani in *The New York Times*.

Wright's first post–September 11 piece for *The New Yorker* was about FBI agent John O'Neill, whose obsession with the al Qaeda terrorist network, and frustrations with the agency's inability to pursue Osama bin Laden, led him to resign from the agency and take a job as the chief of security for the World Trade Center, where he died. "The Counter-Terrorist" [*The New Yorker*, January 14, 2002] is currently being made into an MGM movie, for which

Wright is writing the screenplay. In an odd twist of fate, Wright's first movie, *The Siege,* about an Arab terrorist cell in New York, was one of the most rented videos in the weeks after September 11. "There was this haunting feeling at the beginning of the attacks that this looks like a movie," Wright remembers. "And then I thought: '*It looks like my movie,*'" he says.

His next two *New Yorker* pieces reintroduced him to the Middle East. "The Man Behind bin Laden" [September 16, 2002], Wright's profile of Dr. Ayman al-Zawahiri, took him to Cairo, where he traced the origins of al Qaeda and its terrorist ideology. In the spring of 2003, after lobbying Saudi diplomats for a year for a journalist's visa (the kingdom is famously selective about who is allowed to travel there), Wright got a three-month job training young Saudi reporters at the *Saudi Gazette,* an English-language daily newspaper in Jeddah. "The Kingdom of Silence" [*The New Yorker,* January 5, 2004] paints an ominous picture of a socially repressed and psychologically depressed culture. "I had begun to look at Saudi society as a collection of opposing forces: the liberals against the religious conservatives, the royal family versus democratic reform-ers, the unemployed against the expats, the old against the young, men against women. The question is whether the anger that results from all this conflict will be directed outward, at the West, or inward, at the Saudi regime."

What kinds of subjects are you drawn to?

I'm interested in why people believe what they believe. America has a huge supermarket of beliefs to choose from. It's liberating, but there's also a terrifically dangerous quality to it. The times when people are led into trouble—via political or religious movements—they're *always* animated by strong beliefs.

Yet reporters rarely take beliefs seriously. The status of a religion reporter at a newspaper is comparable to that of an obituary writer's. Reporters are skeptics, so the whole idea of belief is a little repug-nant to them. When they are confronted with someone who is *gen-uinely* captivated by belief, reporters take pity on them by *not* writing about their beliefs.

What elements do you look for in a story?

I like stories that are keyholes into a huge room. At first my stories often seem very small and confined. But when you put your eye down and look through it, it is a *tiny* window on an *enormous* universe.

A lot of your stories take place in the Middle East. Are you more drawn to stories in certain parts of the world than others?

I was a conscientious objector during the Vietnam War and my alternative service was teaching at American University in Cairo. I formed deep ties in Egypt and, given my interest in faith and belief, I've remained intrigued by that part of the world. After all, it is the homeland of religious extremism of all kinds.

How do you get story ideas?

I often stumble onto them. At the outset, my stories may not seem to be about belief. But once I get going, that is the angle I tend to pursue.

For example, in 1991 my therapist told me about the plague of multiple personality disorders (MPD). Both he and his wife, who is also a therapist, were treating a number of young women with MPD. And when they started probing it, they almost always uncovered memories of satanic abuse in the woman's childhood. The scale of what he described was astounding. He said that Satanists in Austin, Texas, alone were responsible for fifty murders a year—a figure that actually *exceeded* Austin's *total* murder rate! I thought, "What's going on here?"

That's fascinating information, but how did you develop it into a story?

I started reporting. I attended a workshop at which a policeman claimed that Satanists were responsible for fifty thousand murders a year in the U.S.—a figure which exceeded the entire *national* murder rate. And this guy was a well-respected cop!

That's when I knew there was a story there: a story about believers and those who believed them. I went to Tina Brown, then editor of *The New Yorker,* and told her I wanted to write about MPD. She wasn't that interested until I told her that most people with MPD claimed to have been victims of satanic abuse. *That* got her excited.

Okay, you've got a story idea and an assignment. How do you go about finding a particular story, such as the one that became Remembering Satan?

I wanted a story that would encompass both the satanic abuse and MPD. So I did a Nexis search and found over a thousand reported cases nationally. I read the articles and started calling the lawyers, victims, or other people who were involved.

The only case in which someone had actually been tried and convicted was Paul Ingram's. He was a fundamentalist Christian and the deputy sheriff of a small town in Washington state, and had *confessed* to committing these crimes. I figured that if there was ever a test case to see whether satanic ritual abuse existed, *this* was it.

Is this instance typical of the way you find stories?

Not necessarily. I also keep large files full of clippings on stories I'd one day like to write. For instance, this morning's *Times* has a story about an Israeli boy who was killed in a suicide bombing whose parents donated his kidneys to a seven-year-old Palestinian girl. This isn't the first time something like this has happened. I got interested in this kidney story when I was in Cairo and Jerusalem on a USIA tour in 1997. I was debating an Israeli Arab, who is now a member of the Knesset, who later had a kidney replaced and is now promoting an organ bank for this kind of exchange.

Why are you interested in a story about kidney transplants?

Again, it's a story about belief. Both communities—Orthodox Jews and Muslims—frown upon organ transplants because they're not religiously sanctified. But if *your* daughter is dying of kidney failure, you make a choice between your religious beliefs and your love for your child. It is an existential crisis. I'd like to write about this because this is a transgression of faith, and it's also one way "enemy" peoples are struggling toward peace. The ideal would be to follow one Israeli kidney and one Muslim kidney.

Do you report international stories differently from the way you report domestic ones?

I try not to. Writers are often misled by the exoticness of foreign places. Their perceptions are distorted by it. As a result, they don't consider the people they meet there as truly human in an everyday sense they would ascribe to people "back home." So when I'm reporting an international story I do my best to strip away the exotic veneer of the place in order to write about my characters in a fashion that is recognizable in *any* context. Then, once I've established their everyday humanity, I can get at the *truly* exotic dimension of the story.

But don't you run the risk of diminishing the genuine "foreignness" of these characters?

There is a real tension. On the one hand, we *over*estimate the exoticness of a foreign culture. On the other hand, we fail to grasp the *profound* differences between cultures—differences which are sometimes so alienating that two people from different cultures can't really see each other at first. So I try to strip away those *superficial* differences, the obvious cultural things, and render the character recognizable, human, and sympathetic in his own terms. Once I've done that I can explore the kinds of differences that are unique to him.

For instance, I wrote a novel about Manuel Noriega [*God's Favorite*, 2000] and his search for love and salvation. What drew me to him was the fact that he was a Buddhist, vegetarian, bisexual, Central American dictator. But before I could get to those topics, I had to demystify his Central Americanness, because Americans are reluctant to read about Latin Americans. Noriega's cultural exoticness was only window dressing. It was his interior life that was *truly* exotic.

How many projects do you juggle at a time?

I prefer writing one thing at a time, although I'll occasionally divide my day between two projects. One might be an article, while the other might be a screenplay or a book. I'm fortunate at the moment because I'm working on a screenplay about John O'Neill, whom I wrote about in *The New Yorker* ["The Counter-Terrorist," January 14, 2002]. At the same time, I'm writing a book about the events that led to the tragedy of September 11. What I learn from writing the screen-play will enrich the book, and vice versa.

You write articles, screenplays, and novels. How do you decide through which genre to pursue a story?

Usually when an idea comes to me it is *already* in a particular form. It is pretty intuitive, although I got the Noriega idea completely wrong. It started out as a two-man play, a dialogue between Noriega and the papal nuncio who gave him asylum when the U.S. invaded Panama. It seemed perfect in Greek dramatic terms: the wickedest man in the world talking with the Pope's official representative—all this while the American army blasted rock music outside. But the play didn't work. I couldn't get the nuncio to shut up, and I couldn't get Noriega to say a word!

So I decided to write a screenplay about it. I had a *blast,* and the screenplay just roared out of me. Oliver Stone was going to make it. He cast Al Pacino as Noriega and Jennifer Lopez as his girlfriend. Then the whole thing fell apart, as movies so often do. So I wrote it as a novel. The experience taught me that my intuition isn't infalli-ble. [The movie was eventually made for Showtime, starring Bob Hoskins.]

Let's talk about research. Some writers say that they don't want to start a story knowing too much for fear that all this information will dull their own impressions. Do you agree?

I've never understood that philosophy. What are you adding to the world of knowledge if you simply give the reader your impressions? They are bound to be superficial. They might be brilliant and insightful if you are a brilliant and insightful person. But I believe they'd be *even more* brilliant and insightful if you really *worked* at understanding your subject by doing a lot of research.

Do you have a research routine?

Yes, I have one I swear by. The first thing I do is a Nexis search, and then I read everything I can on the subject. As I read, I make a list of the people in the clips I'd like to talk to.

For instance, here is the list I made for the John O'Neill story.

[Wright takes out a worn, yellow legal pad, thick with line after line of names, telephone numbers, e-mail addresses, and brief identifying comments.] These are the names of the people at his funeral, here are his colleagues, his girlfriend, his ex-wife. The contact information will eventually become very important to the fact-checkers. As the list grows, I highlight the names of those I've gotten hold of.

At the end of each interview I always ask whom else should I speak to. Or ask for help with contacting other people I know about, but don't have numbers for. I'm mapping the universe of those who know the person I'm writing about.

How long are these lists?

They can be anywhere from fifteen to twenty single-spaced pages and contain hundreds of names.

What other kinds of research do you do?

I read a lot of books. Here are the books I'm using for my 9/11 project. [Wright gestures to three six-foot-long shelves of books.] As I read them I highlight certain passages. Then I have an assistant write down each quote on an index card and note where it came from.

Okay, now that you've got an idea, an assignment, and have done some research, how do you start the interview process?

I usually start by asking someone how he knows the person I'm writing about. The goal of my first interview is to establish a relationship, not squeeze anything out of him. I don't want to scare him off.

How much time do you like to spend with the people you interview?

When I find a *really* good source—somebody who is close to the subject, and is both authoritative and interesting—I'll interview him dozens of times. Although I don't expect instant information, I want to establish a few things immediately. I want my source to know that I am going to write this article, that I want it to be right, and, since he is the authority, that I need his help.

How do you get people to give you such enormous access?

I let them know that I've spent a tremendous amount of time preparing and that I take this subject extremely seriously. People are naturally interested in talking about themselves and their pursuits, and if you can convince them of the genuineness of your interest, it's a rare person who doesn't want to satisfy your curiosity.

I don't want to overwhelm them, but it is helpful to tell them straightaway about the kind of commitment I'll need from them. I say, "There are a lot of things I don't know yet, and I'd like to talk to you about this topic. You're an authority and I hope you won't mind if I come back in the future with more specific, informed questions. In fact, I'd like to have a series of long interviews over a period of time. Then, when I'm writing the piece, I will be back in touch to ask you some very short, pointed questions. And finally, a fact-checker will call you to make sure I haven't made any egregious errors, and I hope you'll extend the same courtesy to him."

Do people ever balk at the amount of time you request?

Sure, sometimes they get a little fed up. Talking to me is a little like going to a doctor. I've imposed a regimen on them and I know what's best for the story. But they may not want to go to the doctor every day of the week. I can tell by their voice when they're getting tired, and I give them a few days off. I try not to be frivolous with their time.

Once you've got access, how do you get people to open up to you?

One way I get them to talk is to show them the lengthy list of the other people I've talked to. Even hardened FBI agents get wide-eyed when they see how many names are there. They think, "Shit, he's talked to *everybody*!" It softens them up a little. First, because they respect me for the effort I've made. And, second, they feel it's pointless to hide anything from me, because somebody else is going to tell me anyway. It's a visual aid that lets people know I'm on the case, and that I'm not likely to be shaken off it.

Do you prefer approaching someone directly or via an acquaintance?

It's not always necessary to go through someone, but in the claustrophobic world I've been working in recently—Islamists and FBI agents—an introduction really helps. Having an intermediary speak on your behalf is key in the Arab world.

For instance, the first time I met al-Zawahiri's uncle Mahfouz Azzam, he was cold, dismissive, and even a little angry. I really needed his help on the story, so his reluctance to talk openly with me was a problem. In the meantime, I interviewed and established a good rapport with someone who turned out to be a friend of his. I told my new source that I felt bad because I had not made a good impression on the uncle, and this man offered to give him a call. Well, the next time I interviewed the uncle it was as if the gates of paradise had opened. He was welcoming and expansive.

How much do you reveal about yourself during an interview?

I always tell people what I'm working on. I don't like being the kind of reporter who curries favor with his subjects by inflating his own importance, although I will do it if it's useful. My goal is to be a receptive vessel into which they can pour their stories, and that's more likely to happen if I focus my attention entirely on them, rather than the other way round.

Where do you most and least like conducting interviews?

I like to see people where they work and live. It relaxes them because they feel they're masters of the situation. They don't feel defensive.

I don't like conducting interviews over dinner. It's awkward to eat while I'm writing and taping, and there are plates and glasses clanking. I don't like being exposed, with people gawking at us from other tables. But sometimes going out and getting somebody drunk is an absolute necessity.

Do you drink during these interviews as well?

Unfortunately, I do. I am *no way* a match for these FBI guys! But it does facilitate the flow of information, and it's a bonding experience.

Do you ever arrange scenes?

If it's productive, I'll do it. My main goal is to get the information. Sometimes you can get information outside of a person's office that you can't get when you're sitting there.

When I was reporting *Remembering Satan*, there was a fellow named Jim Rabie who had been accused of taking part in these absolutely bizarre rituals and child sacrifices as a member of a satanic ring. It had ruined his life. The community hated him, he'd been in jail for six months, he'd lost his job. He was desperate to prove his innocence and offered to take a lie detector test. And he failed it.

I don't put a lot of weight on lie detector tests, but I figured that from the reader's point of view, Rabie's failing the test would be a haunting question that I wouldn't be able to explain away. I realized I would have to give him another lie detector test and then live with the result. I arranged for the best polygraph person I could find to administer a new test. And he passed it this time. I had an obligation on behalf of the reader. As it turned out, the scene where he fails the test became a nice little dramatic point in the story, since it creates tension in the mind of the reader, who *wants* to believe that Rabie is innocent. Later, I was able to relieve that tension by having Rabie take the second test. Because the whole event was outside of the usual role of the reporter, I explained exactly what I did in an author's note.

Do you ever send questions ahead?

Occasionally. The last time I did was when I interviewed the president of the Mormon Church. His office insisted, but it was just a PR department gambit to pressure me. He didn't even look at them.

Do you do interviews by phone, mail, or e-mail? Or only in person?

I do a lot of my *corresponding* with sources via e-mail. It is an easy way to fire off queries to factual questions. Then I'll print out the e-mail correspondence and put it in my files. But I do major interviews face-to-face.

Do you tape your interviews or take notes?

Both. My note-taking skills aren't great. My handwritten notes are only an approximation of the interview.

Do you take notes in front of the people you're interviewing?

I prefer to, but I can't always. Sometimes people get intimidated. They are nervous about being identified and slow to trust outsiders. But the next time we meet, they are usually more relaxed about note-taking and tape recorders.

Do you use shorthand?

No, just sloppy quick notes. I can read my writing, but the fact-checkers often can't, which is another reason I tape. The fact-checkers, whom I love, spend hours and hours listening to my tapes. It's like having the KGB looking over your shoulder, but it can be very helpful.

Do you ask permission before you tape an interview?

Yes. Sometimes they simply blanch and tell me to put it away. Then I explain that I'm not a great note-taker, and that taping helps ensure accuracy. I explain that it is as much for *their* protection as it is for my convenience. However reluctant they are at first, once they've agreed to allow me to tape, they usually forget about the recorder's presence after five minutes.

Will you negotiate about what quotes and information can and can't be used?

Once in a while someone will ask me to turn off the tape in order to tell me something they don't want to be held responsible for. I'll do it and then write "NFA" (not for attribution) in my notes so I'll know it is "off the record." We then go back "on the record." I don't like doing that. I much prefer an interview to be entirely "on the record."

Do you allow your subjects to vet their quotes?

Because *The New Yorker* fact-checkers are going to go over the substance of their quotes with them anyway, I don't mind telling people what I'm going to say about them. I don't particularly like reading exact quotes back to a subject, but I sometimes do it in order to get more information out of him.

For instance, when I was working on a piece about Dr. Ayman al-Zawahiri ["The Man Behind bin Laden," *The New Yorker*, September 16, 2002], I would send small passages of the article-in-progress to members of his family—some of whom I had interviewed in Cairo, and some who had refused to talk to me. I'd simply ask whether I was accurate. Even if it made them mad, which it did on a couple of occasions, this would open them up and get more information out of them. My main interest is getting it right, so I'm happy to make changes if something is incorrect.

Do you transcribe the tapes?

If they're key interviews, I have the tapes transcribed by someone else. I used to do it myself, but they have become too voluminous. And keeping track of all those tapes is difficult. I've found these special plastic cases that hold four cassettes at a time. They are hard to find, but they enable me to line them up like you'd do with CDs, and keep an index of the interviews they hold on the spine of the case. It is much neater than having hundreds of loose cassettes in a box, the way I used to.

But if you both take notes and tape, how do you keep track of all your different sources of information?

On the left-hand column of the front page of every legal pad I take interview notes on, I create a rough index of whose interviews are located on that pad. I then have an assistant make colored tabs with the names of each person on them. I stick them on the side of the pages where their interviews occur so that I can find them readily. When you put the tablets on their sides, leaning against each other, it looks like a neat file.

Then on each tape I make a notation to tell me where I can find the corresponding interview notes. For instance, this interview with Azzam Tamimi is marked "23i," which means that it is the first tape on the twenty-third legal pad. And if I have more than one interview with Azzam Tamimi on the same legal pad, I would mark it "23ai," "23bi," and so on.

How do you know when you've interviewed enough people?

When I realize I know more than the people I'm interviewing. When they start interviewing *me* about the story—when *I'm* perceived as the "expert"—I know I've talked to enough people.

How do you organize this vast cache of research and report-ing material?

I take the notes from my research and create card files on each character, as well as subfiles on specific topics in his life. Eventually, if a character's file gets as big as, say, Osama bin Laden's here [the box is about three feet deep], it gets a box of its own. An individual file might contain twelve hundred cards, but they are broken down into manageable divisions.

I have files on Bush and Clinton under my "America" file. There's a general file on "Islam." I have the terrorists and hijackers filed alphabetically, starting with "Mohammed Atta." Then a big file on "al Qaeda," and subfiles on its presence in Algeria, Afghanistan, Iraq, Egypt, and so on.

Then, I go back through my interview notes and highlight the things that are the most important. I then take the highlighted infor-mation and transfer it to the note cards as well. These note cards then become the *final* resource I consult while writing. So when I'm writing about al-Zawahiri and his family, for instance, it's all right here—in a subsection under Zawahiri in my card file. And the other thing about making note cards like this is that as I'm reading and interviewing, finding out things, I am intuitively creating categories for the files. Okay, these categories are to some extent arbitrary, but you have to have *something*, you know—family, marriage, beliefs, those kinds of things—and those categories form an outline. Eventually, those are the things I'm going to write about, because those are the things I was interested in and found out about. It seems a more organic way of developing the information than beginning with an outline and trying to impose that structure on the material.

Another organizational tool I've developed for this 9/11 project is a color-coded, month-by-month timeline. It starts in 1992 because a lot of the things that culminated in 9/11 started then.

Why colors?

Because it is easier for my eye to follow a single thread of narra-tive. I've got Mohammed Atta in purple, the other hijackers in red, al-Zawahiri in blue, John O'Neill in green. Then I have the source (whether an interview or a publication) of the information listed next to the color.

For instance, what if I want to know where al-Zawahiri was in 1999? I just look for the blue marker, and when I find it, I consult the source of the information to see how credible it is. If the information comes from *The Wall Street Journal,* I know it's a fairly reliable public source. If it comes from the Internet, it's difficult to know whether it's true or not.

Given the sophisticated computer software at your disposal, why do all of this organization on paper?

I know I should have gotten to that point by now, but I just find that, in the end, I need everything on paper. People reading this will think I'm *insane* to put so much labor into organizing the material. But because I do, the actual writing goes very quickly. Everything's right at hand. I developed this method because I used to remember facts, but not where I'd learned them. That was a problem when I had to document the sources.

How long have you used this method?

I started using it for my book about growing up in Dallas [*In the New World: Growing Up with America, 1960–1984*]. It is, essentially, a history of this twenty-year period in America, and I drew on a lot of different material. My faith in the method increased when I was writing profiles of various religious leaders for *Saints & Sinners.*

For instance, it helped me when I wrote about Madalyn Murray O'Hair (America's foremost proponent of atheism). In my interviews with her and my research, I discovered that over the years she had claimed to have earned twenty-six different graduate degrees—in law, nursing, social work, etc.—from various institutions. I called each institution she mentioned and discovered that she didn't have *any* advanced degrees. My note card system was like a finely spun net I could pull through a mass of material. Then, when I hauled it on board, I had all those fish: ironclad proof that she had misrepresented herself for decades. She later sued me for $18 million, and I was real happy I had done my research so thoroughly.

*Okay, you're done with your research, interviewing, and orga-
nizing. How do you start writing?*

I make a rough, two-to-three-page outline and tack it up on the
wall over my desk. As I said, the headings and subheadings of my
note card files usually determine what goes into the outline. In the
case of the al-Zawahiri piece the outline is roughly chronological. I
start with the lead, and then move on to the "gospel graph."

What's a "gospel graph"?

It is the graph that tells the reader why he is reading the story. At
some magazines it is called the "nut graph."

Does the outline become more detailed as you write?

Yes, because the reporting doesn't stop once the writing begins. In
the past, one of my major mistakes was starting to write too soon. I
didn't really know what I was trying to say, and had to stop, go back
to my sources, and fill in the gaps. So even when I'm officially "writing," my day is probably divided evenly between writing and doing
additional interviewing.

*Do you try to write a piece from start to finish? Or do you
write isolated sections?*

I start at the beginning and try to go straight through to the end.

So you write section after section, day after day, until you finish?

No, I go back over what I've written. Almost everything can be
improved the next day. Sometimes, when I get to those sections that
seem like boilerplate, I'll deliberately write poorly and quickly, just to
force myself to make progress. Then I clean it up later.

At the end of each day I stop a *little* before I'm spent, just so I leave
myself something easy to write first thing the next morning. If I don't
know what I'm going to say tomorrow I don't stop. There's nothing
more confounding than confronting a knotted-up problem first thing
in the morning.

What do you do if you get knotted up during the day?

I sometimes go for a run because I find it mentally liberating.
Oftentimes I'll solve the problem that is frustrating me after only five

hundred yards. I get so many ideas when I run that I bring along notepaper and a pencil.

Do you spend a lot of time thinking about the structure of your pieces?

I tend to tell my stories in a linear, although not always chronological, fashion. When I'm putting a character on the stage, I make sure to spend some time fleshing him out, establishing him as a vivid presence in the reader's mind. I like to advance a character to a certain point, and then, at a moment of decision, I put him on hold. The tension this creates is pleasurable for the readers. And that pause allows me to double back and march the readers through all this essential information—information that might kill their interest if you started with it. But since they know you've got something good waiting for them down the road—the character's moment of decision—they'll dutifully read this stuff. *Then* you can resume the delicious business of bringing the character back to life and having him confront the situation.

Do you need to be in any particular place when you write?

Yes, I'm picky. I'm not one of those guys who can write in a coffee shop with people chatting all around him. Back in Texas, I have a nice office that's dark and quiet. I'm a birder and the only thing that distracts me are the birds in the trees outside the office window. I keep a pair of binoculars handy and always jump up and look at a magnolia warbler.

What does a perfect writing day look like?

I start my day with a cup of coffee and the newspaper. One of the reasons I like to write at home is that I want to start in a place that's real quiet and calm. When I'm working in *The New Yorker* offices I have to wait for the subway, jostle with people on the street. Things might happen along the way, and I don't want to see anything that's unsettling. I just want to begin as quietly as possible. I tend not to be very productive in the morning, so I get my e-mail interviewing out of the way in the morning. I don't start clicking until the afternoon, when I'm the most productive. Although my day lasts from nine to six, most of the words are produced in the last two or three hours.

How many drafts do you typically go through?

After I'm "done" with a piece I like to do a completely new second draft. When I finish a draft it has a kind of rigidity to it, a fixed rigor mortis. I need someone to come along with a sledgehammer and say, "This doesn't work. This belongs here. Your ending is obscure," etc. I'm grateful for these criticisms because I'm not able to loosen it up by myself. But when I get that criticism, everything loosens up and is moveable again, like an ice floe after a ship goes through it. That's when I like to rewrite the whole thing entirely.

Are there certain people you show your work-in-progress to?

I have a very dear friend in Texas named Stephen Harrigan, who also writes novels, screenplays, and magazine articles. We sometimes talk several times a day, whether it is to run a word by the other, or read a sentence, or set a scene.

How did you learn to be a reporter?

When I got back from Cairo in 1971, I got a job at the *Race Relations Reporter* in Nashville, Tennessee. I had no formal training and I'm a little embarrassed by my early stories. They were smart-ass and partisan, the kind of impressionistic journalism I was alluding to a moment ago.

The editor was this very difficult guy named Jim Leeson, who taught me the value of going deep into a story. I learned that if you were writing about conflict-ridden subjects, like race, it was important to be a calm center that people from both sides could vent to. I learned that a useful role for a reporter is just to be there and hear what people have to say.

How would you describe your reportorial persona?

I think of a reporter as a professional witness. His job is to report on conflict, and then to return to his community to tell them what is happening and what the community ought to do about it. But the default position for the reporter is usually impartial neutrality—at least for me.

There's an incredible moment in your profile of Walker Railey, the Methodist minister in Dallas who is suspected of killing his wife. You tell him, "I think you're guilty . . . Confess or it will haunt you forever, it will drive you crazy." That doesn't sound very impartial or neutral to me.

I just couldn't maintain a dispassionate stance with him. But I don't think a reporter *should* allow his humanity to be compromised. If you're in a situation that's fundamentally wrong you have to make a stand. Sure, you're a "witness," but you're also a representative of your community. You represent what the community wants to know, which means you sometimes have to abandon neutrality in order to elicit the response your reader is waiting to hear. In the case of Walter Railey, most people in Dallas knew, or believed, that he was guilty. By challenging him directly, I gave him an opportunity to respond to the question everyone wanted to ask.

Other than in your memoir, you rarely appear in your books. Why?

My first editor, Jim Leeson, pounded an ironclad rule into me: the reporter has no place being in his story. So when I wrote my autobiography, it was very charged for me to actually cross the line and enter the universe of "I," "me," and "mine." Plus, nobody had ever thought Dallas worth chronicling in a memoir. I never felt like I had the literary authority of someone growing up in Paris or even Brooklyn. Important and interesting people had passed through *those* places, but Dallas wasn't a place you could "come from," in a literary sense. I had a great deal of trouble granting myself the permission to write a memoir. But once I started it was incredibly energizing.

When I'm writing straight journalism, however, I don't put myself into the narrative unless there's a damn good reason. I want to enhance the reader's appreciation of the subject, and if being there helps accomplish that—or is impossible to avoid—then I'll do it.

For instance, in the piece about al-Zawahiri I have a scene in which I take a tour of the Cairo prison in which al-Zawahiri, and my guide, were once held. In that scene my guide has to be talking to *someone*, he has to be pointing things out to *someone*. I put myself in it because it would have been phony to try to hide myself.

According to *New Yorker* style, they prefer us to write, "he told me," rather than, "he said." The editors believe it makes the piece more authoritative. This drives me nuts because it feels like a mirror

454   THE NEW NEW JOURNALISM

in front of the reporter's face. To stand in front of the reader and say, "Look at me. I'm going to show you this. I'm going to take you by the hand"—that's insulting and it rarely leads the reader to trust the writer more than he would otherwise.

How do you conceive of your authorial presence?
For me the authorial presence is in my *voice*. That's how the reader knows me. When you're reading the work of a writer you admire, and you're wondering what it is that's holding your attention, it's usually the author's comforting and confidential voice inside your head.

Describe your writing voice.
I try to be companionable and firm. Sure, friendly, honest.

What writers have influenced your choice of voice?
I'm a big fan of John McPhee. He was very influential in drawing my attention to journalism as a literary calling. I adore A. J. Liebling. He is a good example of someone who really used his voice, which is so exuberant and playful. I wanted so much to write like him. In terms of pure style, Robert Penn Warren was a big influence. And he's interested in very similar subjects—power, spirituality, and belief. He's drawn to human darkness, and I am too.

Do you think a lot about the sound of words as you write?
Yes, I'm obsessive about grooming the sound of my prose. I like it when editors help me, when they say, "I notice you're doing a lot of word repetition here." I melt with gratitude. I spend a lot of time polishing.

Do you think about language differently, depending on whether you are writing nonfiction, fiction, or a screenplay?
One of the reasons I wanted to write a novel is that there are certain limitations on how far you can go with the prose when writing nonfiction, how far you can go into the character's mind. Fiction gives you license to go as far as you like.

Do you believe that journalism can lead to truth?
Truth is one of those subjective terms that are pointless to get too tied up about. "Truth" has this absolute quality, and yet everybody

hangs on to *his own* truth. A better word might be "understanding." The whole point of a reporter is to sympathize with different perspectives. But I don't think sympathy leads to truth.

For instance, in the recovered memory debate, there was more truth on the side of those who said, "This is an hysterical outbreak," than on the side of those who said, "No, these people are suffering from real memories and experiences." I felt obligated to report on what I believed, while trying to understand both camps.

Another example is the 9/11 book I'm working on. Three thousand people dead and two civilizations are locked in a violent conflict. Virtually everybody claims to have access to "the truth," and a number of them are even willing to die for it. I can't presume to say that my truth is any truer than their truth. But I *do* have a stance, and I *do* think that as a journalist I can help the reader understand the conflicting beliefs.

The problem I have with the word "truth" is that it sounds very simple. And when things get simple, they get dangerous—they don't get easier. We're sliding toward an era of radical simplicity: good versus evil, us versus them, etc. The reporter's job in such a situation is to complicate the issue because complexity leads to more understanding whereas simplicity creates stereotypes.

Do you consider yourself a New Journalist, along the lines that Tom Wolfe described in his essay of that name?

Wolfe had a big influence on me. I have always loved his writing, and he showed me how journalism could take real stories, real people, and put them together in a literary manner. While I wouldn't say that I practice precisely the same kind of journalism Wolfe does, I've certainly been informed by it, especially in my screenplays. One of the most important things Wolfe put on the table was the importance of social rank.

What do you call the kind of journalism you practice?

I don't label it. But if you're asking what I add to the tradition of the New Journalism I'd say it is attention to the interior life. Wolfe is concerned with where people stand in society. I'm more engaged with the subterranean, sometimes deeply dangerous urges, and how these beliefs steer individuals and cultures into conflict.

BY LAWRENCE WRIGHT:

God's Favorite, Simon & Schuster, 2000

Twins: And What They Tell Us about Who We Are, John Wiley & Sons, 1997

Remembering Satan: A Case of Recovered Memory and the Shattering of an American Family, Knopf, 1994

Saints & Sinners: Walker Railey, Jimmy Swaggart, Madalyn Murray O'Hair, Anton LaVey, Will Campbell, Matthew Fox, Knopf, 1993

In The New World: Growing Up with America, 1960–1984, Knopf, 1988

City Children, Country Summer, Scribner, 1979

ABOUT THE AUTHOR

Robert S. Boynton is the director of NYU's magazine journalism program. He has been a senior editor at *Harper's* and a contributing writer for *The New Yorker*. He has also written for *The Atlantic Monthly, The New York Times Magazine, Lingua Franca, The New Republic, The Nation, Rolling Stone,* and many other publications. A graduate of Haverford College and Yale University, he lives with his wife and son in New York. A selection of his work can be found at www.robertboynton.com. For a complete bibliography of the authors discussed in *The New New Journalism,* visit www.newnewjournalism.com.

THE TERROR YEARS
From al-Qaeda to the Islamic State
by Lawrence Wright

These powerful investigative pieces, which take us from the religious police of Saudi Arabia to the rise of the Islamic State, comprise an essential primer on jihadist movements in the Middle East—and the attempts of the West to contain them. Lawrence Wright examines al-Qaeda as it experiences a rebellion from within and spins off a growing web of worldwide terror. He shows us the Syrian film industry before the civil war—compliant at the edges but already exuding a barely masked fury. He gives us the heart-wrenching story of American children kidnapped by ISIS—and *Atlantic* publisher David Bradley's efforts to secure their release. And he details the roles of key FBI figures John O'Neill and his talented protégé Ali Soufan in fighting terrorism. Rigorous, clear-eyed, and compassionate, *The Terror Years* illuminates the complex human players on all sides of a devastating conflict.

History

LONE PATRIOT
The Short Career of an American Militiaman
by Jane Kramer

In *Lone Patriot*, acclaimed *New Yorker* correspondent Jane Kramer delivers an intimate look into the life and mind of a militia leader and his followers, exploring the volatile mix of personalities and politics that shapes their extreme world view. Through a series of exclusive interviews with them both before and after their 1997 arrests, Kramer paints an incredible portrait of a rural America that is rarely glimpsed but strikingly relevant.

Current Affairs

WHISKEY TANGO FOXTROT
Strange Days in Afghanistan and Pakistan
by Kim Barker

From tea with warlords in the countryside to parties with drunken foreign correspondents in the "dry" city of Kabul, journalist Kim Barker captures the humor and heartbreak of life in post–9/11 Afghanistan and Pakistan in this profound and darkly comic memoir. As Barker grows from awkward newbie to seasoned reporter, she offers an insider's account of the region's "forgotten war" at a time when all eyes were turned to Iraq. Candid, self-deprecating, and laugh-out-loud funny, Barker shares both her affection for the absurdities of these two hapless countries and her fear for their future stability.

Memoir

FLIRTING WITH DANGER
Confessions of a Reluctant War Reporter
by Siobhan Darrow

Former star correspondent for CNN, Siobhan Darrow covered the world's hottest war zones over the last two decades, reporting from the front lines in Moscow, Chechnya, the Balkans, Albania, Israel, and Northern Ireland. Her fearless pursuit of stories placed her in countless life-threatening situations, prompting Darrow to wonder what about her character so attracted her to adrenaline, and so alienated her from the family life a part of her longed for. Darrow approaches this question with the same honesty—and seat-of-the-pants courage—that established her reputation as a premiere reporter, and the answers at which she arrives form this riveting memoir of a woman assigned to cover history in the making, even as she chases down the most elusive "get" of all: her own happiness.

Memoir/Current Affairs

THE ROUTES OF MAN
Travels in the Paved World
by Ted Conover

Roads bind our world—metaphorically and literally—transforming landscapes and the lives of the people who inhabit them. With his marvelous eye for detail and his contagious enthusiasm, Ted Conover explores six of these key byways worldwide. In Peru, he traces the journey of a load of rare mahogany over the Andes to its origin, an untracked part of the Amazon basin soon to be traversed by a new east-west route across South America. In East Africa, he visits truckers whose travels have been linked to the worldwide spread of AIDS. In the West Bank, he monitors highway checkpoints with Israeli soldiers and then passes through them with Palestinians, witnessing the injustices and danger borne by both sides. From the passenger seat of a new Hyundai piling up the miles, he describes the exuberant upsurge in car culture as highways proliferate across China. *The Routes of Man* is a spirited, urgent book that reveals the costs and benefits of being connected—how, from ancient Rome to the present, roads have played a crucial role in human life, advancing civilization even as they set it back.

Current Affairs